CW01512076

THE WORKS

OF

ALEISTER CROWLEY

WITH PORTRAITS

VOLUME III

ISBN: 979-8-89096-154-9

Printed: June 2023

Published and Distributed By:
Lushena Books
607 Country Club Drive, Unit E
Bensenville, IL 60106
www.lushenabks.com

ISBN: 979-8-89096-154-9

CONTENTS OF VOLUME III

THE STAR AND THE GARTER

1904

[The simplicity of this exquisite poem renders all explanations superfluous.]

ΑΓΝΩΣΤΩ

ΘΕΩ*

ARGUMENT.

THE poet, seated with his lady, perceives (i.) that he is in some disgrace, arguing the same (ii.) from a difference in the quality of the subsisting silence. Seeking a cause, he observes (iii.) a lady's garter in one corner of the room. His annoyance is changed (iv.) to joy at the prospect of an argument, and of a better understanding. He will (v.) be frank : no poet truly cares what may happen to him. He sketches (vi.) his argument ; but letting fall the word "love" is rapt away into a lyrical transport (vii. and viii.). Further, bidding her (ix.) to fly with him, he points out the value of courage, and its rarity among the bourgeoisie. He calls upon her to awake her own courage, and (x.) bids her embark. His appeal fails, since (xi.) the garter still demands explanation. He then shows (xii.) that mental states are not independent of their physical basis, and casts doubt (xiii.) upon Immortality and Freewill. He asks her (xiv.) to accommodate herself to the facts instead of wasting life upon an Ideal, and to remember that all his acts truly subserve his love for her. He reinforces this (xv.) by a distinction of the important and the unimportant, assures her of his deep passion, and appeals to her. He will (xvi.) show her the picture of the owner of the garter, and gives her (xvii.) the first hint that he does not consider her a rival, any more

than dinner is a rival. As (xviii.) she cannot grasp that idea, he states it plainly and describes (xix.) the lady whose forgetfulness has caused the whole trouble. The spell broken, as it were, he describes (xx., xxi.) two other mistresses, a model and an acrobat, and then again flings at her (xxii.) the frank question : Are these rivals in *Love?* He argues that the resemblances are superficial. For (xxiii.) there is no taint of passion in his Love for his Lady. But she (xxiv.) sees that as a fault in her, and offers her person. He refuses it, fearing to destroy Love, and proves (xxv.) that sexual intimacy is no truer than virginal intimacy. He recalls (xxvi.) the hour when their love stood confessed and (xxvii.) that in which the first promptings of passion were caught and smothered in a higher ecstasy. He complains (xxviii.) that he should have needed to voice all this. He urges (xxix.) that the necessary duties of sex should be performed elsewhere. But, should those duties become unnecessary, let them voyage to solitude and peace. Or (xxx.) no ! it is well to have the ever-present contrast ; let us, however, not despise other folk, but pity them, and for this pity's sake, retire (xxxi.) to meditate, and by this means to achieve the power of redeeming them. He formulates lyrically (xxxii.) this conclusion ; and sums up the whole (xxxiii.), insisting finally on the value of the incident as a stepping-stone to the ultimate.

---

* *I.e.*, Eros. The quotation is from Acts xvii. 23, "To the Unknown God."

THE STAR AND THE GARTER.

I.

WHAT sadness closes in between
Your eyes and mine to-day, my Queen?
In dewfall of our glance hath come
A chill like sunset's in hot lands
Mid iris and chrysanthemum.
Well do I know the shaken sands
Within the surf, the beaten bar
Of coral, the white nenuphar
Of moonrise stealing o'er the bay.
So here's the darkness, and the day
Sinks, and a chill clusters, and I
Wrap close the cloak : then is it so
To-day, you rose-gleam on the snow,
My own true lover? Ardently
I dare not look : I never looked
So : that you know. But insight keen
We (laugh and) call not "love." Now
          crooked
The light swerves somehow. Do you mean—
What? There is coldness and regret
Set like the stinging winter spray
Blown blind back from a waterfall
On Cumbrian moors at Christmas. Wet
The cold cheek numbs itself. A way
Is here to make—an end of all?
What sadness closes in between
Your eyes and mine to-day, my Queen?

II.

YOU are silent. That we always were.
The racing lustres of your hair
Spelt out its sunny message, though
The room was dusk : a rosy glow
Shed from an antique lamp to fall
On the deep crimson of the wall,
And over all the ancient grace
Of shawls, and ivory, and gems [1]
To cast its glamour, till your face
The eye might fall upon and rest,

[1] The description is of Crowley's rooms in
the Quartier Montparnasse.

The temperate flower, the tropic stems.
You were silent, and I too. Caressed
The secret flames that curled around
Our subtle intercourse. Profound,
Unmoved, delighting utterly,
So sat, so sit, my love and I.
But not to-day. Your silence stirs
No answering rapture : you are proud,
And love itself checks and deters
The thought to say itself aloud.
Oh ! heart of amber and fine gold
Silverly darting lunar rays !
Oh ! river of sweet passion rolled
Adown invisible waterways !
Speak ! Did I wound you then unguessed?
What is the sorrow unexpressed
That shadows those ecstatic lids?
A word in season subtly rids
The heart of thoughts unseasonable.
You are silent. Do they speak in hell?

III.

Is it your glance that told me? Nay !
I know you would not look that way.
Seeing, you strove to see not. Fool !
I have ruined all in one rash deed.
Learnt I not in discretion's school
The little care that lovers need ?
For see—I bite my lip to blood ;
A stifled word of anguish hisses :—
O the black word that dams thought's
          flood !
O the bad lip that looked for kisses !
O the poor fool that prates of love !
Is it a garter, or a glove?

IV.

A FOOL indeed ! For why complain,
Now the last five-barred gate is ope,
Held by a little boy ? I hope
The hour is handy to explain
The final secret. Have I any?
Yes ! the small boy shall have a penny !

Now you are angry? Be content!
Not fee the assistant accident
That shows our quarry—love—at bay?
My silver-throated queen, away!
Huntress of heaven, by my side,
As moon by meteor, rushing, ride!
Among the stars, ride on! ride on!
(Then, maybe, bid the boy begone!)

V.

I AM a boy in this. Alas!
Look round on all the world of men!
The boys are oft of genus "ass."
Think yourself lucky, lady, then,
If I at least am boy. You laugh?
Not you! Is this love's epitaph,
God's worm erect on Herod's throne?
"Ah, if I only had not known!"
All wrong, belovèd! Truth be ours,
The one white flower (of all the flowers)
You ever cared for! Ignorance
May set its puppets up to dance;
We know who pulls the strings. No
   sage;
A man unwashed, the bearded brute!
His wife, the mother-prostitute!
Behind the marionetted stage
See the true Punch-and-Judy show,
Turn copper so to silver! Know,
And who can help forgiving? So
Said some French thinker.[1] Here's a
   drench
Of verse unquestionably French
To follow! so, while youth is youth,
And time is time, and I am I,
Too busy with my work to lie,
Or love lie's prize—or work's, forsooth!—
Too strong to care which way may go
The ensuing history of woe,
Though I were jaw, and you were tooth;
So, more concerned with seeking sense
Than worried over consequence,
I'll speak, and you shall hear, the truth.

[1] "Comprendre, c'est pardonner."
   —MME. DE STAEL.

VI.

TRUTH, like old Gaul, is split in three.[1]
A lesson in anatomy,
A sketch of sociology,
A tale of love to end. But see!
What stirs the electric flame of eyes?
One word—that word. Be destinv's
Inviolate fiat rolled athwart
The clouds and cobwebs of our speech,
And image, integrate of thought,
This ebony anthem, each to each :—
To lie, invulnerable, alone,
Valkyrie and hero, in the zone,
Shielded by lightnings of our wit,
Guarded by fires of intellect
Far on the mountain-top, elect
Of all the hills divinely lit
By rays of moonrise! O the moon!
O the interminable tune
Of whispered kisses! Love exults,
Intolerant of all else than he,
And ecstasy invades, insults,
Outshines the waves of harmony,
Lapped in the sun of day; the tides
Of wonder flow, the shore subsides;
And over all the horizon
Glows the last glimmer of the sun.
Ah! when the moon arises, she
Shall look on nothing but the sea.

VII.

O LOVE! and were I with thee ever!
Come with me over the round earth,
O'er lake and fountain, sea and river!
Girdle the world with angel girth
Of angel voyage! Shall we roam
In teeming jungles poisonous?
Or make ourselves an eyrie-home
Where the black ice roars ravenous
In glittering avalanche? Or else
Hide in some corrie on the fells
Of heather and bracken, or delight
In grottos built of stalactite?

[1] "Gallia est divisa in tres partes."
   —Cæsar de Bello Gallico, i. 1.

Or be our lonely haunt the sand
Of the Sahara : let us go
Where some oasis, subtly planned
For love, invites the afterglow !
There let us live alone, except
Some bearded horseman, pennoned, ride
Over the waste of ochre, swept
By wind in waves, and sit beside
Our tent a little, bring us news
Of the great world we have lost for—this !
What fool exclaims—"to lose !"?   To
     lose ?
Ay ! earth and heaven for one small kiss !
But he shall sing beside our fire
The epic of the world's desire ;
How Freedom fares, how Art yet revels
Sane in the dance of dogs and devils.
His thunder voice shall climb and crash,
Scourge liars with tongue's lightning lash,
Through ranks of smitten tyrants drive,
Till bosoms heave, and eyes outflash,
And it is good to be alive.
He shall ride off at dawn, and we
Shall look upon our life again ;
You old, and all your beauty be
Broken, and mine a broken brain.
Yet we shall know ; delighting still
In the sole laughter death derides
In vain ; the indomitable will,
Still burning in the spirit, guides
Our hearts to truth ; we see, we know
How foolish were the things he said,
And answer in the afterglow
How good it is that we are dead.
Will you not come ? Or, where the surf
Beats on the coral, and the palm
Sways slowly in the eternal calm
Of spring, I know a mound of turf
Good for our love to lie on ; good
For breezes, and for sun and shade ;
To hear the murmur of the flood ;
To taste the kava subtly made
To rouse to Bacchic ecstasy,
Since Dionysus silently
Faded from Greece, now only smiles
Amid the soft Hawaian isles ;
Good, above all the good, to keep
Our bodies when we sleep the sleep.

VIII.

MAKE me a roseleaf with your mouth,
And I will waft it through the air
To some far garden of the South,
The herald of our happening there !

Fragrant, caressing, steals the breeze ;
Curls into kisses on your lips :—
I know interminable seas,
Winged ardour of the stately ships,

Space of incalculable blue
And years enwreathed in one close crown,
And glimmering laughters echoing you
From reverend shades of bard's renown :--

Nature alive and glad to hymn
Your beauty, my delight : her God
Weary, his old eyes sad and dim
In his intolerable abode.

All things that are, unknown and known,
Bending in homage to your eyes ;
We wander wondering, lift alone
The world's grey load of agonies.

Make me a roseleaf with your mouth,
That all the savour steal afar
Unto the sad awaiting South,
Where sits enthroned the answering Star.

IX.

WILL you not come : the unequal fever
Of Paris hold our lives for ever?
Were it not better to exceed
The avenging thought, the unmeaning deed,
Make one strong act at least ? How small,
How idiot our lives ! These folk
That think they live—which dares at all
To act ? The suicide that broke
His chain, and lies so waxen pale
In the Morgue to-day ? Did he then fail?
Ay, he was beaten. But to live,
Slink on through what the world can give,

That is a hound's life too. For me,
The suicide stands grand and free
Beside these others. Was it fear
Drove him to stand upon the bank?
The Paris lights shone far and drear;
The mist was down; the night was dank;
The Seine ran easily underneath;
The air was chill: he knew the Seine
By pain would put an end to pain,
And jumped,—and struggled against death,
I doubt not. Ye courageous men
That scorn to flee the world, ye slaves
Of commerce, ye that ply the pen,
That dig, and fill, and loathe your graves!
Ye counter-jumpers, clergy, Jews,
All Paris, smug and good, that use
To point the index scorn, deride
The courage of that suicide—
I ask you not to quit us quite,
But—will you take a bath to-night?
Money might make you. Well: but he,
What was his wage, what was his fee?
Fear fiercer than a mortal fear.
Be silent, cowards, leave him here
Dead in the Morgue, so waxen pale!
He failed: shall ye not also fail?
Ah! love! the strings are little;
The cords are over strong;
The chain of life is brittle;
And keen the sword of song.
Will you not seize in one firm grip
Now, as I hold you, lip to lip,
The serpent of Event, hold hard
Its slipping coils, its writhe retard,
And snap its spine? Delicate hands
You have: the work is difficult;
Effort that holds and understands
May do it: shall our foes exult,
The daughters of Philistia laugh,
The girls of Askalon rejoice,
Writing for us this epitaph:
"They chose, and were not worth the
    choice"?
You are so pure: I am a man.
I will assume the courage tried
Of yonder luckless suicide,
And you—awaken, if you can,
The courage of the courtezan!

X.

To sea! To sea! The ship is trim;
The breezes bend the sails.
They chant the necromantic hymn,
Arouse Arabian tales.

To sea! Before us leap the waves;
The wild white combers follow.
Invoke, ye melancholy slaves,
The morning of Apollo!

There's phosphorescence in the wake,
And starlight o'er the prow.
One comet, like an angry snake,
Lifts up its hooded brow.

The black grows grey toward the East:
A hint of silver glows.
Gods gather to the mystic feast
On interlunar snows.

The moon is up full-orbed: she glides
Striking a snaky ray
Across the black resounding tides,
The sepulchre of day.

The moon is up: upon the prow
We stand and watch the moon.
A star is lustred on your brow;
Your lips begin a tune,

A long, low tune of love that swells
Little by little, and lights
The overarching miracles
Of love's desire, and Night's.

It swells, it rolls to triumph-song
Through luminous black skies;
Thrills into silence sharp and strong,
Assumes its peace, and dies.

There is the night: it covers close
The lilies folded fair
Of all your beauty, and the rose
Half hidden in your hair.

There is the night : unseen I stand
And look to seaward still :
We would not look upon the land
Again, had I my will.

The ship is trim : to sea ! to sea !
Take life in either hand,
Crush out its wine for you and me,
And drink, and understand !

XI.

I AM a pretty advocate !
My speech has served me ill. Perchance
Silence had served : you now look straight
On that clear evidence of France,
The embroidered garter yonder. Wait !
I had some confidence in fate
Ere I spoke thus. For while I spoke
The old smile, surely helpless, broke
On your tired lips : the old light woke
In your deep eyes : but silence falls
Blank, blank : the species that appals,
Not our old silence. I devise
A motto for your miseries :
"There an embroidered garter lies,
And here words—they lie too ?" I see
Your intuition of the truth
Is still in its—most charming—youth.
You need that physiology !

XII.[1]

I LOVE you. That seems simple ? No !
Hear what the physiologist
Says on the subject. *To and fro*
The motor axis of the brain

[1] In view of the strange uproar which this
harmless section created, one person supposing
it to testify Crowley's ignorance, another that
it was a correct physiological description of the
action of the erector penis muscle (! ! !), it should
be explained that the speaker wishes to explain
that consciousness is a function of the brain,
and that, talking to an ignorant girl, he allows
himself to talk what is in detail extravagant
nonsense.

Hits on the cerebellum hard,
Makes the medulla itch : the bard
Twitches his spinal cord again,
Excites Rolando's fissure, and
Impinges on the Pineal gland.
Then Hippocampus major strikes
The nerves, and we may say " He likes,"
But if the umbilical cord
Cut the cerebrum like a sword,
And afferent ganglia, sensory bones,
Shake in the caecum : then one groans
" He likes Miss What's your Name." And if
The appendix vermiformis biff
The pericardium, pleura shoves
The femur—we may say : " He loves."
Here is the mechanism strange
(But perfectly correct) to change
My normal calm—seraphic dew !
Into an ardent love for you.

XIII.

Is there a soul behind the mask ?
What master drives these slaves to task
Thus willing ? Physiology
Wipes the red scalpel, scorns reply.
My argument to please you swerves,
Becomes a mere defence of nerves.
Why they are thus, why so they act,
We know not, but accept the fact.
How this for my peccation serves ?
Marry, how ? Tropically ! Pact
I bind with blood to show you use
For this impertinence—and add
A proverb fit to make you mad
About the gander and the goose,[1]
Till you riposte with all your force
A miserable pun on sauce.
The battle when you will ! This truce
I take in vantage, hold my course.
I see mechanic causes reach
Back through eternity, inform
The stellar drift, the solar storm,
The protoplasmic shiver, each

[1] What is sauce for the goose, is sauce for
the gander.

Little or great, determinate
In law from Fate, the Ultimate.
If this be meaningless, much more
Vacant your speech and sophic skill
(My feminine and fair Escobar ! [1])
To prove mere circumstance is no bar
Against the freedom of the will.
However this may be, we are
Here and not otherwhere, star to star !
Hence then act thou ! Restrain the " Damn !"
Evoked by " I am that I am."
Perpend ! (Hark back to Hamlet !) If
You stand thus poised upon the cliff
Freewill—I await that will ; (One) laughter ;
(Two) the old kiss ; (Three) silence after.
No ? Then vacate the laboratory !
Psychology must crown the event,
And sociology content,
Ethics suffice, the simple story !
(Oh ! that a woman ever went
Through course of science, full and whole,
Without the loss of beauty's scent,
And grace, and subtlety of soul.
Ah God ! this Law maketh hearts ache,
" Who eateth shall not have his cake.")

XIV.

ACCEPT me as I am ! I give
All you can take. If you dislike
Some fragments of the life I live,
They are not yours : I scorn to strike
One sword-swift pang against your peace.
See ! I'm a mountaineer. Release
That spirit from your bonds : or come
With me upon the mountains, cease
This dull round, this addition sum
Of follies we call France : indeed
Cipher ! And if at times I need
The golden dawn upon the Alps,
The gorges of Himalayan rock,
The grey and ancient hills, the scalps
Of hoary hills, the rattling shock
Of avalanche adown the hills—
Why, what but you, your image, fills

[1] A mediæval logician.

My heart in these ? I want you there.
For whom but you do I ply pen,
Talk with unmentionable men
Of proofs and types—dull things !— for whom
But you am I the lover ? Bloom,
O flower, immortal flower, love, love !
Linger about me and above,
Thou perfumed haze of incense-mist !
The air hath circled me and kissed
Here in this room, on mountains far,
Yonder to seaward, toward yon star,
With your own kisses. Yes ! I see
The roseate embroidery
Yonder—I know : it seems to give
The lie to me in throat and teeth.
That is the surface : underneath
I live in you : in you I live.

XV.

WILL you not learn to separate
The essential from the accidental,
Love from desire, caprice from fate,
The inmost from the merely mental ?
Our star, the sun, gives life and light :
Let that decay, the æons drown
Sense in stagnation ; death and night
Smite the fallen fragments of the crown
Of spring : but serves the garter so ?
What wandering meteor is this
Across the archipelago
Luminous of our starry bliss ?
Let that be lost : the smile disputes
The forehead's temple with the frown,
When gravitation's arrow shoots,
And stockings happen to slip down.
You are my heart : the central fire
Whereby my being burns and moves,
The mainspring of my life's desire,
The essential engine that approves
The will to live : and these frail friends,
The women I shall draw you, fail
Of more importance to earth's ends
Than to my life a finger-nail.
'Twere pain, no doubt, were torn away
One, a minute distemperature.

I spend a fraction of the day
Plying the art of manicure.
But always beats the heart : the more
I polish, tint, or carve, I ask
Strength from the heart's too generous store
To bend my fingers to the task.
Cease : I am broken : nought remains.
The brain's electric waves are still ;
No blood beats eager in the veins ;
The mind sinks deathward, and the will.
It is no figure of boy's speech,
Lover's enthusiasm, rhyme
Magniloquent of bard, to reach
Truth through the husk of space and time :
No truth is more devout than this :
" In you I live : I live in you."
Had Latmos not known Artemis,
Where were the faint lights of that dew
Of Keats ? O maiden moon of mine,
Imperial crescent, rise and shine !

XVI.

I WAS a fool to hide it. Here
Phantoms arise and disappear,
Obedient to the master's wand.
The incense curls like a pale frond
Of some grey garden glory about
This room ; I take my sceptre out,
My royal crown ; invoke, evoke
These phantoms in the glimmering smoke ;
And you shall see—and take no hurt—
The very limb yon garter girt.

XVII.

I AM a man. Consider first
What we may learn, if but we will,
From that small lecture I rehearsed
With very Huxley's strength and skill
And clarity. What do I mean,
Admitting manhood ? This : to-day
I fed on oysters, ris-de-veau,
Beefsteak and grapes. Will you repay
My meal with anger, rosy grow

With shame because instead of you
I went to feed chez Lavenue ?[1]
The habit anthropophagous,
Nice as it is, is not for us.
I love you : will you share my life,
Become my mistress or my wife ?
Agreed : but can your kisses feed me ?
Is it for dinner that you need me ?
But think : it is for you I eat.
Even as the object that I see,
The brain 'tis pictured in ; the beat
Of nerves that mean the picture are
Not like it, but dissimilar.
How can a nervous current be
Like that Velasquez ? So I find
Dinner a function of the mind,
Not like you, but essential to
(Even it) my honest love of you.
Consider then yon broidered toy
In the same aspect ! Steals no joy
Glittering beneath the sad pale face ?

XVIII.

STILL grave, my budding Arahat ?
I see the crux of my disgrace
Lies in the mad idea that—that !—
Is not dissimilar, usurps
The very function I have given
Blissful beyond the bliss of heaven—
Aha ! there is a bird that chirps
Another song. Here's paint and brush
And canvas. I will paint anon
The limb yon garter once was on ;
Sketch you a nude—my soul—and nude
The very human attitude
We all assume—or else are posers.
Such winners are the surest losers.
I paint her picture, recognise—
Dare you ?—one glimmer of her eyes
Like yours, one shimmer of her skin
Like that your flesh is hidden in,
One laugh upon her lips enough
Like yours for me to recollect,

[1] A famous restaurateur in the Place de Rennes.

Remind, recall, hint ? Never ! Stuff !
You are, as aye, alone, elect.
Shall we then dive in Paris sewers ?
Ay ! but not find you there, nor yet
Your likeness. Did you then forget
You are my love ? Arise and shine !
It was your blasphemy, not mine.

XIX.

A FAINT sweet smell of ether haunts
Yet the remembrance. Hear the wizard
His lone and melancholy chaunts
Roared in the rain-storm and the blizzard !
The ancient and devoted dizzard !
Appear, thou dream of loveliness !
She wore a rose and amber dress,
With broidery of old gold. Her hair
Was long and starry, gilded red.
Her face was laughter, shapen fair
By the sweet things she thought and said.
Her whiteness rustled as she walked.
Her hair sang tunes across the air.
She sighed, laughed, whispered, never talked.
She smiled, and loves devout and rare
Flickered about the room. She stayed
Still in the dusk : her body sang
Out full and clear " O love me ! " Rang
The silver couplets undismayed,
Bright, bold, convincing. In her eyes
Glittered enamelled sorceries.
She was a piece of jewel work
Sold by a Christian to a Turk.
She had fed on air that day : the flowers
About her curled, ambrosial bowers
Of some divine perfume : the soul
Of ether made her wise ; control
Of strong distilled delight. She showered
Wit and soft laughter and desire
About her breasts in bliss embowered,
And subtle and devouring fire
Leapt in live sparks about her limbs.
Her spirit shields me, and bedims
My sight : she needs me : I need her.
She is mine : she calls me : sob and stir
Strange pulses of old passionate
Imperial ecstasies of fate.

Destiny ; manhood ; fear ; delight ;
Desire ; accomplishment ; ere night
Dipped her pale plumes to greet the sun
She was not ; all is past and done.
A dream ? I wake from blissful sleep,
But is it real ? Well, I keep
An accidental souvenir
Whence thus to chronicle small beer ; [1]
There is the garter. Launched our boat,
The stately pinnace once afloat,
You shall hear all ; we will not land
On this or that mediate strand,
Until the voyage be done, and we
Pass from the river to the sea,
And find some isle's secluded nook
More sacred than we first forsook.

XX.

YES, there are other phases, dear !
Here is a pocket-book, and here
Lies a wee letter. Floral thyrse ? [2]
Divine-tipped narthex of the pine, [2]
Or morphia's deceitful wine ?
The French is ill, the spelling worse !—
But this is horrible ! This, me ?
The upholder of propriety,
Who actually proposed to form
A Club to shield us from the swarm
Of common people of no class
Who throng the Quartier Montparnasse !
I wear a collar : [3] loudly shout
That folk are pigs that go without,—
And here you find me up a tree
To make my concierge blush for me !
A girl " uncombed, so badly dressed,
So rudely mannered—and the rest ;
Not at all proper. Fie ! away !
What would your lady mother say ? "
I tell you, I was put to it
To wake a wonder of my wit

[1] See *Othello*, II. i.
[2] The thyrsus and narthex were carried by the Mænads, the maiden devotees of Bacchus.
[3] The poet libels himself ; he rarely did so.

Winged, to avail me from the scorn
Of my own concierge.   Adorn
The facts I might ; you know them not ;
But that were just the one black blot
On this love's lesson : still, to excuse
Myself to you, who could not choose
But make some weak apology
Before the concierge's eye !
True, you are far too high to accuse—
Perhaps would rather not be told ?
You *shall* hear.   Does a miner lose
If through the quartz he gets to gold ?
Yes: Nina was a thing of nought,
A little laughing lewd gamine,
Idle and vicious, void of thought,
Easy, impertinent, unclean—
Utterly charming !   Yes, my queen !
She had a generous baby soul,
Prattled of love.   Should I control,
Repress perhaps the best instinct
The child had ever had ?   I winked
At foolish neighbours, did not shrink.
Such café Turc I made her drink
As she had never had before ;
Set her where you are sitting ; chatted ;
Found where the fires of laughter lurk ;
Played with her hair, tangled and matted ;
Fell over strict nice conduct's brink,
Gave all she would, and something more.
She was an honest little thing,
Gave of her best, asked no response.
What more could Heaven's immortal king
Censed with innumerous orisons ?
So, by that grace, I recognised
A something somewhere to be prized
Somewhat.   What portress studies song ?
My worthy concierge was wrong.

XXI.

THEN let not memory shrink abashed,
Once started on this giddy whirl !
Hath not a lightning image flashed
Of my divine boot-button girl ?
She is a dainty acrobat,
Tailor-made from tip to toe ;

A tiniest coquettish hat,
A laughing face alight, aglow
With all the fun of life.   She comes
Often at morning, laughs aloud
At the poor femm' de ménage ; hums
Some dancing tune, invades my cloud
Of idle dreams, sits poised upon
The couch, and with a gay embrace
Cries out " Hullo, my baby ! "   Shone
Such nature in a holier face ?
We are a happy pair at least :
Coffee and rolls are worth a feast,
And laughing as she came she goes !
The dainty little tuberose !
She has a lithe white body, slim
And limber, fairy-like, a snake
Hissing some Babylonian hymn
Tangled in the Assyrian brake.
She stole upon me as I slept :
Who wonders I am nympholept ?
Her face is round and hard and small
And pretty—hence the name I gave her
Of the boot-button girl.   Appal
These words ?   Ah, would your spirit save
    her ?
She's right just as she is : so wise
You look through hardly-opened eyes
One would believe you could do better.
Ma foi !   And is your God your debtor ?
So, my true love, I paint you three
Portraits of women that love me.

XXII.

THESE portraits, darling, are they yours ?
And yet there sticks the vital fact
That these, as you, are women.   Lures
The devil of the inexact
With subtle leasing ?   Nay ! O nay !
I'll catch him with a cord, draw out
By a bent fish-hook through his snout,
Give to my maiden for a play.
You, they, and dinner and—what else ?—
However unlike, coincide
In composition verified
Of final protoplasmic cells.

Shall this avail to stagger thought,
Confuse the reason, bring to nought
The rosebud, in reflecting: Hem !
What beauty hath the flower and stem ?
Carbon we know, and nitrogen,
And oxygen—are these a rose ?
But this though everybody knows,
That this should be the same for men
They know not.   Death may decompose,
Reduce to primal hyle perchance—
I shall not do it in advance !
So let the accidental fact
That these are women, fall away
To black oblivion : be the pact
Concluded firm enough to-day,
Not thus to err.   So you are not
In essence or in function one
With these, the unpardonable blot
On knighthood's shield, the sombre spot
Seen on the photosphere of sun.

XXIII.

" NAY ! that were nothing," say you now,
Poor baby of the weary brow,
Struggling with metaphysic lore ?
" But these, being women, gave you more :
You spoke of love ! "   Indeed I did,
And you must counter me unbid,
Forgetting how we must define
This floral love of yours and mine.
That love and this are as diverse
As Shelley's poems and my verse.
And now the bright laugh comes in spite
Of all the cruel will can do.
" I take," you say, " a keen delight
In Shelley, but as much in you."
There, you are foolish.   And you know
The thing I meant to say.   O love !
What little lightnings serve to show
Glimpses of all your heart !   Above
All, and beneath all, lies there deep,
Canopied over with young sleep,
Bowered in the lake of nenuphars,
Watched by the countless store of stars,
The abiding love you bear me.   Hear
How perfect love casts flying fear

Forth from its chambers !   Those and this
Are utterly apart.   The bliss
Of this small quarrel far exceeds
That dervish rapture, dancer deeds
Strained for egregious emphasis.
These touch you not !   You sit alone
Passionless upon passion's throne,
And there is love.   Look not below,
Lest aught disturb the silver flow
Of harmonies of love !   Awake !
Awake for love's own solar sake !
Diverse devotion we divide
From the one overflowing tide.
Despise this fact !   So lone and far
Lies the poor garter, that I gaze
Thither ; it casts no vivid rays.
But hither ?   I behold the star !

XXIV.

NOW your grave eyes are filled with tears ;
Your hands are trembling in my own ;
The slow voice falls upon my ears,
An undulating monotone.
Your lips are gathered up to mine ;
Your bosom heaves with fearful breath ;
Your scent is keen as floral wine,
Inviting me, and love, to death.
You, whom I kept, a sacred shrine,
Will fling the portals to the day ;
Where shone the moon the sun shall shine,
Silver in scarlet melt away.
There is yet a pang : they give me this
Who can ; and you who could have failed ?
Is it too late to extend the kiss ?
Too late the goddess be unveiled ?
O but the generous flower that gives
Her kisses to the violent sun,
Yet none the less in ardour lives
An hour, and then her day is done.
Back from my lips, back from my breast !
I hold you as I always will,
You unprofaned and uncaressed,
Silent, majestical, and still.
Back ! for I love you.   Even yet
Do you not see my deepest fire
Burn through the veils and coverings set
By fatuous phantoms of desire ?

Back ! O I love you evermore.
But, be our bed the bridal sky !
I love you, love you. Hither, shore
Of far unstained eternity !
There we will rest. Beware ! Beware !
For I am young, and you are fair.
Nay ! I am old in this, you know !
Ah ! heart of God ! I love you so !

XXV.

O WHAT pale thoughts like gum exude
From smitten stem of tropic tree !
I talk of veils, who love the nude !
Witness the masterpieces three
Of Rodin that make possible
Life in prosaic Paris, stand
About the room, its chorus swell
From the irritating to the grand.
Shall we, who love the naked form,
The inmost truth, to ourselves fail,
Take shelter from love's lightning-storm
Behind some humbug's hoary veil ?
Ah ! were it so, love, could the flame
Of fast electric fervour flash,
Smite us through husk of form and name,
Leave of the dross a little ash,
One button of pure fusèd gold
Identical—O floral hour !
That were the bliss no eyes behold,
But Christ's delighted bridal dower
Assuming into God the Church.
But—oh ! these nudes of Rodin ! I
Drag one more linnet from its perch
That sang to us, and sang a lie.
Did Rodin strip the clothes, and find
A naked truth fast underneath ?
Never ! Where lurks the soul and mind ?
What is the body but a sheath ?
Did he ply forceps, scalpel, saw,
Tear all the grace of form apart,
Intent to catch some final law
Behind the engine of the heart ?
He tried not ; whoso has, has failed.
So, did I pry beneath the robe,
Till stubborn will availed, nor quailed,
Intimate with the naked probe ?

I know the husks [1] to strip ; name, form,
Sensation, then perception, stress
Of nature thither ; last, the swarm
Of honey-bees called consciousness.
These change and shape a myriad shapes.
Diverse are these, not one at all,
What gain I if my scalpel scrapes,
Turning before some final wall
Of soul ? Not so, nothing is there.
The qualities are all : for this
I stop as I have stopped ; intrude
No science, for I love the fair ;
No wedlock, for I love the kiss ;
No scalpel, for I love the nude.
And we await the deep event,
Whate'er it be, in solitude ;
Silent, with ecstasy bedewed ;
Content, as Rodin is content.

XXVI.

I WILL not, and you will not. Stay !
Do you recall that night of June
When from the insufferable day
Edged out the dead volcanic moon
Solemn into the midnight ? You
Shone your inviolate violet eyes
Into my eyes less sad, and drew
Back from the slender witcheries
Of word and song : and silence knew
What splendour in the silence lies,
The soul drawn back into itself.
It was the deep environing
Wood that then shielded us : the elf
And fairy in an emerald ring,
And hamadryad of the trees,
And naiad of the sleepy lake,
That watched us on the mossy leas
Look on each other's face, and take
The secret of the universe
To sleep with us : you knew, and I,
The purport of the eternal curse,
The ill design of destiny.
You know, and I, O living head
Of love ! the things that were not said.

---

[1] The Buddhist "Skandhas." See "Science
and Buddhism," vol. ii. p. 244.

XXVII.

Do you recall ? Could I forget ?
How once the full moon shone above,
Over the houses, and we let
Loose rein upon the steeds of love ?
How kisses fled to kisses, rain
Of fiery dew upon the soul
Kindled, till ecstasy was pain ;
Desire, delight : and swift control
Leapt from the lightning, as the cloud
Disparted, rended, from us twain,
And we were one : the aerial shroud
Closed on us, shall not lift again
For aught we do : O glamour grown
Inseparable and alone !
And then we knew as now the tune
Our lives were set to, and sang back
Across the sky toward the moon
Into the cloud's dissolving wrack,
Vanished for ever. And we found
Coprolite less than chrysolite,
Flowers fairer than their food, the ground ;
We knew our destiny, saw how
Man's fate is written on his brow,
And how our love throughout was hewn
And masked and moulded by the moon.

XXVIII.

And who is then the moon ? Bend close,
And clothe me in a silken kiss,
And I will whisper to my rose
The secret name of Artemis.
Words were not needed then : to-day
Must I begin what never I thought
To do : mould flowers in common clay ?
Mud casket of mere words is nought,
When by love's miracle we guess
What either always thinketh. Yes ?

XXIX.

So, love, not thus for you and me !
And if I am man, no more, expect
I shall remain so, till, maybe,
The anatomist, old Time, dissect

Me, nerve from flesh, and bone from
    bone,
And raise me spiritual, changed
In all but love for you, my own ;
The little matter rearranged,
The little mind refigured. This
Alone I hope or think to keep :—
The love I bear you, and the kiss
Too soft to call the breath of sleep.
And, if you are woman, even there
I do decline: we stand above.
I ask not, and will take no share
With you in what mankind call love.
We know each other : you and I
Have nought to do with lesser things.
With them—'tis chance or destiny :
With us, we should but burn our wings.
We love, and keep ourselves apart :
Mouth unto mouth, heart unto heart,
Thus ever, never otherwise.
The soul is out of me, and swings
In desperate and strange surmise
About the inmost heart of things.
This is all strange : but is not life,
Death, all, most strange, not to be told,
Not to be understood by strife
Of brain, nor bought for gleaming gold,
Nor known by aught but love?   And
    love
Far from resolving soul to sense,
Stands isolated and above
Immaculate, alone, intense,
Concentrate on itself. But should
The lesser leave me, as it might ;
The lesser never touch you ; would
Your will be one with my delight?
Leave all the thoughts and miseries !
Invade the glowing fields of sun !
Cross bleak inhospitable seas,
Until this hour be past and done,
And we in some congenial clime
Are then reborn, where danger's nought
To mock the old Parisian time
When fear was still the child of thought !
So we could love, and love, and fate
Never clang brutal on the gong,
And lunch, man-eating tiger, wait
Crouched in the jungles of my song ;

My gaze be steadfast on the star
And never to the garter glide,
And I on rapture's nenuphar
Sit Buddha-like above the tide.

XXX.

O BLUEBELL of the inmost wood,
Before whose beauty I abase
My head, and bind my burning blood,
And hide within the moss my face,
I would not so—or not for that
Would so : the gods knew well to save
The mountain summit from the flat,
Youth's laughter from its earlier grave.
It is a better love, exists
Only because of these below it :
Mountains loom grander in the mists :
The lover's foolish to the poet.
I know. Far better strive and earn
The rest you give me than remain
Ever upon the heights that burn
Sunward, and quite forget the plain.
Beauteous and bodiless we are ;
Rapture is our inheritance ;
You shine, an everlasting star,
I, the rough nebula : but whence,
Whither, we know not. But we know
That if our joy were always so
We might not know it. Strange indeed
This earth where all is paradox,
Pushed to the truth : what lies succeed
When every truth essential mocks
Its truth in figure of a phrase ?
How should I care for this, and tire
Body by will to sing thy praise,
Who take this lute, throw down the
        lyre
As I have done to-day, to win
No guerdon differing from the toil,
Were that accomplished : pain and sin
Are needed for the counterfoil
Of joy and love : if only so
All men had these in keen excess
Those were forgotten : indigo
Is amber's shadow, but—confess
For all men but ourselves the tint

Of all the earth is dull and black !
Only some glints of love bestow
The knowledge of what meteor wrack
Trails pestilence across the sky.
But we are other—you and I !
So shall we live in deep content,
Unchanging bliss, despise them still
Groping on isle and continent
Wreathed in the mesh of woe and ill ?
Ah ! Zeus ! we will not : be the law
Of uttermost compassion ours !
Our snows it shall not come to thaw,
Nor burn the roses from our bowers.

XXXI.

AY ! There's a law ! For this recede,
Hide with me in the deepest caves
Of some volcanic island ; bleed
Our hearts out by the ambient waves
Of Coromandel ; live alone,
Hermits of love and pity, far
Where tumbled banks of ice are thrown,
Watched by yon solitary star,
Sirius ; there to work together
In sorrow and in joy but one,
In black inhospitable weather,
Or fronting the Numidian sun,
Equally minded ; till the hour
Strike of release, and we obtain
The passionless and holy power,
Making us masters over pain,
And lords of peace : the rays of light
We fling to the awakening globe ;
The cavern of the eremite
Shall glow with inmost fire, a robe
Of diamond energy, shall flash
Even to the confines of wide space ;
Comets their tails in fury lash
To look on our irradiate face.
And we will heal them.   Dragon men
And serpent women, worm and clod,
Shall rise and look upon us then,
And know us to be very God,
Finding a saviour in the sight
Of power attaining unto peace,
And meditation's virgin might
Pregnant with twins—love and release.

Are you not ready ?   Let us leave
This little Paris to its fate !
Our friends a little while may grieve,
And then forget : but we, elate,
Live in a larger air : awake,
Compassion in the Halls of Truth !
Disdain love for love's very sake !
Take all our beauty, strength, and youth,
And melt them in the crucible
To that quintessence at whose gleam
Gold shudders and grows dull ; expel
The final dross by intimate stream
Of glowing truth, our lunar light !
Are you not ready ?   Who would stay ?
Arise, O Queen, O Queen of Night !
Arise, and leave the little day !

XXXII.

LADY, awake the dread abyss
Of knowledge in impassioned eyes !
Fathom the gulfs of awful bliss
With the poised plummet of a kiss !

Love hath the arcanum of the wise ;
Love is the elixir, love the stone ;
The rosy tincture shall arise
Out of its shadowy cadences.

Love is the Work, and love alone
Rewards the ingenious alchemist.
Chaste fervours chastely overthrown
Awake the infinite monotone.

So, Lady, if thy lips I kissed ;
So, lady, if in eyes of steel
I read the steady secret, wist
Of no gray ghosts moulded of mist ;

I did not bid my purpose kneel,
Nor thine retire : I probe the scar
Of self, the goddess keen and real
Supreme within the naked wheel

Of sun and moon and star and star,
And find her but the ambient coil,
Imagination's avatar,
A Buddha on his nenuphar

Elaborate of Indian toil ;
A mockery of a self ; outrun
Its days and dreams, its strength and spoil,
As runs the conquering counterfoil.

Thou art not ; thou the moon and sun,
Thou the sole star in trackless night,
The unguessed spaces one by one
That mask their Sphinx, the horizon :

Thou, these ; and one above them, light,
Light of the inmost heaven and hell :—
Art changed and fallen and lost to sight,
Who wast as waters of delight.

And I, who am not, know thee well
Who art not : then the chain divides
From love-enlightened limbs, and swell
The choral cries unutterable.

Out of the salt, out of the tides,
The sea, whose drink is death by thirst !
The triumph anthem overrides
The ocean's lamentable sides,

And we are done with life ; accurst
Who linger ; lost who find ; but we
Follow the gold wake of the first
Who found in losing ; who reversed

The dictates of eternity.
Lo ! in steep meditation hearsed,
Coffined in knowledge, fast we flee
Unto the island from the sea.

XXXIII.

THE note of the silence is changed ; the
    quarrel is over
That rather endeared than estranged : lover
    to lover
Flows in the infinite river of knowledge and
    peace :
Not a ripple or eddy or quiver : the monitors
    cease
That were eager to warn, to awaken : a sleep
    is opposed,
And the leaves of the rose wind-shaken are
    curled and closed,

Gone down in the glare of the sun ; and the
twilight perfumes
Steal soft in the wake of the One that abides
in the glooms.
Walking he is, and slowly ; thoughtful he
seems,
Pure and happy and holy ; as one would
who dreams
In the day-time of deep delights no kin to
the day,
But a flower new-born of the night's in
Hecate's way.
Love is his name, and he bears the ill quiver
no more.
He has aged as we all, and despairs ; but
the lady who bore
Him, Eros, to ruin the ages, has softened at
heart ;
He is tamed by the art of the sages, the
magical art.
No longer he burns and blisters, consumes
and corrodes ;
He hath Muses nine for sisters ; the holy
abodes
Of the maiden are open to him, for his wrath
is grown still ;
His eyes with weeping are dim ; he hath
changed his will.
We know him ; and Venus sinks, a star in
the West ;
A star in the even, that thinks it shall fall
into rest.
Let it be so, then ! Arise, O moon of the
lyrical spears !
Huntress, O Artemis wise, be upon him who
hears !
I have heard thy clear voice in the moon ;
I have borne it afar ;
I have tuned it to many a tune ; thou hast
showed me a star,
And the star thou hast showed me I follow
through uttermost night.

I have shaken my spear at Apollo ; his
ruinous might
I have mocked, I have mastered. All hail
to the Star of Delight
That is tender and fervid and frail, and
avails me aright !
Hail to thee, symbol of love, assurance and
promise of peace !
Stand fast in the skies above, till the skies
are abolished and cease !

And for me, may I never forget how things
came well as they are !
It was long I had wandered yet ere my eyes
found out the star.
Be silent, love, and abide ; the wanton
strings must go
To the vain tumultuous tide of the spirit's
overflow.
I sing and sing to the world ; then silence soon
Be about us clasped and furled in the light
of the moon.
Forget not, never forget the terrible song I
have sung ;
How the eager fingers fret the lute, and loose
the tongue
Tinkles delicate things, faint thoughts of a
futile past—
We are past on eagle wings, and the silence
is here at last.
The last low wail of the lyre, be it soft with
a tear
For the children of earth and fire that have
brought us here.
Give praise, O masterful maid, to Nina, and
all as they die !
The moon makes blackest of shade ; the
star's in the swarthiest sky.
Be silent, O radiant martyr ! Let the world
fade slowly afar !
But—had it not been for the Garter, I might
never have seen the Star.

ΟΝ ΟΥΝ ΑΓΝΟΩΝ ΕΤΣΕΒΕΙΣ
ΤΟΥΤΟΝ ΕΓΩ ΡΟΔΟΝ[1] ΚΑΤΑΓΓΕΛΛΩ ΣΟΙ

[1] The quotation is altered from Acts xvii. 23, " Whom therefore (*i.e.* because of the poem)
thou dost ignorantly worship, him do I Rose declare unto thee." Rose was the name of the
poet's wife.

APPENDIX

À MADEMOISELLE LE MODÈLE—DITE JONES

(*To serve as Prelude to a possible Part II.*)

[The humour of this curious poem is partly personal, and Crowley wished to omit it for this reason. But some of the criticism is so apt, and the satire so acute, that we were unwilling to let it drop.]

In order to avoid the misunderstanding, which I have reason to believe exists,[1] I append this simple personal explanation : let it serve, moreover, as the *hors d'œuvre* to a new feast. For it is not manifest that who wrote so much when all was mystery, should write yet more now all is clear ? It is perhaps due to you, the bedrock of my mountains of idealism, that I attained the magical force to make all those dreams come true : for that, then, this.

Further, should Nietzsche play you false, and supply no key to this Joseph confection ; a kid glove and an ortolan are alike to him—and, if this be a haggis, much more is this the case !—you may apply to the only educated man in your neighbourhood, as you applied before in the matter of the Bruce Papyrus (I do not refer to the Bruce Papyrus which all who run may read—all honour to the scribe !), and he will take pleasure in explaining it to you line by line, and letter by letter, if that will serve.

Possess yourself in patience, that is to say, and, should I return from the wilds into which my restless destiny so continually drives me, you may hope for a second part which shall excel the former as realism always must excel idealism.

I have no hope for your brain, and, I am sorry to add, as little for your heart ; but there must be a sound spot in you somewhere [could you not be *natural ?*—But no, no !], and that spot may yet be touched and healed by the Homocea[3] of irritable, if never yet by the Lanoline[3] of amoroso-emasculatory, verse. With this, then, farewell !

I.

There is an eye through which the Kabbalist
Beholds the Goat.
There is an eye that I have often kissed.
(That hath a throat.)

[1] A young lady in the Montparnasse Quarter chose to imagine that she was the " Star " itself ; not merely the model for that masterpiece, as was the case.
[2] Latin, Homo, a man ; cea, waxen : hence, an angry man.—A. C.
[3] Tibetan, La, a pass ; English, no, No ! Greek, Linos, a dirge : hence, a temporary pæan.—A. C.

There is an eye that Arab sages say
Weeps never enough.
There is an eye whose glances make the day
The day of Love.
There is an eye that is above all eyes,
That is no eye.
(Stood proud Anatta on the Bridge of Sighs
And thundered " Why ? ")
Which eyes are mine, which thine, poor ape, discover,
And even yet thou hast not lost thy lover.

II.

Khephra, thou Beetle-headed God !
Who travellest in thy strength above
The Heaven of Nu, with splendour shod
Of Thoth, and girt about with Love !
O Sun at midnight ! in thy Bark
The cynocephali proclaim
Thy effulgent deity, and mark
The adorations of thy name
In seemly stations one by one,
As thou encirclest blinder poles
Than Khem or Ammon showed the sun
In one-eyed sight of secret goals.
So I adore, and sing : for I
This magic monocle avow,
Distorted from Divinity
And wrought in subtler fashion now.
An invocation shrined and sealed
Be this ! The many hear me not,
Though I be vocal, thou revealed.
I scorn the eye, uphold the—what
Gods call the lotus poppy-hued,
Brave wound of weeping Isis !—eye
Of Demiourgos, understood
Of none, O Lily, ladily
Laden with lays of Buddhist bard,
Maiden with ways and bays of mirth,
And music—is the saying hard ?
Shall " Cryptic Coptic " block the birth
Of holy ecstasy ? Forbid,
Ye Gods, forbid ! Posed block, you fail
Of bulging heart by drooping lid.
Can you not serve as finger-nail ?

B

Ay! God of scissors! barber God!
  My earlier mystery did you learn?
Unshoe the aching pseudopod!
  Mysterious donkey, chew or churn
Your human-kindness-milk to butter!
  I gave you gratis God's advice
(Since God's responsible) to—mutter
  In gutter, pay your tithe to vice
Since virtue kicks you down its stairs.
So thus I clothed it in strange word
To catch you thinking unawares.
  Think? do you think? Then, thinks a bird.
Read your Descartes! Nietzsche demurred?
To you, who give yourself such airs,
  This riddle cannot offer snares!
" Love's mass is holier than wine and wafer.
Thou couldst not beetle be: then, be cock-
    chafer!"
Hence my address, this swoodier Swood
  To Khephra, hence the ambiguous speech,
The alluring analogue, the good,
  The loftiest heaven Art hopes to reach,
The highest goal of man as man ;
  The sly Paraprosdokian.
You could not love! You could not serve
  The scouring of Love's scullery! You,
ἴσος θέοισιν? Ha, you swerve
  Back to that subtler meaning! Few
Can guess that miracle of reserve,
  That sacrament of mathematics,
That threescore glee, that three times three,
  That added scream of hydrostatics !
Not I, for one! Be assured, to fail
  With me no arrière-pensée lends.
Fall once the penny, head or tail,
  I care not—all the less my friends !
Faultlessly faulty! Regular
  In ice or fire, 'tis nullness counts.
So, spring of those Parnassian founts,
  A thousand garters heralded
Thy flawless solitary star :
A million garters shall bestead
  The poet's turn, when, lone and far,
All are dismissed : Some man, low brute,
Cry " Shame, O star that would not shoot,
  And yet went out !" But I, my dear,
(Good-bye!) get neither shriek nor groan :
  Kiss, curse, cat's hiss, I shall not hear,
My dear, for I shall be alone.

III.

What change of language! Ah, my dear,
  The reason is not far to seek.
You know of old how oft I veer
  From French to Zend, from Jap to Greek.
Teste der titre polyglot
  Del Berashith, καλος kitab !
I trust you take me, do you not?
  But change of thought—ay ! there's the barb
To stick and quiver in your heart !
Well, little lady, what of art?

IV.

All things are branded change. My thought
  Long ran in one delicious groove.
Now newly sits the appointed court
  To try another case, to prove
Another crime. Last week the law
  Dealt with the garter's gross offence.
You were the Judge, enthroned on awe :
  I wove that eloquent defence,
Unwove that Rhadamanthine frown
  Which I had made myself, my star ;
For I was counsel for the crown,
  And I the prisoner at the bar.
Did you not see—the sight is sad !—
  How tiny was the part you played,
How little use the poet had
  Even in Maytime for a maid?
Why! all's a whirl; but I, be sure,
  Am axle, if at all I be ;
So you, if yet your light endure,
  Are model, and no more, to me.
So well you sit, though, you shall earn
  Beyond your hourly increment
A knowledge. Are you fit to learn,
  Or will you rather be content
With muddled mighty talk of Teutons
  Evolving from the tangled Skein,
Nietzsche's research compared to Newton's
  In some one's enervated brain.
(Did I say—brain?) I'll talk, and you
  Listen or not, as best beseems
Your lily languor. Irish stew
  Shall float like dewdrops in your dreams.
So shall my new Apocalypse
  Appear to you, my model ! Once
You saw a languor on my lips,
  A dawn of many molten suns,
And laughed in springtide of delight ;
  But now eclipse inveils your mood
Of me : descends artistic night ;
  I see a sun called solitude.
So models kiss, and understand
  So far : the picture moves them not.
By label they approve the grand ;
  By critic's candour rave o'er rot.
But, let me hoist you Thornycroft,
  And cry " Behold this Rodin !" bring
Some Poynter, lift the thing aloft,
  Announce a Morice, see you fling
Your soul on knees in fervid praise :—
  If so—Off, Lilith ! runs the phrase.
Now, is no barb upon the dart?
  Now, little lady, What of art ?

v.

Moreover (just a word) this chance
  I fling you over space—for luck !
This Scotland yet may catch your France,
  My crow grow germane to your cluck,

See art : see truth as I who see,
(Am wellnigh fallen in the fight !)
Then the last lie, duality,
May break before the victor sight.
Then, and then only, That. Sweet hours
Of trivial passion deep as death,
Ye are past : I face the solemn powers
Of sex and soul, of brain and breath.
For you I lift the veil : discover
The actual, for I was your lover.
What should such word imply? I showed
Late, in the earlier dithyramb.
But—in yon stone there lurks a toad !—
The Quarter bleats no palinode ;
Goat it may be, no woolly lamb.
Arithmetic assuage your wrath
Should Cambridge wit write quarter " fourth " !
What said the unctuous slime of art,
Scrapings of beauty's palette, pimps
Of serious studios, stews or mart
Of filth, not vice ? Those painter shrimps !
What did they gloat upon, delight
To think of better folk than they ?
Hear then their oracle of might,
The sortes of a Balaam bray.
Through muddy glasses Delphi squints ;
Cowards lack words and glut on hints.

VI.

Sibyl says nothing—she's a Sphinx !
I wonder, though, what Sibyl thinks.
She argues " he would have her grow
So fell a Trixy—point device !—
His Dante to her Beatrice
Should seem—let music's language show :—
Andante move to Allegro,
Alas for pianissimo ! "
And, in return, suspects I don
One glory more than Solomon :
" Rocks cannot satisfy the coney ;
Lingerie's always worth the money."
In fine, flop, German, from thy throne !
Leave Greek and Papuan alone !
What foreign tongues be worth our own ?
Is Armour jointed unawares ?
Is Canning King, as Carlyle swears ?
This is indeed Cumaean lore—
Ah well, 'tis pity !—say no more !

There's one and twenty for your score,
Ah, how your divination slewed awry,
Ye prurient guttersnipes of prudery !
We know as much, my girl ! We laughed,
And still can laugh at Barbercraft
Plied thus askew. Then leave them so !
Evoke the ancient afterglow
Rose on our sacramental snow
Of silent love, of mountain grace.
Remember the old tenderness
Even in these bitter words that press
Their ardent breast, their iron face,
Out to expression. Ay ! remember
The ancient phantom fire of flowers,
The Druid altars of December,
The Virgin priestess, the dread hours
Of solemn love. Then quail before
The deadly import of my word !
Forget your silly self, and store
Its vital horror, stabbed and spurred
To fearful pace and torture wild
Deep in your true heart's core, my child !
For though I strip you bare, and run
My red-hot iron through your flesh,
There is a citadel that none
May touch—not God ! The rotten rest
Evacuate ; be seated there.
Let there be music, and Rome burn !
Then you may climb to be aware
How well you serve my idle turn,
Yet to yourself avail. There too
Lies a last doubtful chance for you.
Behold who dare ! (Ay, you are fain !)
Purblind with prejudice ? No vision.
Palsied with passion ? Sight in vain.
Stupid with sense of self ? Division.
Picture, not model ? Then you win.
I painted soul, who saw your skin :—
Be soul ! That saves you. If you fail,
Why, then, you fail ! Enough of this—
(Read not again Macbeth amiss !)
Give me one customary kiss—
An end of it ! I rend the veil.
The flag falls for the Stakes of Song.
Run, filly, for the odds are long ! [1]

[1] [This " possible Part II." is still *in nubibus*
unless we are to suppose from the Greek Dedications
(pp. 1 and 16) that " Rosa Mundi " is to be taken as
such.]

WHY JESUS WEPT

A STUDY OF SOCIETY AND OF THE GRACE OF GOD

1905

PERSONS STUDIED.

THE MARQUIS OF GLENSTRAE, K.G,
TYSON, *a farmer.*
SIR PERCIVAL DE PERCIVALE, *Bart., K.C.B.*
SIR PERCY DE PERCIVALE, *his son.*
JOHN CARRUTHERS, *his friend and steward of his house.*
GREUMOCH, *a Highland gillie.*
ARNOLD, } *household servants,*
RITSON, }
SIR HERPES ZOSTER, M.D., *a celebrated physician.*
SIR GRABSON JOBBS, Q.C., *Solicitor-General.*
Mr. G. K. CHESTERTON.
LORD RONALD GOWER, *as Chorus.*
A Horny-Handed Brother (Plymouth).
A conscientious Chemist.
A Theatre-Goer.
Large but unseen body of retainers.

MAUD, MARCHIONESS OF GLENSTRAE.
ANGELA, LADY BAIRD.
HORTENSE, *her maid.*
MOLLY TYSON, *daughter of Tyson.*
Aged (Plymouth) Sisters, &c,, &c.

The action of the play occupies three years.

DEDICATIO MINIMA.

My dear Christ,

A person, *purporting to be a friend and disciple of yours, and calling himself John, reports you to have wept. His testimony is now considered by the best authorities to be of a very doubtful order. But if you* did *weep, this (vide infra) is why. Or if not, surely it would have made you weep, had it met your eye. Excuse the rhyme !*
You ask me *(on dit) to believe you. I shall*

be willing to do so—merely as a gentleman—
till you betray the trust ; but at present nobody
worthy of serious consideration can give me
any clear notion of what you actually assert.
*I labour under no such disadvantages. So
have no diffidence in asking you to believe me.*
Yours affectionately,

ALEISTER CROWLEY.

DEDICATIO MINOR.

My dear Lady S——,

I quite agree with your expressed opinion
that no true gentleman would (with or without reason) compare any portion of your
ladyship's anatomy to a piece of wet chamois
leather ; the best I can do to repair his rudeness is to acknowledge the notable part your
ladyship played in the conception of this
masterpiece by the insertion of as much of
your name as my lawyers will permit me.
I am your ladyship's most humble and
obedient servant,

ALEISTER CROWLEY.

DEDICATIO MAJOR.

My Friends,

To you, Eastern of the Easterns, who have
respectively given up all to find Truth ; you,
Jinawaravansa,[1] who esteemed the Yellow Robe

[1] A Siamese prince who became a Buddhist monk.

20

more than your Princedom ; you, Achiha,[1]
*by sticking manfully to your Work in the
World, yet no more allowing it to touch your
Purpose than waters may wet the lotus leaf
(to take the oldest and best simile of your
oldest and best poets), must I dedicate this
strange drama ; for, like you, I would abandon all ; like you, I see clearly what is of
value ; or, if not, at least what is worthless ;
already something ! Thus do I wish you
and myself the three great boons Sila, Samadhi,
and Salam.*

DEDICATIO MAXIMA.

To my unborn child,

*Who may learn by the study of this drama
to choose the evil and avoid the good —* i.e.
*as judged by Western, or "Christian"
standards.*

DEDICATIO EXTRAORDINARIA.

Dear Mr. Chesterton,

*Alone among the puerile apologists of your
detestable religion you hold a reasonably mystic
head above the tides of criticism. You are the
last champion of God ; with you I choose to
measure myself. Others I can despise ; you
are a force to be reckoned with, as Browning
your intellectual father was before you.*

*Whether we are indeed friends or enemies
it is perhaps hard to say : it has sometimes
seemed to me that human freedom and happiness are our common goal, but that you
found your muddied oafs in Gods, ministers,
passive resisters, and all the religious team—
the " Brixton Bahinchuts," we might call
them ; while I, at once a higher mystic and
a colder sceptic, found my Messiah in Charles
Watts, and the Devil and all his angels.
While* נחש *and* משיח *alike add to* 358,
indeed, it is no odds : did you once see this

[1] A metathesis of Crowley's own name ;
"spelt in full," it adds up to 666 ; as does
Aleister E. Crowley. See the signature to the
" Dedicatio Extraordinaria."

[2] Nechesh is the word for serpent used in
Genesis iii. Messiach is the expected Re-
deemer. Their identity is the Vindication of
the Serpent and the revelation of Jehovah as
the arch-enemy of man. The above doctrine
is the most secret of Qabalistic arcana.

*you were not far off from the Heart of the
Qabalah.*

*The occasion of this letter is the insertion
of a scene equivalent to an "appreciation of the
Brixton Chapel" in my masterpiece " Why
Jesus Wept." You asked me for it ;*[1] *I promised
it ;*[2] *and I hope you will like it. Can I do more
than make your Brixton my deus ex machinâ ?
You see, when I wrote " The Soul of Osiris,"
Europe was my utmost in travel. To-day,
what country of the globe has not shuddered
with the joy of my presence ? The virgin
snows of Chogo Ri, the gloomy jungles of
Burma, filled with savage buffaloes and murderous Chins ; the peace of Waikiki, the
breeding hopeful putrefaction of America, the
lonely volcanoes of Mexico, the everlasting
furnace sands of Egypt—all these have known
me. Travel thou thus far, thou also ! Somewhat shalt thou learn ! But otherwise ; gird
on thine armour for thy Christ, O Champion
of the dying faith in a man dead !*

*Arm ! arm, and out ; for the young war-
rior of a new religion is upon thee ; and his
number is the number of a man.*

אלהיסטהדההכדעולהי

WHY JESUS WEPT.

IN vain I sit by Kandy Lake.
The broad verandah slides to mist.
No tropic rapture strikes awake
The grim soul's candour to insist
The pen reluctant. Beauty's task
Is but to praise the peace of earth ;
If Horror's contrast that should ask,
Off from this Paradise of mirth !
Let Kandy Lake, the white soul, mirror
The generalised concept, limn clear
England, a memory clean of error,
A royal reason to be here.
Therefore no reminiscence stirs
My heart of when I lived in Kandy.
Europe's the focus now ! that blurs
The picture of my Buddhist dandy,

[1] *Vide* vol. ii. p. 203, *supra.*
[2] " I promise Mr. Chesterton | A grand
ap-pre-ci-a-ti-on | Of Brixton on Ascension
Day."—*The Sword of Song.*

Allan, who broke his wand of flame,
Discharged his faithful poltergeist,
Gave up attempts to say The Name,[1]
Ananda Maitriya became,
By yellow robes allured, enticed ;
Leaving me all alone to shame
The cunning missionary game ;
And, by bad critics topped and sliced,
Put the ky-bosh on [2] Jesus Christ.

I sing a tale of modern life
(Suited for reading to my wife)
Of how Sir Percy Percivale
Grew from a boy into a man ;
Well ware of every metric plan
A bard may dream, a rhymester scrawl,
Avoiding with deliberate "Damn !"
(Ut supra) In Memoriam ;[3]
For such suggestion would suffice
To turn your blood to smoke or ice,
Dismissing with a hearty curse
Eunuch psychology, pimp verse.
Moreover, lest my metre move
From year to year in one dull groove,
Invention, hear me !   Strange device
Hatch from this egg a cockatrice
Of novel style, that you who read
The Sword of Song—(your poor, poor head !)
Shall stand amazed (at the new note
Flung faultless from this trembling throat)
That Crowley, ever versatile
And lord of many a new bad style
Should still in's gun have one more cartridge,
And who Ixtaccihuatl's [4] smart ridge
Achieved should still be full of mettle
To go up Popocatapetl.[4]

As song then chills or aches or burns,
The metre shall slew round by turns.

[1] The great task of Western occultism is to
" pronounce the name" of Jehovah ; if this be
correctly done, the universe (i.e. of sense) is
annihilated, and the true universe, of spirit, is
made present to the consciousness.
[2] To stop or silence ; to spoil the plans of.
[3] The four lines above are in the metre of
Tennyson's poem "In Memoriam." Its lack
of manliness prompts Crowley's satire.
[4] Mountains in Mexico climbed by Crowley
in 1901.

The gross and bestial demand prose.
(Glance at the page, lass, stop your nose,
And turn to where short lines proclaim
That purity has won the game !)
But stow your prudery, wives and mothers,
You know as much muck as—those others !
Your modest homes are dull ; you need
     me !
Don't let your husbands know ; but—read me !

SCENE I.

The Poet inducts his matter.

I draw no picture of the Fates
(Recitativo—rhyming 8s)
Presiding over birth and so on.
I leave the Gods alone, and go on.
Sir Percival de Percivale
Sat in his vast baronial hall
(All unsuspicious of the weird :
" One day a person with a beard
Shall write of thee, and write a lot
Too like the late Sir Walter Scott.")[1]
Sir Percival de Percivale
(Begin again !) was over all
The pangs of death foreseen ; his eye
Sought the high rafter vacantly.
A week, and he would see no more !
His lady long had gone—O Lor' !
I hear " St. Agnes' Eve "[2] suggest
To this 8's better a far best ;
Spenserian solemnitie
Fits this part of my minstrelsie.

Now is the breath of winter in the hall.
The logs die out — the knight would be
     alone !
The brave Sir Percival de Percivale
Sits like an image hewen out of stone.
Ay ! he must die.   The doctors all are
     gone,

[1] Many of Scott's narrative poems are in the
same metre as this passage.
[2] By John Keats, written in Spenserian
stanzas.   What follows is in part a parody
of this style.

And he must follow to the dusk abode,
The solemn place inscrutable, unknown,
Meeting no mortal on that crowded road ;
All swift in the one course, ions to the kathode.[1]

Sir Percival de Percivale was brave.
There doth he sit and little cheer doth get.
He doth not moan or laugh aloud or rave !
The dogs of hell are not upon him yet.
He was the bravest soul man ever met
In court or camp or solitude—then why
Stands his pale forehead in an icy sweat ?
He mutters in his beard this rune awry :
"There lives no soul undrugged that feareth
        not to die."

Lo ! were it otherwise, mere banishment,
I deem he had feared more ! He had an heir.
This was a boy of strength with ardour blent,
High hope embowered in a body fair.
Him had he watched with eager eye, aware
Of misery occult in youth, awake
At the first touch of the diviner air
Of manhood, that could bane and blessing
        make,
The Lord of Life and Death, the secret of
        the Snake.

The snake of Egypt hath a body twin ;
It hath bright wings wherewith it well can fly ;
It is of virtue and of bitter sin ;
It beareth strength and beauty in its eye ;
Beneath its tongue are Hate and Misery ;
Love in its coils is hidden, and its nature
Is double everyway ; dost wonder why
The poet worships every scalèd feature,
And holds him lordliest yet of every kingly
        creature ?[2]

Sir Percival nor moved nor spoke ; awhile
There is black silence in the ancient hall.
Then cometh subtly with well-trainèd smile
The courteous eld, the agèd seneschal.

[1] When an electric current is passed through
water, and many other fluids, a decomposition
is effected, the component atoms finding their
way to one or other pole of the battery. These
atoms are called "ions" and the poles
"anode" and "kathode."
[2] See note *supra* to "Dedicatio Major."

On bended knee " Sir Percy ! " he doth call
To the young boy, and voweth service true.
Whereat he started, spurning at the thrall ;
But then the orphan truth he inward knew,
And on the iron ground his sobbing body
        threw.

It was a weary while before they raised him
Boy as he was, none dare disturb his grief.
And for his grief was strong, they loved and
        praised him
For son's devotion to their dear dead chief.
Long, long he wept, nor bought with tears
        relief.
He knew the loss, the old head wise and grey
Well to assoil him of his spirit's grief,
The twilight dangers of a boy's dim way,
His dragons to confront, his minotaurs to slay.

Yet, when he knew himself the baronet,
He took good order for the house, and bore
Him as beseemed the master ; none may fret
All are as well bestowed as aye before.
His father's eighty was with him fourscore.
His father's old advisers well he groups
Into a closer company ; their lore
He ardently acquires—he loops no loops,[1]
But—Bacon[2]—grapples them to's soul with
        steely hoops !

You, lass, may see here for this Boy's com-
        panions
Virtue and Peace of Mind, Prudence, Respect,
Throwing new roots down like a clump of
        banyans,[3]
Of Early Training Well the just Effect !

[1] A reference to "looping the loop," an acro-
batic feat popular at the time. Hence, to go
a wild and dangerous, as well as an indirect,
course.
[2] A sarcastic reference to the inane theory
that the plays of Shakespeare were written by
Bacon. The misquotation is from *Hamlet*—
" Those friends thou hast, and their adoption
        tried,
Grapple them to thy soul with hoops of
        steel."
[3] The banyan tree puts forth branches which
droop to the earth and take root. A single
tree may thus spread over many acres.

I would applaud thee, camel gracious-necked!
Confirm thee in thy reading of my task,
Were it not foreign to the fact.   Select
Another favour !—this too much to ask.
The boy's exemplar deeds were but an iron
     mask.

("Ay ! for deception !" Mrs. Sally G—d,
The gawk and dowdy with the long grey teeth,
Jumps to conclusion, instant, out of hand :
" There is some nasty secret underneath ! "
None nastier than thy name ! This verse, its
     sheath,
Thou poisonous bitch, is rotten. Fact, atone !)
Such magic liquors in his veins there seethe
As, would he master, need strong order known
In life's routine, ere he may dare to be alone.

So there alone he was, and like a comet,
Leaps on the utmost ridges of the hills.
Then, like a dog returning to his vomit,
Broods in the hall on all creation's ills !
An idle volume with mere bosh he fills ;
He dreams and dozes, toils and flies afar,
Apace—the body by a thousand wills
Of fire cross-twisted, bruised, is thrust, a spar,
Wreckage of some wild sea, to seas without
     a star.

Listen, O lady, listen, reverend Abbot,
Lord of the Monastery, Fort Augustus ![1]
Hear an awakening spirit's a. b, ab ! but
Let not thy mediæval logic thrust us
Into contempt ; nor, lady, can we trust us
Wholly to thy most pardonable failing,
Sentiment ; one will rot, the other rust us.
Let us just listen to the spirit ailing :—
'Tis like a God in bliss, or like a damned soul
     wailing ! [2]

[1] This monastery is chosen because of its
unpleasant proximity to Crowley's home.

[2] (A word to bid you notice with what
     mastery
Of technique that last stanza there was
     written.
I risk a poet's license on one cast, Ery !
(Pet name for thee, Eros !) The lines are
     smitten
Into due harmony double-rhymed, well-
     knitten.

SCENE II.[1]

SIR PERCY PERCIVALE (*on a mountain
summit*).

No higher ?   No higher ?
All hell is my portion.
My mouth is as fire ;
My thought an abortion.
This is the summit ?
Attained is the height.
Down like a plummet
To blackness and night
Hope goes.   Not here,
Not here is Desire,
The ease from fear,
The ice from fire.
Not here—O God !
I would I were dead
Under the sod !
My brain is as lead.
My thoughts are as smoke.
My heart is a fire ;
I know not what fuel
Is feeding its fury !
In vain I invoke
The Lord of Desire !
He is evil and cruel.
The spells of Jewry
Are poured in his ear
In vain : he may hear not.
O would I were dumb !
For the pestilent fever
That bites my blood
Forces like fear
These babblings : I near not
The secret, nor come
To my purpose for ever.

Wherefore, to show I can repeat the effort,
This verse inserted like a playful kitten
To usher in the youth's c. d. e. f., ert
Or inert as may be ; it can't the lucky deaf
     hurt.)—A. C.

[1] These three *soliloquies* (Scenes *II.*, *III.*,
and *VI.*) perhaps represent the self-torture of
the poet's own youth, much of which he spent
in the Lake district.

A turbulent flood
Whispers and yells,
Alight in my breast.
God ! for the spells
That unseal men—a rest !
No higher ?   I have climbed
This pinnacled steep.
It mocks me, this heaven
Of thine, Adonai !
Rather be limed
In the dusk, in the deep,
Seven times seven
Thy hells, O Jehovah !
I tune the great Name
To a million vowels :—
It escapes me, the flame !
But deep in my bowels
Growls the deep lust,
The bitter distrust,
The icy fear,
The cruel thought !
O ! I am here—
And here is nought.
I must rave on.
I hate the sun.
Anon !   Anon !
Let us both begone,
Thou fiend that pourest
One by one
These evil words
In my ear, in my heart !
Here on the summit
The air is too thin.
Wild as the winds
Let me ride !   Let me start
Over the plains ;
For here my brain's
Numb, it is dumb, it
Is torn by this passion.
Down !   Eagle-fashion
Drive to the level !
Teeth ! you may gnash on !
My body's anguish
Is help to my soul.
Hail to the revel !
The dance of the devil,
The rhythms that languish,
The rhymes that roll!

Down like the swine
Of the gross Gadarene
In a maddening march
From the snow to the rock,
From the rock to the pine,
From the pine to the larch,
From the tree to the green !
   [*He leaps down, then pauses.*
O Devil !   To mock
With echo the roar
Of a young boy's spirit !
And yet (as before)
I know I inherit
The wit of the mage,
The blood of the king,
The age of the sage !
Ah ! all these sting
Through me—this rage
Is the strength of my blood,
The heat of my body,
The birth of my wit.
To hell with the flood
Of words !   Were I God, he
Had made me as fit
For all things as now,
But added a brow
Cool—O how cool !
Fool ! Fool ! Fool !
   [*With a terrible laugh he springs
   out of sight down the crags.*

SCENE III.

SIR PERCY PERCIVALE (*in the Hall*).

O the gloom of these distasteful tomes !
The horror of the secrets here discovered !
Awake,   ye   salamandrines ;[1]   sleep, ye
   gnomes !
Were those   the sylphs that   round   me
   hovered
On the mountain, and destroyed my peace ?
O the misery of this world ; the fear
And folly that is unattained desire !
I would be master ; I, the lord of Greece ;

[1] The spirits of fire, air, water, and earth
were respectively named salamanders (fem.
-drines), sylphs, undines, and gnomes.

I the bright Deva [1] of the golden sphere ;
I the swift spirit of the primal fire :—
All these I am, not will be.   O blind ape !
All these are shapeless ; thou art but a shape,
A blind, bad-blooded bat !   Ugh !   Ugh !
The snake
Wriggling to death amid his burning brake
Is wiser, holier, lordlier.   Open, page
Of the old Rabbi ! [2] tell me of the mage ;
Of him who would ; of him who dared and
did ;
Of him who feared and failed ; of him who
fell ;
One peëring lightwards through a coffin-lid,
One aching heavenwards—and achieving
hell !
O let me do and die as they !   The wand,
The lamp, the sword, come eager to my
hand ;—
Or, if I wander now upon the moor,
An old red-hatted witch will come, for sure,
And teach me how the dragon deeds are done
Or truck my spirit to the Evil One ;
Or else,—I wot not what.   I am drunk with
will,
Will toward some destiny most high, most
holy !
Some of those glories sung with awful skill
By the loud brabble of the monster Crowley,
That poet of the muck-heap !   Oh, enough !
The wind is harsh and vital on the hills.
Forth let me fare !   I am other than the stuff
His dreams are made of !   Aye !   I shall
endure !
I am destined Lord of many magic wills.
Another Rosencreutz another order
Founds—to a better end than his, be sure !
Away ! away, my lad ! and o'er the border
I shall get myself a buxom bride,
And ride—ride—ride !   [*He rises.*
Ride to the blacksmith at Gretna Green,
Kiss a fair lady and find her a queen !
O a Queen, for certain !   It is I that ride,
Ride in my youth and pride

[1] The Indian generic term for any good
spirit.
[2] Rabbi Schimeon, who first wrote down the
Zohar, the most sacred book of the Qabalah.

With a long sword girt to my waist,
And a strawberry mare sweet-paced,
And a long night with no moon, no star !
I will plunder the traveller from afar ;—
Aye ! and find him an ancient sage,
Learn all his wisdom, marry his daughter,
Become a king and a mage,
Lord of Fire, Earth, Air, and Water !
Ho ! my horse, lads !   Away !   To the
moor !
Ho ! there's a fox i' the hole, that's sure.
          [*Flings swaggering out of the room.*

SCENE IV.

ANGELA, LADY BAIRD (*regarding
herself in a mirror*).

I thank you, M. Davenport ! [1]   This smile
Is worth a husband.   Here, one touch of
pink
Completes a perfect picture—Are these eyes
Dark eno' to look love or sin, and large
(O Atropine ! [2]) to beam forth innocence !
Innocence, a grim jest for sixty years !
Nay, sixty-three ; I lie not to myself ;
Else one sins lying ; thus is virtue mixed,
A bubbling draught that soon lies still and
flat ;
While my great lust runs deep and dark, nor
changes
For all that time can do.   What of this
boy ?
I knew his father ; the man feared me well
For all his open laughter ; would he were
Alive !   I dream one torture writhed about
His heart he'll miss in hell.   I hated him.
This boy of his I saw but yesterday
Ride barehead by me like a madman would,
Is strong and well-set—aye ! desirable.
I would be better of his virgin lips :—
          [*She puts her lips against the mirror.*

[1] A famous dentist in Paris.
[2] The alkaloid of belladonna.   It dilates the
pupil, and is abused to this end by many
foolish women.

(Nay, you are cold ! Like a dead man,
    perhaps !)
I would get gladness of the royal force
Of armed insistence against my restraint.
What is worth while, though, to a woman
    found
Fragrant and fearful to a host of men
Even yet ? they throng me, hunt me ! Why
    should I
Do this unutterable wickedness ?
Because that Moina Marjoribanks grins and
    boasts
She will achieve him ? Angela, not so !
For its own sweet, most damnable sake,
    say yes !
Look to those cheeks, redress the red-gold
    hair,
Awake the giant wit, the master sin
That is, for an apple's sake, Lord of us all :
These shall despoil her ; these shall ruin
    him.
Yes, I shall clutch him to these sagging
    breasts
Stained, bruised,—enough !—and take his
    life in mine—
Ugh ! pleasure of Hell ! Sir Percy Percivale,[1]
Here is a strumpet. Ha ! have you a
    sword ?
Enough. I am dressed. I am lovely, have
    communed
With my dark heart : I see my way to it :—
Oh joy ! joy ! joy !—Hortense, these candles
    out !
[*The maid blows out the mirror candles.*
I will go down. Prepare my scented
    paper,
My rosy wax against my coming here—
When, girl ? I' th' morn, i' th' morn ! When
    else ? I'd write.
    [*She goes out, with a set smile on her
    face, yet a gleam of real laughter
    beneath it.*

[1] Sir Percivale, in *Morte d'Arthur*, being
enamoured of a lady, caused a bed to be prepared. But laying his sword therein—and in
that sword was a reed cross and the sign of
the crucifix—she was discovered to be the
devil. See Malory, xiv. 9.

SCENE V.

To CARRUTHERS, *in the Office of* SIR PERCY'S
Ancestral Hall, enter GREUMOCH.

GREUMOCH.

Ay, sir. The laddie's in the thick o't ! Weel !
She'll be off tae th' muir, a'm thinkin, sin'
    the dee.

CARRUTHERS.

He goes to solitude ?

GREUMOCH.

    Weel, weel, sir, na !
She wadna say the laddie wad gang yon.

CARRUTHERS (*smiling*).

He is ever alone ?

GREUMOCH.

    Oo ay, sir, by his lanes.

CARRUTHERS.

Go now, and tell me ever of his doings.
    [*Exit* GREUMOCH.
The hour is nigh, but when that hour may
    strike
None, not the wisest, may foretell. I fear
A moment's mischief may destroy these years
Of grave solicitude, their work. This boy
Thinks his grey father dead. These words
    (*tapping a letter*) shall speak
Even from the tomb. These words shall be
    obeyed
By force of ancient habit : these give me
Supreme authority to exercise
By stealth, not overt till the hour be come
Should madness seat herself upon the lad,
And he turn serpent on his friends. But
    no !
There is too strong a discipline of sense,
Too cool a brain, too self-controlled a
    heart :—
Well, we shall see.
    [*Turns to his books.*

SCENE VI.

Sir Percy Percivale (*on Wastwater*).

God, I have rowed !
My hands are one blister ;
My arms are one ache ;
But my brain is a fire,
As erst on the fell,
In the hall ; let me dive
To the under-abode,
Where the sweet-voiced sister
Of the Screes[1] shall forsake
Her home for desire
Of me !   Say the spell !
Down then ! to drive—
          [*He dives.   The waters close over
               him.   He rises.*
Misery ever !
I dived, and the best
Could dive no deeper.
Did I touch bottom ?
Never, O never !
I stand confessed
A footler, a creeper.
These spells—'Od rot 'em !—
Are vain as the world,
As all of the stars.
This mystery's nought.
But for cold !   The lake
Is hot as the curled
Flames at the bars
Of Hell ; it is wrought
Of fire : what shall slake
This terrible thirst,
This torment accurst ?
          [*He looks into the water.*
Yet, in my face
As I gaze on the water
Is something calmer.
What if the king
Of the Screes should see me,
Give me for grace
His beautiful daughter,
Voluptuous charmer ?

[1] The mountain which bounds Wastwater
on the south.

A golden ring
Should bring her to me ;
No marriage dreamy ;
Identity, love !
          [*He looks up.*
Stay !   In the wood
By the waterway, stands
A delicate fairy !
          [Molly Tyson *is discovered*
I'll steal from above,
Watch her.   How good !
How sweet of her hands !
How dainty and airy !
How perfect, how kind !
How bright in her thoughts !
How subtle, refined,
The least light of her mind !
Let me approach !
O fear !   O sorrow !
I fear to encroach.
Scree-king, I borrow
Thy frown, thy pride,
Thy magical targe.
To her side I glide,
To the mystical marge
Of this lake enchaunted.
O waters elf-haunted,
Bear me toward her,
A cruel marauder,
A robber of light !
O beauty !   O bright !
How shall I sing thee ?
Nay !   do not fly me !
My bird, why wing thee ?
Be kind !   O be nigh me !
She speaks not.   I'll follow !
[*Leaps from boat and wades in to shore.*
The world is my bower.
By height and by hollow
I'll seek thee, O flower !
I'll not turn back !
          [*He pursues her.*
I'll go on for ever.
The strength of a giant
Is in my limbs —
          [*He reels.*
My body is slack ;
My muscles sever ;

My limbs are pliant ;
My eyesight swims.
Come to me ! Come to me !
Thee have I sought !
Thou that wast dumb to me,
Come—I am nought !
[*Striving ever to follow her, he
faints and falls. The girl
stops.*

MOLLY.

Dear me ! The young gentleman's ill
too. What a nice boy it is ! I must go and
help him. Why did he call to me ? (*Goes
back.*) I was afraid—Yes, but I must go.
Something calls me. Is anything the
matter, sir ? (*He does not answer. She lifts
his head to her lap.*) How pale he is ! Poor
boy ! Shall I run to the Hall and get help,
I wonder ? (*Puts him gently down and half
rises. His eyes open.*)

SIR PERCY.

Oh ! I am but a coward. I am not ill,
I was awake. I let you hold me. Forgive
me !

MOLLY.

Forgive you, sir ? I am a poor girl of the
dale.

SIR PERCY.

Your voice is like an empress—no, a
nightingale. You do not speak like a
daleswoman.

MOLLY.

I was at school, sir, at—

SIR PERCY.

O but I love you !
There is none above you,
Not God ! I renounce Thee,
O maker ! Dissolve,
Ye hopes of delusion !
Mage, I will trounce thee !

Sage, to confusion !
Problems to solve ?
Here is my life !
My secret is told—
What is your name,
O fairest of women ?
Bosom of gold !
Faultless your fame !
An aeon were shame
Your beauty to hymn in !
Will you be mine,
Mine and mine only !
Beauty divine,
How I was lonely !
How I was mad !
Say, are you glad,
Glad of me, happy here,
Here in my arms ?
I kiss you, I kiss you !
Say, is it bliss, you
Spirit of holiness ?
Holy I hold you !
Swift as a rapier
Stabbed me your charms,
Broken with lowliness,
Smitten with rapture :—
All is so mixed ;
All is a whirl ;—
(Let me recapture
This lock ; 'tis unfixed.)
Ay, little girl,
Bury my head
In the scent of your hair !
Would I were dead
In your arms ever fair,
Buried and folded
For aye on your breast :—
That were delight,
Eternity moulded
In form of your kiss !
That were the rest
I have sought for, the bliss
I have ached to obtain :—
Ah ! it was pain !

MOLLY.

Ay ! sir, but can you love me ? Me, poor
girl !

SIR PERCY.

Love you? Ah, Christ! I love you so!
Say you love me, love me! Say so! Again!
Again! Aloud! I must hear, or I shall
die.

MOLLY.

I love you. Oh, you hurt me, you do
indeed.

SIR PERCY.

I love you, love you. Yes, you love me!
Love! Christ! Yes, oh! I love you so,
dear heart.

MOLLY.

Dear love, I love you.

SIR PERCY.

Ah, love, love, how I love you. This is
the world! Love! Love! I love you so,
my darling. Oh my white golden heart of
glory!

MOLLY.

I love you, love you so.

SIR PERCY.

Ah, God! I love you! I shall faint
with love. I love you so.

[ANGELA, LADY BAIRD, *is discovered
behind the trees. She suffers the
torments of hell.*

ANGELA (*while the duet continues*).

Ah! if there were a devil to buy souls,
Or if I had not sold mine! Quick bargain,
  God!
Hell catch the jade! Blister her fat red
  cheeks!
Rot her snub nose! Poison devour her guts!
Wither her fresh clean face with old grey
  scabs,
And venomous ulcers gnaw the baby breasts!
Vermin upon her! Infamous drab! Gr!
  Gr!
I would I had her home to torture her.
I would dig out those amorous eyes with
  gimlets,

Break those young teeth and smash that gaby
  grin!
I am utterly wretched! Ah, there is aye
  hope left!—
For see, they part!

SIR PERCY.

Ah, love, at moonrise!

MOLLY.

At my door!

SIR PERCY.

Hell belch
Its monsters one by one to stop the way!
I would be there.

ANGELA.

Christ! he shall not be there!

MOLLY.

Farewell!

SIR PERCY.

O fairest, fare thee well!

MOLLY.

Farewell!
[ANGELA *draws nearer, yet remains
  concealed.*

SIR PERCY.

O but the moon is laggard!

MOLLY.

Hard it is!

SIR PERCY.

Time matters not. I am so drunk with love.

MOLLY.

One kiss, one kiss!

SIR PERCY.

A million! Ay, slack moon,
Dull moon, haste, haste!

MOLLY

Kiss me again, again!

ANGELA.

Would I had the kissing of her with vitriol !

SIR PERCY.

Your kisses are like young rain.

ANGELA.

The slobbery kisses of virginity.
He shall soon know these calculated, keen,
Intense, important kisses,—mine ! Hell's
worm !

MOLLY.

Yes, do not leave me. Let us away now !
No, I must tell them, fetch my—

SIR PERCY.

No ! No ! No !
Nothing is necessary unto love,
Not even light. In chaos love were well.
I love you, love you so, my love, my love.

MOLLY.

How I love you ! Oh, kiss me again !

SIR PERCY.

Yet you were best to go. This bites like
Hell's worst agony.

ANGELA.

Amen !

MOLLY.

God be with you !

SIR PERCY.

Till we meet again.

MOLLY.

At moonrise.

SIR PERCY.

At your door.

ANGELA.

At moonset he shall crawl away from mine.
The dog ! I hate him ! So much the more
sure

To have him. Damn them ! Are they cock
and hen
To make this cackling over their affairs ?
Muck ! Muck !

SIR PERCY.

I love you so, dear heart, dear love.

MOLLY.

Oh yes, I love you ! Percy !

SIR PERCY.

Molly ! Molly !

MOLLY.

Dear boy, how I love you !

SIR PERCY.

And I you, sweetheart.

MOLLY.

Good-bye, then !

SIR PERCY.

Good-bye ! Good-bye ! At moonrise.

MOLLY.

At my door.

ANGELA.

Better write it down, and then you won't
forget.

SIR PERCY.

One kiss for good-bye.

MOLLY.

Good-bye.
[*Slowly retires, looking over her
shoulder. They run back to meet
each other, and embrace anew for
some minutes. Eventually* SIR
PERCY PERCIVALE *tears himself
away,* MOLLY *disappears, and* SIR
PERCY *goes sorrowfully back to his
boat, which he now manœuvres to
the landing stage.*

ANGELA.

Now let him find it ! This will puzzle him.
When Limburger replaces Patchouli,
Why—moonrise !

[SIR PERCY, *radiant, reaches the landing stage, moors his boat and
mounts. He sees a pink note on
the wharf.*

SIR PERCY.

Ah ! she has dropped this !
A cruel fool am I ;
I took an honied kiss ;
I revelled in true bliss ;
Yet never thought to try
A keepsake to obtain
To wear my heart upon.
Now God is great and gracious ;
Here's medicine for my pain.
She has left it ; she has gone !
How sweet the air and spacious !
I am happy—let me see !
I guess some verse inspired
By all her soul desired,
Purity, love, well-being—ay ! and me !
[*He opens the note, reads :—*
" To love you, Love, is all my happiness ;
To kill you with my kisses ; to devour
Your whole ripe beauty in the perfect hour
That mingles us in one supreme caress—" [1]
Why, here is love articulate, vital ! I
thought that only poets, not lovers, could
so speak. And that poets, poor devils,
speaking, could never know.
" So Percy to his Angela's distress—"
Then it is not my Molly that writes this
—who is this Percy ?—not me, at all events,
for there is no Angela that loves me. (*A
sound of sobbing in the trees.*) Whom have
we here ? (*Advances.*) 'Fore God, the most
beautiful woman in the world, except my
Molly ! And her scent ! O she is like some
intimate tropical plant, luring and deadly !

[1] See above, " The Temple of the Holy
Ghost," vol. i. p. 181.

—I am afraid. (*He discovers* ANGELA,)
Madam, can I aid you ?

ANGELA.

Leave me ! Leave me ! I am the wretched-
est girl on the wide earth.

SIR PERCY.

The comeliest, mademoiselle.
(*Aside.*) I see this is a woman of the
world. To her with speeches fit for such,
then.

ANGELA.

I have seen all. Pity me ! Your flattery
is a sword in my heart !

SIR PERCY.

Seen ?

ANGELA.

Your love—you call it so !

SIR PERCY.

Have you, then—

ANGELA.

I saw all. Ah me ! Poor Angela !

SIR PERCY.

Angela is your name ?

ANGELA.

My name.

SIR PERCY.

A lovely name. No doubt your disposi-
tion runs parallel.

ANGELA.

Meets never ? You are no courtier, sir !

SIR PERCY.

Do not say " sir ! "

ANGELA.

What shall I say! Oh leave me! I am ashamed.

SIR PERCY (*very pale*).

Is this your writing?

ANGELA.

Oh shame! shame! shame!
Tell me you have not read it, Sir Percy!

SIR PERCY.

Some I did read—How know you my name?

ANGELA.

I read it in my heart. O but I am ashamed to speak to you! Or would be were not that name as a brand to blot out all feeling from me for evermore.

SIR PERCY (*aside*).

How she speaks! It is indeed an angel singing.
(*Aloud.*) Indeed, I read too far.

ANGELA.

Pity me!

SIR PERCY.

Dear lady, the joy to know, and so perfectly to express such love is enough.

ANGELA.

You mock me! That girl—do you in truth love her? She is most beautiful.

SIR PERCY.

O she is my love, my dove, my star, my— Ah!—I hurt you! (*Aside.*) O beast! What is this doubt?

ANGELA (*very close to him*).

I hear another anthem in those eyes. By God, lad, you are wonderful!

SIR PERCY

What would you say?
VOL. III.

ANGELA.

What would I not do? Listen, I am Angela, Lady Baird. I am rich. That wealth now for the first time yields me some pleasure.

The moon rises late, after ten o'clock: you shall come with me. We are—neighbours, are we not? You shall come to my castle, I say; there I will prepare all for you and your young bride: my chaplain shall marry you at midnight; my name and power shall shield you from all mischance.

SIR PERCY.

I am my own master.

ANGELA.

You think so? They have kept it from you, but you have a guardian: ask him if you may marry a mere country lass—and you now not yet seventeen.

SIR PERCY.

And you—how old are you?

ANGELA.

That is a rude, rude boy!

SIR PERCY.

Oh, I am so sorry, I forgot.

ANGELA.

I will tell you, though. I am all but twenty-two!

SIR PERCY.

That is young yet.

ANGELA.

Ah, in your eyes I see sadness—I breathe; I hope.
Think deeply in yourself, if you love this girl!
I am older than you, to be sure; but not so much.
May be you would find my love a better thing than you think!

C

Do I perspire now? Do my cheeks run down nasty wet tears? Is my love a monotonous harping on one word? Love, Percy—dare I call you Percy?

SIR PERCY.

If I may call you Angela.

ANGELA.

Love, Percy (*she lays one hand on his shoulder and looks deeply in his eyes*), is wit, and laughter, and wisdom; all of love, and in it; but love without these is a mawkish, moonish distemper of folly—and will pass. I shall not pass, my love!—Ah! you feel my breath upon your face!

SIR PERCY.

Yes—do not!

ANGELA.

I shall do so—you dare not move away from me! I have you? No? Ah, Percy, Percy, will you break a heart that only beats for you?

SIR PERCY.

You woo so well that I think you must have loved before.

ANGELA.

Ay! but not like this. If I have loved it was but to study love, to learn his arts; to make myself the queen I am, that I might have strength to win you — never before has my heart been touched. Now my arts fail me. I am a poor and simple girl; and my eyes are aching with the sight of you, and my lips are mad to kiss you!

SIR PERCY.

Your breath is like a mist of rose-dawn about me.

ANGELA (*aside*).

O true apothecary! Thy drugs are[1] expensive, but well worth the money.

[1] Here and repeatedly below she quotes or alters a well-known passage in Shakespeare.

(*Aloud.*) Nay! but I will go. You have shamed me enough. Go! Go!

SIR PERCY.

Nay! I know better of a sudden. It is you that I love!

[*He would kiss her. She draws away.*

ANGELA.

False, fickle wretch!

SIR PERCY.

I will! I will!

ANGELA.

No! No!

SIR PERCY.

Yes, I was a fool, an ass, a brute. A village girl!

ANGELA.

Blood will have blood, they say.

SIR PERCY.

You are my equal, Angela! You shall be mine, mine, mine!

ANGELA.

If I will not?

SIR PERCY.

You will. You have written more than this.

ANGELA.

If I must—

SIR PERCY.

You must.

ANGELA.

Ah love! (*She yields herself up to him. A long pause.*) Learn my first lesson; at these great moments of life, silence is the best. (*Aside.*) There is a more important one. Had that silly gowk but the wit to lead him—*à fin*—where were I now? Not a drain on his stores, but a—Professor Spooner,[1]

[1] A well-known Oxford Professor, who enjoys the reputation of having invented the blunder of the class "half-warmed fish" for "half-formed wish."

in your next lecture warn the girls to go slow : it is dangerous as well as cruel to leave a lover standing.

SIR PERCY.

Oh I have learnt that lesson and a thousand others.

ANGELA.

You must go now. The moon—

SIR PERCY.

This love is not of the moon. To-morrow—

ANGELA.

" And to-morrow and to-morrow." Speak not that idle word !

SIR PERCY.

What of this chaplain ?

ANGELA.

What of your guardian ?

SIR PERCY.

Curses of hell !

ANGELA.

Hush ! hush ! sweet words must come from such sweet lips.

SIR PERCY.

What shall I do ?

ANGELA.

You leave your fate already in my hands ? Nay, but once married, you'll be master then !

SIR PERCY.

Shame, sweetheart !

ANGELA.

You have the strength of mind to defy convention : we dine together : we—O love, how dare you look such looks as these ?—

At moonset ride you back, and none the wiser. This always : for did we marry, the law would have its word to say.

SIR PERCY.

But this you speak of, is it not sin ? (*She looks at him.*) And what if it were ?

ANGELA.

My carriage waits—yonder.

SIR PERCY.

Ah come, come, come !

ANGELA.

Dare I ?

SIR PERCY.

Dare all things ! I will this delight ; it shall be. And in five years we can marry, or my guardian will consent before.

ANGELA.

Come !

(*They go off slowly, closely entwined, kissing and whispering.*)

SIR PERCY.

You are faint with passion, love. You walk heavily.

ANGELA.

Ay, love, it is to feel your strength support me ! (*Aside.*) Will the doctors never catch up with the coiffeurs ?

GREUMOCH (*coming forward, as he sees them go*).

The de'il an' a' ! The de'il an' a' ! Yon grimly auld beetch !

Meester Caroothers, Gude guide thee the nicht ! Y'ere auld bones shall auche sair wi' sorrow ! Weel, weel, it's an ill warld after a' ! Greumoch wad be slow wi' sic ill news, an' she wull maun haste. Weel, weel !

[*Exit hastily.*

SCENE VII.

MOLLY, *outside* TYSON'S *Cottage.   Moonrise.*

MOLLY TYSON.

O there is edged the waning moon
Out of the hollow of Sty Head Pass ! [1]
Gable [1] is grander for the gloom.
Lingmell [1] is silver ! Ah, the bloom
Of the rose of night ; oh, dulcet tune
Of the dew falling on the grass !

I am the veritable Queen
Of Night : my king is hither bound.
A moment and he comes—oh, breast !
Heave if thou wilt !—such stir is rest.
He comes, ah ! steals to me unseen.
The trees are high, the shades profound.

Together over moor and lake !
Together over scaur and fell !
For ever let us travel so ;
To stop so sweet a flight were woe.
Even to stop for love's own sake ;
Save my love did it—Then ? well ! well !

Better to rest together, hard
Hidden in a corner of the ghyll,
Some cavern frosted over close,
Some gully vivid with the rose
Of love ! The frost our years retard !
The rose—perfume our wonder-will !

But while I sing the moon is up.
False moon ! False moon ! So fast to ride.
He is not here ! Sure, he is dead !
O moon, reveal that holiest head !
There is much sorrow in love's cup :
Pleasure goes ever iron-eyed.

Who are these fierce and eager forms
That race across the untrodden moor,
The dark-browed horsemen lashing, crying,
Urging their weary steeds ?   Half-dying
The beasts bend bitter to the storm's
Assault : they hunt ? A man, be sure !

> [1] A   pass,   and   mountains,   in   the   Lake
> district.

These figures touch my soul with fear.
What of my love ?   These caitiffs chase him,
May be.   Who rides ?   I'll catch his bridle,
Plough with his heifer, learn his riddle.
> [*Enter* CARRUTHERS, *riding madly,*
> *crying " Sir Percy ! Sir Percy !"*
You, sir, what makes your honour here !
Sir Percy ?   Who then dares to face him ?

CARRUTHERS.

Let go my bridle, girl, I save a life.

MOLLY.

You hunt Sir Percy Percivale !

CARRUTHERS.

To save him.

MOLLY.

God save all honest men from knaves like
you !
Stay, though, you are his friend ?

CARRUTHERS.

His guardian.

MOLLY.

And I his promised wife.

CARRUTHERS.

Mad girl, be off !

MOLLY.

Ay, strike me, coward !

CARRUTHERS (*after thinking a moment*).
Then, come here, behind me !
Quick, if you love him !

MOLLY.

I will see him safe.
What is this danger ?

CARRUTHERS.

Danger of your sort.
> [*She mounts.*   OLD TYSON *comes out*
> *into the open.*

TYSON.

Eh, less, wheer off noo ?

MOLLY.

Father ! Father !

CARRUTHERS.

Now.
[*Spurs on the horse.*

TYSON.

What, ye'll abdooct my darter ?

CARRUTHERS.

Ha ! Ha ! Ha !
[*Gallops off.*

SCENE VIII.

Dawn.   Outside Castle Baird.   To CAR-
RUTHERS, GREUMOCH, MOLLY, *and
retainers on horseback enter* LADY BAIRD
and SIR PERCY PERCIVALE *on the
battlements.*

CARRUTHERS.

Be a man, Greumoch boy, be a man !

GREUMOCH.

Sir, did she'll no be thinking ye were
greeting yersel', mon, she'll could find it
in her heert to whang ye, whatetfer.

ANGELA.

You are early hunting, gentlemen.   Come
in !
My steward shall serve somewhat.
[*Sees* MOLLY.
Ha ! Ha ! Ha !
You bring a lady, then, Carruthers !

CARRUTHERS.

Madam !
Give me that boy !

ANGELA.

You fool, you are too late !
This is a man.

CARRUTHERS.

I warn you, Lady Baird.
The law calls this abduction.

ANGELA.

Pish ! the law !
Go, my dear (*whispers*) husband—ah !
how proud you look !
Come when you will !

CARRUTHERS.

Sir Percy Percivale,
I stand here in your dear dead father's name.

ANGELA.

You stand here, Percy, for yourself—and
me.

CARRUTHERS.

Come down ; I am your guardian.   Know
this !
Without me you do nought, say nought,
spend nought.
Obey me !

SIR PERCY.

Silence, sir, I am your master.
Whatever powers my   father may have
given
To you, there's one that I inherit from him ;
Namely, to tame the insolent.
[*Turns to* ANGELA.
Dear wife !
I go, as a tooth torn from a jaw.   Expect
I quell this folly in a little while
And come again—to Paris, said you, sweet ?

CARRUTHERS.

Leave your mad chatter with that ghastly
hag !
You fool, the woman is sixty if an hour.

SIR PERCY.

My answer to my promised bride is this.
[*He kisses her.*
So, sir !   To you, this to remember by.
[*He shoots Carruthers in the leg.*

MOLLY.

Oh, Percy, Percy, am I not your love?

SIR PERCY.

I am sorry, heartily, Miss Tyson.

MOLLY.

O!

SIR PERCY.

I did indeed speak foolishly.

ANGELA (aside).

Your purse !

SIR PERCY (aside).

O that were devilish—she's a good girl !

ANGELA.

I hate her.

SIR PERCY.

Buy yourself a pretty hat !
Forget my pretty speeches !

[Flings his purse down.

CARRUTHERS.

O Lord Christ !
In one short day—he was a gentleman !
Sir Percival ! Would God I were dead too !
If he had lived—thank God he died ! Sir
Percy,
Lend me your pistol ; here's a heart to hit !

[SIR PERCY descends, after taking farewell of ANGELA, and appears again
on horseback among his men.

SIR PERCY.

Arnold and Ritson, tend the wounded man !
To breakfast, gentlemen !

[Looks up.

Farewell !

ANGELA (waves her handkerchief and
throws a kiss).

Farewell !

[Exeunt.

ANGELA.

Ah, were such nights thy gift, dear Christ,
all maids
Were well thy servants. This is past all
speaking !
The utmost triumph of a life well spiced
With victory---this beats all. Hortense !
Hortense !
Bring me the brandy—pour a double dram !
Here's luck—ah, Satan, give me fifty such !

[Drinks off the brandy.

And now to bed again—to sleep, I am tired.

[She goes in.

While the scene is being shifted, enter
GOWER as Chorus.

The figure of the Marquis of Glenstrae
Demands the kind attention of the spot
Of consciousness that readers shift away
In awe of such a high exalted pot,
In England's upper Witenagemot
A figure bright enough to make the sun dun,
Yet common—to conceive him asketh not
Imagination's waistcoat buttons undone !
Any old gentleman in any club in London.

SCENE IX.

Enter the MARQUIS OF GLENSTRAE,
Outside TYSON'S Cottage.

GLENSTRAE.

Here, then, lives the pretty piece of goods
Angela wrote me of. (MOLLY appears at doorway.) Ah ! my pretty lass, can you give a
poor old man a glass of milk ?

MOLLY.

Yes, sir, I will fetch you one. Pray you,
set you down awhile.

[He sits down. She goes.

GLENSTRAE.

Ugh ! Ugh ! This rheumatism at me
again. I wish I had left the business to
Arthur.—But there, there, one never knows.
(MOLLY comes in with the milk.) There,
there ! what have you been crying for ?

MOLLY.

O sir!

GLENSTRAE.

I am the Marquis of Glenstrae, my pretty wench. If my name and fortune can serve you—there, there! I never could bear to see a pretty lass cry.

MOLLY.

O my lord! I am the most unhappy girl in the world.

GLENSTRAE.

Tell me about it—there, there, don't cry!

MOLLY.

'Twas but yestreen s'ennight.

GLENSTRAE.

A green wound is easiest cured.

MOLLY.

My lord, yestreen s'ennight I was wooed and won, and ere the moonrise he deserted me.

GLENSTRAE.

Dear, dear! That's bad, bad, bad. There, there, no doubt we shall be able to do something.

MOLLY.

My father thinks it is worse—oh, far worse! I am to go away into service—oh! oh!

GLENSTRAE.

And so you shall, my dear, so you shall. Come and live with my wife as her companion, and we will try and find your lover for you. No doubt the arts of this—er—designing female will soon lose their power —there, there, no thanks, I beg! I never could bear to see a pretty wench cry—there, there!

MOLLY.

O sir, my lord, how can I thank you?

GLENSTRAE.

Come in, my dear, and let us see your father about it. . . . Can you spare an old man a kiss?

MOLLY.

O my lord!

GLENSTRAE (*kissing her*).
There, there! Where is your father? · [*They go in.*

SCENE X.

Paris. Night. SIR PERCY *and* ANGELA *in bed, the latter asleep.*

SIR PERCY.

O Rose of dawn! O star of evening!
O glory of the soul of light!
Let my bright spirit speed on urgent wing!
Let me be silent, and my silence sing
Throughout the idle, the luxurious night!
How soft she breathes! How tender
Her eyes beam down on me! How slender
Her pale, her golden body lies!
Even asleep the dark long lashes move,
And the eyes see. She dreams of me, of love,
Of all these bridal ecstasies
That have been ours this month, this month
    of joy.
I am a foolish boy;
Did not the golden starred Ambassador
Come like a father to me and implore
I would look straight on truth?
" This is no love-sick youth !"
He cried, " she is nigh sixty years of age ;
Her lovers are a mangled multitude ;
You are one duckling of an infinite brood
This vixen hath up-gobbled!" Am I mage?
Ay, for I grant the aged diplomat
His truth—the truth for him! To me she is
The rosy incarnation of a kiss,
The royal rapture of a young delight,
The mazy music of virginity,
Sun of the day, moon of the night,
All, all to me!
Angela, angel! Thou hast made me man,

And poet over-man ! To thee,
To thee I owe transfiguration, peace,
The wide dominion of the wan
Abyss of air. I can look out and see
Beyond the stars, black seas
Wherein no star may swim,
Thence, far beyond the vast revolving spheres
Dark, idle, grim, .
Full of black joys and shadowy unspoken fears,
Wherein I am master.
There is no place for tears.
Cold adamant disaster
Is lord there, and I overlord.
So flits out, like a sword
Flashed through a duellist's live heart,
My thought ; in all the abodes of sense,
The shrines of love and art,
The adytum of omnipotence,
I am supreme, through thee, sweet Angela !
For all the beauties of the universe,
The glories hidden in the flower's cup,
All, all that wakes the soul to worship, verse,
Ripe verse, all wines, all dreams that the soft
    God lifts up :
All these are eidola,
Mere phantom will o' the wisps, thy love the
    real !
There is no more ideal
For me ; romance hath shot its bolt ;
The badger Jesus skulketh in his holt,
Whence let no dog dare draw him ; let him
    skulk !
All is an empty broken hulk
Floating on waters of derision,
Save for the sole true vision,
Angela, star in chaos !   Breathe, breathe
    deep !
Dear heart of gold, beat slowly in soft sleep !
Her lover watches over Angela.
Angela ! O thou wondrous woman,
Thou chaste pale goddess blooded to the
    human,
Artemis rosy like Hippolyta ![1]
Ay, my lord, were it true, your liar's lore,
(Oh blasphemy !) were my young love an
    whore,

[1] Possibly the Hippolyta in " Midsummer
Night's Dream."

An hag of sixty ; I were greater so.
He who doth know
And fears and hates,
Is not as he who cares not, but creates
A royal crown from an old bonnet string,
A maiden from a strumpet : that is to be
    like God,
Who from all chaos, from the husks of
    matter,
Crusts shed off putrefaction, shakes a wing
And flies ; bids flowers spring from the dull
    black sod,
Is not the scientist to shatter
Beauty by dint of microscope,
But wakes a wider hope
And turns all to the beautiful ; so I.
Angela, wake ! The midnight hour is nigh :—
Let us renew the vows of love ! appease
These amorous longings with grave ecstasies,
The holy act of uttermost communion,
The sacrament of life ! Awake, awake !
There is a secret in our subtle union
That masters the grey snake.
Ay ! let him lurk ! The Tree of Knowledge
    we
Have fed our fill of ; this is Eden still.
Awake, O Love ! and let me drink my fill
Of thee—and thou of me !
                            [ANGELA *wakes.*

ANGELA.

Ah, Percy, bend you over me ! Bend deep !
Kiss my own eyelids out of tender sleep
Into exasperate love ! Bend close !
Fill me, thy golden rose,
With dew of thy dear kisses !

SIR PERCY.

Ay, again !
Love, love, these raptures are like springtide
    rain
Nestling among green leaves.

ANGELA.

The Lady of Love weaves
Fresh nets of gossamer for thee and me.
O take not back thy lips, even to sing !

SIR PERCY.

Come, rich, come overrolling ecstasy !
I am like to die with joy of everything.

ANGELA.

Die, then, and kiss me dead !

SIR PERCY.

I die ! I die !

ANGELA.

Thy flower-life is shed
Into eternity,
A waveless lake.

SIR PERCY.

Sleep, sleep !   [*He sleeps.*

ANGELA.

I am awake—
And being awake I weary somewhat of
these jejune platitudes, these rampant ulula-
tions of preposterous puberty. These are
the very eructations of gingerbread ; they are
the flatulence of calf-sickness. I thought I
had taught the boy more sense. He weakens,
and I weary. As you will, my Lady Glenstrae ! Hortense ! (HORTENSE *enters with
a glass of brandy.*)   Brandy !

HORTENSE.

Here, milady.

ANGELA.

Not enough, you she-devil. More ! More !
[*Exit.* ANGELA *falls back to sleep.*

SCENE XI.

Paris. ANGELA, LORD *and* LADY GLEN-
STRAE, SIR PERCY DE PERCIVALE.

ANGELA.

You will not believe what I tell you?
These friends will tell you what I mean, and

if I mean it ! You had your dismissal this
morning. Never dare to address me again !

SIR PERCY.

What ! I have loved you, and you me—
No?—it cannot be so ! and now—I am ill—
you cast me away ! (*Turns his face away.*)
Forgive me, I am very weak.

ANGELA (*goes to him and stands over him*).

You shall have truth, you blind little fool.
I hate you. From the hour you kissed that
village drab, I hated you. I wanted your
youth, your strength, your life, your name
on my list, your scalp at my girdle. Enough !
Do you understand ? These friends will
teach you. May I never see your pale pasty
face again !
[*She spits at him and goes.*

SIR PERCY (*half rises and falls back*).

Oh ! oh ! It is impossible. Lord Marquis, you are a good man. Tell me, it is a
hideous dream.

GLENSTRAE.

No dream, my boy. You are the hundredth
she has treated after this fashion. But cheer
up now. There ! There ! Women are all
the same. Eh, Maud ?

LADY GLENSTRAE.

Who calls? What do you want ? Leave
me alone !

GLENSTRAE.

Ah, nothing ! Nothing, my dear.

LADY GLENSTRAE.

Pull down the blinds.

GLENSTRAE.

Certainly, certainly, my dear, I will ring.
[*Rings.*

SIR PERCY.

I am sick and sane now. God do so to me and more also if I look at a woman again. What a fool I have been !

GLENSTRAE.

Ah, my boy, you will keep clear of the old ones, I know. (*Enter a footman.*) These blinds down ! (*The man obeys.*) But a tasty little morsel like your Molly—your first love. —Eh, my lad ? There ; there, don't be angry !

SIR PERCY.

Pshaw ! You disgust me.
[*The footman turns to go.*

GLENSTRAE (*to footman*).

Wait ! (*To* SIR PERCY.) Would you tell *her* so ?

SIR PERCY.

If I deigned speech.

GLENSTRAE.

Simmons, ask Miss Tyson to step here for a moment. (*Exit servant.*) After which I shall leave you for an hour, my boy. I am to do some business — aha ! some rather pleasant business. There ! there !
[*Enter* MOLLY TYSON.

MOLLY.

O ! Sir Percy ! My lord, could you not have told me of this ?

GLENSTRAE.

Now, your condition !

MOLLY.

Sir Percy, do you, can you love me ? You promised to love me for ever.

SIR PERCY.

Who is this woman ? I am weary of these women.

MOLLY.

Sir, sir, acknowledge me. You know not what hangs on it—my honour even !

GLENSTRAE.

A speech of this breed is not in the bond —but let it pass. There ! there !

MOLLY.

Sir, I beseech you—for an hour—take me away. I am in terrible trouble of body and soul—danger, misery.

SIR PERCY.

O, go ! to the devil for me ! What do I care ? I am tired, I tell you.

GLENSTRAE.

You see, Molly, I told you true.

MOLLY (*turns to the* MARCHIONESS *and kneels by her*).

O, my lady Marchioness ! You are a great lady. Spare me this shame, your lord's shame, your own shame. . . .

LADY GLENSTRAE.

Take her away. Less light !

GLENSTRAE.

Ha ! Ha !

SIR PERCY.

I cannot see your humour, Glenstrae— forgive me so far ! And to tell the truth of it, I can do nothing and care to do less.

GLENSTRAE.

Come, Molly !

MOLLY.

Must I, must I ? Oh, sir, have pity !

GLENSTRAE.

A bargain's a bargain—but there ! there ! —what are you growling at ? A thousand a year and a flat in Mayfair is better than farmer Tyson's butter and eggs.

MOLLY.

Must it be now?

GLENSTRAE.

Much better now. There, there! Wish me good luck, Percy!

SIR PERCY.

I know nothing of your devil's game. Good luck!

GLENSTRAE.

Caste, John Burns.[1]

[*Exeunt* MARQUIS *and* MOLLY.

LADY GLENSTRAE.

Hist! Percy, hither to me. Is no one looking?

SIR PERCY.

No, there is no one here.

LADY GLENSTRAE.

I can cure you. I can make you strong and happy again. O what rapture!

SIR PERCY.

What is it?

LADY GLENSTRAE.

Here, let me give you this medicine. A little prick of pain, and then—pleasure—Oh! [*She bends caressingly over the arm of* SIR PERCY DE PERCIVALE, *and stabs it with a needle.*

Get a doctor to give you a prescription like this—they ask a hundred francs—oh! it is a shame! Buy a little syringe; and that is Heaven for all your life.—How do you feel?

SIR PERCY.

Why, I am well at once. I never felt better in my life. The devil take my trouble

[1] A demagogue of the period.

now! I shall go out and conquer the whole world. I shall be the great magician, the Lord of the Stars. I have it in me to write poetry. Yes, that, first. (*Goes to table and takes pen and paper.*) In praise of—what is your medicine called, dear Marchioness?

LADY GLENSTRAE.

Who calls me? What is it? Leave me alone!

SIR PERCY.

Tell me, dear Lady—Maud!

LADY GLENSTRAE.

Ah! you are the boy.

SIR PERCY.

Your boy, queen!

LADY GLENSTRAE.

Oh, yes, my boy.

SIR PERCY.

What is this medicine called?

LADY GLENSTRAE.

What medicine? I never take medicine!

SIR PERCY.

But you gave it me—with a needle.

LADY GLENSTRAE.

Oh, that medicine! You like it?

SIR PERCY.

It is heaven, heaven! It is called—

LADY GLENSTRAE.

Morphia.

[*They rest.*

SCENE XII.

TWO YEARS LATER.

Night : The Strand, opposite the Hotel Cecil. A chemist's shop behind. A grey, old, wizened man staggers into the shop.

CHEMIST.

This prescription has been made up before, sir.

THE MAN.

Yes, I want it renewed, quickly, quickly.

CHEMIST.

I am afraid, sir, it is marked "once only."

THE MAN.

You won't? O if you knew what I suffer! I will pay you double.

CHEMIST.

I'm afraid not, sir. You may try elsewhere.

THE MAN.

O God! O God!
[Goes out. To him enter on the pavement a bedraggled female.

THE WOMAN.

Come home, ducky, won't you?

THE MAN.

O God! O God! I cannot bear it any longer. It is the last I have.
[He fumbles awhile inside his coat.

THE WOMAN (*catching hold of him*).

Come, stand me a glass of wine, there's a dear.

THE MAN.

Ah! that is well. Can I use this woman, I wonder?

THE WOMAN.

O God! I am punished. Sir Percy here! What is the matter, dear my love?

SIR PERCY.

Never mind love—you are?

MOLLY.

O sir, your Molly, that you broke the heart of. See what has come to me!

SIR PERCY.

Ah, if you knew. You are the lucky one! I am in grips with a more dread disease Than all your wildest nightmares figure you!
[A carriage rolls by, as from the theatre. It stops owing to a block in the traffic.

MOLLY.

O sir! I am so sorry for you.

SIR PERCY.

And a lot of good that does!

Enter, on the pavement, the MARQUIS OF GLENSTRAE, in his fur coat. The occupant of the carriage, ANGELA, LADY BAIRD, recognises him and leans out to greet him.

GLENSTRAE.

Ah, my dear lady, how do you do this cold weather?

ANGELA.

Well, very well, thank you—and you?

GLENSTRAE.

Well enough—a little rheumatic, perhaps. H'm!

ANGELA.

And the dear Marchioness?

GLENSTRAE.

Oh, very sad—there—there! She has had to be, ah!—er—under treatment.

ANGELA.

Dear, dear, how very sad! Hullo! Look here on this picture and on that!

[MOLLY *and* SIR PERCY *are discovered.*

GLENSTRAE.

Oh! Ah! I think I must go on. I have an appointment at the club.

SIR PERCY.

Yet your lordship walks East.

MOLLY.

Oh, I am not revengeful. Give me a fiver, my Lord Marquis, and we'll call it square.

SIR PERCY.

For me, my angel, get this prescription filled.

ANGELA.

Oh, go to the devil, both of you! Marquis, shall we sup at the Carlton?

GLENSTRAE.

With pleasure — ha! a most amusing meeting—ha!

ANGELA.

Where have you been this evening?

GLENSTRAE.

O most dull, indeed! I had to give the Presidential address at St. Martin's Town Hall for the Children's Special Service Mission.

ANGELA.

Yes, your Lordship is indeed a true friend to the little ones. A curious coincidence. I am the new president of the Zenana Mission.

GLENSTRAE.

You!

ANGELA.

Think of the poor heathen women kept in such terrible seclusion!

GLENSTRAE.

Ah! I had not thought your sympathy was genuine; but there, there! There is more real good in human nature than—

ANGELA.

Genuine enough! But what a jest is this!

GLENSTRAE.

A most remarkable coincidence—a very pleasant reminder. Shall we sup?

ANGELA. .

Yes; a magnum of Pol Roger, '84—

GLENSTRAE.

With a dash of brandy in it—

ANGELA.

Will clothe our old loves in a halo of romance again.

GLENSTRAE.

Ha! Ha! We wear well, eh? There, there! (*Opens the carriage door.*) The Carlton. (*Follows and shuts door.*)

[SIR PERCY *and* MOLLY *part. The effect of his last dose is worn off; clutching his prescription, he goes off with set teeth.* MOLLY *goes the other way: to her enter a theatre-goer.*

MOLLY.

Won't you come with me, ducky?

THEATRE-GOER.

Not to-night. See you some other night.

MOLLY.

Oh, do come, dearie!

THEATRE-GOER.

No, I tell you—try Liverpool Street!

[*Curtain.*

*What follows is strictly by request in the
interest of " healthy optimism."*

So far my pen has touched with vivid truth
The constant story of the eternal struggle
Of age and sense with flatulence and youth.
Now—see the venal poet start to juggle !
Young ladies, you desire to see a comedy !
The poet's master pen shall twist the river
Of song into a simple to-and-from eddy,
And you shall laugh where once you feared
        to shiver.
So listen to the happy termination
Of this apparently so sad relation !
'Twill suit your rosy dreams to admiration !
But, be the gatepost witness ! it is rot.
Still, if I hide my face with due decorum
Behind a silken kerchief in the forum,
And laugh aloud—at home—
At the silliness of Rome,
You'll forgive me, will you not ?

SCENE XIII.[1]

The Meeting-House of the Brethren
Gathered Together To The Name Of The
Lord Jesus, sub-section Anti-Ravenite of
the Exclusive section. They are of course
Anti-Stewart, and sound on the Ramsgate
Question, while observing an armed neu-
trality in the matter of Mr. Kelly's action.[2]
In the midst a table with a loaf and a bottle :
also, by their own account, Jesus Christ.
Forms, varnished yellow, around it, them,
and (I suppose) Him. On one of them is a
blackboard with the notice in white paint :

---

1 This scene, with the exception of the introduction of Mr. Chesterton, and (of course)
Sir Percy and Molly, is an accurate description
of the "meeting" at Streatham. The inci-
dents and style are authentic.
2 Themselves must be consulted for elucida-
tion of these historic controversies. Outsiders,
who merely noticed the horripilation of the
Universe, but saw no obvious reason, have
the key in their hands, and may pursue the
research on these lines. Geological papers
please copy.—A. C.

"Those not in fellowship please sit behind
this board." Accepting this dread limitation
are several miserable, well-dressed children
with active minds, who, finding nothing to
interest them in the proceedings, are point-
ing out to each other the obscene passages
in the Bible ; or, this failing from insufficient
acquaintance with the sacred volume, are
engaged in the Sisyphean task of getting rid
of the form in front by deglutition. There
is also an anæmic and pimply youth with a
sporadic beardlet and a dirty face—if it is a
face—who is vastly interested : one would
say an habitual reader of the *Daily Mail*
watching nobility at lunch.

In front of the board, around the table,
are several dear old ladies and gentlemen,
a beautiful, overdressed, languid woman,
some oilily lousy, lop-eared, leprous, lack-
brained, utterly loathsome tradespeople who
gurgle and grin, and a sprinkling of horny-
handed sons of toil, very shiny.

Above, with an olive-branch in one hand
and a copy of the *Daily News* in the other,
floats Mr. G. K. Chesterton in the position
Padmasana,[1] singing " Beneath the Cross
of Jesus" with one voice, and attempting
"God save the Queen !" with the other in
a fashion calculated to turn any marine, if
but he be filled with honourable ambition
to excel in the traditional exploits of his
corps, green with envy.

Behind, and for this reason not previously
observed by the vigilant eye of the reader,
are Sir Percy Percivale and Molly Tyson.

Near the " Lord's Table " a brother is
standing and praying ; he intersperses his
prayer with repeated " you know's," like
the Cairene bore in Marryat's novel.

IST AGED SISTER (*sotto voce*).

Yes ! it's all so blessèd and romantic,
my dear, thank the Lord ! They were both
brought to Jesus on one night, Ascension
Day, as the poor Pagan[2] bodies call it,
through the ministration of Mr. Hogwash,

---

1 The "lotus" position, in which Buddha is
commonly represented as sitting.
2 By Plymouth Brethren all so-called Christian festivals are (rightly, of course, from a
historical standpoint) considered mere aliases
of pagan feasts.—A. C.

the Baptist minister at Brixton (*Mr. Chesterton executes the cake-walk*), who they say is a good man, and very much blessed of the dear Lord, my dear, in his ministrations, though of course he has not been brought out of sect as yet.[1]

2ND AGED SISTER (*sotto voce*).

Dear! Dear! Very sad! Perhaps the dear Lord will open his eyes.
[*The praying brother sits down suddenly, satisfied with himself.*

A HORNY-HANDED BROTHER (*who rises grunting, as if the action were painful or unfamiliar*).

Matthew Twenty-fourth and Forty-third and he said unto them: Whither of the twins will ye that I deliver unto you, Barabbas, or Djeesas that is cawled Croist? Deer Brotheren -
[*But let him expound it to himself while we listen to the aged sisters!*

1ST AGED SISTER (*sotto voce*).

So now they're come out of sect, a most marvellous example, my dear, of the wonderful workings of the Holy Ghost, don't you think so, my dear? and I hear they're to be received into fellowship next Lord's Day.

2ND AGED SISTER (*do.*).

The young people are interested in one another,[2] are they not?

1ST AGED SISTER (*do.*).

Yes! it's all very dear and blessèd. But hush! how beautifully Mr. Worcester is expounding about Barabbas!

[1] Godly for "become a Plymouth Brother."
—A. C.
[2] Godly for "are in love with one another."
—A. C.

MR. G. K. CHESTERTON (*altogether inaudibly*).

This scene is all description and no drama, and ought to satisfy Mr. Bernard Shaw's idea of a dramatic scene.
[*The beautiful woman gets up and goes. The poet hastily follows her out.*

SCENE XIV.

TEN MONTHS LATER.

SIR PERCY DE PERCIVALE'S *Ancestral Hall.*

SIR HERPES ZOSTER, M.D.
SIR GRABSON JOBBS, Q.C.

SIR HERPES Z.

Yes, indeed, a most fortunate event. The children weigh 46 lbs. between the three of them. All boys!

SIR GRABSON J.

Good! Good! No chance of heirs failing—ha!
But a word in your ear. This morphia?

SIR HERPES Z.

Not a sign of relapse, old friend, and never will be now. Sir Percy is as sound a man as lives in England—I took four other opinions.

SIR GRABSON J.

None as weighty as your own.

SIR HERPES Z.

You are polite, very polite. Where is Carruthers?

SIR GRABSON J.

He is away to Windsor—the King (*they beat their foreheads eighty-seven times upon the ground*) knights him to-day.

SIR HERPES Z.

I knew he had the O.M. and the F.Z.S.; but this knighthood?

SIR GRABSON J.

He has taken up political economy. He will marry a duchess. Greumoch, too, is doing well. After the—ah—event we all deplored so, he entered the Benedictines at Fort Augustus; and to-morrow they instal him as Lord Abbot.

SIR HERPES Z.

What? And he a Highlander?

SIR GRABSON J.

It seems that was a mere disguise; his true name was Johann Schmidt.[1]

SIR HERPES Z.

So? Why the deception?

SIR GRABSON J.

A Jesuit, no doubt! But about Lady Percivale now?

SIR HERPES Z.

Better and better. Old Farmer Tyson, luckily enough, as it turned out, insisted on examination, and no less than twenty-three skilled surgeons—all men of note!—declared her to be *virgo intacta*.

SIR GRABSON J.

Eh? What?

SIR HERPES Z.

You see, Englishmen—ah!

SIR GRABSON J.

Er—ah?

[1] The Abbot of the Fort-Augustus Abbey was at this time a German.

SIR HERPES Z.

Ah!

SIR GRABSON J.

Er—ah! As Whistler said, "You put out your arm, and you hit three"[1]—eh?

SIR HERPES Z.

Probably. At least the anatomical detail is certain. Here is a ph—

SIR GRABSON J.

Tush, tush, old friend, I can take your word for it.

SIR HERPES Z.

You have some good news to announce, I think, as well as I.

SIR GRABSON J.

Sad for the general commonwealth, but of particular joy in this house. The Marquis of Glenstrae had the misfortune yesterday to fall against a circular saw in motion.

SIR HERPES Z.

Dear, dear! and how was that?

SIR GRABSON J.

His lordship was very fond of children, as you may know. It seems he was pursuing

[1] Certain of our little-instructed surgical readers have expressed themselves dissatisfied with the explanation given by Sir G. Jobbs. They argue that it requires to be amplified, since the Marquis of Glenstrae must have had normal habits, otherwise so pure a poet as Crowley would never have introduced him. This is true; but Sir R. Burton has pointed out that the outcry against Greek Art comes chiefly from those who are personally incapable of it.

Englishmen and Virgins are then like Alpine guides and mountains; some can't go, and the rest lose the way.

Hence Mr. Kensit.

Further Note.—The silly cavillers now observe that this is no solution of the difficulty, Sir P. Percivale being English. This is absurd: (1) Lady Percivale is just as likely to have remained *virgo intacta* as any other mother. (2) The English law, cognisant of the dilemma set forth above, permits the use of a poker in the relations of man and wife. (3) If God's Grace can break a habit, it can surely rupture a hymen.—AUTHOR.

— it is, I am told, an innocent child's game!—one of the factory hands; and—he stumbled. He was sawn slowly into no less than thirty-eight pieces.

SIR HERPES Z.

But how does this bear on the case?

SIR GRABSON J.

Dying without issue, he has left all to Sir Percy here; the King (*cheers from large but unseen body of retainers, who have been eavesdropping*), moreover, unwilling that the Marquisate should die out, will bestow it on the same lucky young fellow.

SIR HERPES Z.

This is marvellous news!

SIR GRABSON J.

Again, Lady Baird has just perished in awful agony. Having suffered for twenty years from a hideous and incurable disease, she brought matters to a climax last night by falling into a barrel of boiling sulphuric acid.

SIR HERPES Z.

How so?

SIR GRABSON J.

It was her bath-night.

SIR HERPES Z.

Ah! enamel! But why did it hurt her?

SIR GRABSON J.

(*Impressively.*) It is the finger of God!

The Poet concludes.

Now I have written four-and-twenty hours
Without a decent rest by Kandy Lake.
VOL. III.

I invoke the urgent elemental powers
To bring all to an end for Buddha's sake.
I must bid all ye matrons fond farewell,
Knowing your inmost thoughts; that, had
ye dared,
Ye would be just as far *en route* for hell
As Angela, the gentle Lady Baird;
And all ye youths, aware that Percy's fall
Is something to be envied of ye all;
And all ye parsons, seeing that ye pray
Your Father for the Luck of Lord Glen-
strae.

Enough of this! Insistent Fates
Bid me return to rhyming 8s.
I say what I have seen ill done
In honest clean-lived Albion;
And if these things the green tree grows,
What price the dry, my lords? Who
knows?
You say that I exaggerate;
That "we are not as bad as that."
(Excuse the doubtful tag of verse!)
Au contraire, you are vastly worse.
I see the virtuous and the vicious,
The *sans reproche* and the suspicious,
All tarred with the same nasty tar,
Because—I see you as you are.
Permit me to reduce the list
Of optimist and pessimist
By just my name! I am neither, friends,
I know a stick has got two ends!
Nothing were easier than to show
That Lady Baird avoided woe;
And Lord Glenstrae, that worthy peer,
Saved whisky by supplying beer.
For what is good, and makes for peace,
What evil, wisdom must increase
Well near omniscience before
One guesses what it all is for.
Still, since *de gustibus non est*—
(My schoolboy readers know the rest!)
I much prefer—that is, mere I—
Solitude to Society.
And that is why I sit and spoil
So much clean paper with such toil
By Kandy Lake in far Ceylon.
I have my old pyjamas on:

D

I shake my soles from Britain's dust :
I shall not go there till I must ;
And when I must—ah, you suppose
Even I must !—I hold my nose.
Farewell, you filthy-minded people !
I know a stable from a steeple.
Farewell, my decent-minded friends !
I know arc lights from candle-ends.

Farewell !　A.poet begs your alms,
Will walk awhile among the palms.
An honest love, a loyal kiss,
Can show him better worlds than this ;
Nor will he come again to yours
While he knows champak-stars [1] from sewers.

　[1] The champak, one of the most beautiful
of tropical flowers, has a star-shaped blossom.

ROSA MUNDI

AND OTHER LOVE-SONGS

1905

I

1. ROSE of the World !
Red glory of the secret heart of Love :
Red flame, rose-red, most subtly curled
Into its own infinite flower, all flowers above !
Its flower in its own perfumed passion,
Its faint sweet passion, folded and furled
In flower fashion ;
And my deep spirit taking its pure part
Of that voluptuous heart
Of hidden happiness !

2. Arise, strong bow of the young child Eros !
(While the maddening moonlight, the
    memoried caress
Stolen of the scented rose
Stirs me and bids each racing pulse ache,
    ache !)
Bend into an agony of art
Whose cry is ever rapture, and whose tears
For their own purity's undivided sake
Are molten dew, as, on the lotus leaves
Silver-coiled in the Sun
Into green-girdled spheres
Purer than all a maiden's dream enweaves,
Lies the unutterable beauty of
The Waters. Yea, arise, divinest dove
Of the Idalian, on your crimson wings
And soft grey plumes, bear me to yon cool
    shrine
Of that most softly-spoken one,
Mine Aphrodite ! Touch the imperfect
    strings,
Oh thou, immortal, throned above the moon !
Inspire a holy tune
Lighter and lovelier than flowers and wine
Offered in gracious gardens unto Pan
By any soul of man !

3. In vain the solemn stars pour their pale
    dews
Upon my trembling spirit ; their caress
Leaves me moon-rapt in waves of loveliness
All thine, O rose, O wrought of many a muse
In Music, O thou strength of ecstasy
Incarnate in a woman-form, create
Of her own rapture, infinite, ultimate,
Not to be seen, not grasped, not even imagi-
    nable,
But known of one, by virtue of that spell
Of thy sweet will toward him : thou, unknown,
Untouched, grave mistress of the sunlight
    throne
Of thine own nature ; known not even of me,
But of some spark of woven eternity
Immortal in this bosom. Phosphor paled
And in the grey upstarted the dread veiled
Rose light of dawn. Sun-shapen shone thy
    spears
Of love forth darting into myriad spheres,
Which I the poet called this light, that
    flower,
This knowledge, that illumination, power
This and love that, in vain, in vain, until
Thy beauty dawned, all beauty to distil
Into one drop of utmost dew, one name
Choral as floral, one thin, subtle flame
Fitted to a shaft of love, to pierce, to endue
My trance-rapt spirit with the avenue
Of perfect pleasures, radiating far
Up and up yet to where thy sacred star
Burned in its brilliance : thence the storm
    was shed
A passion of great calm about this head,
This head no more a poet's ; since the dream
Of beauty gathered close into a stream

Of tingling light, and, gathering ever force
From thine own love, its unextended source,
Became the magic utterance that makes Me,
Dissolving self into the starless sea
That makes one lake of molten joy, one pond
Steady as light and hard as diamond ;
One drop, one atom of constraint intense,
Of elemental passion scorning sense,
All the concentred music that is I.
O ! hear me not ! I die ;
I am borne away in misery of dumb life
That would in words flash forth the holiest
      heaven
That to the immortal God of Gods is given,
And, tongue-tied, stammers forth—my wife !

4. I am dumb with rapture of thy loveliness.
All metres match and mingle ; all words tire ;
All lights, all sounds, all perfumes, all gold
      stress
Of the honey-palate, all soft strokes expire
In abject agony of broken sense
To hymn the emotion tense
Of somewhat higher—O ! how highest !—
      than all
Their mystery : fall, O fall,
Ye unavailing eagle-flights of song !
O wife ! these do thee wrong.

5. Thou knowest how I was blind ;
How for mere minutes thy pure presence
Was nought ; was ill-defined ;
A smudge across the mind,
Drivelling in its brutal essence,
Hog-wallowing in poetry,
Incapable of thee.

6. Ah ! when the minutes grew to hours,
And yet the beast, the fool, saw flowers
And loved them, watched the moon rise,
      took delight
In perfumes of the summer night,
Caught in the glamour of the sun,
Thought all the woe well won.
How hours were days, and all the misery
Abode, all mine : O thou ! didst thou regret ?
Wast thou asleep as I ?
Didst thou not love me yet ?

For, know ! the moon is not the moon until
She hath the knowledge to fulfil
Her music, till she know herself the moon.
So thou, so I ! The stone unhewn,
Foursquare, the sphere, of human hands
      immune,
Was not yet chosen for the corner-piece
And key-stone of the Royal Arch of Sex ;
Unsolved the ultimate x ;
The virginal breeding breeze
Was yet of either unstirred ;
Unspoken the Great Word.

7. Then on a sudden, we knew. From deep
      to deep
Reverberating, lightning unto lightning
Across the sundering brightening
Abyss of sorrow's sleep,
There shone the sword of love, and struck,
      and clove
The intolerable veil,
The woven chain of mail
Prudence self-called, and folly known to who
May know. Then, O sweet drop of dew,
Thy limpid light rolled over and was lost
In mine, and mine in thine.
Peace, ye who praise ! ye but disturb the
      shrine !
This voice is evil over against the peace
Here in the West, the holiest. Shaken and
      crossed
The threads Lachesis wove fell from her
      hands.
The pale divided strands
Were taken by thy master-hand, Eros !
Her evil thinkings cease,
Thy miracles begin.
Eros ! Eros !—Be silent ! It is sin
Thus to invoke the oracles of orde.
Their iron gates to unclose.
The gross, inhospitable warder
Of Love's green garden of spice is well
      awake.
Hell hath enough of Her three-headed
      hound ;
But Love's severer bound
Knows for His watcher a more fearful shape,
A formidable ape

Skilled by black art to mock the Gods
    profound
In their abyss of under ground.
Beware ! Who hath entered hath no boast
    to make,
And conscious Eden surelier breeds the snake.
Be silent ! O ! for silence' sake !

8. That asks the impossible. Smite ! Smite !
Profaned adytum of pure light,
Smite ! but I must sing on.
Nay ! can the orison
Of myriad fools provoke the Crowned-with-
    Night
Hidden beyond sound and sight
In the mystery of His own high essence ?
Lo, Rose of all the gardens of the world,
Did thy most sacred presence
Not fill the Real, then this voice were
    whirled
Away in the wind of its own folly, thrown
Into forgotten places and unknown.
So I sing on !
            Sister and wife, dear wife,
Light of my love and lady of my life,
Answer if thou canst from the unsullied
    place,
Unveiling for one star-wink thy bright face !
Did we leave then, once cognisant,
Time for some Fear to implant
His poison ? Did we hesitate ?
Leave but one little chance to Fate ?
For one swift second did we wait ?
There is no need to answer : God is God,
A jealous God and evil ; with His rod
He smiteth fair and foul, and with His
    sword
Divideth tiniest atoms of intangible time,
That men may know he is the Lord.
Then, with that sharp division,
Did He divide our wit sublime ?
Our knowledge bring to nought ?
We had no need of thought.
We brought His malice in derision.
So thine eternal petals shall enclose
Me, O most wonderful lady of delight,
Immaculate, indivisible circle of night,
Inviolate, invulnerable Rose !

9. The sound of my own voice carries me on.
I am as a ship whose anchors are all gone,
Whose rudder is held by Love the indomi-
    table —
Purposeful helmsman ! Were his port high
    Hell,
Who should be fool enough to care ? Suppose
Hell's waters wash the memory of this rose
Out of my mind, what misery matters then ?
Or, if they leave it, all the woes of men
Are as pale shadows in the glory of
That passionate splendour of Love.

10. Ay ! my own voice, my own thoughts.
    These, then, must be
The mutiny of some worm's misery,
Some chained despair knotted into my flesh,
Some chance companion, some soul damned
    afresh
Since my redemption, that is vocal at all,
For I am wrapt away from light and call
In the sweet heart of the red rose.
My spirit only knows
This woman and no more ; who would
    know more ?
I, I am concentrate
In the unshakable state
Of constant rapture. Who should pour
His ravings in the air for winds to whirl,
Far from the central pearl
Of all the diadem of the universe ?
Let God take pen, rehearse
Dull nursery tales ; then, not before, O rose,
Red rose ! shall the beloved of thee,
Infinite rose ! pen puerile poetry
That turns in writing to vile prose.

11. Were this the quintessential plume of
    Keats
And Shelley and Swinburne and Verlaine,
Could I outsoar them, all their lyric feats,
Excel their utterance vain
With one convincing rapture, beat them
    hollow
As an ass's skin ; wert thou, Apollo,
Mere slave to me, not Lord—thy fieriest
    flight
And stateliest shaft of light

Thyself thyself surpassing ; all were dull,
And thou, O rose, sole, sacred, wonderful,
Single in love and aim,
Double in form and name,
Triple in energy of radiant flame,
Informing all, in all most beautiful,
Circle and sphere, perfect in every part,
High above hope of Art :
Though, be it said ! thou art nowhere now,
Save in the secret chamber of my heart,
Behind the brass of my anonymous brow. [1]

12. Ay ! let the coward and slave who writes
    write on !
He is no more harm to Love than the grey
    snake
Who lurks in the dusk brake
For the bare-legged village-boy, is to the Sun,
The Sire of Life.
The Lover and the Wife,
Immune, intact, ignore.   The people hear ;
Then, be the people smitten of grey Fear,
It is no odds !

13. I have seen the eternal Gods
Sit, star-wed, in old Egypt by the Nile ;
The same calm pose, the inscrutable, wan
    smile,
On every lip alike.
Time hath not had his will to strike
At them ; they abide, they pass through all.
Though their most ancient names may fall,
They stir not nor are weary of
Life, for with them, even as with us, Life
    is but Love.
They know, we know ; let, then, the writing go!
That, in the very deed, we do not know.

14. It may be in the centuries of our life
Since we were man and wife
There stirs some incarnation of that love.
Some rosebud in the garden of spices blows,
Some offshoot from the Rose
Of the World, the Rose of all Delight,
The Rose of Dew, the Rose of Love and Night,
The Rose of Silence, covering as with a vesture
The solemn unity of things

[1] This poem was issued under the pseudonym
of H. D. Carr.

Beheld in the mirror of truth,
The Rose indifferent to God's gesture,
The Rose on moonlight wings
That flies to the House of Fire,
The Rose of Honey-in-Youth !
Ah !   No dim mystery of desire
Fathoms this gulf !   No light invades
The mystical musical shades
Of a faith in the future, a dream of the day
When athwart the dim glades
Of the forest a ray
Of sunlight shall flash and the dew die away !

15. Let there then be obscurity in this !
There is an after rapture in the kiss.
The fire, flesh, perfume, music, that outpaced
All time, fly off ; they are subtle : there
    abides
A secret and most maiden taste ;
Salt, as of the invisible tides
Of the molten sea of gold
Men may at times behold
In the rayless scarab of the sinking sun ;
And out of that is won
Hardly, with labour and pain that are as
    pleasure,
The first flower of the garden, the stored
    treasure
That lies at the heart's heart of eternity.
This treasure is for thee.

16. O ! but shall hope arise in happiness ?
That may not be.
My love is like a golden grape, the veins
Peep through the ecstasy
Of the essence of ivory and silk,
Pearl, moonlight, mother-milk
That is her skin ;
Its swift caress
Flits like an angel's kiss in a dream ; remains
The healing virtue ; from all sin,
All ill, one touch sets free.
My love is like a star—oh fool ! oh fool !
Is not thy back yet tender from the rod ?
Is there no learning in the poet's school ?
Wilt thou achieve what were too hard for God?
I call Him to the battle ; ask of me
When the hinds calve ?   What of eternity

When he built chaos? Shall Leviathan
Be drawn out with an hook? Enough; I see
This I can answer—or Ernst Haeckel can!
Now, God Almighty, rede this mystery!
What of the love that is the heart of man?
Take stars and airs, and write it down!
Fill all the interstices of space
With myriad verse——own Thy disgrace!
Diminish Thy renown!
Approve my riddle! This Thou canst not do.

17. O living Rose! O dowered with subtle
dew
Of love, the tiny eternities of time,
Caught between flying seconds, are well filled
With these futilities of fragrant rhyme;
In Love's retort distilled,
In sunrays of fierce loathing purified,
In moonrays of pure longing tried,
And gathered after many moons of labour
Into the compass of a single day,
And wrought into continuous tune,[1]
One laughter with one languor for its neigh-
bour.
One thought of winter with one word of June,
Muddled and mixed in mere dismay,
Chiselled with the cunning chisel of despair,
Found wanting. well aware
Of its own fault, even insistent
Thereon; some fragrance rare
Stolen from my lady's hair
Perchance redeeming now and then the distant
Fugitive tunes.

18.   Ah! Love! the hour is over!
The moon is up, the vigil overpast.
Call me to thee at last,
O Rose, O perfect miracle lover,
Call me! I hear thee though it be across
The abyss of the whole universe,
Though not a sigh escape. delicious loss!
Though hardly a wish rehearse
The imperfection underlying ever
The perfect happiness.

[1] It will be noticed in fact that this poem
is in an original metre, no stanza being complete in itself, but one running on into the
next.

Thou knowest that not in flesh
Lies the fair fresh
Delight of Love; not in mere lips and eyes
The secret of these bridal ecstasies,
Since thou art everywhere,
Rose of the World, Rose of the Uttermost
Abode of Glory, Rose of the High Host
Of Heaven, mystic, rapturous Rose!
The extreme passion glows
Deep in this breast; thou knowest (and love
knows)
How every word awakes its own reward
In a thought akin to thee, a shadow of thee;
And every tune evokes its musical Lord;
And every rhyme tingles and shakes in me
The filaments of the great web of Love.

19. O Rose all roses far above
In the garden of God's roses,
Sorrowless, thornless, passionate Rose, that
lies
Full in the flood of its own sympathies
And makes my life one tune that curls and
closes
On its own self delight;
A circle, never a line! Safe from all
wind,
Secure in its own pleasure-house confined,
Mistress of all its moods,
Matchless, serene, in sacred amplitudes
Of its own royal rapture, deaf and blind
To aught but its own mastery of song
And light, shown ever as silence and deep
night
Secret as death and final. Let me long
Never again for aught! This great delight
Involves me, weaves me in its pattern of
bliss,
Seals me with its own kiss,
Draws me to thee with every dream that
glows,
Poet, each word! Maiden, each burden of
snows
Extending beyond sunset, beyond dawn!
O Rose, inviolate, utterly withdrawn
In the truth:—for this is truth: Love
knows!
Ah! Rose of the World! Rose! Rose!

II.

THE NIGHTMARE.

Up, up, my bride ! Away to ride
Upon the nightmare's wings !
The livid lightning's wine we'll drink,
And laugh for joy of life, and think
Unutterable things !

The gallant caught the lady fair
Below the arms that lay
Curling in coils of yellow hair,
And kissed her lips.   "Away !"

The lover caught his mistress up
And lifted her to heaven,
Drank from her lips as from the cup
Of poppies drowsed at even.

"Away, away, my lady may !
The wind is fair and free ;
Away, away, the glint of day
Is faded from the ghostly grey
That shines beyond the sea."

The lordly bridegroom took the bride
As giants grasp a flower.
"A night of nights, my queen, to ride
Beyond the midnight hour."
The bride still slept ; the lonely tide
Of sleep was on the tower.

"Awake, awake ! for true love's sake !
The blood is pulsing faster.
My swift veins burn with keen desire
Toward those ebony wings of fire,
The monarchs of disaster !"
The golden bride awoke and sighed
And looked upon her master.

The bride was clad in spider-silk ;
The lord was spurred and shod.
Her breasts gleamed bright and white as
     milk,
Most like the mother of God ;
His heart was shrouded, his face was clouded,
Earth trembled where he trod.

"By thy raven tresses ; by those caresses
We changed these five hours past ;
By the full red lips and the broad white brow
I charge thee stay ; I am weary now ;
I would sleep again—at last."

"By thy golden hair ; by the laughter rare
Of love's kiss conquering,
By the lips full red and the ivory bed
I charge thee come, I am fain instead
Of the nightmare's lordly wing !"

The bride was sad and spoke no more.
The tower erect and blind
Rocked with the storm that smote it sore,
The thunder of the wind.

Swift to their feet the nightmare [1] drew
And shook its gorgeous mane.
"Who rideth me shall never see
His other life again.

"Who rideth me shall laugh and love
In other ways than these."
"Mount, mount ! " the gallant cried, "enough
Of earthly ecstasies ! "

The pale bride caught his colour then :
The pale bride laughed aloud,
Fronting red madness in her den :
"The bride-robe be my shroud !

"The bride-robe gave me light and clean
To kisses' nuptial gold.
Now for a draught of madness keen !
The other lips are cold."

They mount the tameless thundering side ;
They sweep toward the lea ;
The mare is wild ; they spur, they ride,
Mad master and hysteric bride,
Along the lone grey sea.

The pebbles flash, the waters shrink !
(So fearful are those wings !)
The lightning stoops to let them drink.
They see each other's eyes, and think
Unutterable things.

[1] Night-mare has of course nothing to do
with the horse, etymologically.   Mare is from
A.S. *mara*, an incubus.—A. C.

And now the sea is loose and loud ;
  Tremendous the typhoon
Sweeps from the westward as a shroud,
Wrapping some great god in a cloud,
  Abolishing the moon.

And faster flying and faster still
  They gallop fast and faster.
" Turn, turn thy rein ! " she shrieked again,
" 'Tis edged with sore disaster."
He looked her through with sight and will :—
  The pale bride knew her master.

And now the skies are black as ink,
  The nightmare shoreward springs ;
The lightning stoops to let them drink.
They hold each other close, and think
  Unutterable things.

The roar of earthquake stuns the ear ;
  The powers volcanic rise,
Casting the lava red and sheer
A million miles in ether clear
  Beyond the labouring skies.

Ghastlier faces bend around
  And gristlier fears above.
They see no sight : they hear no sound ;
But look toward the chill profound
  End and abyss of love.

The water and the skies are fallen
  Far beyond sight of them.
All earth and fire gasp and expire :
The night hath lost her starry host,
  Shattered her diadem.

Eternity uplifts its brink
  To bar the wizard wings.
The lightning stoops to let them drink.
They silently espouse, and think
  Unutterable things.

The nightmare neighs !   The untravelled
    ways
Are past on fervid feet.
The limits of the limitless
Flash by like jewels on a dress,
  Or dewdrops fallen in wheat.

" O love !   O husband !   Did you guess
  I did not wish to go ?
And now—what rapture can express
  This ?—do you feel and know ? "
The girl's arms close in a caress ;
  Her lips are warm aglow ;
She looks upon his loveliness :—
The night has frozen the old stress ;
  His mouth is cold as snow !

But closer to the corpse she links,
  And closer, closer clings.
Her kiss like lightning drops and drinks.
She burns upon his breast, and thinks
  Unutterable things.

Now half a moment stayed the steed ;
  And then she thought he sighed ;—
And then flashed forward thrice the old
    speed :—
And then she knew he had died.

But closer to him clings she yet,
  And feeds his corpse with fire,
As if death were not to forget
  And to annul desire.

And therefore as the utter space
  Sped past by hour and hour,
She feeds her face upon his face
  Like a bird upon a flower.

" Awake, awake ! for love's own sake !
  I grow so faint and cold ;
I charge thee by the bridal bed,
The violet veins, and the lips full red,
  And the hours of woven gold ! "

And colder now the bride's lips grow
  And colder and yet colder,
Until she lies as cold as snow,
  Her head against his shoulder.

The nightmare never checked its pace.
  The lovely pair are gone
Together through the walls of space
  Into oblivion.

III.

THE KISS

I BEHOLD in a mist of hair involving
Subtle shadows and shapes of ivory beauty.
Gray blue eyes from the spherèd opal eyelids
Look me through and make me a deep con-
tentment
Slow dissolving desire. We sit so silent
Death might sweep over sleep with flowers
of cypress
(Gathered myriad blossoms, Proserpina's),
Stir us not, nor a whisper steal through love-
trance.
Still we sit ; and your head lies calm and
splendid
Shadowed, curve of an arm about it whisper-
ing.
Still your bosom respires its sighs of silver ;
Still one hand o' me quivers close, caresses,
Touches not. O a breath of sudden sad-
ness
Hides your face as a mist grows up a
mountain !
Mist is over my eyes, and darkness gathers
Deep on violet inset deep of eyepits.
Neither holds in the sight the lovely vision.
Slow the mist is dissolved in the wintry
sunlight
On the fells, and the heather wakes to
laughter :—
So sight glimmers across the gulf of sorrow.
You the lily and I the rose redouble,
Bend, soft swayed by a slow spontaneous
music,
Bend to kiss, are alight, one lamp of moon-
rays
Caught, held hard in a crystal second.
Swiftly
Touch, just touch, the appealing floral sisters,
Brush no bloom off the blossom, lift no lip-
gleam
Off the purple and rose, caressing cressets,
Flames of flickering love.   They draw
asunder.
Thus, and motionless thus, for ages. Hither !

IV.

ANNIE.

ANEMONES grow in the wood by the stream ;
And the song of the spring in our garden
Wakes life to the shape of an exquisite dream ;
And reason of passion asks pardon.

I made up a posy by moonlight, a rose,
And a violet white from its cranny,
And a bluebell, and stole, on the tips of my
toes,
At the dark of the night to my Annie.

Her window was open ; she slept like a child ;
So I laid the three flowers on her breast,
And stole back alone through the forest deep-
aisled,
To dream of the lass I loved best.

And the next night I lay half awake on my bed,
When—a foot-fall as soft as the breeze !
Oh ! never a word nor a whisper she said
To disturb the low song of the trees.

But she crept to my side. Awhile we lay
close :
Then : " Have pardon and pity for me ! "
She whispered—" your bluebell and violet
and rose--
I can give but one flower for three."

V.

BRÜNNHILDE.[1]

THE sword that was broken is perfect: the
hero is here.
Be done with the dwarfs and be done with
the spirit of fear !

Hark ! the white note of a bird ; and the
path is declared ;
The sword is girt on, and the dragon is
summoned and dared.

[1] See Wagner, from whose " Ring of the
Nibelungs " the symbolism of this poem is
taken.

Be done with the dragons ! Awaits for the
    lord of the sword
On the crest of a mountain the maid, the
    availing award.

The spear of the Wanderer shivers, the God
    is exhaust.
Be done with the Gods ! the key of Valhalla
    is lost.

The fires that Loki the liar built up of deceit
Are like roses that cushion the moss for the
    warrior's feet.

Be done with the paltry defences ! She
    sleeps. O be done
With the mists of the mountain ! Awake to
    the light of the sun !

Awake ! Let the wave of emotions conflict-
    ing retire,
Let fear and despair be engulfed in delight
    and desire.

There is one thing of all that remains : that
    the sword may not bite :
It is love that is true as itself ; and their
    scion, delight.

True flower of the flame of love : true bloom
    of the ray of the sword !
The lady is lost if she wit not the name of
    her lord.

Awaken and hither, O warrior maiden !
    Above
The Man is awaiting. Be done with the lies !
    It is love.

VI.

DORA.

Dora steals across the floor
    Tiptoe ;
Opens then her rosy door,
    Peeps out.
"Nobody ! And where shall I
    Skip to ?"
Dora, diving daintily,
    Creeps out.

"To the woodland ! Shall I find
    Crowtoe,
Violet, jessamine ! I'll bind
    Garlands.
Fancy I'm a princess. Where
    Go to ?
Persia, China, Finisterre ?
    Far lands ! "

Pity Dora ! Only one
    Daisy
Did she find. The sulking sun
    Slept still.
Dora stamped her foot. Aurora
    Lazy
Stirred not. Hush ! A footstep. Dora
    Kept still.

What a dreadful monster ! Shoot !
    Mercy !
('Twas a man.) Suppose the brute
    Ate her ?
By-and-by the ruffian grows
    " Percy."
And she loves him now she knows
    Better.

VII.

FATIMA.[1]

FRAUGHT with the glory of a dead despair,
My purple eidola, my purple eidola
March, dance—through hyacinthine spheres
Moaning : they sweep along, attain, aware
How frail is Fatima.
They bathe the Gods with stinging tears.
They weave another thread within the mystic
    veil.
They are drawn up anon in some great hand.
They shudder and murmur in the web of Kama.
They hear no music in the white word Rama.
They rush, colossi, liquid swords of life
Strident with spurious desire and strife.
Mocked ! I am dumb : I await the gray
    command :
I wait for Her :

[1] Written in collaboration with S. M.

Inscrutable darkness through the storm
Loomed out, with broidered features of gold :
   its form
Wing-like lay on the firmaments,
River-like curves in all its movements
Swift from inertia of vast voids rolled, stirred
Gigantic for roar of strepitation : whirred
   The essential All
That was Her veil : her voice I had heard
Had not large sobbing fears surged ; will
   and word
     Fall
Down from the black pearls of the night,
   down, back
   To night's impearléd black ;
Down, from chryselephantine wall
And rose-revolving ball,
Doomed, fierce through Saturn's aeons to
   tear,
Fraught with the glory of a dead despair.

VIII.

FLAVIA.

I KISSED the face of Flavia fair,
   In the deep wet dews of dawn,
And the ruddy weight of my lover's hair
Fell over me and held me there
   On the broad Italian lawn.

And the bright Italian moon arose
   And cleft the cypress grove ;
For sadness in all beauty grows,
And sorrow from its master knows
   How to appear like love.

Alas ! that Flavia's gentle kiss,
   And Flavia's cool caress,
And Flavia's flower of utter bliss
Must fade, must cease, must fall and miss
   The height of happiness.

The moon must set, the sun must rise,
   The wind of dawn is chill.
Oh, in this world of miseries
Is one hour's pleasure ill to prize ?
   Is love the means of ill ?

Oh, if there were a God to hear !
   Or Christ had really given
His life ! Or did a Dove appear
Bearing a rosebud, we might fear
   Or hope for hell or heaven.

Alas ! no sign is given. But short
   Bliss of the earth is ours ;
The kiss that stops the avenging thought ;
The furtive passion shrewdly caught
   Between the summer flowers.

So, Flavia, till the dawn awake
   Cling close, cling close, as this is !
While moonlight lingers on the lake,
Our present happiness we'll take
   And fill the night with kisses !

IX.

KATIE CARR.

'TWAS dark when church was out ! the
   moon
   Was low on Rossett Ghyll ; [1]
The organ's melancholy tune
   Grew subtle, far, and still.

All drest in black, her white, white throat
   Like moonlight gleamed ; she moved
Along the road, towards the farm,
   Too happy to be loved.

" O Katie Carr ! how sweet you are ! "
   She only hurried faster :
She found an arm about her waist :
   A maiden knows her master.

Through grass and heather we walked to-
   gether ;
   So hard her heart still beat
She thought she saw a ghost, and fast
   Flickered the tiny feet.

" O Katie Carr, there's one stile more !
   For your sweet love I'm dying.
There's no one near ; there's nought to fear."
   The lassie burst out crying.

    [1] A pass in Cumberland.

" From Wastdale Head to Kirkstone Pass
     There's ne'er a lass like Kate : "—
The gentle child looked up and smiled
     And kissed me frank and straight.

The night was dark, the stars were few :—
     Should love need moon or star ?
Let him decide who wins a bride
     The peer of Katie Carr.

X.
NORAH.

NORAH, my wee shy child of wonderment,
     You are sweeter than a swallow-song at
          dusk !
You are braver than a lark that soars and
     trills
     His lofty laughter of love to a hundred
          hills !
You lie like a sweet nut within the husk
     Of my big arms ; and uttermost content
I have of you, my tiny fairy, eh ?
     Do you live in a flower, I wonder, and
          sleep and pray
To the good God to send you dew at dawn
     And rain in rain's soft season, and sun
          betimes,
And all the gladness of the afterglow
     When you come shyly out of the folded
          bud,
Unsheath your dainty soul, bathe it in blood
     Of my heart ? Do you love me ? Do you
          know
How I love you ?   Do you love these
     twittering rhymes
I string you ? Is your tiny life withdrawn
Into its cup for modesty when I sing
     So softly to you and hold you in my hands,
You wild, wee wonder of wisdom ? Now
     I bring
     My lips to your body and touch you
          reverently,
Knowing as I know what Gabriel under-
          stands
     When he spreads his wings above for
          canopy

When you would sleep, you frail angelic thing
     Like a tiny snowdrop in its own life
          curled—
But oh ! the biggest heart in all the world !

XI.
MARY.

MARY, Mary, subtle and softly breathing,
Look once eager out of the eyes upon me,
Draw one sigh, resign and abide in maiden
          Beauty for ever !

Love me, love me, love me as I desire it,
Strong sweet draughts not drawn of a well of
          passion,
Truth's bright crystal, shimmering out of
          sunlight
          Into the moon-dawn.

Closer cling, thou heart of amazed rapture,
Cords of starlight fashioned about thee net-
          wise,
Tendrils woven of gossamer twist about us !
          These be the binders !

Night winds whirl about the avenger city ;
Darkness rides on desolate miles of moor-
          land ;
Thou and I, disparted a little, part not
          Spirit from spirit.

Strange and sister songs in the middle ether
Grow, divide ; they hover about, above us.
We, the song consummate of love, give music
          Back to the mortal.

Here, my love, a garden of spice and myrtle ;
Sunlight shakes the rivers of love with
          laughter ;
Here, my love, abide, in the amber ages,
          Lapped in the levin.

Linger, linger, light of the blessed moonrise !
Full-orbed sweep immaculate through the
          midnight !
Bend above, O sorrowful sister, kiss me
          Once and for ever !

Let the lake of thought be as still as dark-
      mans [1]
Brooding over magian pools of madness !
Love, the sun, arise and abide above us,
      Mary Mavourneen.

XII.

XANTIPPE.

SWEET, do you scold ?   I had rather have
      you scold
Than from another earn a million kisses.
The tiger rapture on your skin's Greek gold
Is worth a million smiles of sunken cold
And Arctic archangelic passion rolled
      From any other woman.   Heaven misses
The half of God's delight who doth not see
      Some lightning anger dart like love and
         strike
Into the sacred heart its iterant glee
Of scathing tortures worth Hell's agony
To melt—ah, sweet, I know ! in foam and free
Lustre of love redoubled.   Come to me !
   I will avenge that anger, like to like,
With gentle fires of smitten love, will burn
Into your beauty with the athletic rush
Of conquering godhead ; and your cheek
      shall burn
      From red of wrath to shame's adorable
         blush,
And so in tears and raptures mix the cup
      Of dreadful wine we are wont to drain and
         —well !—
Needs but one glance to lift the liquor up,
   One angry grip to wake me, and to swell
The anguish into rapture—come, to sup
   The liquid lava of the lake of Hell !

XIII.

EILEEN.

THE frosty fingers of the wind ; the eyes
Of the melancholy wind : the voice serene
Of the love-moved wind: the exulting secrecies
Of the subtle wind : lament, O harmonies
Of the most musical wind !   Eileen !

[1] Night—an old English canting word.

The peace of the nameless loch : the waiting
      heart
Of the amorous loch : the lights unguessed,
      unseen,
Of the midnight loch ; the winter's sorrow
      apart
Of the ice-bound loch : O majesty of art
Of the most motionless loch !   Eileen !

The gleam of the hills : the stature of the
      hills
Facing the wind and the loch : the cold and
      clean
Sculpture of the stalwart hills ; the iron wills
Of the inscrutable hills !   O strength that
      stills
The cry of the agonised hills !   Eileen !

Come back, O thought, alike from burn and
      ben
And sacred loch and rapture strong and keen
Of the wind of the moor.   A race of little
      men
Lives with the little.   The exalted ken
Knows the synthetic soul.   Eileen !

Close in the silence cling the patient eyes
Of love : the soul accepts her time of teen,
Awaits the answer.   Midnight droops and
      dies,
A floral hour ; what dawn of love shall rise
On a world of sorrow ?   Peace !   Eileen !

Mazed in a Titan world of rock and snow ?
Horsèd among the bearded Bedawin ?
Drowsed on a tropic river in the glow
Of sunset ?   Whither ?   Who shall care or
      know,
When one and all are this ?   Eileen !

XIV

THE night is void of stars : the moon is full,
Veiling their radiance with her beautiful
Mist of still light.   O slumbrous air !
Wings of the winter, droop to-night !   Behold
The mirror of shuddering silver in the gold
Setting of loose involving hair !

Closer and closer through the dusk of sense
Avails the monotone omnipotence.
Steady, in one crescent tune,
Rises the virgin moon ;
And from the depth of eyes flooded with
love
Shines ecstasy thereof.

Words pass and are not heard. The ear,
awake
Only for its master's individual sake,
Strains only for three whispered songs,
Hears naught beside, interprets silence so,
Till liquid melodies of music flow
"I love you." We afford to wait ; who
longs
That knows ? And we know ; for the moon
is full.

Steals in the ambient aura of delight
That quivering ray intense and cool
Self centred. Woven of a million lines
There is a curve of light,
A pure, ideal curve, single, that shines
Amid the manifold night
Of all the flowery dreams that build it up.
So from the azure cup
Of heaven inverted is the white wine poured.
Stay, O thou vivid sword
Of soul, and cease, and be not ! Unto me
Through all eternity
Let me be not, and this thing be !

XV.

O THE deep wells and springs of tears !
O the intenser rays of blue,
Fleeting through gray unaltering spheres,
Like skies beholden through the dew !
O pearls of light ! O sombre meres
Wherein a waterwitch is hid,
And chants of sunset rise unbid,
Your eyes, your eyes ! They read me through,
Sphinx ; and your soul, the Pyramid,
Burns upward, and I worship you.

2.

But had I moulded beauty's eyes
I had not touched the carving tool
Thus tenderly : my spirit dies
Before you, but my life still lies
Salient, unwounded, and to dule
Wakes : I had rather you were now
Medusa, of the awful brow,
The snaky hair, the face of fear.
So could I shut my eyes ; feel how
Your hair fell back on me and bit,
Your lips descended on my face
In one exenterate kiss : and wit
I should abide a little space—
So little a space !—and solemn rise,
Face the black vaults of the alone,
And, knowing, lift to you mine eyes,
Look on your face, and turn to stone.

XVI.

THE schoolboy drudges through his Greek ;
Plods to the integral calculus ;
Makes sulphuretted hydrogen ;

And, if the poor dumb thing could speak,
He'd say : Hic labor omnibus
Prodest : vitae verae limen.

Deinde missa juventute
Ave ! cum otio dignitas ! [1]
So I : and strove and did not shirk.

But now ? Confront me life and duty ;
Toil is my daily hap, alas !
And work is still the sire of work.

Shall I repine ? What joys are hid
In weariness of idleness ?
Rich, young, beloved, shall I recede ?

Enjoy ? Not I ! I work unbid ;
Book follows book : ideas press
Hurrying over the green mead

[1] This work is good for all men, the thres-
hold of real life. Then, once youth is past,
Hail ! Ease and dignity.

Of mind : they roll, a rippling stream
Hurrying, hurrying : hour by hour
The brain throbs : shall I never rest ?

Ay ! for a little : peace supreme
Receives my head that lies a flower
Borne on the mountain of thy breast.

XVII.

SPEAK, O my sister, O my spouse, speak,
    speak !
Sigh not, but utter the intense award
Of infinite love ; arise, burn cheek by cheek !
Dart, eyes of glory ; live, O lambent sword
O' the heart's gold rushing over mount and
    moor
Of sunlit rapture ! rise all runes above,
Dissolve thyself into one molten lure,
    Invisible core of the visible flame of love ;
Heart of the sun of rapture, whirling ever ;
    Strength of the sight of eagles, pierce the
        foam
Of ecstasy's irremeable river,
    And race the rhythm of laughter to its home
In the heart of the woman, and evoke the
    light
Of love out of the fiery womb of night !

XVIII.

FRIENDSHIP.

BETTER than bliss of floral kiss,
Eternal rapture caught and held ;
Better than rapture's self is this
To which we find ourselves compelled,
The trick of self-analysis.

Thoughts fetter not true love : we weld
No bands by logic : on our lips
The idle metaphysic quibble
Laughs : what portends the late eclipse ?
What oracle of the solar sybil ?

Orion's signal banner dips :
"This is the folly of your youth,
Achieving the exalted aim ;
Because you have gained a higher truth
To call it by a lower name."

XIX.

ROSE on the breast of the world of spring,
    I press my breast against thy bloom,
My subtle life drawn out to thee : to thee
    its moods and meanings cling.
I pass from change and thought to peace,
    woven on love's incredible loom,
Rose on the breast of the world of spring !

How shall the heart dissolved in joy take
    form and harmony and sing ?
How shall the ecstasy of light fall back to
    music's magic gloom ?
O China rose without a tnorn, O honey-bee
    without a sting !

The scent of all thy beauty burns upon the
    wind. The deep perfume
Of our own love is hidden in our hearts,
    the invulnerable ring.
No man shall know. I bear thee down unto
    the tomb, beyond the tomb,
Rose on the breast of the world of spring !

XX.

LIE still, O love, and let there be delight !
Lie on the soft banks of ambrosial air,
The roseate marble of invisible space.
Secure and silent, O caressing night,
We are in thee ; and thou art everywhere.
Lie still, and read thy soul upon my face.

Swayed slowly by the wind, made crafts-
    men of
The mystery of happiness, we lie
And rock us to and fro, and to and fro.
Shrined in the temple of the world, O love,
We wait self-worshipped through eternity,
Until " to ignore " is equal to " to know."

Lie still, O love, and let me hide my brows
In the deep bosom and the scented vales.
Thy deep drawn breath embrace my hair,
    resume
My life in thine ! Here is an amber house
With gateways of old gold. Far nightin-
    gales
Sing like smooth silence through the extreme
    perfume.

Moving, flying, exulting, on we go,
Borne on blue clouds of glory. On the river,
Over the mountains of the night, above
The stars of the night, above the floral glow
Of the sun dawning now for us for ever
Who rest content in the abode of love !

Lie still, O love, and let the fragrant sleep
Perfume our eyelids with dew-dropping
    death,
And silence be the witness of the will.
Fall, fall, fall back in the uprolling deep
Wrapt in rose mist of unsuccessive breath
Of love, of love. Lie still, O love, lie still.

XXI.

UNDER the stars the die was cast to win.
The moonrays stained with pale embroidered
    bars
The iridescent shimmer of your skin,
        Under the stars.

Great angels drove their pearl-inwoven cars
Through the night's racecourse : silence stood
    within
The folded cups of passion's nenuphars.

You were my own ; sorrowless, without sin,
That night—this night.   Sinks the red eye[1]
    of Mars ;
The hand of Hermes[1] guides us as we spin
        Under the stars.

[1] Tibetan astrologers give these symbols to
the planets Mars and Mercury.

XXII.

DROOP the great eyelids purple-veined !
Stand, pure and pale and tremulous !
Dare to believe, O soul unstained,
The truth unguessed and unexplained !

The unquiet air monotonous
Wreathes the sad head in whirring mist.
Hath the delicate will disdained
The delicate lips that would be kissed ?

Like far blue snows by sunrise caught
Love lights the enlightened eyes of blue.
Dare to believe the child-heart's thought,
And wake in wonder ! For I knew
From the first hour that This was true.

XXIII.

PROTOPLASM.

ALTHOUGH I cannot leave these bitter leas,
And whisper wiser than the southern breeze,
And mix my master music with the sea's ;

Although I shiver and you smile ; heap coal
And you stand laughing where the long
    waves roll ;
There is a sympathy of soul to soul.

Not Scylla, not the iron Symplegades
Shall bar that vessel, in delighted ease
Winning her way by stainless sorceries.

Though I be melancholy and thou fair,
And I be dark and thou too high for care ;
Both yet may strive in a serener air,

Clasping the vast, the immeasurable knees ;
Searching the secrets of the calm decrees
Of Hermes gray or gold Musagetes !

Is there another ? Unprofane, aware,
See me secreted, silent, everywhere.
And then consider ! Dost thou dare to dare ?

The live sun leaps by invisible degrees ;
The blessèd moon grows slowly through the
    trees ;
And fire has fire's ingressive agonies.

I everywhere abide, and I control
Olympian glories and the Pythian goal.
What isle unfurls yonder life's glimmering
    scroll?

This be thy shrine, and all its splendours
    these!
Awake to dream! Two desolate nudities
Woven through sculpture into ecstasies.

XXIV.

Aum! I unfold the tinted robe,
My love's embroideries one by one,
Unveil her glories, globe on globe,
And find beneath the quivering probe
    A shaking skeleton.

The smile of vermeil lips is past ;
The skull's black grin awhile remains ;
The fallen flesh displays aghast
Ribbed bars of bone : was Venus cast
    For this? What Mars attains?

Where is the poesy that shed
Its dewfall downward through her eyes?
Gaunt sockets stare from bony head.
Moves she? Ah me ! the living dead !
    The poet loves? He lies.

Others perceive thee, peerless maid
Broidered with beauty, starred and gemmed
With purity and light, arrayed
In wit—like moonlight down a glade
    With flowers diademed.

But I remember ; see the form
Serene sink slowly to the dust.
'Tis but a date: the eventful storm
Comes : then or now? What odds? They
    swarm,
    The winds : this breath, one gust.

Ah ! in the spiritual soul
Is there no essence to abide
When flesh and bone alike shall roll
From shape to shape, from goal to goal,
    On time, the envious tide?

All tire, all break, all pass. Beware
False thirst, false trust, false doubts of truth
Whilst thou art young, whilst thou art fair,
Awake and see the sepulchre
    For beauty yawn and youth.

Strive to cessation. Only this
Is the true refuge : this alone
Be implicit in our subtle kiss,
Be master of the imperfect bliss
    We call perfection's throne.

Then, if we strive, not all in vain
This vision of the barrèd bones ;
This knowledge in a poet's brain,
Daring to sing its own deep pain
    In shapeless semitones.

Ah ! if we strive, we attain. In sooth,
The effort is of old begun,
Or I had hardly seen the truth
Beneath thy beauty and thy youth :—
    A mouldering skeleton !

XXV.

I am so sad and, being alone to-night,
I will not see you. Self-disdain forbids.
I wander through the icy hermitage
Of the populous streets, hoping. O might
Some idle God look through his drowsy lids
And will us happiness ! Serene and sage
Therefore I sit, as if I loved you not,
And train a practised pen, and strive to art ;
Accomplish art, and lose the art therein.
I sit, a bitter Witenagemot,[1]
The saint, the poet, the man : the lover's heart
Pleads at the bar. How should he hope to
    win?
The saint is silent while the poet strings
These futile follies, gives for bread a stone,
And the man endures. The lover breaks
    the lyre.
Its death-cry, agony, O agony ! rings
One name. The lover sits in hell alone
Fondling the devil that men call desire.

[1] The ancient parliament of Britain.

XXVI.

WHEN the wearily falling blossom of midnight
Stirs the face of a sleeper, Mother of Sorrow !
Look thou down in the dawn of heavier dewfall.
Tears of widow despair, O mutely lamenting
Crouched in heavenly bowers over the carven
Gateway's ivory flower, tears of revival
Fall, oh fall, to the black abodes of the lonely.
I await, I await, I sing not for sorrow,
Train the fugitive lights of music across me,
Seek by force to avail me, vainly attempting
Song with feather detested, agony futile :
Ply these piteous exercises of cunning,
Hateful—ay ! to myself ! To me it were better
Only to woo in the silence, magical silence,
Silence eloquent, wert thou here or afar, love.
Woo thee, nay ! but abide in certain recession ;
Stilled to the splendid currents fervid of passion ;
Float to seas of an unassailable silence
Down the river of love. The words are awakened :
Let the soul be asleep. The dawn is upon us.

XXVII.[1]

ECSTASY, break through poetry's beautiful barriers,
Intricate webs, labyrinthine mazes of music !
Leap, love, lightning's self, and, athwart the appalling
Evil clouds of an agony bound by existence,
Enter, avail me, exult ! In the masses of matter
Nothing avails ; in the splendour spirit is, nothing.
Give me love ; I am weary of giants colossal,
Royal, impossible things ; I am fain of a bosom
Always breathing sleep, and the symphony, silence.
Years are forgotten ; abide, deep love, I am happy.

[1] An acrostic.

XXVIII.

COULD ivory blush with a stain of the sunset on highlands
Of snow : could the mind of me span
The tenderness born of the dew in immaculate islands
Virgin of maculate man :
Could I mingle the Alps and Hawaii ; Strath Ness and A'pura [1] and Baiæ ;
Kashmir and Japan :
Could lilies attain to the life of the Gods : could a comet
Attain to the calm of the moon :
I would mingle them all in a kiss, and draw from it
The soul of a sensitive tune.
All lovers should hear it and know it : not needing the words of a poet
In ebony hewn.

O beam of discovery under the eyelids awaking
The sense of delight ! O assent
Slow dawning through cream into roses ! O white bosom shaking
The myrtles of magical scent
In the groves of the heart ! O the pleasure that runs over all overmeasure,
The wine of Event !

Overmastered the hurl of the world in the hush of our rapture ;
Entangled the bird of success
In the snare of bewildering fancies. We capture
Delight in the toils of a tress
Rough gilded of sunlight and umber with virginal shadows of slumber—
Ah ! sorrow, regress !

Till the idle abyss of eternity swoon to our pinions
With music of wings as we fly
Through the azure of dreams, and the purple of mighty dominions
Exalted, afoam in the sky ;
And to us it were wiser and sweeter to ruin the race of the metre,
And song were to die.

[1] Anuradapura, the ruined sacred city of Ceylon.

1906

A DRAMATIC VERSION[1] OF

R. L. STEVENSON'S STORY

THE SIRE DE MALÉTROIT'S DOOR

(Written in collaboration with GERALD KELLY)

SCENE I.

The SIRE DE MALÉTROIT *sitting before
the fire. A chime of bells—eleven.*

ALAIN.

'Leven o' th' clock! Plague take these
lovers! What? do they make a Malétroit
wait? [*Picks up letter from table—reads*]
" Mademoiselle " — um, um — " my words
might show that love which I cannot declare
in writing "—very likely—"nor raise a blush
on that alabaster brow"—um! um! ah!—
" embrace of the eyes "—is the fellow an
octopus?— " Tho' you do not respond to my
letters "—ah!—"yet I would not have you
leave me "—I daresay not—" Pity me, moonlike queen "—moonlike? um!—" Leave the
postern door ajar "—well, it is ajar—" that I
may speak with your beauty on the stairs "
—um—can't meet him there. Cold! cold!
[*Sniffs.*] A pretty letter. [*Throws it aside.*]
Andrew! some more logs. [*Enter* ANDREW.]
I expect company. [*Chuckles long.*] The old
Burgundy, Andrew. [*Exit* ANDREW.] I
propose to squeeze Duke Charles' grapes,
though fate and my age forbid me a smack
at his forces — *neu sinas Medos equitare
inultos*—but our good King is no Augustus.
 [*Strikes gong. Enter* PRIEST *quietly
 and quickly.* ALAIN *does not turn
 round.*
Good evening, father. All is ready?

PRIEST.

All, my lord.

ALAIN.

It is near the time. She has remained
in her room?

PRIEST.

All the day.

ALAIN.

Has she attempted no message? eh?

PRIEST.

Sir, she——

ALAIN.

[*Interrupts.*] She has not succeeded, at
least?

PRIEST.

I am still Father Jerome.
 [*Pause.*

ALAIN.

She is ready dressed as I ordered? And
now praying in the Chapel?
 [ALAIN *gets up and can now see* PRIEST.

PRIEST.

As you ordered, my lord.

ALAIN.

Content?
 [PRIEST *puts out his hands with the
 gesture " hardly."*

PRIEST.

Young maids are wilful, my lord.

1 This play has been publicly performed within the United Kingdom. It is entered at
Stationers' Hall. All rights reserved.

ALAIN.

Let her be resigned to the will of Heaven. [*The* PRIEST *smiles subtly.* ALAIN *perceives it.*] And *my* will. [*Strikes gong twice.*] You may retire, father.

[PRIEST *bows and retires. Enter* CAPTAIN *and stands at salute.*]

Ah, Captain, you have your fifty men in readiness?

CAPTAIN.

Yes, my lord. [*Salutes.*]

ALAIN.

Let them be drawn up behind yon door. When I clap my hands you will raise the arras, but let no man move. And let 'em be silent—the man I hear I hang. [CAPTAIN *salutes.*] You may go. [CAPTAIN *salutes, and exit.* ALAIN *reaches to a tome on the table.*] Now, Flaccus, let us spend this night together as we have spent so many. The crisis of my life—my brother's trust, God rest his soul! [*crosses himself and mutters silently in prayer*]—shall not find Alain de Malétroit unready or disturbed.

SCENE CLOSES.

SCENE II.[1]

A narrow dirty street in Paris, fifteenth century. Night pitch black. Passers-by with lanterns.

FIRST PASSER-BY *stumbles into* SECOND.

SECOND PASSER-BY.

Zounds, man! have a care with thy goings.

FIRST PASSER-BY.

Stand, or I strike. Who but a thief goes lanternless o' nights?

[1] The play may be presented in a single scene, by omitting this Scene, and joining Scenes I. and III. by the noise of a banging door.

SECOND PASSER-BY.

The saints be praised, 'tis my good gossip Peter Halse. What, knowest thou not thy old friend? [FIRST PASSER-BY *lifts his lantern to the other's face.*

FIRST PASSER-BY.

Martin Cloche, by the Mass!

SECOND PASSER-BY.

Ay, Martin Cloche! And his lantern hath gone out, and his heart faileth him somewhat. But these be troublous times.

[*Enter* FLORIMOND *and waits.*

FIRST PASSER-BY.

The town is full of these drunken English men-at-arms.

SECOND PASSER-BY.

The English be bad, but God save us from the Burgundians! Their own cousin-germans be we, and for that they are but bitterer.

FLORIMOND.

Devil take them! What, will they stand here gossiping all night?

FIRST PASSER-BY.

'Tis a cold night: I would be home.

SECOND PASSER-BY.

Light me, prithee, to my door: it lieth as thou knowest, but a stone's-throw from St. Yniold's.

FIRST PASSER-BY.

Well, let us be going.

[*Exeunt.*

FLORIMOND.

Now for the moment I have longed for this three months! Blanche! Blanche! I shall see thee, touch thee—who knows what

maiden love may work on maiden modesty?
Ah, fall deeper, ye blessed shadows ! Ye
are light enough for Florimond de Champdivers to move toward his bliss !
> [*Noise of clashing armour, ribald
> laughter, &c. Enter the Watch,
> R., drunk.*

A WATCHMAN.

Ho, boys ! a gay night for thieves.

FLORIMOND.

Curse the sots !
> [*Crouches back in the shadow.*

SECOND WATCHMAN.

(*Sings*)

The soldier's life is short and merry,
His mistress' lips are ripe as a cherry,
Then drink, drink !
The guns roar out and the swords flash clean,
And the soldier sleepeth under the green,
Oh, the soldier's life for me !

But a scurvy night it is, comrades, when the
streets are slippery, and the wine cold in
a man's belly, and never a little white
rabbit of a woman scuttling along in the
dark.

THIRD WATCHMAN.

What ho ! my lads ! Here's a scurvy
Frenchman skulking along. What, will
you make your lass attend you, master ?

FLORIMOND.

Loose me, knave, I am for England, and
a Captain in your army, or rather that of
Burgundy—if you will be precise.

FIRST WATCHMAN.

What do you here, without a lantern,
scaring honest folk ?

FLORIMOND.

Honesty is no word for to-night. Will
you the loyal man's word ?

SECOND WATCHMAN.

That's it, my gallant cock ! The word !

FLORIMOND.

Burgundy and freedom.

THIRD WATCHMAN.

So ! Give a crown to the poor watchmen
then to drink your Excellency's health, and
luck to your honour's love. Ah ! we're
gay when we're young—I've a sweetheart
myself.

FLORIMOND.

And now be off !
> [*Gives money. Exeunt.*

Cold !—the devil ! Ah ! but to-night—
at last I shall touch my Blanche. May
Blanche warm me well with a hearty kiss !
The little white cat ! Three months ! And
I've not so much as exchanged a word.
There must be an end to all that. Faith,
but she makes me think of Biondetta, that
I knew in the Italian campaign. O my
Blanche ! One moment, and I am in thine
arms ! Blanche ! Sweet, sweet Blanche.
O little white-faced rose of France. A
soldier's heart is thine — a soldier's arms
shall be round thee in a moment ! 'Tis a
fine thing this love—the strong true abiding
love of a brave man. How like little Florise
her voice is when she sings !
> [*By this fool's talk he loses his oppor-
> tunity. Enter* DENYS.

DENYS.

Cold is no word for it. [*Shudders.*]
Where the devil have I got to now ? Had
I but vowed St. Denys a candle and put the
same in my pocket, I would not now be in
the dark. Here was a lane, and the folk
had called it Wolf's Throat, and now here's
a door and devil a name to it. Fool I was
to stay winebibbing with Cousin Henri, and
triple knave he to send me forth without
a boy and a light. True ! he was under
the table—and seven times fool was I not to
join him there.

FLORIMOND.

O this miserable sot !

[*Crouches again,* DENYS *sees him.*

DENYS.

O thank God ! Here's another poor devil, a gentleman by his clothes, and a thief by his manner, and I daresay a good fellow. [*Goes to* FLORIMOND *and slaps him on the back.*] Sir, do you know this cursed Paris? My inn, which I have lost, is the Sign of the Green Grass—I should say the Field o' Spring—and 'tis hard by the Church of St. Anselm, that is hard by the river, and the hardest of all is that neither church, inn, nor river can I find this devil of a night.

[*Catches* FLORIMOND *and shakes him by the shoulder.*

FLORIMOND.

Know you are speaking to a captain in the army of Duke Charles ! Moderate thy drunkenness, man, or I will call the watch.

DENYS.

Know me for a captain in the army of His Majesty King Charles of France, whom God preserve !

FLORIMOND.

What, traitor ?

DENYS.

Traitor in thy teeth ! I have a safe-conduct from your pinchbeck duke. Oh, the devil ! 'twill serve me but ill these Paris nights—a fool am I ! Well, sir, I ask your pardon, and throw myself on your kindness.

FLORIMOND.

Ha ! St. Gris ! Then I have you, my fine cock. Watch, ho ! A traitor ! I will pay you your insolence.

[*Calls.*

DENYS.

Oh then, to shut your mouth. [*Draws.*

[FLORIMOND *tries to draw, gets the flat of* DENYS' *sword on his shoulder, and runs away. Exit* DENYS *pursuing and* FLORIMOND *calling out. Distant shouts. Re-enter* DENYS, *L.*

DENYS.

Oh, my inn ! my inn ! What a fool am I ! Where can I hide? The air is full of noises. I would change my safe-conduct for a pair of wings. I must steal back the way I came, and St. Denys lend me prudence the next fool I meet. What a night ! O my God !

Enter WATCH, *R., running and shouting.*

Well, for France, then ! My back to the door, and my sword to the foeman's breast ! [*Puts his back to the door.*] My father's son could never have died otherwise ! [*Enter* WATCH.] St. Denys for Beaulieu ! The door's open. May the luck turn yet !

[*Slides backwards gently through door.* WATCH *cross stage stumbling, cursing, and crying, "A traitor, a traitor !"*

[*Stage being clear for a little, suddenly the door bangs violently.*

DENYS.

[*Inside.*] What the devil was that? The door !

Re-enter FLORIMOND, *R.*

FLORIMOND.

At last ! [*Goes to door and pushes it.*] The devil take all women ! After all, the door is shut. Laugh, thou light little fool, laugh now. One day thou shalt moan upon the stones, and Florimond de Champdivers shall shut his door to thee. Damn and damn and damn ! What served love shall serve hate : 'tis a poor game that only works one way. [*Curtain.*

SCENE III

The SIRE DE MALÉTROIT *as in Scene I.
He is standing alert and intent, listening. From below are growls and muttered curses ; then a sharp sound like the snapping of a sword.*

ALAIN.

Amat janua limen! [*Closes book.*] Now, my friend, whoever you are — for your charming letter does not mention your honourable name—we shall very soon have the pleasure of seeing you. " Embrace of the eyes," eh? You distrust my door already, eh? Why do you knock so? [*Great noise below.*] No honester craftsman ever built a door—you waste time! Why so reluctant to move from the cold night to the " blush of an alabaster brow," and the rest of your accursed troubadour's jargon, to a bliss you little expect. " Gratia cum Nymphis geminisque sororibus audet ducere nuda choros." But your *choros*, Blanche, is but your old uncle, who perhaps loves you better than you think just now. [*A sound of suppressed sobbing from the Chapel.*] Ah! you may weep if you will—but what choice have you left me? And Lord! Lord! what could a loving heart ask more? [*Stumbling on steps, and a muttering, " Perdition catch the fool who invented these circular stairs."*] Ha! He seems a little uncertain of the stair. Hush! [*Enter* DENYS, *who remains behind arras.* ALAIN *sits.*

DENYS.

[*Stumbles and swears.*] O these stairs! They go round and round, or *seem* to go round—faith! I have seen an entire castle do as much—and lead nowhere. [*Pushes against arras and is seen by audience. He hastily withdraws.*] Oh, they do though! Shall I knock? Shall I go in? Shal. I stay here till morning? There are three fools there, and I have a poor choice: to knock is polite, to wait is polite, and to introduce my charming self is the politest of all. [*Peeps in.*] Can't see anybody! It's clearly a gentleman's house—and a fool he is to leave his postern door ajar. Whoever he is, he can hardly blame me for a misadventure—and a curious tale is a passport the world over. Well, let me go in! To go in boldly is to slap Luck the courtezan on the shoulder, and 'tis Venus o' the dicebox to an ace and a deuce but she call me a tall fellow of my hands and bid me sit to supper. Warily now! . . .
[*Pushes past arras.*

ALAIN.

Good evening, good evening, my dear young friend. Welcome, very welcome! Come to the fire, man, and warm yourself. " Jam satis terris nivis,"—if you know your Horace as you know your Ovid, we shall get along splendidly.
[DENYS *stands stupefied.* ALAIN *waits.*

DENYS.

I fear, sir, I don't know my Ovid. [*With the air of one primed to repeat a lesson.*] I beg a thousand pardons, Monsieur.

ALAIN.

Don't apologise, don't apologise. I've been expecting you all the evening.

DENYS.

Excuse me, sir, there is some mistake— !

ALAIN.

No! No! There is no mistake. Be at ease, my young friend.

DENYS.

[*Shrugs his shoulders.*] But I had no wish to be here—er—er !—Nothing was further from my thoughts than this most unwarrantable intrusion.

ALAIN.

Well, well, that's all right. Here you are, which is the great thing after all, isn't it? Sit down, my dear young friend [DENYS *uncomfortably and slowly takes a chair*], and we shall—er—arrange our little affair. You arrived uninvited, but believe me, most welcome.

DENYS.

Sir, you persist in error. I am a stranger : Denys de Beaulieu is my name, and I am here under a safe-conduct. That you see me in your house is only owing to—your door.

ALAIN.

Ah! my door—a hospitable fancy of mine!

DENYS.

I don't understand. I did not wish . . . oh!

ALAIN.

My dear sir, we old gentlemen expect this reluctance from young bloods. [*With bitter irony.*] We bear it. But [*flaming out*] if the matter touches one's honour—[*rises and looks sternly at* DENYS].

DENYS.

Your *honour?*
[DENYS *is amazed out of all measure.*

ALAIN.

We try to find some means of overcoming such modesty.

DENYS.

Is this Ovid or Horace?

ALAIN.

To business, then, if you will affect ignorance. [*Strikes gong ; enter* PRIEST, *who gives* DENYS *a long keen glance and speaks in an undertone to* ALAIN.] Is she in a better frame of mind?

PRIEST.

She is more resigned, my lord.

ALAIN.

Now a murrain o' these languishing wenches in their green - sickness! By 'r Lady, she is hard to please. A likely stripling, not ill-born, and the one of her own choosing. Why, what more would she have?

PRIEST.

The situation is not usual to a young damsel, and somewhat trying to her blushes.

ALAIN.

She should have thought of that before. This devil's dance is not to my piping, but since she is in it, by 'r Lady, she shall carry it through.
[*Motions* PRIEST *to retire. Exit* PRIEST, *with a low reverence to* ALAIN *and a courteous bow to* DENYS.

DENYS.

[*Rises and clears his throat.*] Sir, let me —explain that——

ALAIN.

Don't explain. May I beg you to be seated, my *dear* young friend. We've been expecting you all night : the lady is ready, though I believe a little tearful : a bride has so much to fear, you know — *et corde et genibus tremit*—eh, my Gaetulian lion?

DENYS.

[*Raises his hand authoritatively to check speech.*] Sir! this misunderstanding, for such I am convinced it is, must go no further. I am a stranger here—

ALAIN.

Well, well, you'll get to know the old place in time. Blanche——

DENYS.

Sir! pray let me speak. I know you not——

ALAIN.

We know *you.*

DENYS.

[*Ironically.*] I am too honoured.

ALAIN.

Well?

DENYS.

You speak of a lady to me. You mistake me——

ALAIN.

I hope so.

DENYS.

Do not entrust a stranger with your family secrets, is my advice—as a man of the world.

ALAIN.

But my nephew !—

DENYS.

I do not even know your lordship's honourable nephew.

ALAIN.

I may yet show you a sneaking rascal in his person.

DENYS.

This really cannot go on. I must beg you, sir, to allow me to go from your house. I came here by an ill chance enough—though it saved my life in sooth.

ALAIN.

And secured you a splendid marriage.

DENYS.

[*Aside.*] Never, never again will I mix my drinks. [ALAIN *surveys* DENYS *from head to foot, emitting satisfied chuckles at*

irregular intervals, while DENYS *clears his throat repeatedly. This continues long,* DENYS *fidgeting more and more.* DENYS, *politely :*] The wind has gone down somewhat.

[ALAIN *falls into a fit of silent laughter.* DENYS *rises and puts on his hat with a flourish.*

DENYS.

Sir, if you are in your wits, I find you insolent : if not, I will not stand here parleying with a madman.

ALAIN.

I must apologise, no doubt, but the circumstances are peculiar. Is it your custom to steal into the houses of gentlemen after midnight, and accuse the owners of lunacy ? [*Chuckles.*] Well—let us be polite if we cannot be friendly.

DENYS.

Then, sir, you will permit me to explain my intrusion.

ALAIN.

[*Laughing.*] Ha ! Ha ! a fine story, I wager. 'Twill interest me much, i' faith. [DENYS *shows signs of impatience ;* ALAIN *begins to look a little doubtful. With sudden interest :*] Well, how *did* you come here ?

DENYS.

[*With much quaint lively gesture—his story-telling powers are much in request by his mess, and he is very proud of them.*] Aye, sir ! by 'r Lady, when I think of it, 'tis a curious adventure enough. [*Pause to collect thoughts. Then dashes off lively :*] Lost my way in this cursed town—night like hell's mouth—groped about your dirty little black narrow streets—no lantern—quarrelled with an officer—I draw—captain bolts—up run guard—see open door—your door, sir !— in I go ! and then all of a sudden bangs to the door and I am caught like a rat in a

trap. I break my sword on the old beast—
give it up—up come stairs—ah ! stairs come
up—I mean *I come*—a murrain on these
courtly phrases ! and here I stand [*rises and
bows*], Denys de Beaulieu, Damoiseau de
Beaulieu, in the Province of Normandy, at
your lordship's service.

ALAIN.

That is your way of looking after the
lady's reputation. Hear mine ! Allow me
first to introduce myself as Alain de Malétroit, Sire de Malétroit, and Warden of the
Marches under his Majesty King Charles—

DENYS.

Whom God preserve !
        [*Waves his broken sword.*

ALAIN.

What excellent sentiments, and what an
unfortunate omen—dear, dear me ! And
I have the honour to offer you the hand—
I presume you already possess the heart—of
the Lady Blanche de Malétroit.

DENYS.

You—what ?

ALAIN.

Tut ! Tut ! The marriage, if you please,
will take place in an hour.

DENYS.

[*Aside.*] Oh, he is mad after all ! [*Aloud.*]
What nightmare is this ?

ALAIN.

You are not very polite to the lady—not
as polite as your letter.

DENYS.

My letter ?
      [ALAIN *takes up letter from table and
      reads.*

ALAIN (*reads*).

"O white-bosomed Blanche ! I am pale
and wan with suffering for thy love. Pity
me, moonlike queen. Leave to-night the
postern door"—my postern door—"ajar
that I may speak with your beauty on the
stairs"—my stairs. "Beware of thy lynx-
eyed uncle "—me—ah ! yes ?

DENYS.

Sir, do you take me for the pernicious
idiot that wrote that stuff ?

ALAIN.

Sir, I know that there is a lady and a
letter and a door and—a marriage.
    [*Indicating the appropriate four
      quarters of the universe.*

DENYS.

And a sword. If it *be* broken—

ALAIN.

Integer vitæ scel—

DENYS.

I know *that* tag at least.
    [ALAIN *claps his hands, walks toward
      door behind* DENYS. *The arras
      swings back and armed men appear.*

ALAIN.

O maior tandem parcas, insane, minori.

DENYS.

A truce to all this theatrical folly, Monsieur de Malétroit. Let me do you the
honour to take your words seriously. I
decline this marriage. I demand free
passage from your house.

ALAIN.

I regret infinitely that I cannot comply
with Monsieur's most moderate demands—
at least [*quickly*] in the sense he means.

DENYS.

I am a prisoner then?

ALAIN.

I state the facts, and leave the inference to Monsieur's indulgence. But before you altogether decline this marriage, it would be perhaps properer did I present you to the lady.

DENYS.

[*Sees that he must humour his strange host; rises and bows in acquiescence with inane smile and phrase.*] Ah, Monsieur, you make me too happy!
> [*This speech is not ironical but conventional and absurd.* ALAIN *strikes the gong. Enter* PRIEST *and bows.*

ALAIN.

Require the presence of the Lady Blanche de Malétroit, if you please, father.

PRIEST (*bows*).

My lord.
> [*Retires. Enter* BLANCHE *in a bridal dress, very shy and ashamed, with downcast eyes.*

DENYS.

[*Aside.*] Ah! but she is beautiful!

ALAIN.

Mademoiselle de Malétroit, allow me to present you to the Damoiseau Denys de Beaulieu. Monsieur Denys, my niece. [BLANCHE *hears the strange name and is shocked, looks up and only sees the back of* DENYS' *head, so low is he bowing. She understands that he has given another name and regains her self-possession.*] Forgive the formality of this introduction, but, after all, your previous acquaintance—[DENYS *stares wildly.*] Under the circumstances, Blanche, I think I should give your little

hand to kiss. [*A pause.*] It is necessary to be polite, my niece.
> [BLANCHE, *tormented beyond endurance, rises up as if to strike her uncle, sees* DENYS, *screams, covers her face with her hands, and sinks on the floor.*

BLANCHE.

That is not the man!—my uncle—that is not the man!

ALAIN.

[*Chuckles.*] So? Of course not. I expected as much. It was so unfortunate you could not remember his name.

BLANCHE.

This is not the man.

ALAIN.

A man, niece. [*Turns airily to* DENYS.] *Tempestiva sequi viro,* Monsieur Denys.

BLANCHE.

Indeed, indeed, I have never seen this person till this moment. [*Turns to* DENYS *imploringly.*] Sir, if you are a gentleman, you will bear me out. Have I seen you— have you ever seen me—before this accursed hour?

DENYS.

I have never had that pleasure. [*Turns to* ALAIN.] This is the first time, my lord, that I have ever met your engaging niece. [*Aside.*] But he doesn't care, he's mad— by 'r Lady, perhaps I'm mad myself.
> [*Goes off into silent laughter.* ALAIN *checks him sternly.*

ALAIN.

Sir, you will find I mean no jest.

DENYS.

Mademoiselle, I ask you a thousand pardons for this scene—none of my making, but of my strange fortune's.

ALAIN.

This gentleman drank a little too much for dinner.

DENYS.

Nay, by St. Denys, not enough, else had I been now along under Cousin Henri's table, and not in this house of maniacs and men-at-arms, and beauties in distress. Oh, pardon me, I am rude. [*With lively gallantry.*] Mademoiselle! I wrong myself when I forget myself: what I would say is that if the arm or brain of Denys de Beaulieu can save you, it is at your disposal [*starts: but serious, struck*]—I mean—[*Aside.*] St. Denys, what a coil is here! Is it possible that I love her?

[*He stands back, aside, amazed. His attitude vibrates between tender pitiful courtesy, lighted with love, and ironical appreciation o^f his own dilemma.*]

ALAIN.

I will leave you to talk alone.

[*Turns to leave.*]

BLANCHE.

[*Jumps up, and flings her arms around him. He repulses her not ungently. She clasps his knees, and he for the first time appears a little awkward and at a loss.*] Uncle, you cannot be in earnest. Why, I'll kill myself first—the heart rises at it—God forbids such marriages. Will you dishonour your white hair?

ALAIN.

Nay, mistress, I will save my brother's memory from shame.

BLANCHE.

O sir, pity me. There is not a woman in the world but would prefer death to such an union. Is it possible [*falters*] that you still think this [*points to* DENYS, *who stands embarrassed and ashamed*] to be the man?

ALAIN.

Frankly, I do. But let me explain to you once for all, Blanche de Malétroit, my way of thinking about this affair. [*Sternly.*] When you took it upon yourself to dishonour my family [BLANCHE *slides to floor and sobs*] and the name I have borne stainless in peace and war for more than threescore years, you forfeited not only the right to question my designs, but that of looking me in the face. I am a tenderer man than your father —he would have spat on you and thrust you from his door. But married you shall be, and that to-night. [*Turns to* DENYS.] And you, Monsieur, will best serve her if you save her. What devil have I saddled your life with that you look at me so black?

[*Turns on his heel and exit. A short silence of embarrassment.*]

BLANCHE.

[*Turns on* DENYS *with flashing eyes.*] And what, sir, may be the meaning of all this?

DENYS.

God knows; I am a prisoner in this house, which seems full of mad people. But I understand one thing, [*doubtfully*] I *think :* that you are to be married to me, and that your wishes are to be consulted as little as mine.

BLANCHE.

Monsieur, I blame myself cruelly for the position I have placed you in.

DENYS.

Mademoiselle, I have at least the delicacy to refrain from asking any answer to these riddles. But—

BLANCHE.

O how my head aches! It is only fair to you to tell you—

DENYS.

A moment, of your grace, Mademoiselle. Do not think that I am some obscure fortune-hunter who will jump at the chance so strangely offered him. My name is as noble as your own—ay! were things otherwise, I would still spare you. As it is, I have but to do as my duty and my interest—and yours—demand. We will see if Monsieur de Malétroit can cage me here for ever. [*Looks at sword meditatively.*] That is unfortunate.

BLANCHE.

I am so afraid, sir : I know my uncle well : but—thank you,—thank you !

DENYS.

Is Monsieur de Malétroit at hand?

BLANCHE.

There is a servant within call.
[*Strikes gong thrice.*
[*A pause. Enter* ANDREW.

DENYS.

Ask Monsieur the Sire de Malétroit to honour us with his presence.
[ANDREW *bows and exit.*

BLANCHR.

Monsieur, I don't know what we—you—will do, but thank you—thank you.

DENYS.

[*Draws himself up.*] Ah ! Mademoiselle, trust me, all will be well.
[*Enter* ALAIN *and ironically bows.*

DENYS.

[*Grandly.*] Messire, I suppose that I am to have some say in the matter of this marriage, so let me tell you without further ado, I will be no party to forcing the inclinations of this lady. [ALAIN *smiles,* DENYS *pauses.*] I—er—you understand me, sir? [ALAIN *still smiles.*] Had it been

freely offered to me, I should have been proud to accept her hand, for I perceive she is as good as she is beautiful [ALAIN *still smiles*], but as things are—er—I have the honour, Messire, of refusing [ALAIN *smiles more and more*]—I—er—er--
[ALAIN'S *smile becomes positively insupportable.* BLANCHE *smiles through her tears in gratitude and is secretly tickled at his confusion.* DENYS *gets annoyed, and swings away on his heel with an expression of disgust.*

ALAIN.

I am afraid, Monsieur de Beaulieu, that you do not perfectly understand—the alternative. Follow me, I beseech you, to this window. [*They cross to the window,* DENYS *shrugging his shoulders.*] Look out ! [DENYS *looks out into the blackness.* ALAIN *points to just below.*] Here are hooks. Iron hooks. Fastened into the wall. Strong. [*They turn back into room.*] And there [*points*] is the Lady Blanche. And so, Monsieur Denys de Beaulieu, Damoiseau de Beaulieu, in the province of Normandy, I do myself the honour to inform you that unless you are married to my niece in an hour's time, from these hooks you will hang. [BLANCHE *screams aloud, and falls half fainting into a chair.*] I trust your good sense will come to your aid, for of course it is not at all your death that I desire, but my niece's establishment in life. Your family, Monsieur de Beaulieu, is very well in its way, but if you sprang from Charlemagne you should not refuse the hand of a Malétroit with impunity—not if she had been as common as the Paris road, not if she were as hideous as the gargoyles on my roof. Neither my niece, nor you, nor my own private feelings move me in this matter. The honour of my house has been compromised : I believe you to be the guilty person : at least you are now in the secret ; and though it will be no satisfaction to me to have your interesting relics kicking their heels from my battlements [*jerks his thumb toward the window*], if I cannot wipe out the dishonour, I shall at least stop the scandal.

DENYS.

Frankly, sir, I think your troubles must have turned your brain ; there are other ways of settling such imbroglios among gentlemen.

ALAIN.

Alas, sir ! I am old. When I was younger I should have been delighted to honour you ; but I am the sole male member of my ancient house. Faithful retainers are the sinews of age, and I were a fool did I not employ the strength I have.

DENYS.

Oh, hang me now, and have done with it !

ALAIN.

No haste. An hour of life is always— an hour. And though one half that time is nigh lapsed already, yet—if you will give me your word of honour to do nothing desperate, and to await my return before you fling yourself from the window,—or, as I guess, —on the pikes of my retainers, I will with- draw myself and them that you may talk in greater privacy with the Lady Blanche. I fought at Arcy, and know what wonders may happen in an hour. [DENYS *turns bitterly, almost savagely, toward* BLANCHE.] You will not disfigure your last hour by want of politeness to a lady ?

[DENYS *flushes, accepts the rebuke, bows to both and says simply :*

DENYS.

I give you my word of honour.
[*His decision is not uncoloured by the pathetic petitioning of the mute* BLANCHE.

ALAIN.

I thank you, sir ; then I will leave you. [*Turns to go, stops.*] Sir, you are young, you think me a hard man, and perhaps a coward. Remember, pray, that the tears of age are frozen at the heart ere they can spring to the eyes. You may yet think better of the lonely old Sire de Malétroit, and the honour of his house may one day be your own.   [*Exit.*
[BLANCHE *comes over to* DENYS, *who remains leaning heavily on the table.*

BLANCHE.

Oh, sir, how cruelly have I done in my girl's folly, to bring a gallant gentleman to such a pass.

DENYS.

Ah ! life is a little thing, fair lady. [*Sighs, gradually getting pleased with himself as a martyr.*] My mother is married again—she needs neither my arm nor my affection ; my brother Guichard will inherit my fiefs, and unless I am mistaken, that will console him amply for my death : as for my father— why, I go to join him in an hour. Ay ! lady, we are soon forgotten. It is barely ten years since he fell, fighting desperately, with many noble gentlemen around him, and—to-day—I doubt me if the very name of the battle lingers in men's minds ! I go to join him in an hour.

BLANCHE.

[*Sighs.*] Ay ! sir, you speak sad, but you speak true.

DENYS.

Will there be memory *there?* [DENYS *now fancies himself as a philosopher.*] For I would not marry you—nay ! not though I loved you with my soul. In an hour you will be rid of me.

BLANCHE.

Oh, sir, do not be more cruel than our fate itself—to speak as if I could think so.

DENYS.

[*Pities himself.*] You will perhaps sigh once—I hope you will sigh once!—and then you will forget, and laugh, and go back to your old life. Ah! what can I think of all this?

BLANCHE.

I know what you must think, Monsieur de Beaulieu; you dare not say it—but you wrong me. Oh! before God, you wrong me.

DENYS.

[*Distressed.*] Don't! Don't!

BLANCHE.

Do yield: do marry me! Let me tell you how it all came about—you are so brave and young and handsome—I will not have you die.

DENYS.

You seem to think I stand in great fear of death.

BLANCHE.

[*Flushes at this boyish rudeness.*] But *I* will not have you die. I *will* marry you. [*With determination.*

DENYS.

[*Aside.*] Here is love's language—and Lord knows who's meaning. [*Aloud.*] What you are too generous to refuse I may be too proud to accept.

BLANCHE.

[*Controls her indignation.*] O sir! listen! I have no mother—no father. I am very lonely—how can I tell you? [*Goes over and crouches on chair half-sobbing.*] Three months

ago a young man began to stand near me in church. I—I could see I pleased him—and that pleased me; so I listened, when, as I went down the aisle, he whispered me such words as I passed—like poetry, they were so beautiful. I didn't know it was any harm—I let him write me letters, I was so glad that any one should love me. And yesterday he asked me to meet him on the stairs, so that he might tell me with his own voice; but Uncle Alain found the letter, and oh! oh! [*Cries.*]

DENYS.

Poor child! [*Aside.*] By heaven, I do love her. Was ever a man so ill-placed to win a woman?

BLANCHE.

I would not have answered it—oh! Monsieur, I swear to you. I thought no wrong. But uncle shut me up in the chapel, and said I was to be married to-morrow—and—and —set a trap for you.

DENYS.

Mademoiselle, I never thought ill of you, believe me!

BLANCHE.

Then oh, sir! marry me! You shall never see me again, and I will—yes! I will —kill myself, and you shall be free and happy again. It can't hurt you much to say a few words in the chapel with me— and then go back. But pray for me when I am dead.

DENYS.

[*Struggling long with emotion, stops himself from crying and gives a forced laugh.*] Here's romance, if ever there was any. Dog that I am! To laugh when your pale sweet little body is all shaken with weeping. Mademoiselle—Blanche—listen to me, and do not talk such wild nonsense. I will not

marry you. I do not love you, or you me.
[*Aside.*] Half a lie is better than no truth.
[*Aloud.*] I will not ruin your life—and I
can commit suicide by merest idleness, a
talent I am master of, and one most agree-
able to my nature.

BLANCHE.

Oh ! Monsieur Denys, but I love you.
[*Comes and clings to his knees.*] I do ! I
do ! I will not kill myself, but I will make
you love me——

DENYS.

A harder task than you think, little one.

BLANCHE.

Or tolerate me at least. [*Cries.*

DENYS.

O bother ! I shall cry too in a minute.

BLANCHE.

You are very unkind. I hate you.

DENYS.

How much of all this is truth? What
with pity and drawing-room manners and
so on, Truth is the kernel of a devilish hard
nut. They say she lives at the bottom of
a well—where one is drowned. [*Looks
down, craning, as if into a well.*] St. Denys
grant I may find her at the end of a rope—
where one is hanged. [*With gesture ap-
propriate.*]
[BLANCHE *curls herself up in chair
and sobs bitterly.* DENYS *goes to
window and looks gloomily out.*
[*Mimics* ALAIN.] Hooks. Iron hooks.
Fastened into the wall. Strong. H'm !
and there is the Lady Bl— oh ! curséd
luck—do you clap me on the shoulder like
a good comrade? No ! you get round my
neck like a lover ! Oh ! was ever gallant
VOL. III.

in such a scrape before? But dawn cannot
be far off : I shall—swing myself lightly
out of it.

BLANCHE.

[*Sobbing.*] Monsieur Denys ! Monsieur
Denys !

DENYS.

She has my name pat enough. O poor
little girl ! If only I didn't love her, with
what a good will would I marry her. The
nearer one comes to it, the clearer one sees
that death is a dark and dusty corner, where
a man lies hidden and forgotten till the
archangel's — broom. I have few friends
now : once I am dead I shall have none.

BLANCHE.

[*Falters.*] You forget Blanche de Malétroit.

DENYS.

You have a sweet nature, Mademoiselle,
and you are pleased to estimate a little
service far beyond its worth.

BLANCHE.

No, sir, I say more : I recognise in you
a spirit that should not give the *pas* to the
noblest man in France.

DENYS.

And yet here I die in a mousetrap—with
no more noise about it than my own
squeaking. [*A pause.*

BLANCHE.

I cannot have my champion think so
meanly of himself.

DENYS.

[*Aside.*] Ah ! could I forget that I was
asked in pity and not in love !
[*Advances, checks himself, swings
round and goes to window.*

F

BLANCHE.

I know how you must despise me—oh!
you are right. I am too poor a creature
to occupy one thought of your mind.
Alas! although you must die for me to-
morrow--[*She stops short, and waits for
him to respond, but* DENYS *is indeed thinking of something else.*] What! You are
too proud to link yourself with the dis-
honoured house of Malétroit? I too have
my pride : and now—and now—I would
no more marry you than I would marry
my uncle's groom.

[*Stamps her foot.* DENYS *turns round
and looks at her inquiringly. He
has not heard what she has been
saying ; he becomes again absorbed
in his own thoughts.* BLANCHE
*gets angrier and angrier, stamps
again, and, not attracting his attention, falls into the chair and cries
petulantly.*

BLANCHE.

It's too hard. To ask and be refused--
I, a Malétroit. [DENYS *comes back into the
room and faces her. She rises and strikes
him across the face with her glove.*] Cowardly
boy! [DENYS *turns furiously red, catches
her suddenly in his arms and kisses her,
flings her away, drops to the floor and groans
in an agony of shame and love.*] Double
coward! [*She reels away as if he had struck
her : comes back to where he crouches, bends
over him and strokes his hair.*] Denys!
Monsieur Denys! I am so sorry. You are
going to die so soon and I am rude to you—
when it is all my fault.

[DENYS *rises and stands facing her
manfully.*

DENYS.

Die! Not I! Blanche, when I kissed
you I loved you : I loved you when I saw
you in the doorway, and I know you love
me now.

BLANCHE.

Sir! I do not love you. How dare you
speak to me so?

DENYS.

You love me. [*Laughing.*] Why, you
said so!

BLANCHE.

You pass my patience, sir. I was acting,
acting for your own safety. I made the
most shameful declaration a maid can make
for your sake—and you fling it in my teeth.

[DENYS *knows his triumph, and proceeds to enjoy it with laughing
speech, as one with a petulant child.*

DENYS.

I fail to see that my safety is any the
more assured now--without it. Yes, Monsieur de Maladroit, I accept your offer with
the best will in the world.

BLANCHE.

O you despicable coward! I will kill
you at the very altar-steps.

DENYS.

Yours is a wonderful strong family for
killing, little one.

BLÁNCHE.

Mademoiselle de Malétroit is my name.

DENYS.

For half-an-hour—nay! barely that.

[BLANCHE *stamps her foot and turns
away angry. Breaks down and
kneels in chair, crying.* DENYS
follows and stands above her.

DENYS.

O Blanche! Blanche! Do you not see
how every tear is like a drop of poisonous

dew falling on my heart? You have seen whether I fear death. No love worth Love's name ever yet needed to be asked. And yet—in words! If you care for me at all, do not let me lose my life in a misapprehension! Tho' I would die for you blithely, faith, I had rather live on—in your service. Can you love me a little? Fool! Fool! Ay, there's a pair of us—why do we wait here and let our happiness stand in the cold and knock at our door all night?

BLANCHE.

Don't! Don't make me more miserable and hopeless than I am.
[DENYS *determines to make a general advance.*

DENYS.

[*Tenderly.*] Little fool!
[*He waits. She struggles in herself; and at last rueful and pouting, gets up and stands before him downcast, rubbing her eyes. He takes full advantage of his position.*
[*With mock severity.*] Aren't you ashamed of yourself?

BLANCHE.

[*Sobbing.*] After all you have heard?

DENYS.

[*With double entendre.*] I have heard nothing.
[*He opens his arms to her. She still stands about to sob again, breaks down, but this time flings herself on him and sobs on his breast. Enter* ALAIN *unseen.*
[*Softly.*] My darling!
[BLANCHE *raises her face.* DENYS *goes to kiss her, but she draws back.*

BLANCHE.

The captain's name was Florimond de Champdivers.

DENYS.

I did not hear it. [*A pause.*] Blanche, will you kiss me?
[*They take one long look and then tenderly and very deliberately kiss. They remain so, silently delighting in each other.*

ALAIN.

[*Comes forward with a chuckle.*] Good morning, nephew!
[*They leap up covered with confusion, recover their self-possession, and curtsey and bow respectfully, hand in hand.*

CURTAIN.

GARGOYLES

BEING STRANGELY WROUGHT IMAGES OF LIFE AND DEATH

1907

TO L. BENTROVATA.

Nec tamen illa mihi dextra deducta paterna
Fragrantem Assyrio venit odore domum
Sed furtiva dedit muta munuscula nocte.

Go sunnily through my garden of flowers, dear maiden o' mine, and once in a while you shall come upon some grotesque Chinese dragon with huge and hideous eyes leering round the delight of the daffodils ; or it may be some rude Priapus looking over the calm rock-shadowed beauty of the lake ; or even, hanging amid the glory of elm or beech, an human skeleton, whose bones shall rattle in the breeze, and from whose eyeless sockets shall glare I dare not bid you guess what evil knowledge.

Then, an you be wise, you shall know that a wise gardener wisely put them there. For every garden is the world ; and in the world these are.

So every cathedral is the world, and the architect of Notre Dame deserved his heaven.

To me life and death have most often appeared in majesty and beauty, in solemnity and horror ; in emotions, to be brief, so great that man had no place therein. But there are moods, in which the heights are attained indirectly, and through man's struggle with the elemental powers.

In these poems you shall hear the laughter of the gods and of the devils ; understand their terrors and ecstasies ; live in their heavens and hells.

But I not only heard and understood and lived ; I sounded and imposed and begat : you must also do both, or the universe will still be a mystery to you as to the others.

IMAGES OF LIFE

PROLOGUE.

VIA VITÆ.

I.

My head is split. The crashing axe
Of the agony of things shears through
    The stupid skull : out spurt the brains.
The universe revolves, then cracks,
    Then roars in dissolution due ;
    And I am counting up the gains
And losses of a life afire
With dust of thought and dulled desire.

II.

So, all is over. I admit
    Futility the lord of will.
    Life was an episode, for me

As for the meanest monad, knit
    To man by mightier bonds than skill
        Of subtle-souled psychology
May sever. Aim in chaos ? None.
The soul rolls senseless as the sun.

III.

Existence, as we know it, spins
    A fatal warp, a woof of woe.
        There is no place for God or soul.
Works, hopes, prayers, sacrifices, sins
    Are jokes. The cosmos happened so :
        Innocent all of guide or goal.
Else, what were man's appointed term ?
To feed God's friend, the coffin-worm !

IV.

Laugh, thou immortal Lesbian !
  Thy verse runs down the runic ages.
    Where shalt thou be when sun and star,
My sun, my star, the vault that span,
Rush in their rude, impassive rages
    Down to some centre guessed afar
By mindless Law ? Their death-embrace
A simple accident of space ?

V.

Where is thy fame, when million leagues
  Of flaming gas absorb the roll
  Of many a system ruinous hurled
With infinite pains and dire fatigues
  To build another stupid soul
  For fools to call another world ?
Where then thy fame, O soul sublime ?
Where then thy victory over Time ?

VI.

Wilt thou seek deeper than the fact ?
  Take refuge in a city of mind ?
    Build thee an house, and call it heaven ?
Rush on ! there foams the cataract,
  Blind steersman leader of the blind,
  Sole devil herald of the seven
Thy garnished halls should house, O Christ,
Thou being dead, thou sacrificed

VII.

Not for atonement, not for bliss ;
  Truly for nothing : so it was.
    Nay, friends, think well ! Renounce
      the dream !
Seek not some mystery in the kiss,
  Some virtue in the chrysopras,
    Some nymph or undine in the stream.
Things as we know them should be enough
To glut our misery and our love.

VIII.

Why must despair to madness drive
  The myriad fools that fear to die ?
    God's but a fervid phantom drawn
Out of the hasty-ordered hive
  Of thoughts that battle agony
  In the melancholy hours of dawn.
When vital force at lowest ebbs
Anæmic nerves weave frailest webs.

IX.

So, be content ! Should science cleave
  The veil of things and show us peace,
    Well :—but by wild imagining
Think not a golden robe to weave !
  Such moulder. By fantastic ease
  Ye come not well to anything.
Work and be sober : dotage thinks
By worth of words to slay the Sphinx.

X.

Things as they are—of these take hold,
  Their heart of wonder throb to thine !
    All things are matter and force and
      sense,
No two alone. All's one : the gold
  Of truth is no reward divine
  Of faith, but wage of evidence.
The clod, the God, the spar, the star
Mete in thy measure, as they are !

XI.

So lifts the agony of the world
  From this mine head, that bowed awhile
    Before the terror suddenly shown.
The nameless fear for self, far hurled
  By death to dissolution vile,
  Fades as the royal truth is known :
Though change and sorrow range and roll
There is no self—there is no soul !

XII.

As man, a primate risen high
  Above his fellows, work thou well
    As man, an incident minute
And dim in time's eternity,
  Work well ! As man, no toy for hell
  And heaven to wrangle for, be mute !
Let empty speculation stir
The idle fool, the craven cur !

XIII.

Myself being idle for an hour
  I dare one thing to speculate :
    Namely, that life hath cusps yet higher
On this our curve : a prize, a power
  Lies in our grasp : unthinking Fate
  Shall build a brain to nestle nigher
Unto the ultimate Truth : I burn
To live that later lives may learn.

XIV.

Simple to say ; to do complex !
That we this higher type of man
May surely generate, o' nights
Our lesser brains we vainly vex.
Our knowledge lacks ; we miss the plan.
Fools hope our luck will set to rights
Our skill that's baulked. Yet now we know
At least the way we wish to go.

XV.

This task assume ! Colossal mind
And toil transcending, concentrate
Not on the metaphysic wild ;
Not on the deserts vast and blind
Of dark Religion ; not on Fate,
The barren ocean ; but the Child
Shows us a beacon in the night ;
A lens to lure and lend the light.

XVI.

Wisdom and Love, intenser glow !
Beauty and Strength, increase and burn !
Be brothers to the law of life !
Things as they are—their nature know !
Act ! Nor for faith nor folly turn !
The hour is nigh when man and wife,
Knowing, shall worship face to face,
Beget and bear the royal race.

THE WHITE CAT.

HAIL, sweet my sister ! hail, adulterous
    spouse,
  Gilded with passionate pomp, and gay with
    guilt :
Rioting, rioting in the dreary house
  With blood and wine and roses splashed
    and spilt
About thy dabbling feet, and aching jaws
  Whose tongue licks mine, twin asps like
    moons that curl,
Red moons of blood ! Whose catlike body
    claws,
  Like a white swan raping a jet-black girl,

Mine, with hysteric laughter ! O white cat !
  O windy star blown sideways up the sky !
Twin cat, twin star, 'tis night ; the owl and
    bat
  Hoot, scream ; 'tis us they call—to love
    or die.
Twin cat, our broomsticks wait : we'll fly
    afar !
  We'll blaze about the unlighted sky, twin
    star !

ALI AND HASSAN.

FROM THE ALF LAYLAH WA LAYLAH.

ALI bade Hassan to his house to sup.
They ate, passed round the full forbidden
    cup,
Till, in an interval of dance and song,
Hassan forgot his manners—loud and long.
Struck with confusion, forth he fares, takes
    ship
To utmost Ind and far-off Serendip.
Full forty years he there abides : at last,
Rich and respected, he contemns the past :—
" If I declare myself, there's hope, I wot,
Hassan's remembered, and his fault forgot !—"
Determines to revisit home. Sweet airs
Accomplishing the voyage, he repairs
Unto the barber. " Tell me of the state !
Haroun still holds the royal Caliphate ? "
" Nay," said the barber, " long ago he passed
Where all delights are 'stinguished at the last,
And all good things forgotten, wallahy !
He died—aha now !—no—yes—let me see !
Ten years, three months, four days, as I'm a
    sinner,
Since Hassan let the — shame — at Ali's
    dinner."

AL MALIK.

A GHAZAL OF AL QAHAR.

AL MALIK the magnificent
Was sitting in his silken tent.

But when he saw the boy Habib
I wis his colour came and went.

Quoth he : By Allah, 'tis a star
Struck from the azure firmament !

Habib : I pour the wine of love
For Al Awaz the excellent.

The king : I envy him thy shape,
Thy voice, thy colour, and thy scent.

Habib : In singing of his slave
Hath Al Awaz grown eminent.

The king : But I, to taste thy lip,
My kingdom willingly had spent.

Habib : Asylum of the World !
My master bade me to present

My loveliness to thee, whose brows
Like to a Scythian bow are bent.

The king accepted him to bear
His cup of wine, and was content.

Let Al Qahar their praises sing :
Three souls, one love, one element.[1]

SONG.

1.

Dance a measure
Of tiniest whirls !
Shake out your treasure
Of cinnamon curls !
Tremble with pleasure,
O wonder of girls !

[1] This poem is very much taboo in Persia, as it is supposed to be little better than a pamphlet in favour of Christianity. The later work of Al Qahar, and especially his masterpiece, the Bagh-i-muattar, are, however, if not quite above suspicion, so full of positive piety of the Sufi sort that even the orthodox tolerate what the mystic and the ribald silently or noisily admire.

II.

Rest is bliss,
And bliss is rest,
Give me a kiss
If you love me best !
Hold me like this
With my head on your breast !

ANICCA.

He who desires desires a change.
Change is the tale of life and death.
Matter and motion rearrange
Their endless coils ; the Buddha saith :
"Cease, O my sons, to desire !
Change is the whole that we see
By the light of a chaos on fire.
Cease to desire—you are free !"
Your words, good Gotama, are brave and true ;
Easy to say, but difficult to do !

TARSHITERING.

NEPALI LOVE-SONG.[1]

O kissable Tarshitering ! the wild bird calls
    its mate—and I ?
Come to my tent this night of May, and
    cuddle close and crown me king !
Drink, drink our full of love at last—a little
    while and we shall die,
    O kissable Tarshitering !

Droop the long lashes : close the eyes with
    eyelids like a beetle's wing !
Light the slow smile, ephemeral as ever a
    painted butterfly,
Certain to close into a kiss, certain to fasten
    on me and sting !

Nay ? Are you coy ? Then I will catch
    your hips and hold you wild and shy
Until your very struggles set your velvet
    buttocks all a-swing,
Until their music lulls you to unfathomable
    ecstasy,
    O kissable Tarshitering !

[1] Possibly the original of the well-known Hindustani song :—
    "Thora thairo, Tenduk ! thora thairo, tum !
    Thora thairo, thairo thora, thora thairo tum !"
                                        A. C.

A FRAGMENT.[1]

*In the midst of the desert of Libya, on a
mound of sand, lieth a young man alone
and naked. Nightfall.*

NIGHT the voluptuous, night the chaste
Spreads her dark limbs, a vaulted splendour,
Above the intolerable waste.
Night the august one, night the tender
Queens it and brides it unto me.
I am the soul serenely free ;
I dare to seek the austere ordeal
That drags the hoodwink of the Real
Back from the Maker's livid eyes
Lustred with hate.   At noon I came
Blind in the desert, saw the sun
Leap o'er the edge, a fury of flame
Shouting for rapture over his prize,
The maiden body of earth.   Outrun
The violent rays ; the dawn is dashed
In one swift moment into dust.
Long lies the land with sunlight splashed,
Brutally violate to his lust.
Alone and naked I watched through
The appalling hours of noon ; I parched ;
I blistered : all the ghastly crew
Of mind's sick horror mocked me ; arched
The flaming vault of hell and pressed
Its passionate murder in my breast.
Seven times I strove to slay me : filled
My mouth with sand to choke my breath.
In vain !   No loftier purpose willed
The iron miracle of death.
So, blind and strangled, I survive.
So, with my skin a single scar,
I hail the night, the night alive
With Hathor for the evening star.
O beauty ! See me broken, burned
Lone on the languorous Lybian plain !
Is there one lesson to be learned
From this my voluntary pain,
My dread initiation, long
Desired and long deferred ?   The Master—
Is he the secret of the song,
Portent of triumph or disaster

[1] Intended as the prologue to a history of
an initiate in semi-dramatic form.

The night wind breathes upon the air
Still shimmering from the fearful heat ?
Can I still trust who have learned to dare ?
All others I have known effete,
Bid them await.   Who knows to-day
The purpose of the dread essay ?
Surely I, earlier, further fared !
I knew the deed that closes clay,
Division's sword by sense unbared,
A living lie.   The deep delusion !
Dividuality—confusion !
These I unmasked of yore.   To-day
The hideous blue, the hideous gold
Of sky and sand their wrath unrolled,
Their agony and hate proclaimed.
Is it that night shall kiss to peace
The furious carnival that flamed
Its ruinous ardour from the sun !
Nay, let all light, all things, but cease !
Sense is the seal of double rule.
The million oracles that run
Out of the mouth of God the fool
Are not myself.   To nothing turn !
To nothing look !   Then, then !—discern
Nothing, that one may one remain.
So I am paid the horrible pain
That these my brothers ordered me.
I look upon their brows—I see
Signs many and deep of torture past ;
A star, yon star, true peace at last.

(*There approacheth an aged man, riding
upon an ass, with a led ass, and a
Nubian servant.*)

The Adept. In the name of God, the One,
        the Great,
Merciful and compassionate,
Acclaim the perfect period
Of ordeal past !
    The Neophyte. There is no God !
    A. Rise ! in the name of obscure Fate,
Ruthless and uncompassionate.
    N. Of endless life, of toil and woe
I am the burned and branded foe.
I came this torture to endure
That I might make my freedom sure.
    A. No soul is free.

N.   There is no soul.
See yonder gleams the starry shoal
Of orbs incalculably vast.
They are not present : they are past,
Since the long march of shuddering light
Made years the servants of its might.
There is no soul.
   A.   These stars thou seest
Are but the figuring of thy brain.
   N. Then of all things the soul were freest.
   A. Move then the centre of thy pain !
   N. 'Tis done.
   A.   A trick to cheat a child.
   N. It is the truth that I am nought.
Hear what I have gathered in the wild,
Flowers of imperishable thought
With glory and with rapture clothed.
This being, thinking, loved or loathed,
Hath attributes. This sand is gold :—
Deem'st thou a gilder lurks within
The atom ? What should Nature hold
Of aureate save a mind begin
Colour-conception ? Then we win
To think our thought itself a chance
Grafted upon the circumstance
Of cerebrin and lethicin.
   A. Ill fares the rifleman that holds
The muzzle to his eye. Yon gold's
Mental : enough ! the mind is all.
   N. No : this is but a slave in thrall
To matter's motion. We deny
A causeless cause, an entity
Beyond experience, that tricks
Our folly with its idle claim
To be because we feel it.
   A.   Sticks
The reason there ?
   N.   We choose a name
To cover all the host of facts
Comprised in thought.
   A. (aside)   The elixir acts.
Then backward work ; the name becomes
With pomp of metaphysic drums
A *causa causans*—God, soul, truth.
So raves the riot, age and youth,
The cart before the horse. Revered
And reverend master, is your beard
Darwin's survival of some tail ?

Who rants of soul were best to saddle
His face, his arms the ass to straddle,
Since for his voice the part thus bare
Would serve as well to scent the air.
   A. Where reverence ceases, ribald jest
Breaks forth, the wise allow the rest.
The perfect master stands confessed.
   N. Why ! I supposed your wrath would
    burst ;
My name and number stand accurst
In the great Order of the West !
   A. Nay : Buddha smiles; 'twas Jesus wept !
Arise, O brother and adept !
   N. Master !
   A. The torture-hours are past.
   N. The peace of pain is mine at last.
   A. Ere the moon rise, the brethren meet.
Come, let us turn toward the South.
   N. Lord, I embrace thy holy feet.
   A. Nay, let me kiss thee on the mouth.
         Desunt cetera.

THE STUMBLING-BLOCK.

I ALMOST wonder if I ought
   To hymn this height of human pain :
   To enter into Jones's thought
      I'd have to work with Jones's brain.

Terrestrial speech is wholly vain
   To carry meaning as it ought :—
   To enter into Jones's thought
      I'd have to work with Jones's brain.

This is the High God's cruel sport :
   To enter into Jones's thought
   And make its inner meaning plain,
      I'd have to work with Jones's brain.

WOODCRAFT.

THE poet slept. His fingers twine
In his wife's hair. He dreams. Divine
His dream ! Nay then, I'll tell you it.

He wandered in a forest dim.
A woodcutter encountered him
Where a felled oak required his wit.

This man with a light axe did lop
The little branches at the top.
Then said the poet: " Thus why tax
Your force? This double-handed axe
Were better laid to the tree-trunk."
"Friend, are you natural, or drunk?"
Replied the woodsman; " leaf and twig
Divert the impact of the big
Axe ; chop them first, the trunk is fit
For a fair aim, a certain hit.
How do you work yourself?" He spoke
To empty space—the poet woke ;
And catching up a carving-knife
He slit the weasand of his wife.

A NUGGET FROM A MINE.

A MINER laboured in a mine.
(The poet dreamed) By coarse and fine
He shovelled dust into a trolley.
" But this " (the poet said) "is folly !
Take up your pick, engage in shock
At the foundation of the rock ! "
The miner swore. " You —— fool !
You clever —— ! go to school
And college and be —— ! Strike you !
There ain't no sense in forty like you !
If I don't clear this muck, the pick
Will foul and jam, slip, swerve, or stick.
Clear off the chips, the blow goes true.
Now, mister, off, my —— to you !"
The last oath faded in the air.
The poet woke and was aware
Of property and children. Claims
His breech a vesta. Up the flames
Leap ; he stalks forth, free among men,
With just a notebook and a pen.

AU CAVEAU DES INNOCENTS.

Oct. 28, 1904.

NIGHT, like a devil, with lidless eyes,
Stands avenging over the Halls.
Sleep there is none, for day awaits
Tokens of toil ; there is none that dies,

Death being rest ; there is none that calls,
Voice being human ; only the Fates
Rattle the dice at a sombre game,
Game without goal of peace or fame.
Sinister, sombre, horrors and hates
Lurk in the shadows, under the walls.
Light deceives, and the darkness lies.

Love there is none ; he is child of peace :
Joy there is none ; she is bride of force :
Thought there is none ; it is birth :—there
    fell
Ages ago all hope of these.
Lust is awake, and its friend remorse.
Crime we snatch, between spell and spell.
Man is aglare, and is off unheard.
Woman hath speech, of a single word.
Hell may be heaven, for earth is hell !
So do I laugh, and the hideous coarse
Peals like applause re-echo and cease.

Here in the close and noisome cave,
Drunk on the breath of the thieves and
    whores
Close as they cram in the maw of the pit,
Sick with the stench of the kisses that
    rave
Round me, surfeiting sense, in scores ;
Mad with their meaning, I smoke and sit
Rhyming at random through my teeth,
Grey with the mire of the slough beneath,
Deep in the hearts that revel in it,
Drowned in the breath of the hell that
    pours
In the heart of Paris its infamous wave.

Damning the soul of God, I rise,
Stumble among the dissolute bands,
Grope to the steep inadequate stairs
Scrawled with villainous names. My eyes
Loathe the flare of the flickering brands.
Out I climb through the greasy airs
Into the cold and desolate road.
Horror is sure of a safe abode
Here in this heart, too pale for prayers,
While over the Halls avenging stands
Night, like a devil, with lidless eyes.

ROSA INFERNI.[1]

> "Ha ha ! John plucketh now at his rose
> To rid himself of a sorrow at heart.
> Lo,—petal on petal, fierce rays unclose ;
> Anther on anther, sharp spikes outstart ;
> And with blood for dew, the bosom boils ;
> And a gust of sulphur is all its smell :
> And lo, he is horribly in the toils
> Of a coal-black giant flower of hell !"
> —BROWNING, *Heretic's Tragedy*, ix.

I.

Rose of the world ! Ay, love, in that warm
    hour
Wet with your kisses, the bewitching bud
Flamed in the starlight ; then our bed your
    bower
Heaved like the breast of some alluring flood
Whereon a man might sleep for ever, until
Death should surprise him, kiss his weary will
Into the last repose, profounder power
Than life could compass. Now I tax my
    skill
To find another holier name, some flower
Still red, but red with the ecstasy of blood.
Dear love, dear wife, dear mother of the child
Whose fair faint features are a match for
    mine,
Lurks there no secret where your body smiled,
No serpent in the generous draught of wine ?
Did I guess all, who guessed your life well
    given
Up to my kiss ? Aha ! the veil is riven !
Beneath the smiling mask of a young bride
Languorous, luscious, melancholy-eyed ;
Beneath the gentle raptures, hints celestial
Of holy secrets, kisses like soft dew,
Beneath the amorous mystery, I view
The surer shape, a visage grim and bestial,
A purpose sly and deadly, a black shape,
A tiger snarling, or a grinning ape
Resolved by every devilish device
Upon my murder. This I clearly see
Now you are—for an hour—away from me.
I see it once ; no need to tell me twice !

[1] Being the necessary sequel to Rosa Mundi.
—A. C.

II.

Some Yankee yelled—I tag it to a rime—
" You can't fool all the people all the time."
So he of politics ; so I of love.
I am a-many folk (let Buddha prove !)
And many a month you fooled the lot of us—
Your spell is cracked within the ring !
    Behold
How Christ with clay worth more than any
    gold
Cleared the man's eyes ! So the blind
    amorous
Is blinded with the horror of the truth
He sees this moment. Foolish prostitute !
You slacked your kiss upon the sodden youth
In some excess of confidence, decay
Of care to hold him—can I tell you which ?
Down goes the moon—one sees the howling
    bitch !
The salmon you had hooked in fin and gill
You reel unskilfully—he darts away.
Alas ! you devil, but you hold me still !

III.

O first and fairest of Earth's darling
    daughters !
How could I sing you?—you have always
    seemed
Unto the saucy driveller as he dreamed
Like a rich sunset seen on tropic waters—
(Your eyes effulgent from a thousand
    slaughters
Looked tenderly upon me !) all the red
Raving round you like a glory shed
Upon the excellent wonder of your head ;
The blue all massed within your marvellous
    eyes ;
The gold a curtain of their harmonies
As in a master canvas of de Ryn ;[1]
But ever central glowed the royal sun,
A miracle cartouche upon the edge
Of the opalescent waters slantwise seen.
This oval sealed with grave magnificence
Stamped you my queen. Thus looked your
    lips to one

[1] Rembrandt.

Who stood a casual on life's slippery ledge,
A blind bat hanging from the tree of sense
Head downward, gorged with sweet banana
   juice,
Indifferent to—incapable of—aught
Beyond these simple reflexes. Is thought,
Even the highest thought, of any use ?

IV.

We are not discussing metaphysics now.
I see below the beautiful low brow
(Low too for cunning, like enough !) your lips,
A scarlet splash of murder. From them drips
This heart's blood ; you have fed your fill on
   me.
I am exhaust, a pale, wan phantom floating
Aimless in air, than which I am thinner. You
I see, more brilliant, of that sanguine hue
(If anything be true that I can see)
Full fed ; you smile, a smile obscenely gloating
On the voluptuous wreck your lust hath
   wrought.
See the loose languor of precipitate thought
These versicles exhale ! How rude the rime !
There is no melody ; the tune and time
Are broken. Thirteen centuries ago
They would have said, "Alas ! the youth !
   We know ·
This devil hath from him plucked the im-
   mortal soul."
_I_ say : you have dulled my centres of control !

v.

If you were with me, I were blind to this :
Ready to drain my arteries for your kiss,
Feel your grasp tighten round my ribs until
You crush me in the ecstasies that kill.
Being away and breathing icy air
I am half lover, caring not to care ;
Half-man again—a mere terrestrial ball
Thus breaking up a spiritual thrall—
Eh, my philosophers ?—half-man may yet
   determine
To get back manhood, shake the tree from
   bats :

To change the trope a shade—get rid of
   vermin
By using William Shakespeare's " Rough on
   Rats." [1]

VI.

Ah, love, dear love, sole queen of my affec-
   tion,
Guess you not yet what wheel of thought is
   spun ?
How out of dawn's tumultuous dejection
And not from noon springs up the splendid
   sun ?
Not till the house is swept and garnished well
Rise seven other devils out of hell.

VII.

This is the circle ; as the manhood rises
And laughter and rude rhyme engage my pen ;
As I stalk forth, a Man among mere men,
The balance changes ; all my wit surprises
That I who saw the goblins in your face,
That I who cursed you for the murderous
   whore
Licking up life as a cat laps its milk,
Now see you for a dream of youth and grace,
Relume the magic aura that begirt you,
Bless you for purity and life—a store !
An ever-running fountain-head of virtue
To heal my soul and buckler it and harden !
Your body is like ivory and silk !
Your lips are like the poppies in the garden !
Your face is like a wreath of flowers to
   crown me !
Your eyes are wells wherein I long to drown
   me !
Your hair is like a waterfall above me,
A waterfall of sunset ! In your bosom
I hear the racing of a heart to love me.
Your blood is beating like a wind-blown
   blossom
With rapture that you mingle it in mine !
Your breath is fresh as foam and keen as
   wine !
Intoxicating glories are your glances !
Your bodily beauty grips my soul and dances

[1] Meaning that by study of Shakespeare he
would resume higher interests, and baffle the
sensual seductions of this siren.

Its maddening measures in my heart and
    brain !
Is it that so the wheel may whirl again,
That some dull devil in my ear may show
    me :
" For John the Baptist's head—so danced
    Salome !" ?

VIII.

Then, in God's name forbear ! It does not
    matter.
Life, death, strength, weakness, are but
    idle chatter.
Nothing is lost or gained, we know too well.
For heaven they balance us an equal hell.
We discard both ; an infinite Universe
Remains ; we sum it up—an infinite curse.
So—am I a man ? I lack my wife's embrace.
Am I outworn ? I see the harlot's face.
Is the love better and the knowledge worse ?
Shall I seek knowledge and count love dis-
    grace ?
Where is the profit in so idle a strife ?
The love of knowledge is the hate of life.

DIOGENES.

" ALL things are good " exclaimed the boy.
Who taste the sweetmeat find it cloy.

" All things are ill " the dotard sang.
Who stir the serpent feel the fang.

" All is a dream !" the wise man spake.
Who grasp the bubble find it break.

Aye, to all three the saga saith :
There is no joy in life but death.

There is this limit set to lust :
Ashes to ashes, dust to dust.

O fools and blind that sickly strive
To amass, to glut yourselves, to swive,

To drink, to acquire respect and praise :—
These visions perish as you gaze.

Eternal mockery is the real ;
Eternal falsehood, the ideal.

Choose : nay, abstain from choice of these.
Go, be alone, and be at ease !

Retire : renounce : the hermit's cell
Hath all of earth, and nought of hell.

Renouncing all, keep nought enshrined
A lurking serpent in the mind.

Deem not to catch some goodlier gain
Than these ; the goodliest prize were pain.

Know that the utmost heaven is void
Of aught save star or asteroid !

Or, an it please thee, idly dream
A God therein, a force supreme,

A heart of love, a crown of light,
An infinite music of delight ;—

This, but no more ; let fancy sway
But never fix the transient ray !

All things are lawful, so they be
At most a marshalled imagery.

Dream of Earth's glories higher and higher,
Mounting the minaret, desire ;

Never attaining to the sky,
Realization—lest thou die.

So dream, possessing all ; so dream,
Possessing nothing : I esteem

These twain as one, since dreams they are.
Thus mayst thou journey far and far

And far ! to climes unguessed, to seas
Proud with seignorial argosies,

To mountains strange with golden snows,
To gardens green with many a rose,

To secrets past the sense of sense,
Skies virgin of experience,

Untrodden avenues of mind,
Things far from hurrying humankind.

Thus spins out life its splendid charm :—
Live, love, enjoy, yet do no harm.

No rose of thought may bear or breed
The poisonous thorn of word and deed.

Call " homo sapiens " him who thinks ;
Talkers and doers—missing links !

 . . . .

Such songs are twilight's, when I stretch
My limbs, and wander down to fetch

My water from the cool cascade,
My wood from the enchanted glade,

My berries from the rustling bough :—
Return, and eat, and sleep. Allow

For me, the silence and the night ;
Life, peace ; and death, a welcome wight.

SAID.

THE spears of the night at her onset
Are lords of the day for a while,
The magical green of the sunset,
The magical blue of the Nile.
 Afloat are the gales
 In our slumberous sails
On the beautiful breast of the Nile.

We have swooned through the midday, exhausted
By the lips—they are whips—of the sun,
The horizon befogged and befrosted
By the haze and the greys and the dun
 Of the whirlings of sand
 Let loose on the land
By the wind that is born of the sun.

On the water we stand as a shadow,
A skeleton sombre and thin
Erect on the watery meadow,
As a giant, a lord of the Djinn
 Set sentinel over
 Some queen and her lover
Beloved of the Gods and the Djinn.

We saw the moon shudder and sink
In a furnace of tremulous blue ;
We stood on the mystical brink
Of the day as it sprang to us through
 The veil of the night,
 And the babe of the light
Was begotten in the caves of the dew.

My lover and I were awake
When the noise of the dawn in our ears
Burst out like a storm or a snake
Or the rush of the Badawi spears.
 Dawn of desire !
 But thy kiss was as fire
To thy lovers and princes and peers.

Then the ruin of night we beheld
As the sun stormed the heights of the sky
With his myriad swords, and compelled
The pale tremblers, the planets, to fly.
 He drave from their place
 All the stars for a space,
From their bastioned towers in the sky.

Thrilled through to the marrow with heat
We abode (as we glode) on the river.
Every arrow he launched from his seat,
From the white inexhaustible quiver,
 Smote us right through,
 Smote us and slew,
As we rode on the rapturous river.

Sweet sleep is perfection of love.
To die into dreams of my lover,
To wake with his mouth like a dove
Kissing me over and over !
 Better sleep so
 Than be conscious, and know
How death hath a charm to discover.

Ah ! float in the cool of the gloaming !
Float wide in the lap of the stream
With his mouth ever roving and homing
To the nest where the dove is adream.
 Better wake so
 Than be thinking, and know
That at best it is only a dream.

So turn up thy face to the stars !
In their peace be at peace for awhile !
Let us pass in their luminous cars
As a sob, as a sigh, as a smile !
 Love me and laze
 Through the languorous days
On the breast of the beautiful Nile !

May 1905.

EPILOGUE.

PRAYER.

THE light streams stronger through the lamps
of sense.
          Intelligence
Grows as we go. Alas : its icy glimmer
          Shows dimmer, dimmer
The awful vaults we traverse. Were the sun
          Himself the one
Glory of space, he would but illustrate
          The night of Fate.
Are not the hosts of heaven in vain arrayed ?
          Their light dismayed
Before the vast blind spaces of the sky ?
          O galaxy
Of thousands upon thousands closely curled !
          Your golden world
Incalculably small, its closest cluster
          Mere milky lustre
Staining the infinite darkness ! Base and
          blind
          Our minion mind
Seeks a great light, a light sufficient, light
          Insufferably bright,
Hence hidden for an hour : imagining
          This vast vain thing,
We call it God, and Father. Empty hand
          And prayer unplanned
Stretch fatuous to the void. Ah ! men my
          friends,
          What fury sends
This folly to intoxicate your hearts ?
          Dread air disparts
Your vital ways from these unsavoury follies,
          Black melancholies
Sit straddled on your bended backs. The
          throne
          Of the unknown

Is fit for children. We are too well ware
          How vain is prayer,
How nought is great, since all is immanent,
          The vast content
Of all the universe unalterable.
          We know too well
How no one thing abides awhile at all,
          How all things fall,
Fall from their seat, the lamentable place,
          Before their face,
Weary and pass and are no more. So we,
          Since hope must be,
Look to the future, to the chance minute
          That life may shoot
Some flower at least to blossom in the night,
          Since vital light
Is sure to fail us on the hideous way.
          What ? Must we pray ?
Verily, O thou littlest babe, too weak
          To stir or speak,
Capable hardly of a thought, yet seed
          Of word and deed !
To thine assured fruition we may trust
          This weary dust.
We who are old, and palsied, (and so wise !)
          Lift up our eyes
To little children, as the storm-tossed bark
          Hails in the dark
Some hardly visible harbour light ; we hold
          The hours of gold
To our own breasts, whose hours are iron
          and brass :—
          So swift they pass
And grind us down :—we hold the wondrous
          light
          Our scattering sight
Yet sees, the one star in a night of woe.
          We trust, and so
Lift up our voices in the dying day
          Indeed to pray :
O little hands that are so soft and strong,
          Lead us along !

IMAGES OF DEATH

PROLOGUE.

PATCHOULI.

LIKE memories of love they come,
  My perfumes in the silver vase:
The fragrant root, the odorous gum,
Myrrh, aloes, or olibanum :—
  Anon, like memories of love, they pass !

They pass, and all the wonder-web
Of thought and being is unrolled.
Like sombre tides there flow and ebb
  Wonderful things ! not to be told :
  Beautiful things ! and images of gold.

The touch of brown Habiba's breast,
  The brimming lip, the cheek of down,
The dainty dovelet in its nest :
These fade, as ever a palimpsest
  Like autumn vanishes from gold to brown.

Zuleikha, on whose marble knees
  My bearded head is lazily lain,
Shows like some stirring of the breeze
  Fluctuant in the poppied grain,
  No more at all : the vulgar sense is slain.

Of all the world alone abides
  The faint perfume of Patchouli,
That subtle death in love ; it glides
Across the opening dream, derides
  The fetich folly, immortality.

Awake, O dream ! Let distant bells
  And vague muezzins haunt the ear,
Gaunt camels kneel by dusky wells,
  Imagination greyly hear :
  Allahu akbar ! Allahu kabir !

Over inhospitable sands
  Let the simoom its columns spin !
In snowy vales, untrodden lands,
Let there be storm, and bearded bands
  Of robbers pass around the bubbling skin !

Let there be caves of treasure rare
  Deep hidden in sepulchral seas ;
And birds unheard-of darken air
  With royal wings, like argosies
  Sailing beneath magnific promontories !

Let Caliphs mete fantastic law
  And ebon eunuchs swing the sword
So swift, so curved,—let voiceless awe
Sit on the palace dome, to draw
  Some god's destruction on its smiling lord !

May many a maiden comely clad
  Revolve in convoluted curls,
Till from each pliant pose I had
  (By virtue of her wondrous whirls)
  The illusion of a thousand dancing-girls !

Let harlots robed in gold and green
  Sit slowly waving ivory plumes
And wings of palm ; the while their queen
Lurks in some horror-house unseen,
  Damned to be smothered in divine per-
    fumes !

Let there be scenes of blood and pain,
  Some Slav beneath the Cossack knout,
Some mother ripped, some baby slain ;
  Let lust move silently about :—
  Soft laughter hid in all, song whispering
    out !

Then let these things of form decay,
  Some subtler dream dissolve their form,
As I have seen a cloudlet lay
Its forehead on the sea, and pray
  Some idle prayer to sunset, or the storm !

Yea ! as a cloud in worship-trance
  Swoons in invisible delight,
Let slave and king, let death and dance
  Shake off their forms, and clothe their
    light
  In shrouds of sepulchre, the starless night !

Let song and cry leave tune and tone,
Perish uncried and die unsung !
Nature, the monotonic moan
Roared by the river, thunder alone :—
 The Hoang-Ho, its note, the monstrous
 Kung !¹

Or let Kailasha's ² godded peak
Summon the oread and the gnome
To leave their toils, the word to speak
That shakes its azure-splitting dome
With the reverberation—listen !—Aum !

Let olive fail, and mangostin !
O'erturn the dark forbidden draught !
Give me the taste, the taste unclean
Of human flesh and blood that mean
 Some infinite horror to the light that
 laughed !

So let the scent of lily and rose,
Of jasmine, taggara,³ pass away !
Let patchouli, patchouli, repose
My nostrils with your odour grey,
Dead darlings exquisite in your decay !

So, silk and velvet, fur and skin,
 Your sensuous touch shall quit me quite :
I am at swiving strain with sin
I'll touch the stars, the blood run thin
 From the torn breast of Night, my mother
 Night.

Nor shall the mind revoke at ease
 These myriad cressets from the sun ;
Constrained in sober destinies
 Thought's river shall its ripples run
 Into the one, the one, the one, the one.

¹ The fundamental tone in Chinese music ;
supposed to be given by the Hoang-Ho river,
according to Professor Rice.
² Sacred mountain in the Himalaya, the
abode of Shiva.
³ An eastern perfume. *Cf.* Max Müller's
Dhammapada.
 VOL. III.

Bursting the universe, a grip
Girds me to God ; aha ! the bliss !
Begone, frail tortures wrung from whip,
Weak joys sucked hard from leman's lip,
Ye are nought at all, are nought at all, in
this !

  .   .   .   .

But brown Habiba's fawn-wide gaze
 And white Zuleikha's drowsy glance
Woo me to waking unto day's
 Delight from night's unmeasured trance :—
 To drink, to dally, to desire, to dance.

Ah ! beautiful and firm your hips,
 Habib ! ah ! coolthsome your caress,
Zuleikha ! soft your honey lips—
The tongue of pleasure subtly sips
 The wine that age distils, and calls dis-
 tress.

Enough ! when all is ended, when
 The poppied pleasure purples pain—
Death—shall I laugh or smile ? Amen !
I'll wake, one last fond cup to drain,
And then—to sleep again, to sleep again !

KALI.¹

THERE is an idol in my house
 By whom the sandal alway steams.
Alone, I make a black carouse
 With her to dominate my dreams.
With skulls and knives she keeps control
 (O Mother Kali !) of my soul.

She is crowned with emeralds like leaves,
 And rubies flame from either eye ;
A rose upon her bosom heaves,
 Turquoise and lapislazuli.
She hath a kirtle like a maid :—
Amethyst, amber, pearl, and jade !

¹ The most popular form, in Bengal, of
Sakti, the Hindu Isis.
 G

Her face is fashioned like a moon ;
    Her breasts are tongues of pointed jet ;
Her belly of opal fairly hewn ;
    And round about her neck is set
The holy rosary, skull by skull,
Polished and grim and beautiful !

This jewelled shape of gold and bronze
    Is seated on my bosom's throne ;
She takes my muséd orisons
    To her, to her, to her alone.
Oh Kali, Kali, Kali, quell
This hooded hate, O Queen of Hell !

Her ruby-studded brow is calm ;
    Her eyes shine like some sleepy flood ;
Her breast is oliban and balm ;
    Her tongue lolls out, a-dripping blood ;
She swings my body to and fro ;
She breaks me on the wheel of woe !

To her eternal rapture seems
    Mere nature ; underneath the crown
Of dusky emeralds there streams
    A river of bliss to sluice me down
With blood and tears, to drown my thought,
To bring my being into nought.

The cruel teeth, the steady sneer,
    The marvellous lust of her, I bring
Unto my body bright and clear
    (Dropped poison in a water spring !)
To fill me with the utmost sense
Of some divine experience.

For who but she, the adulterous queen,
    Made earth and heaven with all its stars,
The storm, the hunger epicene,
    The raging at invisible bars,
The hideous cruelty of the whole ?—
These are of Kali, O my soul !

The sterile force of bronze and gold
    Bends to my passion, as it grips
With feverish claws the metal cold,
    And burns upon the brazen lips
That, parted like a poppy bud,
Have gemméd curves like moons of blood.

The mazes of her many arms
    Delude the eye ; they seem to shift
As if they spelled mysterious charms
    Whereby some tall grey ship should drift
Out to a windless, tideless sea
Motionless from eternity.

This then I seek, O woman-form !
    O god embowelled in curves of bronze !
The shuddering of a sudden storm
    To mix me with thy minions
The lost, who wait through endless night,
And wait in vain, to see the light.

For I am utterly consumed
    In thee, in thee am broken up.
The life upon my lips that bloomed
    Is crushed into a deadly cup,
Whose devilish spirit squats and gloats
Upon the thirst that rots our throats.

Gape wide, O hideous mouth, and suck
    This heart's blood, drain it down, expunge
This sweltering life of mire and muck !
    Squeeze out my passions as a sponge,
Till nought is left of terrene wine
But somewhat deathless and divine !

Not by a faint and fairy tale
    We shadow forth the immortal way.
No symbols exquisitely pale
    Avail to lure the secrets grey
Of his endeavour who proceeds
By doing to abolish deeds.

Not by the pipings of a bird
    In skies of blue on fields of gold,
But by a fierce and loathly word
    The abomination must be told.
The holy work must twist its spell
From hemp of madness, grown in hell.

Only by energy and strife
    May man attain the eternal rest,
Dissolve the desperate lust of life
    By infinite agony and zest.
Thus, O my Kali, I divine
The golden secret of thy shrine !

Death from the universal force
Means to the forceless universe
Birth. I accept the furious course,
Invoke the all-embracing curse.
Blessing and peace beyond may ie
When I annihilate the " I."

Therefore, O holy mother, gnash
Thy teeth upon my willing flesh !
Thy chain of skulls wild music clash !
Thy bosom bruise my own afresh !
Sri Maharani ![1] draw my breath
Into the hollow lungs of death !

There is no light, nor any motion.
There is no mass, nor any sound.
Still, in the lampless heart of ocean,
Fasten me down and hold me drowned
Within thy womb, within thy thought,
Where there is nought—where there is
    nought !

THE JILT.

" WHO is that slinkard moping down the
    street,
    That youth—scarce thirty—bowed like
    sixty ?"   " Oh,
A woman jilted him."   " Absurd ! "   " Con-
ceit !
Some youths take life—are Puritans, you
    know ! "

I heard it, sitting in the window—glowed,
    Rushed to my wife and kissed her.   Lithe
    and young
The rapture of some ardent madness flowed ;
And — bye-and-bye — its miracle found
tongue.

.   .   .   .

Guess, guess the secret why I burn for you
    These years so cold to woman as I was !
Guess why your laugh, your kiss, your touch
    run through
My body, as it were a tunéd glass !

[1] Holy Queen—one of the many thousand
titles of the Goddess.

You cannot guess ?—false devil that you are !
To Cruelty's add calm's analysis !
You love me ?   Yes—then crown me a
    bearded Sar
Bull-breasted by my sleek Semiramis ![1]

Did you not hear those men below ?   They
    spoke
Of one I think you have forgotten long ;
Talked of his ruined life—half as a joke—
    But I— But I—it is my whole heart's
    song !

I love you when I think of his pale·lips
    Twitching, and all his curls of gold awry ;
Your smile of poison as he sighs and sips ;
    Your half-scared laughter as his heart-
    beats die—

Let him creep on, a shattered, ruined thing !
    A ship dismasted on a dreadful sea !
And you—afar—some word of largesse fling
    Pitifully worded for more cruelty !

His death lends savour to our passionate
    life ;
    His is the heart I taste upon your tongue ;
His death-spasms our love-spasms, my wife ;
    His death-songs are the love-songs that
    you sung !

Ah ! Sweet, I love you as I see him stagger
    On with hell's worm a-nuzzling to his
    heart,
With your last letter, like a poisoned dagger,
    Biting his blood, burning his bones apart.

Ah ! Sweet, each kiss I drink from you is
    warm
    With the dear life-blood of a man—a man !
The scent of murder lures me, like a charm
    Tied by some subtlety Canidian.

Ay ! as you suck my life out into bliss,
    Its holier joy is in the deadlier thirst
That drank his life out into the abyss
    Of torture endless, endless and accurst.

[1] Queen of Assyria, famous for glory and
debauchery.   Sar is the royal title.

I know him little ; liking what I know.
  But you—you offer me his flesh and blood.
I taste it—never another vintage owe,
  Nor bid me sup upon another food !

This is our marriage ; firmer than the root
  Of love or lust could plant our joy, my
    wife,
We stand in this, the purple-seeded fruit
  Of yon youth's fair and pitiable life.
     .   .   .   .
Do, I not fear that you may treat me so ?
  One day your passion slake itself some-
    how,
Seek vigour from another murder ?   No !
  You harlot, for I mean to kill you—now.

THE EYES OF PHARAOH.

DEAD Pharaoh's eyes from out the tomb
  Burned like twin planets ruby-red.
Enswathed, enthroned, the halls of gloom
  Echo the agony of the dead.

Silent and stark the Pharaoh sate :
  No breath went whispering, hushed or
    scared.
Only that red incarnate hate
  Through pylon after pylon flared.

As in the blood of murdered things
  The affrighted augur shaking skries
Earthquake and ruinous fate of kings,
  Famine and desperate destinies,

So in the eyes of Pharaoh shone
  The hate and loathing that compel
In death each damnèd minion
  Of Set,[1] the accursed lord of Hell.

Yea ! in those globes of fire there sate
  Some cruel knowledge closely curled
Like serpents in those halls of hate,
  Palaces of the Underworld.

[1] The ass-headed deity of the Egyptians, slayer of Osiris.

But in the hell-glow of those eyes
  The ashen skull of Pharaoh shone
White as the moonrays that surprise
  The invoking Druse on Lebanon.

Moreover pylon shouldered round
  To pylon an unearthly tune,
Like phantom priests that strike and sound
  Sinister sistrons at the moon.

And death's insufferable perfume
  Beat the black air with golden fans
As Turkis rip a Nubian's womb
  With damascenéd yataghans.

Also the taste of dust long dead
  Of ancient queens corrupt and fair
Struck through the temple, subtly sped
  By demons dominant of the air.

Last, on the flesh there came a touch
  Like sucking mouths and stroking hands
That laid their foul alluring smutch
  Even to the blood's mad sarabands.

So did the neophyte that would gaze
  Into dead Pharaoh's awful eyes
Start from incalculable amaze
  To clutch the initiate's place and prize.

He bore the blistering thought aloft :
  It blazed in battle on his plume :
With sage and warrior enfeoffed,[1]
  He rushed alone through tower and tomb.

The myriad men, the cohorts armed,
  Are shred like husks : the ensanguine
    brand
Leaps like a flame, a flame encharmed
  To fire the pyramid heaven-spanned

Wherein dead Pharaoh sits and stares
  Swathed in the wrappings of the tomb,
With eyes whose horror flits and flares
  Like corpse-lights glimmering in the
    gloom,

[1] Accompanied by those sages and warriors who owed him feudal service.

Till all's a blaze, one roar of flame,
Death universal, locked and linked :—
Aha ! one names the awful Name—
The twin red planets are extinct.

BANZAI !

THERE leapt upon a breach and laughed
  A royally maniac man.
A bitter craft
Is mine, he saith,
  O soldiers of Japan !
I am the brothel-knave of death,
  The grimly courtesan.

Now who will up and kiss her lips,
  Or grip her breast and bone ?
The subtle life she shears and snips
  Is harder gained than gone ;
The lover's laughter whom she clips
  Is but a dying groan.

She lieth not on a gilded bed
  In the city without the city.[1]
One kiss is hers full rank and red—
Do you sip at her lip? Hell hangs on her
      fangs !
  She loves ; love laughs at pity !

Then who will up to taste her mouth ?
  Who on her mount and ride ?
Look to the North, the West, the South !
  There is carnage vulture-eyed.
Then who will suck the breath of death,
  The swift and glittering bride ?
The bride that clings as a snare with springs
  To the warrior's stricken side ?

A shudder struck the hidden men
  As the maniac's mouthings ceased.
Then, kindling, rose a roar :
  " Spread, spread the furtive feast !
The wine of agony pour !
The fruit of valour pluck !
The meat of murder suck !

[1] The prostitutes of Japan live in a city by
themselves, whenever they are sufficiently
numerous to make this practicable.

Sweet are the songs of her throat !
Soft are the strokes of her fan !
She hath love by rhyme and rote,
  She is subtle and quick to man !
She danceth ? Say she doth float !
  Rapture is gold in her eyes !
She sigheth honey-sweet sighs
  Of the glory of Japan !
Red are her lips and large,
  The delicate courtesan ! "

Then the officer's voice
  Caught in his throat for joy.
Like birds in spring that rejoice,
  Clearly and softly the boy
Whispered : " Now, let us charge ! "
Then leaping sheer o'er trench and mound,
  They rise as a single man ;
They bound like antelopes over the ground
  For the glory of Japan.

With glittering steel they wheel—they reel ?
  They are steady again and straight !
The dull brute Christians red with the weal
  Of the knout—they will not wait !
The ringing cries of the victors peal
  In, in at the captured gate !

.   .   .   .   .   .

Then o'er the field the maniac passed
  And closed the dead men's eyes.
" They are sleeping close with death at last ! "
  The wanton warrior cries.
But he who saw the dead man's jaw
  Grind at the last was aware
That the harlot's kiss was Paradise
  That the soldier tasted there.
And beyond the magnificent joy of death
  Shears through the sky, as a flame
Ripping the air, the lightning breath
  Of the nation's resonant fame.
Hail ! to the Hachiman [1] deed well done !
  To the virile strength of a man !
To the stainless blaze of the Rising Sun
  The glory of Japan !

[1] Japanese God of War.

LE JOUR DES MORTS.

At Paris upon Dead Man's Day
  I danced into the cemetery.
The air was cool ; the sun was gay ;
The scent of the revolving clay
  Made me most wondrous merry.

Earth, after an agonising bout,
  Had swallowed up a widow clean.
The issue hung for long in doubt :—
—Oh ! anybody can make out
  The mystery I mean.

The dead were dancing with the worms ;
  The live were laughing with their lemans ;
The dead-alive were making terms
With God, and notaries, and germs,
  With house-agents and demons.

All Paris keeping sacrament
  Of musing or of melancholy,
Impatient of the next event,
To spend, to barter, to be spent ;—
  I chuckled at the folly.

" I would that I were dead and damned,"
  Thinks every wiser human.
"Corpses have room, and men are jammed ;
Those offer food, and these are crammed :—
  And cheaper, too, is woman ! "

I, being neither God nor ghost,
  A mere caprice of matter,
Hop idly in the hideous host,
Content to chaff the uttermost,
  To cackle and to chatter.

They bring their wreaths to deck the dead,
  As skipping-ropes the devils use them.
One through the immortelles perks his head.
[These sights to ghosties are as bread ;
  The luckless living lose them.]

Grotesque and grim the pageant struts ;
  We sit a-straddle on the crosses.
Our soulless missiles take for butts
The passers' hats, or in their guts
  Disturb their dinner's process.

Thus one man's work is one man's play ;
  The melancholy help the merry.
All tread the ordered stupid way
At Paris, upon Dead Man's Day,
  In Père Lachaise his cemetery.

AVE MORS.

O virgin ! O my sister ! Hear me, death !
  The tainted kisses of the harlot life
Sicken me ; hers is foul and fevered breath,
  This noisome woman I have made my wife.
She lies asweat, aslime. O hear me, thou !
  Wash with thy tears this desecrated brow !
With cool chaste kisses cleanse me ! Lay
    me out
Wrapped in a spotless winding-sheet, and
    soothe
These nerves ill nuzzled by the black swine's
    snout
  With thine eternal anodyne of truth !

The foul beast grunts and snorts ; but hear
    me, death !
Thy wings are wind-white as her hoofs are
    dunged.
Thy songs are faint and pale with honey
    breath,
Honey and poppy ! as her mouth hot-
    tongued
Spews out its hideous lust. O loathèd life !
Thou nameless horror of the bestial strife
Of love and hate, I straitly charge thee quit
  This bed of nastiness, this putrid sea ;
For not by any amorous tricks of wit
  Shalt thou regain thine empire over me.

O virgin, O my sister ! Hear me, death !
  Thou hast a sleep compelling soul and
    mind.
Thine is the sweet insufferable breath
  That comes like Bessarabia's twilight wind
To bring a quiet coolth from day's long heat,
  Peace to the belly gorged with blood and
    meat,

Stars for the sun that smote, for fire slow
  streams,
For the simoom the zephyr's cooing kiss,
Deep sleep at last from all the evil dreams,
And rest, the possibility of bliss.

THE MORIBUND.[1]

I.

THE Seven Wise Men of Martaban [2]
Sate round the dying man.

They were so still, one would have said :
If he were dying, they were dead !

The first was agéd ; in his beard
He muttered never a weird.

The next was beautiful and gay :
He had no word to say.

The third was wroth and rusty red,
Yet not a word he said.

The fourth was open and bold :
His silence girt him like fine gold.

The fifth was ruddy and fair of face ;
He held his tongue a space.

The sixth was many-coloured, but
He kept his lips well shut.

The last was like a full great moon ;
He knew, but uttered not, his rune.

II.

Now when the time was fully come
The dying man was dumb,

But with his failing hand did make
A sign : my heart doth ache.

[1] A meaning may be found for this poem by
any really profound student of the Qabalah.
[2] Gulf of Martaban, South of Burma.

At that the kingly man, the fourth,
Rose up and spat against the North.

Then made the dying man a sign :
My head is running like strong wine.

The agéd man lifted his mouth
And spat against the South.

He clutched his throat in pang of death,
As if he cried for breath.

Whereat the second beat his breast
And frowned upon the West.

Then the man sighed, as if to say :
The glow of life is gone away.

At this the rusty and wroth released
His eyes against the East.

Then the man touched his navel, as
He felt his life thence pass.

Also he smote his spine ; the base
Of life burnt up apace.

Then rose the many-coloured sage ;
He was right sad with age.

With him arose the ruddy and fair ;
He was right debonair.

They twain to upper air and lower
Advanced the eyes of power.

Ay ! but above the dead man's head
A lotus-flower was spread.

Thence dripped the Amrita, whereby
Life learneth not to die.

The seventh in silence tended it
Against the horror of the pit.

III.

Thus in a cage of wisdom lay
The dead man, live as they.

They hold him sacred from the sun,
From death and dissolution.

Within the charméd space is nought
Possible unto thought.

There in their equilibrium
They float—how still, how numb !

There must they rest, there will they stay
Innocent of the judgment day.

Remote from cause, effect retires.
Act slays its dams and sires.

There is no hill, there is no pit.
They have no mark to hit.

It is enough.   Closed is the sphere.
There is no more to hear.

They perish not ; they do not thrive.
They are at rest, alive,

The Seven Wise Men of Martaban ;
And, moribund, the man.

THE BEAUTY AND THE BHIKKHU :

A TALE OF THE TENTH IMPURITY.

(*From the Pali.*)

I.

LISTEN !   The venerable monk pursued
  His path with downcast eyes ; his thought
    revolved
Ever in closer coils serenely screwed
  About the Tenth Impurity.   Dissolved
All vision of his being but of one
Thing only, his sun-whitened skeleton.

II.

A dainty lady sick of simple life,
  Chained to the cold couch of some vapid
    man,
Put on her jewels, off the word of wife,
  Resolved to play the painted courtesan,

So ran along the village path.   Her
    laughter
  Wooed all the world to follow tumbling
    after.

III.

Then when she met the venerable monk
  Her shamelessness desired a leprous
    wreath
Of poisonous flowers, seducing him.   He
    shrunk
  Back from her smile, seeing her close
    white teeth.
Bones ! he exclaimed, and meditating that,
From a mere Bhikkhu grew an Arahat.

IV.

Her husband found her gone, in fury followed
  Lashing the pale path with his purple
    feet,
Heedless of stones and serpents.   Hail ! he
    holloaed
  To the new Rahan[1] whom he bowed to
    greet
Kissing the earth : O holy master, say
If a fair female hath passed by this way !

V.

The Bhikkhu blessed the irritated man.
  Then the slow sloka[2] serpentine began:
" Friend ! neither man nor woman owns
  This being's high perception, owed
Only to Truth ; nor beams nor stones
  Support the Arahat's abode.
Who grasps one truth, beholds one light,
  Becomes that truth, that light ; discedes
From dark and deliquescent night,
  From futile thoughts and fatuous deeds.
Your girl, your gems, your mournful tones
  Irk not perfection with their goad.
One thing I know—a set of bones
  Is travelling on upon this road ! "

―――――――
[1] Arahat.   [2] Stanza.

IMMORTALITY

" From this tale, Callicles, which I have heard and believe, I draw the following in-
ferences:—Death, if I am right, is in the first place the separation from one another
of two things, soul and body ; nothing else. And after they are separated they retain their
several natures, as in life ; the body keeps the same habit, and the results of treatment
or accident are distinctly visible in it : for example, he who by nature or training or
both was a tall man while he was alive, will remain as he was, after he is dead ; and the
fat man will remain fat ; and so on ; and the dead man who in life had a fancy to
have flowing hair, will have flowing hair. And if he was marked with the whip and
had the prints of the scourge, or of wounds in him when he was alive, you might see the
same in the dead body ; and if his limbs were broken or misshapen when he was
alive, the same appearance would be visible in the dead. And in a word, whatever was
the habit of the body during life would be distinguishable after death, either perfectly,
or in a great measure and for a certain time. And I should imagine that this is equally
true of the soul, Callicles ; when a man is stripped of the body, all the natural or ac-
quired affections of the soul are laid open to view."—PLATO, *Gorgias.*

IMMORTALITY.

I.

I MOVED. Remote from fear and pain
The white worms revelled in my brain.
Who travelled live may travel dead ;
The soul's no tenant of the head.
They had hanged my body by the neck ;
Bang went the trap. A little speck
Shot idly upon consciousness
Unconscious of the head's distress
When with dropped jaw the body swung
So queer and limp ; the purple tongue
Shooting out swollen and awry.
Men cheered to see the poisoner die.
Not he ! He grinned one visible grin,
The last ; then, muffled in his sin,
He lived and moved unseen of those
Nude souls that masquerade in clothes,
Confuse the form and the sensation,
And have the illusion, incarnation.
I bore myself. Death was so dull.
The dead are strangely beautiful
To the new-comer ; it wears off.

II.

They told me I was damned. The Shroff[1]
Gave me ten dollars Mex. (For ease
Of English souls the dead Chinese

[1] Money-changer. Mexican dollars were
long the sole currency on the Chinese coast.

Are taxed) to pay my way in hell.
On one pound sterling one lives well.
For luxuries are cheaply paid
Since Satan introduced Free Trade ;
And necessaries—woe is me !—
Are furnished to the damned soul free.

III.

God's hell, Earth's heaven, are not so far.
Dinner brought oysters, caviar,
Anchovies, truffles, curried rabbit
(Bad for the apoplectic habit),
While ancient brandy and champagne
Washed down the dainties. Once again
I seemed to haunt the Continental.[1]
A saucy little elemental
Flitted across ; I heard it sneer ;
" You won't get water, though, I fear."
That's hell all over. Good-bye, greens,
Water, cold mutton, bread, and beans !
They feed us well, like gentlemen,
On chilis, seasoned with cayenne.
Worse, one must finish every course.
'S truth, I had rather eat boiled horse !

IV.

My first friend was an agéd monk.
He fed on rice and water. Sunk
His cheeks and cold his blood. You see
The fool was a damned soul like me ;

[1] Smart restaurant in London.

He had starved himself on earth in hope
In heaven to banquet with the Pope,
With God and Christ on either hand
And all the angels' choral band
Playing sweet music.   O the fool
To treat earth as a baby's school !
In hell one lives as one is wont.
Punch said to would-be bridegrooms :
       Don't !
Might I advise the same to those
Shapeless and senseless embryos
Who seek to live ?   Yes, God is wise
Enough to set a snare for lies
As well as truths.   The soul content
On earth in his own element
Will be content from flesh released.
But he who strives to be a beast
Or strives to be a god ; would gain
Long bliss for a few hours of pain,
Or struggles for no matter what,
Continues.   I would rather not.

v.

That puzzle's grief I did not share
Because on earth I did not care.
I met a grave philosopher—
'Had sought most nobly not to err
Probing God's Nature.   See his lobes
Swell with hell's torment !   Still he probes
The same fool's problem.   I explain
The simple state of things in vain.
He chose to study God, and die in it.
He made his bed, and he must lie in it.

vi.

After my dinner I debate
(Urged to the task by habit's Fate)
The project of a poisoning.
In hell one finds that everything
Is easy.   Poison to my hand ;
A cunning potion cool and bland
Fit to administer the draught :—
How like old times !   I nodded, laughed,
Poisoned my neighbour, a young girl
Sent here for marrying an earl.
Of course she did not die.   But then
On earth I never killed my men ;

They only die whom one forgets.
Remember that each action sets
Its mark still deeper in the mind !

vii.

O piteous lot of humankind
Whose history repeats itself !
Dinner is cleared by gnome and elf ;
I pay the bill, take Baal's receipt,
And stroll off smoking.   Soon I meet
The fairest foulest whore that burns.
High feeding pays : desire returns.
She willing (for a copper rin) [1]
For any ecstasy of sin
Gaily embraces me.   A room
Starts up in the half-light, half-gloom,
Perfectly purposed for debauch.
In mirrors shines a wicked nautch,
And on the floor Hawaian belles
Rave in a hula-hula [2]—Hell's !
Fragonard, Rops, had lined the walls
With wild indecent bacchanals,
And bawdy photographs attest
The Devil's taste to be the best.

viii.

I did not sleep at all : but she :—
O face of deathless agony !
O torture of hell's worm, to wrest
From peace that miserable breast !
Me, me she strikes in mid-delight
Staggered and shattered at the sight,
The moment that she slept.   I laughed
Thereat : the bowl I idly quaffed
Was nectar : she amused me, so.
You see, my friend, I did not know.
I also slept at morn.   Then, then,
A low voice whispered in the den :
" Lucky young fellow !   Brave and clever !
This sort of thing goes on for ever."

ix.

On earth I dreaded impotence,
Age, death.   You see, I had no sense.
Best be an old man ere you die ;
They wish insensibility,

[1] Japanese coin worth a small portion of a
penny.
[2] The indecent dance of the South Seas.

So are their pains the duller. Hell
Is managed infinitely well
From the peculiar standpoint of
A god who says that he is Love.

x.

That was the poet Crowley's point.
I think *his* nose is out of joint ;
He bet on justice being done ;
And here—it's really rather fun !—
The unlucky devil devil-spurred
Writes, climbs, does Yoga like a bird ;
Just as he was before he " died,"
The ass is never satisfied.
He has only been here forty days,
And has already writ six plays,
Made eight new passes, one new peak,
Is bound to do two more this week,
And as for meditation ! Hard he
Soars from Dhyana to Samadhi ;
Writes wildly sloka after sloka,
Storms the Arupa-Brahma-Loka,
Disdains the mundane need of Khana,[1]
Slogs off, like Buddha, to Nibbana :—
Poor devil !

xi.

One thing makes me weep.
He was wise one way, and scorned sleep.
Wherefore he sleeps not, does not hear
That still small dreadful voice of fear.
Therefore he realises not
That this is his eternal lot.
Therefore he suffers not at all.

xii.

Luckier is he than one, a small
Wild girl, whose one desire on earth
Was to—be blunt with it !—give birth
To children. Here she's fairly in it !
Pumps out her fourteen babes a minute ;
Her (under chloroform) the voice
Bids to be gleesome and rejoice :
" No sterile God balks *thine* endeavour.
This sort of thing goes on for ever."

[1] Dinner.

xiii.

I was a humorous youth enough
On earth ; I laughed when things were
    rough.
Therefore, I take it, now in Hades
The funny side of things—and ladies—
Engages my attention. Well !
You know enough of life in Hell.
I was an altruist, my brothers !
My life one long kind thought for others :
For me six maidens wear the willow :—
Poisoning is a peccadillo.
Hence I'm disposed to give advice
Simple, if possibly not nice ;
Shun life ! an awkward task and deep.
But if you cannot, then—shun sleep !

(Suppose I thus had prophesied,
Gone to my wife to bed, and died !)

EPILOGUE.

THE KING-GHOST.

The King-Ghost is abroad. His spectre
    legions
    Sweep from their icy lakes and bleak
    ravines
Unto these weary and untrodden regions
    Where man lies penned among his Might-
    have-beens.
        Keep us in safety, Lord,
        What time the King-Ghost is abroad !

The King-Ghost from his grey malefic
    slumbers
    Awakes the malice of his bloodless brain.
He marshals the innumerable numbers
    Of shrieking shapes on the sepulchral
    plain.
        Keep us, for Jesu's sake,
        What time the King-Ghost is awake !

The King-Ghost wears a crown of hopes
forgotten ;
Dead loves are woven in his ghastly
robe ;
Bewildered wills and faiths grown old and
rotten
And deeds undared his sceptre, sword, and
globe.
Keep us, O Mary maid,
What time the King-Ghost goes
arrayed !

The Hell-Wind whistles through his plume-
less pinions ;
Clanks all that melancholy host of bones ;
Fate's principalities and Death's dominions
Echo the drear discord, the tuneless tones.
Keep us, dear God, from ill,
What time the Hell-Wind whistles
shrill.

The King-Ghost hath no music but their
rattling ;
No scent but death's grown faint and
fugitive ;
No light but this their leprous pallor battling
Weakly with night. Lord, shall these
dry bones live ?
O keep us in the hour
Wherein the King-Ghost hath his
power !

The King-Ghost girds me with his gibbering
creatures,
My dreams of old that never saw the sun.
He shows me, in a mocking glass, their
features,
The twin fiends " Might-have-been " and
" Should-have-done."
Keep us, by Jesu's ruth,
What time the King-Ghost grins the
truth !

The King-Ghost boasts eternal usurpature ;
For in this pool of tears his fingers fret
I had imagined, by enduring nature,
The twin gods " Thus-will-I " and " May-
be-yet."
God, keep us most from ill,
What time the King-Ghost grips the
will !

Silver and rose and gold what flame re-
surges ?
What living light pours forth in emerald
waves ?
What inmost Music drowns the clamorous
dirges ?
—Shrieking they fly, the King-Ghost and
his slaves.
Lord, let Thy Ghost indwell,
And keep us from the power of Hell !
Amen.

Kneel down, dear maiden o' mine, and let your eyes
Get knowledge with a soft and glad surprise !
Who would have thought you would have had it in you ?
Say nothing ! On the contrary, continue !

RODIN IN RIME

1907

AUTHOR'S NOTE

AUGUSTE RODIN AND THE NOMENCLATURE OF HIS WORKS

A STUDY IN SPITE

WHEN illegitimate criticism is met with a smart swing on the point of the jaw, and has subsided into an unpleasant and unpitiful heap ; when its high-well-born brother has shaken hands—not without many years of friendly sparring—with the new pugilist, all his family are very disappointed, for Society takes no notice of them in its (to them unseemly) adulation of the rising star. Their unfraternal feeling may even lead them to employ a sandbagger and a dark night to rid them of this dreamer Joseph.

In the case of the success, in the heavy weights, of the Meudon Chicken (M. Rodin will forgive us for the lengths to which we carry our analogy), envy has given up hope even of sandbags, and is now engaged in the ridiculous task of attempting to disconcert the eye of the Fancy Boy by flipping paper pellets at him across the arena. They do not reach him, it is true : but as I, who happen to be sitting in a back row, admiring the clean, scientific sequences of rib-punchers, claret-tappers, &c., &c., recently received one of these missiles in the eye, my attention was called to the disturber. I will now do my part as a law-abiding citizen and take my boot to the offender, as a warning to him and all of his kidney. I shall not mention his name : that he would enjoy : that is perhaps what he hoped. I will merely state that he is one of those unwashen and oleaginous individuals who are a kind of Mérodack-Jauneau without the Mérodack, i.e., without the gleam of intention in their work which to the lay mind redeems even the most grotesque imbecility of technique, and the most fatuous ignorance of all subjects connected or unconnected with art. By philosophy he understands "Science and Health" : by poetry Lake Harris or Eric Mackay : he expects a painting to tell a pretty story or to upset a metaphysical position. His conversation is like that of Planchette : or if William Horton were vocal—— But Heaven forbid !

What he said, though parrot-talk, caught up in some fifth-rate sculptor's studio, no doubt, had so much truth in it, carefully concealed by the lying misinterpretation he had put on it, that, as I said, the pellet hit me. This was what it came to. Rodin's works, it is said, *mean* nothing. He makes a study : people see it in his studio : A. goes up and says to the Master: "Ah, how beautiful," &c., *ad nauseam*—"I suppose it is 'Earth and the Spring.'" B. follows, and suggests "Hercules and Cacus"; C. thinks "The Birth of a Flower" ; D. calls it "Despair"; E. varies it with "Moses breaking the Tables of the Law"; F. cocks his eye warily, and asks if it is not meant for "Mary Magdalene"; G. votes for "The Beetle-Crusher and his Muse," and so on, day after day, till Z. comes round and recognises it for Balzac. Rodin shakes him warmly by both hands : Balzac it is for all time—and one ceases to wonder that it was rejected !

Now, of course, this paper pellet is in any case very wide of its mark. Rodin can easily sculp himself a tabernacle and go in with Whistler—and even drag in Velasquez ; but here am I illustrating, however feebly, the Works, in Poetry: and poetry cannot, unfortunately, ever be pure technique. I have long wished to write "A Sonnet in W. and P." (with Whip as the keynote); a triolet in U. and K. ; an ode in S. Sh. Sw. Sp. and Str.—and so on ; but people would merely say "Nonsense Verses" (so they do now, some of them !). So that my work is liable to the most vital misinterpretation. My best friend tells me utterly false, utterly funny story about me that I wrote one sonnet for "L'Ange déchu" and another for "Icare."

The real heart of the attack is, of course, against Rodin's intention, and it is my object to show what rubbish it is, even granting the literary basis of criticism to be valid. I am given to understand that something of the sort described above does sometimes take place in the naming of a statue (of the allegorical description especially). But that is a question of felicity, of epigram ; never of subject.

In "La Main de Dieu," for example, the meaning is obvious, and not to be wrested or distorted. What does it matter if we call it as at present, or

  (a) The Hand of Creation,
  (b) The First Lovers,
  (c) The Security of Love,
  (d) The invisible Guard

—anything in reason ? These are only ways of looking at one idea, and as you are theologian, poet, lover or mystic, so you will choose. And it is the Master's merit, not his fault, if his conception is so broad-based as to admit of different interpretations. The phenomenon is possible because Rodin is the master and not the slave of his colossal technique. The naming of a masterpiece is perhaps harder work than the producing it, and Rodin being a sculptor and not an illicit epigram distiller, is perfectly justified in picking up what he can from the witty and gifted people who throng his studio as much as he will let them.

Let there be an end, then, not to the sordid and snarling jealousy which greatness must inevitably excite, not to the simian tooth-grindings which must always accompany the entrance of a man into the jungle, but to this peculiarly senseless and sidelong attack. One accepts the lion as a worthy antagonist ; one can enjoy playing with a fine dog ; one can sympathise with sincere and honourable labour, though it be in vain ;

one ignores laughingly the attack of tiny and infuriated puppies ; but there are insects so loathsome, so incredibly disgusting, worms whose sight is such an abomination, whose stink is so crapulous and purulent, that, ignoring their malignity, but simply aware of their detestable presence, the heel is ground down in one generous impulse, and the slimy thing is no more. Decomposition, already far advanced, may be trusted speedily to resolve the remains into the ultimate dust of things, mere matter for some new and hopefuller avatar.

Such a worm are you, M. D——, who once, as above described, voided your noxious nastiness in my presence, trusting to conciliate me by the intended compliment that my poems on Rodin were from myself and not from him, and that any other statues would have done as well.

I am as little susceptible to flattery as I am to the venomous dicta of spite and envy, and I resent that when I see it employed as the medium for this. Without your compliment, M. D——, I might have left you to crawl on, lord of your own muck-heap ; with it, I take this opportunity of stamping on you.

NOTE.—I had intended [1] to include reproductions of photographs of those few statues which I have written upon ; but I prefer to pay my readers the compliment of supposing that they possess the originals in either bronze or marble.

[1] _I.e._, in the large first edition, which contains seven of M. Rodin's water-colours. _Vide_ Bibliographical Note.

RODIN IN RIME

FRONTISPIECE

RODIN.

HERE is a man ! For all the world to see
  His work stands, shaming Nature.
    Clutched, combined
In the sole still centre of a master-mind,
The Egyptian force, the Greek simplicity,
The Celtic subtlety. Through suffering free,
  The calm great courage of new art, refined
    In nervous majesty, indwells behind
The beauty of each radiant harmony.

Titan ! the little centuries drop back,
  Back from the contemplation. Stand and span
    With one great grip his cup, the Zodiac !
Distil from all time's art his wine, the truth !
  Drink, drink the mighty health—an age's youth—
    Salut, Auguste Rodin ! Here is a man.

VARIOUS MEASURES

THE TOWER OF TOIL.

(LA TOUR DE TRAVAIL.)

THE old sun rolls ; the old earth spins ;
    Incessant labour bends the stars.
Hath not enough of woes and sins
    Passed? Who shall efface their senseless
    scars?
One makes, one mars. The æons foil
All purpose ; rise, O Tower of Toil.

Rise in thy radiance to proclaim
    The agony of the earth alive !
Stand by the sea, a marble flame,
    A lighthouse wedded to an hive !
Still upward strive ! O tower, arise
An endless spiral to the skies !

Stand on the weather-beaten coast
    A flaming angel in the noon ;
A silver, fascinated ghost
    In midnight's revel with the moon ;
In silent swoon be still ! the spoil
Of years is thine, O Tower of Toil.

Let day, a glowing vigour, male ;
    And night, a virgin bowed and curled,
Stand at the foot ; their ardours pale
    Systole and diastole of the world !
With life impearled (their eyes absorb)
They visibly sustain the orb.

Then let the tower in seven tiers
    Rise in its splendour marmorean,
Unite the chill divided years
    In plain perception of the æon.
Cry clear the pæan ! Its tunes recoil
About thy flanks, O Tower of Toil.

Below be miners fashioned fair,
    And all that labour in the sea
Sepulchred from the ambient air,
    A fatal weird of dole to dree.
No time to be, no light to live.
Earth's need to these hath hope to give.

Above be various shapes of labour,
    The bodily strength, the manual skill ;
They shape the anvil and the sabre,
    The ploughshare and the bolt ; they
    fill
The myriad will of brains that boil :
Their fame be thine, O Tower of Toil !

Here set the travailers of land ;
    Here the young shepherd, fluteless now ;
The mariner with tarry hand ;
    The clerk, with pale and foolish brow,
His brain bought cheap for brainless grind :
The bloodless martyr of the mind !

Grow up the grades, O godlike hand,
    Rodin, most rightly named "August"!
Thy splendid sons and daughters stand
    Obedient to the master "must."
The decadent dust thy spells assoil ;
Death lives in this, thy Tower of Toil.

Grow up the grades ! record the tasks
    These arduous phantoms have achieved !
The growth of mind to mortals asks
    A power not swift to be believed.
What bosoms heaved ere Nature's age
From monkey-man deduced the sage !

So be thy spiral tower the type
    Of higher convolutions drawn
From hunger's woe and murder's gripe
    And lust's revulsion to the dawn
Of days that spawn on holier soil
Thy loftier sons, O Tower of Toil.

There is a flower of native light
    That springs eternal on the earth.
Carve us, O master-hand, aright
    That ecstasy of pain and mirth,
A baby's birth ! That prize of fear
Engrave upon the loftiest tier !

Nor in the solitary woe
  (The silent, the unwitting strain)
Forget the miracles that grow
  In the austerely ordered brain!
Darwin and Taine, Descartes and Boyle,
Inscribe thou on the Tower of Toil!

Those who have striven to limn the mind,
  Paint, model, tune, or hymn the light,
Their vision of the world refined
  By mastery of superior sight:
Honour their might! the gain have these
Of all men's woes and ecstasies!

High soul; no benediction seek
  From any spirit but our own!
Crown not the mighty with the weak!
  The Tower be a Tower, and not a Throne!
In man-carved stone the endless coil
Arise untopped, the Tower of Toil!

Deem not that prayer or sacrifice
  Will ever cause the work to end!
Serene, sufficient, let it rise
  Alone; it doth not ask a friend,
Nor shall it bend a fatuous knee
To a fantastic deity.

What crest or chrism were so good
  To work as Art, the crown upon
Work's brow? Thy will with love endued
  Lift up this loftier Parthenon!
Thine art the consecrative oil
To hallow us the Tower of Toil!

LA BELLE HEAULMIERE.

AGE and despair, poverty and distress
  Bend down the head that once was blithe
    and fair.
Embattled toward the ancient armouress
  Age and despair!

Where is the force of youth? The beauty
    where?
  What two-edged memory of some lost
    caress
Lurks in the sorrowful pose and lingers
    there?

O melancholy mother! Sorceress,
  No more enchantress! What the harvest
    rare
Sprung from the seed of youth and happiness?
  Age and despair.

FEMME ACCROUPIE

SWIFT and subtle and thin are the arrows of
    Art:
I strike through the gold of the skin to the
    gold of the heart.
As you sit there mighty in bronze I adore the
    twist
Of the miracle ankle gripped by the miracle
    wrist.
I adore the agony-lipped and the tilted head,
And I pay black orisons to the breasts
    aspread
In multiple mutable motion, whose soul is
    hid.
And the toils of confused emotion the Master
    bid
Lurk in the turn of the torso for poets to see
Is hid from the lesser and dull—hidden from
    me.
She squats, and is void and null; I know her
    not;
As God is above, but more so, she sits, to
    blot
Intelligence out of my brain, conceit from
    my ken;
And I class myself, idle and vain, with the
    newspaper men.

CARYATIDE

SHALL beauty avail thee, Caryatid, crouched,
    crushed by the weight of a world of woe?
  By birthright the burden is thine: on thy
    shoulders the sorrow hath slid
From the hand of the Healer: behold, in
    the steady, continuous throe,
  Shall beauty avail thee, Caryatid?

Thou wast proud of thy beauty : the burden
  of beauty was hid
  From thy eyes: how is't now with thee,
  now ? By the sweat dropping slow
From the brows of thy anguish, we see what
  the weight of it did
  To the patient despair of the brain. Shall
  no God strike a blow ?
Shall no hero be found the unbearable
  burden to rid ?
  And if these be extinct—'tis a fiend that
  laughs eager and low :
"Shall beauty avail thee, Caryatid ? "

JEUNE MERE

SURELY the secret whisper of sweet life
Shakes in the shell-ear murmurous memories
Of the old wonder of young ecstasies
In the first hours when the white word of
  wife
She won so hardly out of dark wild strife
And mystery of peace ; thine utter ease,
Abandoned rapture ! Caught and cut by
  seas
Of sudden wisdom, stinging as a knife
Swift struck sets all the blood a-tingle. Woe !
What wakes within ? What holiest intima-
  tion
Of intimate knowledge of the lords of nature ?
She sees her fate smile out on her, doth
  know
Her weird of womanhood, her noble station
Among the stars and ages ; and her stature
Soars o'er the system ; so the scarred mis-
  feature
Of death avails her for the isolation
Of high things ever holy ; this the throe
Of swiftly-comprehended motherhood
Once taught her. Now the whisper of the
  child
Bids her be great, who was supremely good.
For, mark you ! babes are ware of wiser
  things,
And hold more arcane matters in their mild
Cabochon eyes than men are ware of yet.
  VOL. III.

Therefore have poets, lest they should forget,
Likened the little sages unto kings.
But look ! the baby whispers—hush ! Nay !
  nay !
We shall disturb them loving—come away !

L'AMOUR QUI PASSE.

LOVE comes to flit, a spark of steel
Struck on the flint of youth and wit ;
Ay, little maid, for woe or weal,
Love comes to flit.

Hermes one whisper thrills. Admit !
Kupris one smile aims—do you feel ?
Eros one arrow—has he hit ?

Why do you sit there immobile ?
A spark extinct is not relit.
Beyond resource, above appeal,
Love comes to flit.

TETE DE FEMME (MUSEE DU LUXEMBOURG).

IT shall be said, when all is done,
  The last line written, the last mountain
Climbed, the last look upon the sun
  Taken, the last star in the fountain
Shattered, that you and I were one.

What shall they say, who come apace
  After us, heedless, gallant ? Seeing
Our statues, hearing of our race
  Heroic tales, half-doubted, being
So far beyond a rime to trace.

What shall they say ? For secret we
  Have held our love, and holy. Splendour
Of light, and music of the sea
  And eyes and heart serene and tender,
With kisses mingled utterly.

These were our ways. And who shall know ?
  What warrior bard our nuptial glories
Shall sing ? Historic shall we go
  Down through our country's golden stories ?
Shall lovers whisper " Even so

As he loved her do I love you " ?
So much they shall know, surely; never
The truth, how lofty and fresh as dew
Our love began, abode for ever :
They cannot know us through and through.

We have exceeded all the past.
The future shall not build another.
This is the climax, first and last.
We stand upon the summit. Mother
Of ages, daughter of ages, cast

The fatal die, and turn to death !
Let evolution turn, involving
As when the gray sun sickeneth—
Ghostly September ! so dissolving
Into the pale eternal breath.

When all is done, shall this be said.
When all is said, shall this be done,
The æon exhaust and finishéd,
And slumber steal upon the sun,
My dear, when you and I are dead.

LA CASQUE D'OR.

A NINA OLIVIER.

You laughing little light of wickedness, low
    ripples round you love and coils
And twists the Casque of Gold about the
    child-face with a child-caress.
O glory of the tangled net ! O subtle vase
    of scented oils !
You laughing little light of wickedness !

Through all the misty wind of light that
    glamours round you, sorceress,
Your face shines out with feline grace, exults,
    a tiger in the toils !
They shall not hold your passion in : fling,
    fling your lips, my murderess,

On mine that I may pass away, a vapour
    that your passion boils,
A rose whose petals flutter down as cruel
    lips and fingers press.
Hear one last careless laugh acclaim my
    corpse the latest of your spoils,
You laughing little light of wickedness.

LES BOURGEOIS DE CALAIS

PERFECTLY sad and perfectly resolved,
    They are ready, ready to be hanged.
    They go
(Forlorn ones !) against Calais' overthrow ;
And all their fate in Calais' is involved
Unto the utmost.   Who will save his folk
    From vengeful ire of the tyrant ? Six are
    these,
Perfectly sad, and steady, and at ease.
Self-slain, they shall save others from the
    yoke.
Seven then are these found faithful unto
    death ;
    From Calais six ; and one from Nazareth.

REVEIL D'ADONIS.[1]

ADONIS, awake, it is day ; it is spring !
It is dawn on the lea, it is light on the lake !
The fawn's in the bush and the bird's on
    the wing !
    Adonis, awake !

Adonis, awake ! We are colour and song
And form, we are Muses most tender to take
Thy life up to Art that was lost over long.
    Adonis, awake !

Adonis, awake ! thou hast risen above
The fear in the forest, the brute in the brake.
Thou art sacred to shrines that are higher
    than Love !
    Adonis, awake !

[1] Properly the sequel to Mort d'Adonis on
p. 122.

LA MAIN DE DIEU

THE Hand. From mystery that is cloud
   control
The mystery that is emptiness of air,
Purpose and power. What blossom do
   they bear?
Stability and strength inform—what soul?

Turn to me, love! the banks of air are soft.
   Turn to me, love! the skies are blue,
Fleeced with the clouds that hang aloft,
   Buds that may blossom into dew.

Turn to me, love! lie close and breathe
   The smooth waves of the wind!
The zephyr in thy locks I'll wreathe,
   The breeze entwined.

We are so safe; so happy we:
   Our love can never falter; fate can never
   close
Hard on the flower of land and sea.
   Lift, O rose petals of my rose,
Toward me, rest, dream on, we are here, we
   love.
There is no shadow above,
   No ghost below: we are here. Kiss! Kiss!
For ever. Who would have believed, have
   thought of this?

Outside is nothing. Let what will uproll,
   Within all's certain. Are we not aware
(Who see the hand) What brain must know
   —and care?
What wisdom formed the racers, find a
   goal?

Careless and confident, let us love on.
Life, one or many, rises from a seed,
   Sprouts, blooms, bears fruit, and then is
   gone—is gone.
Let go the future, ominous and vast!
Loose the bound mind from the unavailing
   past!
   Live, love for ever, now, in every deed!

DESESPOIR.

INTO the inmost agony of things
   She sees, through glamour of untrusty
   sense,
   The full corruption of omnipotence,
The infinite rage of fishes to have wings,
   The lust of beasts for tentacles; caught
   thence
Corollary, syllogism, she strides tense
Into the inmost agony of things.

So, fearless, amid gods and evil kings,
   She sits, poor wretch, eternal scientist,
   Straining mild muscles, leaving to its list
The spasm-shaken body. So she flings
   The teeth-set fate of Fortune's face un
   kissed
Against the fiat: sets her clenchéd fist
In his face: slides spinning with her body's
   twist
Into the inmost agony of things.

EPERVIER ET COLOMBE.

WHEN, at the awful Judgment-day, God
   stands
Shrunken and shaking at my gaze, before
My hollow seat of agony, it may be
He shall discover me the great excuse
For an ill world ill shapen by ill hands,
For unit joy and misery ten score,
For all his work's complaint; I think that
   He,
Twitching his fearful fingers, may let loose
This answer: Thus a kiss I brought to being
Which by no other way were possible.
Measure, O man! Balance with eyes true-
   seeing
If I were right or no to have made Hell!

Then would He stand forgiven — nay!
   acquitted!
I, as I look on this tight coil of bliss,

Swift clasp of Rodin's magical mind love-
    witted,
See all creation fade; abide, one kiss.
Then to my own soul's bow this shaft be
    fitted ;
Thank God for all, seeing that all is this !

RESURRECTION.

FROM youth and love to sorrow is one stride.
So to the thinker; to the lover's self
Rather it glides or swoons ; the idle elf
That plucks a rose, scatters its petals wide,
Is like the wind, is like the moon-wrought
    tide,
Is most like life : so soft to man, so hard
To the all-gathering brain of a great bard !

Christ answered: Peace to man amid the
    strife !
I am the Resurrection and the Life.
Let the graves open : see the woman grip
Her goodly love, her gainful fellowship !
See the man, hungry, grasp the willing
    bride,
Grope through the dark dawn to her glow-
    ing side !
There is the resurrection trump: confess
The mystery of life is happiness !

Rodin discerned. We see the eagle-eyed
Glory of echoing kisses ; hear the sound
Of glutted raptures break in the profound,
The abyss of time : upsurge the dead. Why
    hide
Thy sorrowful god's brow, O sculptor, mage,
Child of eternity, father of an age ?
Thou hast seen, thou hast showed, that as it
    was on earth
So shall it be in resurrection birth.
The cycle of weariness and passionate pain
Is and was ever and must be again.
There is no death ! Ah ! that is misery !
For this, Lord Christ, is it that thou wouldst
    be,
Thou yesterday, to-day, and thou to-morrow ?
The mystery of this our life is sorrow.

L'ETERNEL PRINTEMPS.

I.

THE eternal spring is in the heart of youth.
They are nearest to the secret of the world,
These lovers with their lithe white bodies
    curled
Into the rhythm of a dance ; the truth
Is theirs that feel, not ours that idly see ;
Theirs that inhabit, and not ours that flee
The intimate touch of love and think to
    sleuth
By intellect all the scent of being, whirled
In the wheel of time—roll back, slow years,
    and be
A monument, a memory for me ;
That I may in their passion have a part,
And feel their glory glow within my heart !

II.

This holy rapture is the eternal spring.
Here in the love that tunes the untrammelled
    feet,
Here in the ardour of the arms that cling,
The alluring amber-touch of sweet to sweet,
The ageless awe of the new love revealed,
The reverence of the new love hovering
    nigh ;
These things are mazes flowery on the field,
Measures to trace a-dancing by-and-by.
Here in the statued pose the rhythm is sealed
That all who are human dance to evermore.
Before this ecstasy all ages yield :
Eternity breaks foamless on time's shore.
And I, because of this delight in me,
Am one in substance with eternity.

ACROBATES

MY little lady light o' limb
    Twirls on her lover's twisting toes·
    Lithe as a lynx, red as a rose,
She spins aloft and laughs at him.
So gay the pose, so quaint the whim,
    One stares and stares : it grows and grows.

So swift the air she seems to skim
  One's senses dazzle ; wonder glows
    Warm in one's veins like love—who
      knows ?
One follows till one's eyes are dim
My little lady light o' limb.

L'AGE D'AIRAIN.

FRESH in the savage vigour of the time,
The golden youth stands in the golden
    prime,
Erect, acute, astrain.   We look and long
For those bronze lips to blossom into song.
He is silent.   We reflect.   Ourselves grown
    old
Yearn somewhat toward that sensuous glow
    of gold.

All this is folly.   Rodin made him so,
Evoked the strength, the goodliness, the
    glow.
The form is little : in the mind there dwells
Force to avail the childish heart that swells
With aught that is.   The golden prime is
    past—
Aye ! but a nobler gain is ours at last
Who see man weary, but within our span
The perfect promise of the overman.

FAUNESSE.

THE veil o' th' mist of the quiet wood is
    lifted to the seer's gaze ;
He burns athwart the murky maze beyond
    into beatitude.

A solemn rapture holds the faun : an holy
    joy sucks up the seer
Within its rose-revolving sphere, the orient
    oval of the dawn.

Light's graven old cartouche is sealed upon
    the forest : groves are gray
With filtered glamours of the day, the steely
    ray flung off his shield.

She kneels, yon spirit of the earth ; she
    kneels and looks toward the east.
In her gray eyes awakes the beast from
    slumber into druid mirth.

She is amazed, she eager, she, exotic orchid
    of the glade !
She waits the ripe, exultant blade, life
    tempered by eternity.

And I who witness am possessed by awe
    grown crimson with desire,
Its iron image wrapped in fire and branded
    idly on my breast.

Her face is bronze, her skin is green, as
    woods and suns would have it so.
Her secret wonders grow and glow, limned
    in the luminous patine.

Worship, the sculptor's, clean forgot in
    worship of her body lithe,
And time forgotten with his scythe, and
    thought, the Witenagemot.

Confused in rapture : peace is culled a flower
    from the arboreal root,
The vision dulled, the singer mute, shattered
    the lute, the song annulled.

SONNETS AND QUATORZAINS

MADAME RODIN.

HEROIC helpmeet of the silent home !
Shall who sings Art not worship womanhood ?
There is depth of calm beneath the sea's fine
 foam ;
Behind the great there is ever found the good.
Honour and glory to the sacred house
And ark of the covenant of holy trust,
The unseen mother and the secret spouse
Ever availing in the sorrow and dust
That aye avenge the artist's victory won,
That cover up his monuments of fame,
That twist his sight, once steadfast on the
 sun,
To the fear folded in the robes of shame :—
Lest he, to all the world plain victor, find
Himself mere failure to his own white mind.

LE PENSEUR.

BLIND agony of thought ! Who turns his
 pen
Or brush or lyre to Art, shall see in this
The symbol of his battle against men
For men, the picture of the torturing bliss
Of his necessity : sits clutched and closed
Into himself the adept of wizard thought.
Gripped in his own embrace he sits : keen-
 nosed
The invisible bloodhounds ache upon the
 slot !
Soon, soon they are on him : soon the fangs
 of hate,
The sharp teeth of the infinite are in him !
Shall love, or fame, or gold, those pangs
 abate ?
 What siren with smooth voice and breast
 shall win him ?
Never a one, be sure ! In serene awe
The thinker formulates eternal law.

LA PENSÉE.

EXQUISITE fairy, flower from stone begotten
 Sprung into sudden shape of maidenhood,
Hast thou thy father's anguish all forgotten ?
 Hast thou a balm, who hast hardly under-
 stood ?
Is not thy beauty for his comfort moulded,
 Thy joy and purity his won reward ?
Sweet blush of blood, pale blossom lightly
 folded,
 To thee did he carve his way by right of
 sword ?
Thou who art all delight to all of us,
 Hast thou no special intimate caress
For him whose bloody sweat stood murderous
 On the writhen brow, the bosom of dis-
 tress ?
Ay ! for his anguish thou art gain enough—
One thought, worth all Earth's fame, and
 gold, and love !

LE BAISER.

INFINITE delicacy in great strength
 Holds the white girl and draws her into
 love.
All her lithe subtlety, her lovely length,
 Is sealed in the embrace about, above
Her visible life. What mastery of repose,
 Compulsion of motion lurks for us therein
As we gaze back on Greece, as Nature glows,
 Simple and sacred, with no thought of sin,
Yet born to trouble us, to fascinate.
 Here we are, back i' th' springtime of the
 earth ;
God above man ; and above God, dire fate.
 Ancient cosmogony of peace and mirth !
Careless, we careless, do invoke thy rime
Of the ancient rapture of the olden time.

BOUCHES D'ENFER.

Look how it leaps towards the leaper's
    curl
Of vivid ecstasy, life loosed at last
From the long-held leash! The headlong,
    hot-mouthed girl
Upon her sister like a star is cast,
Pallid with death-in-life achieved. O force
Of murder animal in the dead embrace!
The implacable ardour, unavenged remorse
For time's insulting loss, quickens the pace
Unto its prey that gathers, like a storm
Shrouding invisibly the crater's rim
Whence fury yet shall wake, and fire in-
    form
The inane basalt and coruscations dim
Of smouldering infamy. Bow down in awe!
It is enough. The Gods are at feast. With-
    draw!

LA GUERRE

She sits and screams above the folk of peace,
Deafening their quiet ears with hideous
    clamour.
Abhorred and careless she bids order cease.
Her hate resolves the shriek into a stammer
Of inarticulate rage. The wounded man
Twisted in agony beneath her squirms
To hear her raucous blasphemies outspan
The grip of God at this his last of terms.
Yea! he must die with horror in his ears,
Hate in his heart. The mischief must
    endure.
He hath expiated naught by death. His
    tears,
His thoughts, these strike nor stay her not,
    be sure!
She is Madness, and a fury; though were
    gone
All life to war, she would scream on—scream
    on.

W. E. HENLEY.[1]

Cloistral seclusion of the galleried pines
Is mine to-day : these groves are fit for Pan—
O rich with Bacchic frenzy and his wine's
Atonement for the infinite woe of man!
Is there no God of Vital Art to dwell
Serene, enshrined, incensed, adored of us?
Were not a cemetery His citadel?
His treasure-house some barred sarcophagus?
And here his mighty and reverend high-priest
Bade me good cheer, an eager acolyte,
Poured the high wine, unveiled the mystic
    feast ;—
Swooped the plumed anguish of inveterate
    night ;
Devouring torture of insight shot. Night
    hovered ;
Dawn smote. I bowed—O God declared,
    discovered!

SYRINX AND PAN.

Syrinx is caught upon the Arcadian field.
    The god's grip huddles her girl breasts :
    his grim
    And gnarlèd lips grin forth the soul of him.
The imprint of his bestial heart is sealed
And stamped armorial on her virgin shield,
    Fame's argent heraldry despoiled. Grows
    dim
    For her the universe : supple and slim
She slides in vain. She loathes him—and
    doth yield.

Shame, sorrow, these be sire and dam of
    song.
    Fatality, O Nature, is thy name.
    Along the accursèd river, stagnant shame,
Eddying woe, from rape and godly wrong,
    Springs the immortal reed: the mortal's cry
Rises, an angry anthem, to the sky.

[1] Written on a visit to the late W. E. Henley
at Woking some three weeks before his death.
The influence of the man has perhaps overshadowed that of the bust of him by Rodin.

ICARE.[1]

ICARUS cries : " My love is robed in light
And splendour of the summits of the sun.
Wing, O my soul, thy plumed caparison
Through ninety million miles of space beyond
    sight !
Utmost imagination's eagle-flight
Out-soar ! " But he, by his own force un-
    done,
His peacock pinions molten one by one,
Falls to black earth through the impassive
    night.

Lo ! from uprushing earth arises love
Ardent and secret, scented with the night,
Amorous, ready. Sing the awakening bliss
That catches him, from the inane above
Hurled—nay, drawn down ! What utter-
    most delight
Dawns in that death ! Icarus and Gaia kiss.

LA FORTUNE.

"HAIL, Tyche ! From the Amalthean horn
Pour forth the store of love ! I lowly bend
Before thee : I invoke thee at the end
When other gods are fallen and put to scorn.
Thy foot is to my lips ; my sighs unborn
Rise, touch and curl about thy heart ; they
    spend
Pitiful love. Lovelier pity, descend
And bring me luck who am lonely and for-
    lorn."   •

Fortune sits idle on her throne. The scent
Of honeyed incense wreathes her lips with
    pleasure.
For pure delight of luxury she turns,
Smooth in her goddess rapture. So she
    spurns
And crushes the pale suppliant. Softly bent,
Her body laughs in ecstasy of leisure.

[1] Called " Fille d'Icare " by the distinguished
anatomists, priceless idiots, and pragmatical
precisians, who see nothing but a block of
marble in this most spiritual of Rodin's masterpieces.

PAOLO ET FRANCESCA

PAOLO ignites, Francesca is consumed.
Loosened she lies, and breathes great gasps
    of love ;
He, like an hunter, hungers, leaps above,
Attains, exults, despairs. This love is
    doomed,
Were there no hell. In granite walls en-
    tombed
Lies the true spirit and the soul thereof.
The body is here—yet is it not enough,
These litanies unchanted, unperfumed ?

Live in the shuddering marble they remain :
Here is the infinite credo of pure pain.
Here let life's agony take hold enough
Of all that lives : let partial tears for them
Wake knowledge, brain-dissolving diadem
Of white-hot woe upon the brows of love !

LES DEUX GENIES.

GOOD bends and breathes into the rosy
    shell
Of peace and perfume, love in idleness,
Of pure cold raptures, hymns the mystic
    stress,
Imagining's reiterate miracle.

Evil breathes, bending, the reverberate spell
Conjuring ghosts of the insane address
Of agony lurid in the damned caress,
Exulting tortures of the heart of hell.

The maiden sits and listens, smiles. Her
    breath
Is easy ; over her bowed head fall deep
Glowing cascades of hair ; she combs her
    hair

With subtle ecstasy, electric sweep
Of unimaginable joy ; let life and death
Pass : she will comb, and comb, and will
    not care.

LA CRUCHE CASSEE.

THE waterpot is broken at the well.
Forth rush the waters, bubbling from the
  brim,
Curling and coiling round the riven rim,
Lost beyond hope; and she, her sighs up-
  swell,
And sorrow shakes her: shame's oblivious
  hell
Burns round her body: in her eyes there
  swim
Tears of deep joy, deep anguish ; love's first
  hymn
Is choral in her ear's young miracle.

She knows the utmost now ; what waters
  white
She held from heaven's crystal fountains ;
  flight
Of what celestial birds struck down :—Ah me!
What god or demigod hath struck remorse
Into that close-crouched, cold, and desolate
  corse,
Wailing her violate virginity ?

LA TENTATION DE SAINT-
ANTOINE.

IN mystic dolour wrapt, the ascetic turns
His vague untutored thought to love, and sees
Himself exalted at the amber knees
Of God the Father : his bowed forehead burns
With chastity's white star: no spirit yearns
More keenly from the abyss ; yet, God ! are
  these
Subtle star-sparks of spirit chastity's ?
These deep-set shiverings saint nor sage
  discerns ?

Laughter and love are over him, entice
His life to sweeter scent of sacrifice.
She knows God's will, not he ! Her ardour
  licks
Flowers from the dust. O fool ! that, heavy
  of breath,
Dost rot in worship at the shrine of death !
O mystic rapture of the crucifix !

EVE.

THE serpent glimmered through the primal
  tree,
Full in the gladness of the afterglow ;
Its royal head warred ever to and fro,
Seeking the knowledge of the doom to be.
Eve, in the naked love and liberty
She had not bartered yet, moved sad and
  slow,
Serene toward the sunset, murmuring low
The tyrant's curse, the hideous decree.

Then she, instructed by the Saviour Snake,
Saw once clear Truth and gave her life, and
  love,
And peace, and favour of the fiend above,
For Knowledge, Knowledge pure for Know-
  ledge' sake.
The full moon rose. Creation's voice was
  dumb
For the first woman's shame, strength,
  martyrdom.

FEMMES DAMNEES.

KISS me, O sister, kiss me down to death !
The purple of the passionate hour is flaked
With notes of gold: there swim desires un-
  slaked,
Impossible raptures of expostulate breath.
The marble heaves with longing ; hungereth
The mouth half-open for the unawaked
Mouth of the baby blossom, where there
  ached
Never till now the parched sweet song that
  saith :

"Ah ! through the grace of languor and the
  glow
Of form steals sunset flaming on the snow !
Darkness shall follow as love wakeneth
In moonlight, and the flower, chaste love,
  now bloom
First in the bosom, after in the tomb—
Kiss me, O sister, kiss me down to death !"

NABUCHADNOSOR.

SENSELESS the eyes: the brow bereft of sense.
Hunger is on the throne of pride ; and naught
Fills the gray battlefield of ancient thought,
The market places of intelligence,
Save need and greed ; whose royal words
　　incense
The jealous God of Israel is distraught.
No jewels in the casket nobly wrought.
The shrine is grand ; the god is ravished
　　thence.

On clawing hands and hardened knees the
　　King
Exists, no more ; is it a little thing ?
King Demos, hear my parable ! We pass,
We poets, see you grovel at our feet,
Despise our love, and tender flesh, and
　　wheat,
Clamour for lust, and carrion, and grass.

MORT D'ADONIS.

ADONIS dies. (Imagination hears
The hoarse harsh breathing of the ill-nurtured
　　boar)
Venus bends low, half mother and half
　　whore,
Whole murderess of boy's budhood. Fall,
　　black fears !

Ay ! through her widowed, her unwedded
　　tears,
The foolish filial appeal, " Restore,
O Father Zeus, this tender life once more ! "
Falls the baulked hope of half a million years.

She in her gloom and ignorance will go
Forlorn to Paphos, wrapt in urgent woe,
Her hair funereal swathing her fallen form,
Its wind-swept horror holding him ; his white
Torn body blushing through tempestuous
　　night.
So breaks the life in hell, the year in storm.

BALZAC.

GIANT, with iron secrecies ennighted,
Cloaked, Balzac stands and sees. Immense
　　disdain,
Egyptian silence, mastery of pain,
Gargantuan laughter, shake or still the
　　ignited
Stature of the Master, vivid. Far, affrighted,
The stunned air shudders on the skin. In
　　vain
The Master of " La Comédie Humaine "
Shadows the deep-set eyes, genius-lighted.

Epithalamia, birth-songs, epitaphs,
Are written in the mystery of his lips.
Sad wisdom, scornful shame, grand agony
In the coffin-folds of the cloak, scarred
　　mountains, lie,
And pity hides i' th' heart. Grim knowledge
　　grips
The essential manhood. Balzac stands, and
　　laughs.

LE CYCLOPS SURPREND ACIS ET GALATHEE.

COILED in the hollow of the rock they kiss,
Rolled in one sphere of rapture ; looks
　　intense
With love, and laughter shapen of innocence !
They cling, and close, and overhang the
　　abyss.

But over them ! What monster, then, is this
Crouched for his spring, gross muscles nude
　　and tense,
Bulged eyeballs ready for the rape, immense
In hate, the imminent spectre ? He it is,

The Cyclops. Ay ! thought Zeus, and what
　　of that ?
Were it not well for love, in red rough maw
Swift crunched, to expiate my eldest law ?

Better, far better thus. True love lies flat,
A weary plain beyond the single peak.
I then will pity them. I will not speak.

OCTAVE MIRBEAU.

BRUTAL refinement of deep-seated vice
Carves the coarse features in a sentient
    mould.
The gardens,[1] that were soft with flowers
    and gold
And sickening with murder of lust to entice
The insane to filthier raptures, carrion spice
Of ordure for perfume, bloom there, fixed bold
By the calm of the Master, god-like to behold
The horror with firm chisel and glance of ice.

Ay! and the petty and the sordid soul,
A servile whore's deformed debauchery,[2]
Grins from the image. Let posterity
From Rodin's art guess Mirbeau's heart, extol
The lethal chamber men ere then will find
For the pimp's pen and the corrupted mind.

[1] Le jardin des supplices, par Octave
Mirbeau.
[2] Les mémoires d'une femme de chambre,
par Octave Mirbeau.

SOCRATE.

(L'HOMME AU NEZ CASSE.)

CONSUMMATE beauty built of ugliness,
O broken-nose philosopher, is thine.
Diamonds are deepest in the blue-mud mine ;
So is the secret of thy strong success
Dæmonic-glittering through the wear and
    stress
Of tortured feature ; virtue's soul doth shine,
Genius and wisdom in the force divine
That fills thy face ; magnificence ! no less.

Ay! thou shalt drink the hemlock; thou
    shalt suffer
And die for self-respect, for love of others!
To-day are men indissolubly brothers?
Is my life smoother than the Greek's or
    rougher?
The Greek at least shall stead me in my craft.
Crucify Crowley! Nay, my friends! the
    draught.

COLOPHON.

INCIDENT.

(RUE DE L'UNIVERSITE, 182.)

SPELL-BOUND we sat : the vivid violin
Wailed, pleaded, waited, triumphed. Kingly note
By note imperial from its passionate throat
Vibrates : the shadows fall like pauses in
The workshop of the Master : where there spin
Phrases in marble : fancies fall or float,
Passions exult, despairs abound, loves dote,
Thoughts gallop or abide : and prayer is sin.

Spell-bound we sat : one, young, eagerly moves.
One sits in thought : one listens, dreams, and loves.
One, critical, approves with conscious nod.
But I abode without the spell ; saw these—
Diverse harmonics of identical keys!—
And these were thus : but Rodin heard like God.

ORPHEUS

A LYRICAL LEGEND

[The allusions in this poem to classical legend or myth are too numerous to be dealt with by annotation. A good classical dictionary will enable the reader to trace all the allusions.]

CONTENTS.

BOOK II.

BOOK III

WARNING.

MAY I who know so bitterly the tedium of this truly dreadful poem be permitted to warn all but the strongest and most desperate natures from the task of reading or of attempting to read it? I have spent more than three years in fits of alternate enthusiasm for, and disgust of, it. My best friends have turned weeping away when I introduced its name into conversation; my most obsequious sycophants (including myself) were revolted when I approached the subject, even from afar.

I began Book I. in San Francisco one accursed day of May 1901. I was then a Qabalist, deeply involved in ceremonial magic, with a Pantheon of Egypto-Christian colour, in fact, the mere bouillon of which my "Tannhauser" was the froth. The idea was to do the "biggest thing ever done in lyrics." I bound myself by an oath to admit no rhyme unless three times repeated; to average some high percentage of double rhymes—in brief, to perform a gigantic juggle with the unhappy English language. The whole of this first book is technically an ode (! ! !) and was so designed. So colossal an example of human fatuity truly deserves, and shall have, a complete exposure.[1]

Book I. was finished in Hawaii, ere June expired, and Book II. begun.

I had just begun to study the Theosophic writings—their influence, though slight, is apparent. So intent was I on producing a

[1] *Vide* the Contents. Can the Spirit of Perversity attribute the unwieldiness of the structure to its formal symmetry and perfection?

big book that the whole of my "Argonauts" was written for the shadow-play by which Orpheus wins Eurydice to an interest in mortal joys and sorrows. Also—believe it !—I had proposed a similar play in Book III., to be called "Heracles" or "Theseus," by performance of which Persephone should be moved, or Hades overwhelmed.

But luckily I was myself overwhelmed first, and it never got a chance at Hades. Book II., then, and its Siamese twin, were written in Hawaii, Japan, China, Ceylon, and South India, where also I began Book III. That also I finished in the Burmese jungle and at Lamma Sayadaw Kyoung at Akyab.

During this period I was studying the Buddhist law ; and its influence on the philosophy of the poem is as apparent as that of Hinduism on Book II.

The summer of 1902 asked another kind of philosophy—the kind that goes with glacier travel in the Mustagh Tagh. Orpheus slept.

Book IV. was begun in Cairo on my way to England, and bears marks of confirmed Buddhism up to the death of Orpheus.

But the more I saw of Buddhism the less I liked it, and the first part of Book IV. is flatly contradicted by its climax.

This is a pitiable sort of confession for a man to make !

What was I to do ? I could not rewrite the whole in order to give it a philosophic unity. Gerald Kelly forcibly prevented me from throwing it into the river at Marlotte, though he admitted quite frankly that he could not read even through Book I. and did not see how any one could. Tell me, he said, conjuring the friendship of years, can *you* read it ? Even a poet should be honest ; I confessed that I could not !

Taking it in sections, with relays and an ambulance, we could see no fault in it, however. It is clumsily built ; it is all feet and face ; but you cannot make a Monster symmetrical by lopping at him.

Still, we cut down every possible excrescence, doctored up the remains so as to look as much like a book as possible (until it is examined), and are about to let it loose on society.

The remaining books all share this fatal lack of Architecture; but they are not so long ; there is some incident, though not much ; and they are proportionately less dull. Further, the scheme is no longer so ambitious, and the failure is therefore less glaring.

I might have done like Burton and his Kasidah, and kept the MS. for twenty years (if I live so long), ever revising it. But (*a*) I should certainly not live twenty years if I had the accursed manuscript in all sorts and sizes of type and colour of ink and pencil to stalk my footsteps, and (*b*) I am literally not the man who wrote it, and, and despise him as I may, I have no right to interfere with his work.

But I will not be haunted by the ghost of a Banquo that another man has failed to lay ; and this kind of ghost knows but one exorcism.

One should bury him decently in fine fat type, and erect nice boards over him, and collect the criticisms of an enlightened press, and inscribe them on the tomb.

Then he is buried beyond resurrection ; oblivion takes him, and he will never haunt the author or anybody else again.

Old Man of the Sea, these three years you have drummed your black misshapen heels upon me ; I have had no ease because of you ; I am bepissed and conskited of your beastliness ; and now you are drunk with the idea that you are finished and perfect, I shall roll you off and beat your brains out upon that hardest of flints, the head of the British Public. I am shut of thee. Allah forget thee in the day when he remembereth his friends !

August 14, 1904.

EXORDIUM.

FROM darkness of fugitive thought,
    From problems bewildering the brain,
Deep lights beyond heaven unsought,
    Dead faces seen dimly in rain ;
      From the depths of Mind's caverns,
        the fire
      Reclaims the old magical lyre ;
The ways of creation are nought,
If only, O mother, O Muse, I may measure
    Thy melodies in me again !

How wayward, how feeble the child
  Three watched from the stars at his birth;
Erato the fierce and the mild ;
  Polymnia grave ; and the girth
  Broad-girdled of gold and desire,
  Melpomene's terrible lyre,
That lifts up her life in the wild,
The star-piercing pæan, and floats in mid-
  ether, and sinks to the earth.

These three of the Muses were mine ;
  They nurtured and knew me and kissed.
Erato was hidden in wine ;
  Polymnia dawned in the mist :
  Melpomene shone in the pyre
  Of terrors that burned in her lyre ;
But all of their passion divine
I lost in the life and the stress of the world
  ere ever the soul of me wist.

But, Orpheus, thy splendider light
  Was the veil of thyself the more splendid.
Thou leapedst as a fountain in flight,
  As a bird in the rainbow descended !
  From the sweet single womb risen
    higher
  Did Calliope string thee her lyre,
Thy mother : and veiled her in night :—
For thyself to Herself art a veil till the veils
  of the Heaven be rended and ended.

Now, single myself as thy soul,
  I pray to Apollo indeed !
Fling forth to the starriest goal
  My spirit, invoking his rede ;[1]
  Care nought for his mercy or ire ;
  Reach impious hands to his lyre.
Determined to die or control
Those strings the immortal at last, though
  the strings of this heart of me bleed.

Come life, or come death ; come disdain
  Or honour from mutable men,
I cry in this passionate pain—
  My blood be poured out in the pen !
  Euterpe ! Espouse me ! inspire
  My life looking up to Thy lyre !
Of thy love, thine alone, am I fain !
Be with me, possess me, reveal me the
  melodies never yet given to men.

The starry and heavenly wheels,
  The earth and her glorious dye,
The light that the darkness reveals,
  The river, the sea, and the sky ;

  [1] Counsel.

All nature, or joyful or dire,
  Life, death, let them throng to the lyre,
  All sealed with the marvellous seals !
Let them live in my sob, let them love in my
  song, let them even be I !

Let me in most various song
  Be seasons, be rivers that roll,
  Be stars, the untameable throng,
  All parts of the ultimate whole ;
  All nature in various attire
  Be woven to one tune of the lyre,
  One tune where a million belong—
Multitudinous murmur and moan, melodious,
  one soul with my soul !

One soul with the wail of distress
  The ravished Persephone flung ;
One soul with the song of success,
  Demeter's, that found her and sung ;
  One soul with all spirits drawn nigher
  From invisible worlds to the lyre ;—
They throng me and silently press
The strings as I need them, and quicken
  my fingers and loosen my tongue !

And thou, O supreme, O Apollo !
  I have lived in Thy lands for a year,
Under skies, where the azure was hollow,
  The vault of black midnight was clear.
  Think ! I who have borne Thee, nor
    tire—
  May I not lift up on Thy lyre
Most reverent fingers, and follow
Thy path, take Thy reins, drive Thy chariot
  and horses of song without fear ?

Let the lightning be harnessed before me,
  The thunder be chained to my car,
The sea roll asunder that bore me,
  The sky peal my clarion of war !
  As a warrior's my chariot shall gyre !
  As a lord I will sharpen the lyre !
The stars and the moon shall adore me,
Not seeing mean me, but Thyself in the
  glory, the splendidest star.

Around me the planets shall thunder,
  And earth lift her voice to the sea ;
The moon shall be smitten with wonder,
  The starlight look love unto me.
  Comets, meteors, storms shall admire,
  Be mingled in tune to my lyre,
  The universe broken in sunder,—
And I—shall I burn, pass away ? Having
  been for a moment the shadow of Thee !

LIBER PRIMUS VEL CARMINUM

TO

OSCAR ECKENSTEIN,

WITH WHOM I HAVE WANDERED IN SO MANY SOLITUDES OF
NATURE, AND THEREBY LEARNT THE WORDS AND
SPELLS THAT BIND HER CHILDREN

Τάχα δ' ἐν ταῖς πολυδένδροισιν 'Ολύμπου
Θαλάμαις, ἔνθα ποτ' 'Ορφεὺς κιθαρίζων
ξύναγεν δένδρεα μούσαις, ξύναγεν Θῆρας ἀγρώτας.
—Βακχαι.

Orpheus with his lute made trees,
And the mountain tops that freeze
  Bow themselves when he did sing.
To his music plants and flowers
Ever sprung, as sun and showers
  There had made a lasting spring.

Everything that heard him play,
Even the billows of the sea,
  Hung their heads, and then lay by.
In sweet music is such art,
Killing care and grief of heart—
  Fall asleep, or hearing die.
—*Henry VIII.*

. . . vocalem temere insecutæ
  Orphea sylvæ,
Arte materna rapidos morantem
Fluminum lapsus, celeresque ventos,
Blandum et auritas fidibus canoris
  Ducere quercus.
—*Hor. Carm.*, Lib. I. xii.

INTRODUCTORY ODE.

CALLIOPE, ORPHEUS.

Str. a.

CALLIOPE.

IN the days of the spring of my being,
  When maidenly bent I above
The head of the poet, and, seeing
  Not love, was the lyre of his love ;
When laurels I bore to the harper,
  When bays for the lyrist I bore,
My life was diviner and sharper,
  My name in the Muses was more ;

When virgin I came to him stainless,
When love was a pleasure and painless !
  What Destiny dreams and discovers
  The fragrance men know for a lover's ?
Peace turned into laughter and tears,
Borne down the cold stream of the years !

Ant. a.

ORPHEUS.

O mother, O queen many-minded,
  More beauty than beauty may be,
More light than the Sun ; I am blinded,
  Sink, tremble, am lost in the sea.

The voice of thy singing descended,
  Rolled round me and wrapped me in mist,
Some sense of thy being, borne splendid ;
  I dreamed, I desired, I was kissed.
Some breath from thy music hath bound me ;
Some tune from thy lyre hath found me.
  Thy words are as rushing of fire ;
  But I know not the lilt of thy lyre :—
Thy voice is as deep as the sea ;
Thy music is darkness to me.

Str. β.

CALLIOPE.

Child of Thracian sire, on me begotten,
  Knowest thou not the laughter and the life ?
Knowest thou not how all things are for-
    gotten,
  Being with a maiden wife ?
How a subtle sense of inmost being
  Wraps thee in, and cuts the world away ;
Sight and sound lose hearing and lose seeing,
  All the night is one with all the day ?
Hearken to her sighing !
Life droops down as dying,
  Melting in the clasp of amorous limbs and
    hair ;
All the darkening world
Round about ye furled—
  Dost thou know, or, knowing, dost thou
    care ?

Ant. β.

ORPHEUS.

Mother, I have lain, half dead, half slumber-
    ing,
  Curtained in Eurydice her hair ;
Clothed in serpent kisses, souls outnumbering
  Dewdrops flung in spray through air.
I have lain and watched the night diminish,
  Fade and fall into the arms of day,
Caring not if earth itself should finish,
  Caring only if my lover stay ;
Listening to her breathing,
Laughing, lover-weaving
  All the silken gold and glory of her head,

Kissing as if time
Forgot its steeps to climb,
  Made eternity's, one with all the dead.

Str. γ.

CALLIOPE.

Listen, then listen, O Thracian !
  Oeager lay on the lea :
I, from my heavenly station ;
I, from my house of creation,
  Stooped, as a mortal to be
Passionate, mother and bride ;
Flashed on wide wing to his side,
  Caught him and drew him to me.
Kisses not mortal I lavished ;
Out of the life of him ravished
  Life for the making of thee.
Son, did I lose in the deed ?
Son, did the breasts of me bleed,
  Bleed for pure love ? Did I see
Zeus with his face through the thunder
Frowning with fury and wonder ?
  Love in Olympus is free—
I have created a god, not a mortal of mortal
  degree.

Ant. γ.

ORPHEUS.

Hear me, O mother, descended
  To earth, from the sisterly shrine !
Hear me, a mortal unfriended,
  Save thou, in thy purity splendid
    Indwell me, invoke the divine !
As sunlight enkindles the ocean,
As moonlight shakes earth with emotion,
  As starlight shoots trembling in wine,
So be thy soul for a man !
Teach my young fingers to span
  That musical lyre of thine !
Passion and music and peace,
Teach me the singing of these !
  Teach me the tune of the vine !
Teach me the stars to resemble,
As tide-stricken sea-cliffs to tremble
  Thy strings, as the wind-shaken pine !
Let these and their fruits and the soul of
  their being be mine, very mine !

EPODE

CALLIOPE

As the tides invisible of ocean,
    Sweeping under the dark star-gemmed sea ;
As the frail Caduceus' serpent-motion
    Moves the deep waves of eternity ;
As the star-space lingers and moves on ;
As the comet flashes and is gone ;
As the light, the music, and the thunder
    Of moving worlds retire ;
As the hoarse sounds of the heaven wonder
    When Zeus flings forth his fire ;
As the clang of swords in battle ;
As the low of home-driven cattle ;
As the wail of mothers children-losing ;
    As the clamorous cries of darkening death ;
As the joy-gasp of love's chosen choosing ;
    As the babe's first voluntary breath ;
As the storm and tempest fallen at even ;
As the crack and hissing of the levin ;
As the soft sough of tree-boughs wind-shaken ;
    As the fearful cry of souls in hell,
When past death and blinder life they waken,
    Seeing Styx before their vision swell,
When the bands of earth are broken
As the spirit's spell is spoken
On the vast and barren places
    Where the unburied wander still ;
As the laughter of young faces ;
As the Word that is the will ;
As the life of wells and fountains,
    Of the old deep-seated mountains ;
As the forest's desolate sighing ;
    As the moaning of the earth
Where her seeds are black and dying ;
    As the earthquake's sudden birth ;
As the vast volcano rending
Its own breasts ; as music blending
With young maiden's loving laughter,
    With the joy of fatherhood,
With the cry of Mænads after
    Sacrifice by well or wood ;
As the grave religious throng
Moving silently along,
Leading heifers, snowy-footed,
    Into glades and sacred groves,

Where the altar-stone is suited
    To commemorate the Loves ;
As the choir's most seemly chanting ;
As the women's whispers haunting
Silent woods, or chaster spaces,
    Where the river's water wends ;
As the sound, when the white faces
    Burn from space, and all earth end.
In the presence of the Gods ;
These and all their periods ;
These, and all that of them is,
    I bestow on thee, and this
Also, mine eternal kiss !
In one melody of bliss
These and thou and I will mingle,
Till all Nature's pulses tingle,
Hear and follow and obey thee,
    Thee, the lyrist ; thee, the lyre !
These shall hear and not gainsay thee,
    Follow in the extreme desire,
Mingling, tingling, mixed with thee
Even to all Eternity.
These, and all that of them is,
Take from Calliope in this
Single-hearted, many mouthèd, kiss.

ORPHEUS, SEATED UPON OLYMPUS, TUNES HIS LYRE.

ORPHEUS.

First word of my song,
    First tune of my lyre,
Muse, loved of me long,
    Be near and inspire !
    Bright heart ! Mother strong !
    Sweet sense of desire !
Be near as I lift the first notes impassioned
    of fervour and fire !

    Not ever before
    Since Nature began
Hath one cloven her core,
    Found the soul of her span ;
    No son that she bore
    Her spirit might scan ;
But I, being born beyond Nature, have known
    her and yet am a man.

Ye fieriest flowers,
Life-stream of the world,
In passionate bowers
Of mystery curled,
Come forth ! for the powers
Of my crying are hurled :—
Come forth ! O ye souls of the fire, where
the sound of my singing is whirled !

Ye blossoms of lightning,
Bare boughs of the tree
Of life, where the brightening
Abysses of sea
Reveal ye, the whitening
Swords kindled of me.
Come forth ! I invoke thee, O lightning, the
flames of the Gods flung free !

THE LIGHTNING.

The wand of Hermes, the caduceus
wonder-working,
Sweeps in mid-æther—
Where we are lurking
It finds us and gathers.
By our mother the amber
In her glorious chamber ;
By the flames that enwreathe her ;
By the tombs of our fathers ;
Awake ! let us fly, the compeller is nigh.
Strike ! let us die !

ORPHEUS.

Ye powers volcanic,
Cyclopean forces,
Workers Titanic,
I know your courses.
By fury and panic,
By Dis and his horses,
Come forth ! I invoke ye, volcanoes, arise
from your cavernous sources !

THE VOLCANOES.

The Hephæstian hammer on the anvil
of hell,
In the hollows accurst,
Falls for the knell
Of the children of earth.

By the strength of our fires,
The fierce force of our sires,
Let us roar, let us burst !
By the wrath of our birth,
Up ! and boil over in rivers of lava !
Uncover ! Uncover !

ORPHEUS.

Lift up thine amber
Lithe limber limbs,
Lissome that clamber
Like god-reaching hymns ;
The flame in its chamber
Of glory that swims,
The spirit and shape of the fire, mine eyes
with fine dew that bedims !

Exempt from the bond
All others that binds,
As a flowery frond
The spark of thee blinds,
Within and beyond
As a thought of the mind's
In all, and about, and above ! I invoke thee,
my word as the wind's.

THE FIRE.

I, raging and lowering,
I, flying and cowering,
I, weaving and woven,
Budding and flowering,
Spiring and showering,
Cleaving and cloven !
My being encloses
Fountains of roses,
Lilies, and light !
I wrap and I sunder !
I am lightning and thunder !
The world-souls wonder
At me and my might !

All-piercing, all-winding,
All-moving, all-blinding,
All shaken in my hissing ;
My life's light finding
All spirits, and binding
Their love with my kissing ;

Ruthless, fearless,
Imperial, peerless,
  Creep I or climb.
Nought withstands me,
Bursts me or brands me ;
Nor Heaven commands me,
  Nor Space, nor Time.

Above, the supernal !
Below, the infernal !
  Of all am I master.
On Earth, the diurnal !
In all things eternal !
  Life, love, or disaster !
Abiding unshaken,
I sleep and I waken
  On wonderful wings ;
In depth and in height,
In darkness and light,
In weakness and might,
In blindness and sight,
In mercy and spite,
In day and in night,
Averse or aright,
For dule or delight,
  I am master of things.

ORPHEUS.

O mother, I fear me !
  The might of the lyre !
They tremble to hear me,
  The powers of the fire.
Come near me to cheer me !
  Be near and inspire !
Be strength in my heart and good courage,
  and speed in the single desire !

The fire knows its master !
  They flicker and flare,
Dread dogs of disaster,
  Wild slaves of despair.
Faster and faster—
  My soul is aware
Of a sound that is dimmer and duller, wide
  wings adrift of the air.

Their forces that wander
  No God-voice know they !
Their bridals they squander !
  Unknown is their way !
The sky's heart ? beyond her
  Sweet bosom they stray.
Shall these then obey me and hear ?   Shall
  the tameless ones hear and obey ?

From secretest places
  Whence darkness is drawn,
Where terrible faces
  Enkindle the dawn,
From wordless wide spaces,
  The ultimate lawn,
Come forth ! I invoke thee, O wind, come
  forth to me fleet as a fawn.

THE WINDS.

From fourfold quarters,
  The depth and the height,
We come, the bright daughters
  Of day shed on night ;
The sun and the waters
  Have brought us to light ;
The sound of him slaughters
  Our soul in his sight.
We hear the loud murmur ; we know him ;
  we rest ;
    We breathe in his breast.

ORPHEUS.

By sunlight up-gathered
  As dust of his cars,
By moonlight unfathered,
  Unmothered of stars,
Unpastured, untethered,
  Unstricken of scars,
Come forth ! I invoke ye, O clouds ! ye
  veils ! ye divine avatars !

THE CLOUDS.

Sun's spirit is calling !
  We gather together,
White wreaths, as appalling
  Pale ghosts of dead weather,

The veil of us falling
On snow-height and heather,
Or hovering and scrawling
Strange signs in the æther.
We hear the still voice, and we know him
we come !
We are sightless and dumb.

ORPHEUS.

More frail than your friends,
The clouds borne above,
The light of thee blends
With the moon and her love.
Thy spirit descends
As a white-throated dove.
Come forth ! I invoke thee, O mist, and
make me a sharer thereof !

THE MIST.

From valleys of violet
My shadow hath kissed,
From low-lying islet,
A vision of mist,
The voice of my pilot
Steals soft to insist.
O azure of sky, let
Me pass to the tryst !
I hear the low voice of my love ; and I rest
A maid on his breast.

ORPHEUS.

Thou child of soft wind
And the luminous air,
Thou, stealing behind
As a ghost, as a rare
Soft dew, as a blind
Fierce lion from his lair,
Come forth ! I invoke thee, O rain, look
forth with thy countenance fair !

THE RAIN.

From highland far drifted,
From river-fed lawn,
From clouds thunder-rifted,
I leap as a fawn.

The voice is uplifted,
The lord of my dawn ;
My spirit is shifted,
My love is withdrawn.
I hear the sweet feet of my God ; I know
him ; I fall
In tears at his call.

ORPHEUS.

Cold lips and chaste eyes
Of frost-fall that leap,
That shake from the skies
On the earth in her sleep
Kiss nuptial, arise
As the lyre-strings sweep !
Come forth ! I invoke thee, O frost, the
valleys await thee and weep.

THE FROST.

So silent and wise
In her cerement clothes,
So secretly lies
My soul in my snows ;
I awake, I arise,
For my spirit now knows
The first time in her eyes
That a voice may unclose
My petals : I hear it ; I come ; I clasp the
warm ground
In my passion profound.

ORPHEUS.

In valleys heaped high,
In drifts lying low,
Swift slopes to the sky,
Come forth to me, snow !
Thy beauty and I
Are of old even so
As lover and lover. Come forth ! I invoke
thee ! the hills are aglow.

THE SNOW.

Bright breasts I uncover,
Heart's heart to thy gaze ;
O lyre of my lover,
I know thee, thy praise.

Black heavens that hover,
Blind air that obeys,
I come to thee over
The mountainous ways
As a bride to the bridegroom : I blush, but
I come
And bow to thee dumb.

ORPHEUS.

O blacker than hell,
O bluer than heaven,
O green as the dell
Lit of sunlight at even !
O strong as a spell !
O bright as the levin !
Come forth ! I invoke thee, O ice, by their
anguish, the rocks thou hast riven !

THE ICE.

My steep-lying masses,
Mine innermost sheen,
My soundless crevasses,
My rivers unseen,
My glow that surpasses
In azure and green
The rocks and the grasses.
Above, I am queen.
These know thee ; I know thee, O master,
I hear and obey.
I follow thy lyrical sway.

ORPHEUS.

O tenderest child
And phantom of day !
Gleam fitful and wild
On the flowery way !
Blue skies reconciled
To the kisses of clay !
Come forth ! I invoke thee, O dew ! The
maiden must hear and obey.

THE DEW.

Life trembling on leaves,
Sunrise shed in tears,
Love's arrow that cleaves
The veil of the years,

Light gathered in sheaves
Of tenderest fears
As dayspring enweaves
My soul into spheres—
I hear, and I nestle upon thee, O lyrist
supreme,
Light loves in a dream.

ORPHEUS.

Child of sweet rain,
O fathered of frost !
Bitterest pain
The birth of thee cost.
Passion is slain
When wished of thee most.
Come forth ! I invoke thee, O hail, thou lord
of a terrible host !

THE HAIL.

My father was glad of me
In places unseen ;
My mother was sad of me,
Where wind came between ;
Winter is mad of me,
Earth is my queen ;
Meadows are clad of me,
Nestled in green.
As pearls in the cloudland I slept ; but I hear
the loud call ;
I obey it and fall !

ORPHEUS.

Rain's guerdon and daughter
By sunlight's spies
Divided in water,
O light-stream, arise !
Seven petals that slaughter
The menace of Dis,
Come forth ! I invoke thee, O rainbow ! thou
maid of the myriad eyes !

THE RAINBOW.

In multiple measure
The flowers of us fold
The scarlet and azure
And olive and gold,

Hyperion his treasure
Of light that is rolled
In music and pleasure
Unheard and untold.
We are kisses of light and of tears, love's
triumph on fear.
We obey : I am here !

ORPHEUS.

Dim lights shed around me
In many a form
Like lovers surround me :—
O tender and warm !
They hunt me, they hound me ;
They struggle and swarm—
Come forth ! I invoke ye united, the mani-
fold shape of the storm !

THE TEMPEST.

Wide-winged, many-throated,
Colossal, sublime,
I come and am coated
With feathers of Time.
I hear the deep note, head
My pinions to climb,
The roar of devoted
Large limbs of the mime
That mocks the loud lords of Olympus ; we
mingle ; I wake.
I come with the sound of a snake.

ORPHEUS.

O storm many-winded,
O life of the air,
Thou angry and blinded
Hast sky for thy share.
O mother deep-minded,
My lyre to my prayer
Responds, and the elements answer or ever
my soul is aware.

Ye powers of deep water
And sea-running bays,
Earth's fugitive daughter
In deep-riven ways,

Enamoured of slaughter,
A mirage of grays,
Deep blues, and pale greens unbegotten, I
turn to your lyrical praise.

I tune the loud lyre
To the haunts of the vale
As a sea-piercing fire
On the wings of the gale.
I lift my desire,
I madden, I wail !
Come forth ! I invoke ye, O powers, in the
waters that purple and pale.

Come forth in your pleasure,
O fountains and springs !
Come dance me a measure
Unholpen of wings !
Show, show the deep treasure,
Unspeakable things !
Come forth ! I invoke ye, O fountains, I
· sweep the invincible strings.

THE FOUNTAINS.

In the heather deeply hidden,
From the caverns darkly drawn,
In the woodlands man-forbidden,
In the gateways of the dawn,
In the glad sweet glades descended,
On the stark hills gathered high,
Where the snows and trees are blended,
Kissed at birth by sun and sky ;
We have heard the summons : we are open
to the day-spring's eye.

ORPHEUS.

O broad-bosomed lakes
Whence the mist-tears uprise,
That shed in sweet flakes
The gleam of the skies,
Whose countenance takes
The bird as he flies
In kisses, come forth ! I invoke ye, O lakes,
where the love of me lies !

THE LAKES.

In the hollow of the mountain,
    In the bosom of the plain,
Fed by river, stream, and fountain,
    Slain by sun, reborn of rain ;
In the desert green-engirded,
    Lying lone in waste and wood,
To my breast the many-herded
    Lowing kine in gracious mood
Come, drink deeply, and are glad of me, my
    pleasant solitude.

ORPHEUS.

From the breast of the snow
    As a life-swollen stream,
Your love-rivers flow
    Soft hued as a dream,
Adrift and aglow
    With the sunlight supreme.
Come forth ! I invoke ye, O torrents that fall
    in the mazes and gleam !

THE MOUNTAIN TORRENTS.

Falling fast or lingering love-wise,
    Gathered into mirror-lakes,
Floating sprayed through heaven dove-
        wise,
    Dreaming, dashing ; sunlight shakes
Into million-coloured petals
    All our limpid drops, and wraps
Earth with green, as water settles
    On the rocks and in their gaps,
Mossy rainbow-tinted maidens, flowers and
    fernshoots in their laps.

ORPHEUS.

Low down in the hollows
    And vales of the earth,
What eagle-sight follows
    Your length and green girth ?
Your light is Apollo's,
    Diana's your mirth !
Come forth ! I invoke ye, O rivers, I have
    watched your mysterious birth !

THE RIVERS.

In the lowland gently swelling,
    Born and risen out of rain,
Wide the curves and arrowy dwelling
    Where we rest or roll again.
There our calm sides shield the mortal,
    Bears his bark our breast, and we
Follow to the mystic portal
    Where we mingle with the sea.
Every life of earth we list to : should not we
    then answer thee ?

ORPHEUS.

O see mixt with æther
    In whirls that awake,
Roar skywards and wreathe her
    Bright coils as a snake,
In agony seethe her
    Sad cries for the sake
Of peace—I invoke ye ! Come forth ! O
    spouts in the wave's wild wake !

THE WATERSPOUTS.

Whirling over miles of ocean,
    Lowering o'er the solemn sea,
Hears our life the deep commotion
    That we know—thy witchery.
Wheeling, hating, fearing ever
    As we thunder o'er the deep,
Death alone our path can sever,
    Death our guerdon if we weep.
We obey thee, we are with thee ! Wilt thou
    never let us sleep ?

ORPHEUS.

O rolled on the river
    By might of the moon,
Ye tremble and quiver,
    Ye shudder and swoon !
The cities ye shiver :
    The ships know your tune.
Come forth ! I invoke ye, O eagres ! dread
    rivals of shoal and typhoon !

The Eagre.

Flings my single billow spuming
Into midmost air the world,
As the echo of my booming
To the furthest star is hurled.
Now I hear the lunar clashing
That evokes me from the tide,
Now I rise, my fury lashing,
Rolling where the banks divide—
I obey thee, I am with thee, Lord of Light-
ning, lotus-eyed !

Orpheus.

In sacred grove,
In silent wood,
In calm alcove,
In mirrored mood,
What light of love
Your depth endued ?
Come forth ! I invoke ye, O wells, ye
dwellers of dim solitude !

The Wells.

Deep and calm to heaven's mirror
Through the cedarn grove or ashen,
Willow-woven, or cypress terror,
To the sky's less serene fashion
Still we look : around our margin
Holy priestess, longing lover,
Poet musing, vagrant virgin,
Nor their own mild looks discover,
But the light and glow of that they are
meditating over.

Orpheus.

O curves unbeholden,
Bright glory of bays !
Deep gulfs grown golden
With dawn and its ways !
With sunset enfolden
In silvery praise !
Come forth ! I invoke ye, O gulfs, where
the sea is as children, and plays.

The Bays.

Where the hills reach to heaven behind us
A voice is rolled over the steep,
Some godhead whose glory would bind us,
Reflected far-off on the deep.
We hear the low chant that may blind us,
The song from the ultimate shore.
We come that our lover may find us
His bride as he found us before.
We listen, and love ; and his voice is the
voice of the God we adore.

Orpheus.

Come forth in your gladness,
O end of all these !
O sorrow and madness
And passion and ease,
Sharp joy and sweet sadness,
Deep life and deep peace !
Come forth ! I invoke you, ringed round
earth's girdle, the manifold seas !

The Sea.

I hear but one voice in our voices ;
One tune, multitudinous notes ;
One life that burns low or rejoices,
One song from the numberless throats.
Where ice on my bosom is piled,
Where palm-fronded islands begem
My breast, where I rage in the wild
White storms, where I lap the low
hem
Of earth's mantle, or war on her crags, I am
one, and my soul is in them.

I am mother of earth and her daughter ;
I am father of heaven and his son ;
I am fire in the palace of water ;
I am God, and my glory is one !
I am bride of the sun and the starlight ;
The moonlight is bride unto me ;
I am lit of my deeps with a far light,
My heart and its flame flung free.
I am She, the beginning and end ; I am all,
and my name is the Sea !

ORPHEUS.

Then thou, O my mother,
　　Hast given to me
The power of another,
　　The watery key.
Bright air is my brother,
　　My sister the sea ;
I have called, and they answer and come ;
　and their song is but glory to thee.

One other is left me,
　　The light of the earth.
If Fate had bereft me,
　　Oh Muse, of thy birth,
Still I had cleft me
　　A way in her girth !
I tune the loud lyre once again to the mother
　of men in her mirth.

O mighty and glad
　　In spring-time and summer !
O tearful and sad
　　When the sun is grown dumber,
　　When the season is mad,
And the gods overcome her,
When the sky is fulfilled of the frost and the
　fingers of winter numb her !

O marvellous earth
　　Of multiple mood
That givest men birth
　　And delicate food,
Red wine to make mirth
　　Of thine own red blood,
And corn and green grass and sweet flowers
　and fruits most heavenly-hued !

Borne skyward in swoon
　　By arrowy hours,
Girt round of the moon
　　And the girdling flowers,
The sun for a boon,
　　Sweet kisses of showers,
O mother, O life, O desire, my soul is a
　bird in thy bowers !

My soul is caught up
　　In thy green-hearted waves.
I drink at the cup
　　Of thy sweet valley graves.
My spirit may sup
　　Slow tunes in thy caves.
O hide me, thy child, in thy bosom, that the
　heart in me yearns to and craves.

Most virginally sprung
　　In the shadow of light,
Eternally young,
　　A magical sight,
Wandering among
　　Day, twilight, and night,
As a bride in her chamber that dreams many
　visions of varied delight.

O how shall my lyre
　　Divide thee, dispart
Thy water and fire,
　　Thy soul and thy heart,
Thy hills that spring higher,
　　Thy flowers that upstart,
How quire thee, my limitless love, with a
　lewd and a limited art ?

A fortress, a sphere,
　　An arrow of flame ;
Let thy children appear
　　At the sound of thy name !
In my silence uprear
　　The sweet guerdon of shame !
Be they choral to hymn thee, O mother, thy
　magic ineffable fame !

Last birth of the Sun,
　　Best gift of the giver,
Thou surely art One !
　　As the moon on the river,
Whose star-blossoms run,
　　Kiss, tremble, and shiver,
And roll into ultimate space, and are lost to
　man's vision for ever.

Come forth to the sound
Of the lightning lyre,
Ye valleys profound
As a man's desire,
Ye woodlands bound
In the hills that are higher
Than even the note of a bird as it wings to
the solar fire !

Ye fruits and corn,
Gold, rose, and green,
Vines purple-born,
Pearl-hidden sheen,
Trees waving in scorn
Of the grass between !
Come forth in your chorus, and chant the
praise of your mother and queen !

Ye trees many-fronded
That shake to the wind,
Green leaves that have sounded
My harp in your kind,
Light boughs that are rounded,
Grey tops that are shrined
In the tears of the heaven as they fall in the
blackening storm grown blind !

Ye fields that are flowered
In purple and white,
Embossed and embowered
By the love of the light,
Gold-sandalled and showered,
Dew-kissed of the night,
Your song is too faint and too joyous for
mortals to hear it aright.

Blue pansies, and roses,
And poppies of red,
Pale violets in posies
Where Hyacinth bled,
The flower that closes
Its dolorous head ;—
What song may be sung, or what tune may
be told, or what word may be said ?

All tropical scent,
Blossom-kindled perfume
Love-colours new-lent
By the infinite womb,
Gold subtlety blent
With the scarlet bloom ;—
Shall ye in my melody live ?   Shall my song
be not rather your tomb ?

Most musical moves
The head of the corn ;
Strong glorious loves
Of its being are born.
Dim shadows of groves
Of Demeter adorn
The waves and the woods of the earth, the
heart of the mother forlorn.

Caves curved of the wind,
Deep hollows of earth,
Whence the song of the blind
Old prophet had birth,
The caves that confined
Deep music of mirth,
Thy caves, O my mother, are these not a
gem in thy virginal girth ?

Ye mountains uplift
As an arrow in air ;
Ice-crowned, rock-cliffed,
Snow-bosomed bare,
I give ye the gift
Of a voice more fair.
Leave echo, and wake, and proclaim that ye
stand against death and despair !

Ye hills where I rested
In rapture of life,
From dawn calm-breasted
To evening's strife,
Where skies were nested
With mist for a wife !
Leave echo, and speak for yourselves : let
your song pierce the heaven as a knife !

Olympus alone
  Of earth's glories is taken
For deity's throne
  Deep-frozen, storm-shaken.
What glories are shown
  When their slumbers awaken !
The avalanche thunders adown, and the gods
  of the gods are forsaken.

  To mortals your voices
    Are mighty and glad.
  The maiden rejoices:
    The man is grown mad
  For love, and his choice is
    The choice of a lad
When a virgin first smiles on his suit, and
  the summer for envy is sad.

  Wan grows Aphrodite,
    And Artemis frail ;
  Apollo less mighty,
    Red Bacchus too pale.
  Dark Hades grows bright, he
    Alone may avail
When the god and the mortal are one, as the
  mountain is one with the gale.

THE CHILDREN OF EARTH.

Our hair deep laden with the scent of earth,
The colour of her rosy body's birth,
  Our mother, lady and life of all that is
    divine ;
We gather to the sombre sound, as spring
Had whispered, " Follow," hiding in her
    wing
  Her glorious head and flowing breast of
    wine.
Though in the hollow of her heart be set
So deep and awful a fire, though the net
  Of all her robes be frail as we are fine,
We gather, listening to the living lyre
Like falling water shot with amber fire,
And blown aloft by winds even to heaven's
  desire.

Deep starry gems set in a silver sea,
Sullen low voices of dark minstrelsy,
  Light whispers of strange loves, of silver
    woven,
Dumb kisses and wild laughter following :
All these as lives of autumn and of spring
  We are : we follow across the rainbow
    cloven,
A never-fading path of golden glory,
Whereof the lone Leucadian promontory
  Holds one divinest gate : the other troven
Far, far beyond in interlunar skies,
Where the Himâlayas stir them, and arise
To listen to the song that swells our arteries.

O moving labyrinth sun-crowned, dread maze
Of starry paths, of Zeus-untrodden ways,
  Of mystic vales unfooted of the deep,
Our mother, virgin yet in many places
Unseen of man, beholden of the faces
  Only of elemental shapes of sleep
That are ourselves, her daughters wild and fair
Caught nymphwise in the kisses of the air,
  That flings our songs reverberate from
    steep to steep,
Songs caught in solar light, we are shed
Even down beyond the valleys of the dead,
And smiled upon in groves ruled by the holy
  head.

Great Pan hath heard us, children of his
    wooing,
Great Pan, that listens to the forest, suing
  Vainly His peace that dwells even in the
    desolate halls.
The delicately-chiselled flowers nod,
Look to the skies, and see thee for a God,
  O sightless lyre that wails, O viewless voice
    that calls !
Thy sound is in our death and in her womb,
Far in Spring's milky breast, in Autumn's
    gloom,
  In Summer's feast and song, in Winter's
    funerals.
In the dead hollow of the hills there rings,
Sharp song, like frost hissing on silver wings,
Or like the swelling tune we listen to for
  Spring's.

We come, we mountains, crowned and incense-bringing,
Robed as white priests, the solemn anthem singing ;
  Or as an organ thundering fiery tunes.
We come, we greener hills, and rend the sky,
With happier chorus and the songs that die
  Or mix their subtle joy and being with the moon's.
We come, we pine-clad steeps, we feathery slopes,
With footfalls softer than tne antelope's.
  We listen and obey : the sacred slumberer swoons
More tranced than death in this far following,
Careless of winter, not invoking spring ;
And all the witless woods company us and sing.

But not the glades by song of thee unstricken ?
Not they ? Shall they refuse the pulse to quicken,
  Soft smiting the low melody of light ?
Tuned without fingers, the wild woods lift high
The wordless chant, the murmurous melody,
  The song that dwells like moon-enkindled night.
We draw from low palm groves and cedar hills,
From stern grey slumbers, for thy music fills
  All earth with unimaginable delight.
Have we not brought the leaves dew-diamonded,
The buds fresh-gleaming, star-blossoms, and shed
  Our scent and colour and song around thy sacred head ?

We that are flowers are kindled in thy praise,
Even as thy song shed lustre and swift rays,
  Darting to brighten and open the folded flowers.
The violet lifts its head, the lily lightens,
The daisy shakes its dew, the pansy brightens,
  All cups of molten light upon the twilight hours.

The poppy flames anew, the buttercup
Glows with fresh fire, the larkspur rouses up
  To be the lark indeed amid the azalea bowers.
Magnolia and light blooms of roses mute
Rouse them to gather in one golden lute
  In fairy light and song into the sky to shoot.

The laughing companies of corn awaken,
Their wind-swept waves by Dædal music taken
  Into a golden heaven of festal song.
We shake and glisten in the sun, we see
The very soul and majesty of thee
  Thrill in the lyre and leave the lazy long
Notes for crisp magic of sharp rustling sound,
And thy life quickens and thy loves abound,
  Listening the answer of our dancing throng.
Joy, sleep, peace, laughter, thought, remembrance, came
  Even at our prelude, a death-quickening flame,
And earth rejoiced throughout to hear Demeter's name.

We come, in bass deep-swelling, rocks and caves,
A hollow roar across the golden waves
  Hidden in islands set deep in the untravelled sea.
Across the corn from storm-cleft mountain-sides
Our voice peals, like the thunder of the tides,
  Into the darkling hills that fringe Eternity.
Dire and divine our womb unfruitful bears
Deep music darker than tempestuous airs
  When Heaven's anger wakes : when at our own decree,
With clanging rocks sky-piercing for our tomb,
We call the thunder from our own black womb,
  We hear the voice and we obey—we know not whom !

We hear thee, who are cliffs and pinnacles
Higher than heaven's base, founded far in hell's ;
  We hear, that sunder the blue skies of heaven ;

Our voiceless clefts and spires of delicate hue,
Changing and lost in the exultant blue,
  By fire and whirlwind fashioned and then
    riven,
Invoke fresh song, with deep solemnity
In noble notes of mastery answering thee,
  By some young tumult in our old hearts
    driven ;
And this immortal path of splintered rock
Shall lead the wild chant to the sky, and
    mock
The nectared feast of Gods with its im-
passioned shock.

Deep-mouthed, I, earthquake, wake in
    echoing thunder.
I break my mother's breast ; I tear asunder
  The womb that bore me ; I arise in terror,
Threatening to ruin her, crag, crown, and
    column,
Reverberate music of that mighty and solemn
  Call of creation, Vulcan's awful mirror.
I rend the sky with clamour terrible,
Shaking the thrones of earth and heaven and
    hell,
  Confound the universe in universal error.
I sound the awful note that summons
    mortals,
As I awake, to pass the dreadful portals
And face the gloom of Dis, the unnameable
    immortals.

Soft our mild music steals through thunder-
    ous pauses,
A phrase made magic by the Second Causes,
  The mighty Ones that dwell beneath the
    empyreàn.
We, vines and fruits and trees with autumn
    laden,
Sing as the bride-song of a married maiden
Before the god-like vigour of the man
Breaks the frail temple-doors of love asunder,
And wakes the new life's promise in pale
    wonder,
  Shattering the moulded glass, the shape
    Selenian.
Fruits of the earth, our low song joins the
    crowd.

We need not (to be heard) to thunder loud.
Our hearts are lifted up, our heads with love
    low bowed.

The tenderest light, the deepest hidden, is
    shed
Up through dark earth—your home, O happy
    dead !—
  Crusted in darkness lie the secret lights.
Formed in the agony of earth as tears,
Clothed in the crystal mirror of the years,
  We dwell, sweet-hearted nun-like eremites !
Diamond and ruby, topaz and sapphire,
Emerald and amethyst, one clear bright fire,
  We are earth's stars below, as she above
    hath Night's.
Our sweet clean song pierces the cover,
And thin keen notes of music flit and hover
Like spirit-birds upon the lyre of this our
    lover.

We, children of the mountains, lying low
On earth's own bosom, deep, embowered,
    flow
  In wide soft waves of land : upon us sweep
The mightiest rivers : in our hollows lie
Great lakes : our voices hardly rise, but die
  In the cold streams of air : shallow and
    deep :
Leagues by the thousand, dells a minute
    long ;
All we are children of the mighty throng
  That cluster where the mountains fail, and
    sleep
In such cool peace that even thy lyre awakes
Hardly a soul that tenderer music makes.
Yet we arise and listen for our own sweet
    sakes.

THE LIVING CREATURES OF THE EARTH.

  The heavy hand is held,
    And the whips leave weary blows.
  The mysteries of eld
  Are cancelled and expelled,
    And the miserable throes.

All we are shapen fair
In many forms of grace,
But change is everywhere,
And time is all our share
And all the ways of space.

One lives an hour of day ;
One even man's life exceeds ;
One loves to chase and slay ;
One loves to sing and play ;
Each soul to his own deeds !

A share of joy is ours,
A double share of grief ;
So sum the many hours
In many hopes and powers,
All powers except the chief.

Emotion fills our souls,
And love delights us well,
And joy of sense full rolls ;
But leads us, and controls
Life's central citadel.

Whence we were drawn who knows ?
Of law or Gods or chance ?
But, as life's river flows,
What Sea shall clasp and close
Beyond blind circumstance ?

Such little power we own
Of vague experience,
And instinct to enthrone
The life's mere needs alone,
Nor answer '' why " and " whence."

Nor wandering in the night
Our minds may apprehend
Reflecting in pure light
Of soul, what sound or sight
May lead us to some end.

We hear the dim sound roll
From distant mountains drawn,
We follow, but no soul
Guesses that silver goal,
The sunset or the dawn.

The lyre entices fast
Our willing feet and wings,
We wonder from the past
What spell is overcast
From off the sonant strings.

Awhile we deem our mates
Are calling through the wood ;
Awhile the tune creates
These unfamiliar states
Of thinking solitude.

Awhile we gather clear
A note of promise swell,
A song of fate and fear,
Assuring us who hear
Of other shapes to dwell.

A promise vast and grand
As is the spangled sky !
We dimly understand ;
We join the following band
Of dancing greenery !

We see all Nature bend
To high Olympus' hill.
Our tunes we choose and send ;
We follow to the end,
O Orpheus, all thy will.

Our little love and hate,
Our hunger and our fear,
Pass to a solemn state
Pregnant with hope and fate.
O Orpheus, we are here !

THE EARTH.

Life hidden in death,
Life shrined in the soul,
Life bright for his breath,
Life dark for his goal,
I am Mother, and Burier, and Friend—
Look thou to the end !

I am Light in thy Love,
I am Love in thy Life.
I am cloistered above
Where the stars are at strife.
I am life in thy light, and thy death
Is part of my breath.

My voices are many,
Thy lyre is but one ;
But thou art not as any
Soul under the sun !
Thou hast power for an hour,
The motherly dower.

One voice of my voices
Uncalled and unheard,
No song that rejoices
Of beast or of bird,
No sound of my children sublime,
But the spirit of time.

Fear is his name,
Nor flickers nor dies
His blackening flame.
Beware, were thou wise !
Not him shalt thou hail from the dusk with
thy breath ;
His name—it is Death !

My seasons and years,
Shalt thou traffic with these?
Art thou Fate ? Are her shears
Asleep or at ease?
Though Time were no more than the shape
of thy glass—
Beware ! let him pass !

ORPHEUS.

Not these do I fear,
O Earth, for their peace.
I cry till they hear
O'er the desolate seas.
I call ye ! give ear,
O seasons, to these
Fleet-footed, the strings of the lyre ! Come
forth ! I invoke ye—and cease.

O hours of the day,
And hours of the night,
Pause now while ye may
In your heavenly flight !
Give answer and say,
Have I called ye aright?
Are the strings of my lyre as fire, the voice
of my singing as light?

THE HOURS.

Darkness and daylight in divided measure
Gather as petals of the sunflower,
In many seasons seek the lotus-treasure,
Following as dancing maidens, mute for
pleasure,
The fervent flying footsteps of the Hour.

The sun looks over the memorial hills,
The trampling of his horses heard as wind ;
He leaps and turns, and all his fragrance fills
The shade and silence ; all the rocks and rills
Ring with the triumph of his steeds behind.

The bright air winnowed by the plumeless
leapers
Laughs, and the low light pierces to the
bed
Where lovers linger, where the smiling
sleepers
Stir, and the herds unmindful of their keepers
Low for pure love of morning's dewy head.

The morning shakes its ocean-bathèd tresses,
The bright sun broadens over all the earth.
The green leaves fall, fall into his caresses,
And all the world's heart leaps, again ad-
dresses
Its life, and girds it in the golden girth.

Then noon full-fashioned lies upon the steep.
The large sun sighs and turns his bridle-
rein,
Thinks of the ocean, turns his heart to sleep,
Laughing no longer, not yet prone to weep,
Feeling the prelude of the coming pain.

K

The hills and dales are dumb beneath the
    heat,
And all the world lies tranced or mutely
    dreaming,
Save some low sigh caught up where pulses
    beat
Of warm love waiting in the arboreal seat
Till the shade lengthen on the lawn light-
    gleaming.

Now all the birds change tune, and all the
    light
Glows lowlier, musing on departed day.
Strange wings and sombre, heralding the
    night,
Fleet far across the woods; and gleaming
    bright
The evening star looks from the orient
    way.

Shadow and silence deepen : all the woods
Take on a tenderer phrase of musical
Breezes : the stream-sought homes and
    solitudes
Murmur a little where the maiden moods
Are sadder as the evening's kisses fall.

Like silver scales of serpenthood they fall
Across the blind air of the evening ;
Shadowy ghosts arise funereal
And seek unspeakable things ; and dryads
    call
The satyr-company to the satyr-king.

And all the light is over ; but the sky
Shudders with blanched light of the un-
    risen moon.
The night-birds mingle their sad minstrelsy
For daylight's requiem : and the sea's reply
Now stirs across the land's departed tune.

The moon is up : the choral crowd of stars,
Shapen like strange or unknown animals,
Move in their measure : beyond Æolian bars
The clustering winds, moving as nenuphars,
Gather and muse before the midnight calls.

The darkness is most deep in hollow dells.
There, blacker than Cocytus, lurk the
    shades
Darker than death's, more terrible than hell's,
Uttering unwritten words : the silent wells
Keep their sweet secret till the morning
    maids
Bring their carved pitchers to the moss-
    grown side.
For now beyond, below the east, appears
A hint as if a band, silvern and wide,
The girdle of some goddess amber-eyed,
Rose from the solemn company of the
    spheres.

The sky is tinged, as if the amorous flesh
Of that same queen shone through the
    girdle drawn
By her own kissing fervour through its mesh.
Last, glory of godhead ! flickers, flames the
    fresh
First faint frail rose and arrow of the dawn.

SPRING.

Mild glimpses of the quiet moon, let through
    Tall groves of cedar, stain the glade ;
    gleams mild
The kirtle of the unweaned spring, stained
    blue
From the blue breasts that suckle to the
    child.
    Through the new-leavèd trees
    The hidden stranger sees
The moon's sweet light, the shadows listening
    If a ghost-foot should fall :
    And if a ghost-voice call
Tremble the leaves and light-streaks of the
    spring.
On wavering wing
    The small clouds gallop in the windy sky :
    The hoarse rooks croak and droop them
    to the nest :
One sweet small throat begins to sing,
    Becomes the song, losing identity
    Ere its wail wakes the long low-lying
    crest
    That rears across the west.

Spring, maiden-footed, steals across the
    space,
Sandalled with tremulous light, with flicker-
    ing hair
Blown o'er the sweet looks of the fair child-
    face,
    Like willows drooping o'er the liquid
        mere,
      Whence timid eyes look far,
      Even where her kisses are
Awaited by the tender mother lips,
    Earth's, that is lonely and old,
    Grown sad, fearful, and cold
With bitter winter and the sun's eclipse ;
So the child slips
    From bough to bough between the weep-
      ing trees,
    And with frail fingers smooths and
      touches them.
They murmur in their sleep : the moonlight
    dips
    And laughs, seeing how young buds catch
      life from these
      Child-kisses on the stem.

The leaves laugh low, and frosty-footed
    Time
Shoulders a lighter burden ; in the dale
Some distant notes of lovely music climb,
    Thrown from the golden-throated night-
      ingale,
    Pale sobs of love and life
    With death and fear at strife,
Fiercely beset and hardly conquering,
    When spring's bright eyes at last
    Flash through the sullen past,
And tune its pain to tears, its peace to
    sing.
The earth's lips cling
    To the child's bosom, and low smiles
      revive ;
    Love is new-born upon the golden
      hour,
And all the life of all the exultant spring
    Breathes in the wind that wakes the world
      alive
    Into the likeness of a flower.

SUMMER.

Full is the joy of Maidenhood made strong,
    Too proud to bend to swift Apollo's
      kiss ;
Rejoicing in its splendour, and the throng
    Of gaunt hounds leashless before Artemis.
    In strange exulting bliss
The maiden stands, full-grown, with bound-
      ing breasts
    Bared to the noon, and narrow
Keen eyes that glance, dim fires that veil
      their crests
    To flame along the arrow
Aimed at some gallant of ten tines perched
      high
Branching against the sky
    His cedar-spreading horns : erect she
      stands,
    Holding in glimmering hands
    A silver bow across the shining weather,
    While, bound in pearl-wrought bands,
    Her bright hair streams ; she draws the
      quivering feather
Back to the small ear curved : with golden
    zone
Gathering her limbs she stands alone
    Like a young antelope poised upon a spire
      of stone.

What tender lightning flashes in the bosom
    Heaving with vigour of young life ? What
    storm
Gathers across the brow's broad lotus-
    blossom ?
    What sudden passion fills the fragrant
    form
    With subtle streams of warm
Blood tingling to the finger-tips of rose ?
    Swiftly the maiden closes
The lustre of her look : disdainful glows
    The fire of wreathing roses
In her bright cheeks : she darts away to
    find
Like some uncovered hind
    Shade in the forest from the stag's pursuit,
    Ere the sun's passion shoot

His ray, strange deeps unknown and feared
    to uncover.
  But now the ancient root
Of some wise oak betrays her to her lover:
  She stumbles and falls prone: the forest
    noon
  Guesses life's law; all nature's tune
  Tells that the hour is come when May
    must grow to June.

Then in the broad glare of the careless sun
  Apollo's light is on her and within;
His shafts of glory pierce her one by one;
  His kisses darken, shivering and keen,
  Swift glories cold and clean
Of that chaste bridal, and the earth gets
    gladness,
  Till the last winter's traces
Fall from the spring's last cold wind—shining
    sadness !—
  And from the frail new faces
Blushing through moss; and all the world is
    light
With the unsufferably bright
  Full joy and guerdon of that sunny season
  By Love's sweet trap of treason.
    So the bright girl is now a woman
      brighter;
  And childhood sees a reason
    Beneath the strong stroke of the goodly
      smiter
For all the past: and love at last is hers.
No more the bosom's pride demurs,
While in her womb the first faint pulse of
  motherhood soft stirs.

AUTUMN.

Full amber-breasted light of harvest-moon,
  And sheaves of corn remembering the sun
    Laughing again for love of that caress
When night is fallen, and the sleepy swoon
    Of warm waves lap the shoreland, one by
      one;
    Forgetful kisses like a dream's possess
All the low-lying land,
  And, statelier than the swaying form
  Of some loud God, lifting the storm

In his disastrous hand,
  Steps the sweet-voiced, the mellow
    motherhood
  Glad of the sun's kiss, full of life, well
    wooed
    And won and brought to his bed,
Proud of her rhythm in the lusty kiss,
  Triumphant and exulting in the mood
Wherein her being is
    Crowned with a husband's head,
  And left in solitude which is not soli-
    tude.

She strides with mighty steps across the
    glade
  Laughing, her bosom swelling with the
    milk
    Born of a million kisses: leaps her
      womb
Pregnant with fruits, and latter flowers, and
    shade
  Of the great cedar-groves: soft, soft, as
    silk,
    Her skin glows amber, silvered with the
      bloom
Mist-like of the moon's light,
  A slumberous haze of quietude
  Shed o'er the hardy limbs, and lustihood,
And boldness, and great might.
  Earth knows her daring daughter, and the
    sea
  Breaks into million-folded mystery
    Of flower-like flashes in the pale moon-
      rise,
Exulting also, now the sun is faded,
  With joy of her supreme fertility
And glowing masteries
    Of autumn summer-shaded,
  The golden fruit of all the blossoming
    sky.

And now the watcher to the bright breasts
    blind
  Loses the seemly shape, the loud swift
    song;
    Now the moon falls, and all the gold is
      gone,

And round the storm-caught shape hard
    gusts of wind
Blow, and her leaves are torn, a flying
    throng
Of orange and purple and red ; the
    sombre sun
Shines darkly in her breast
    But wakes no joy therein,
    And all his kisses sharp and keen
Bring only now desire of rest,
    Not their old rapture : the warm violet eyes
    Melt into sweet hot tears ; subtler the sighs
    Are interfused of death ;
The brave bright looks grow duller,
    And fear is mingled with love's ecstasies
Again, and all her breath
    Fails, and the shape and colour
    Fade, fail, are lost in the sepulchral seas.

WINTER.

Know ye my children ? From the old strong
    breast
    Not weary yet of life's grey change, not
    drawn
Into the utter peace of death, the rest
    Of the dim hour that lingers ere the dawn,
Spring these that laugh upon thee. In the
    snow
    See forests bare and gaunt,
    Where winged whispers haunt,
Lighting the dull sky with a slumberous
    glow ;
    Hear the strange sounds of winter
    chaunt ;
Feel the keen wisdom of the winter thrill
    Young hearts with passionate foretaste
    Of death in some wild waste
Of deserts darkening at some wild god's will,
Of frozen steppes awaiting the repose
    That only death discovers, never sleep.
    My misery is this
That I must wake to childhood gold and
    rose,
    And maidenhood, and wifehood, and still
    keep
    Bound on Life's fatal wheel—revolv-
    ing bliss.

O that worn wisdom and the age of sorrow
    Could learn its bitter lesson, and depart
Into some nightfall guiltless of a morrow,
    Into some cave's unprofitable heart
Beyond this curse of birth ! O that dread
    night
    Could come and cover all,
    Even itself to fall
To some abyss past resurrection's might !
    For the old whispers of my old life call
Accursèd hopes, accursèd fears, accursèd
    pleasures.
    Long-suffering of all life !
    Changed consciousness at strife !
No dancer treads the melancholy measures
Unchanged for one short tune : no dancer
    flags,
    The hateful music luring them to move
    Weary and desolate ;
And as the rhyme revolves and shrills and
    drags
    Their limbs insane they smile and call it
    love,
    Or, mocking, call it hatred : it is Fate.

These grey eyes close to the deceitful dream
    Of death that will not take the tired for
    ever.
Again, again, revolves the orb ; the stream,
    The dew, the cloud, the ocean, and the
    river.
My magic wand and cup and sword and
    spell
    Languish, forgotten fears.
    The cup is filled with tears ;
The sword is red with blood ; the pentacle
    Builded of flesh ; the wand its snake-
    head rears
Swift energy : my labour is but lost.
    I, who thus thought all things to end,
    Find in the void no friend.
I have but conjured up the fiend that most
I trusted to abolish : all my toil
    Goes to give rest to life, and build anew
    These pinnacles of pain,
Cupola upon cupola ; the soil
    To comfort, to avail, to assoil with dew,
    To build the year again.

ORPHEUS.

O hours not of day
But of æons that roll !
Earth stretches away
From pole unto pole ;
Four seasons decay,
Ere one sound of thy soul,
O fervent and following years, springs over
the solar goal !

Come forth to the sound
Of the seven sweet strings !
Advance and rebound !
Be your pomp as a king's !
Girdled around
With seasons and stings
As a serpent's encompassing Time.   Come
forth ! on the heavy grey wings !

Ye arbiter lords
That sit as for doom,
Bright splendour of swords
Leaps forth in your gloom !
But stronger my chords
Shall lift in your womb
The love of your passage and time, imme-
morial ages, your tomb.

Ye linger for long,
But ye pass and are done :
But I, my sweet song
Outliveth the sun !
Ye are many and strong ;
I am stronger, and one !
Come forth ! I invoke ye, O years, in my
evening orison.

THE YEARS.

Crowned with Eternity, beyond beginning ;
Sandalled with wings, Eternity's ; the end
Far beyond sight of striving soul or sinning ;
Ourselves see not, nor know, nor compre-
hend.
Reeling from chaos, unto Chronos winning,
Devoured of Him our Father and our
friend,
This is our life, lead winged or footed golden ;
We pass, and each of other is unbeholden.

Ranged in dim spectral order and procession,
We span man's thought, we limit him in
time ;
None of the souls of earth have had posses-
sion
Of larger loves or passions more sublime.
Where the night-caverns hide our solemn
session
The summoning word lifts up our holy
rhyme.
Even as a mighty river, bend to bend,
We rise in turn and look toward the end.

Also, the Gods arisen from the living
Lights of the sky, half hidden in the night,
Vast shapes beholden of men unbelieving,
Staggering the sense and reason with the
sight,
Manifold, mighty, monstrous, no light giving
Unto the soul that is not also light ;—
We rise in ghastly power ; we know the
token,
The speech of silence and the song unspoken.

ORPHEUS.

Come forth to the sound,
Ye lustres of years
That hide in profound
Abysses of fears,
Hidden and bound !
The voice of tears
Implores and impels ye, O lustres, with a
tune that is strong as a seer's.

THE LUSTRES.

Fivefold the shape sublime that lifts its head
Uniform, self-repeating, comparable
At last to a man's life : twice seven times
dead
Ere the light flickers in that citadel,
Or the great whiteness lure his soul instead
Of many-coloured earth : ere the strong
spell
Fail, and the Fates with iron-shapen shears
Cut the frail silver, hide him from the years.

Fivefold: the year that is in darkness hidden,
  Being beginning: then the moving year,
All change and tumult; then the quiet un-
    chidden
  Of deep reflection; then the gladdening
    tear
Or saddening smile, the laughter not for-
    bidden
  And love enfolding the green-woven
    sphere:
Lastly, the burning year of flame and fume
That burns men up in fire's sepulchral womb.

Fivefold: the child, the frail, the delicate:
  Then the strong laughing mischief: then
    the proud
Fight toward manhood and the sense elate,
  Creative power and passion: then the loud
Assertion of young will, the quickening rate
  And strength in blood, in youth with life
    endowed,
And firmness fastening; the last lustre's span
Consolidates and shows the perfect man.

Fivefold: the humour changes as his child
  Calls him first "father"; sense of strength
    divine
Fills him; then man's work in the world,
    and wild
  Efforts to fame: then steadier in the shrine
Burns the full flame: then, turning, the years
    piled
  Seem suddenly a burden; then the fine
Flavour of full maturity is tasted:
The man looks back, and asks if life be
    wasted.

Fivefold: delight in woman altering
  To joy of sunlight only: love of life
Changing to fear of death: the golden spring
  Trembles; he hates the cold, the winter
    strife,
Laughs not with lust of combat: feebly cling
  His old hands: he has sepultured his wife:
Last, palsied, shaking, drawing tremorous
    breath,
He gasps—and stumbles in the pit of death.

ORPHEUS.

O girded and spanned
  By the deeds of time,
Rocks shattered and planned
  In your depth: where climb
The race and the land,
  And the growth sublime
Of worlds—I invoke ye! Come forth, ye
  centuries! Come to the rhyme!

THE CENTURIES.

How hardly a man
  Though his strength were as spring's
Shall stretch out his span
  To the width of my wings!
The years are enfolden
In my bosom golden,
  My periods
Are the hours of the Gods.
They have their plan
  In my seasons; all things
Are woven in the span
  Of the spread of my wings.

My brazen gates cleft
  By shafts shed of time,
Are ruined and left
  As the Gods sing their rhyme.
Buttress and joist are
Effaced of the cloister.
Fane after fane
We lift us again
To the hoarier transept
  Where ages climb,
And ruin is left
  Where the Gods said their rhyme.

The deity-year
  (Whereof I am an hour)
Shall be born and appear
  As the birth of a flower,
Shall fade as they faded,
The flower wreaths braided
In maiden's hair.
The Gods shall fare

As the children of Fear
In the Fear-God's Power,
And their names disappear
As the fall of a flower !

The universe-day
(Whereof I am a second)
Shall fall away
And be no more reckoned ;
Shall fall into ruin.
(Sad garden it grew in !)
Unguessed at, unknown,
Beyond them alone,
Is a space that is grey
As it caught them, and beckoned,
And lost them—their way
Is nor counted nor reckoned !

Inconceivable hollow,
Eternity's womb !
Cataclysmal they follow,
Tomb hidden in tomb.
Reeled off and unspun,
Time's fashion is done
In the ultimate
Abysses of fate.
Æons they swallow,
And swamp in the gloom,
Where Eternities follow
Their biers to their tomb.

ORPHEUS.

O Mother, O hollow
Sweet heart of the moon !
O matchless Apollo
That granted the tune !
Time's children follow
The strings that commune
With Nature well cloven that comes to the
lyre's lilt silver-hewn.

O bays of the wind,
And shoreland of Thrace !
O beaten and blind
In the light of my face !
Heaven thunders behind,
Hell shakes for a space,
As I fling the loud sound to the sky, and the
vaults of the Earth give place.

O mystical tune
Of a magic litten
Of music, the moon,
The stars unsmitten,
The sun, the unhewn
Stones deeply bitten
By runic fingers of time, where decrees of the
Fates are written !

Time listens, obeys me ;
All Nature replies ;
Nought avoids me, nor stays me,
Nor checks, nor defies.
Tribute she pays me
From seas unto skies.
But Death—shall he heed me or hear ? shall
he list to the lyre and arise ?

O thou who art seated,
Invisible king,
The never-defeated,
The shadowy thing !
What mortal hath greeted
Thy shrine, but shall sing
Not earthly but tunes of thine own, in the
vaults of Aornos that ring ?

Nor caring nor hearing
For hearts that be bowed,
Nor hating nor fearing
Man's crying aloud,
Solemnly spearing
The single, the crowd,
Thou sittest remote and alone, unprofane,
with due silence endowed !

I call thee by Nature,
My mother and friend !
By every creature !
By life and its end !
By love, the true teacher,
My chanting I send,
Invoking thy stature immense, the terrible
form of a fiend !

I hear not a word,
  Though my music be rolled
As the song of a bird
  Through fields of gold.
    Hast thou not heard?
    Have I not told
The magic that bridleth the Gods, the Gods
  in their houses of old?

Art thou elder than they
  In their mountain of light?
Is thy fugitive way
  Lost in uttermost night?
    Shalt thou not obey,
    Or my lyre not affright,
If I call thee by Heaven and Earth with a
  God's tumultuous might?

If I curse thee or chide
  Shalt thou tremble not, Thou?
Not move thee and hide
  From the light of my brow?
    Shall my arrows divide
    Not the heart of thee now?
Art thou cased in strong iron to mock the
  spells that all others avow?

Art thou muffled or hidden
  In adamant brass?
Is my music forbidden
  In Orcus to pass?
    Have I cursed thee and chidden?
    My flesh being grass,
I curse not as yet, but command thee; the
  names that avail I amass.

No sound? no whisper?
  No answer to me?
From dawn-star to Hesper
  I call upon thee!
    In the hour of vesper
    I change the key!
I cry on Apollo to aid, I lift up my lyre on
  the sea.

Thou reaper of fear,
  Accurst of mankind,
I charge thee to hear,
  Deaf horror deep-mined
    In hell! O uprear
    On the front of the wind!
I curse thee! Thou hearest my hounds of
  thunder that mutter behind?

How strange is the dark
  And the silence around!
Hardly the spark
  Of my silvery sound
    Moves, or may mark
    The heaven's dim bound.
How strange! I have sought him in vain—
  perchance not in vain have I found!

No! Life thrills in me;
  Vibrates on the lyre;
The Fates still spin me
  Their thread of desire:
    Still, woo and win me
    Soft eyes, and the dire
Low fervour of sensual phrase, song kin to
  the nethermost fire!

In silence I wait
  For his voice to roll,
For the coming of Fate,
  The strength of my soul.
    My words create
    One glorious whole
From the fragments divided that seem past a
  man's or a god's control.

I, seeing the life
  Of the flowers renew,
The victorious strife
  Of the spring run through,
    The child's birth rife
    With loftier dew—
I know the deep truth in myself; see acacia
  in cypress and yew.

Death is not at all !
'Tis a mask or a dream !
The things that befall
Only slumber or seem !
They fear ; they appal—
They are not as ye deem !
Death died when I dipped my lyre in the
sweet Heliconian stream !

Give praise to your lord,
All souls that draw breath,
All flowers of the sward !
For the song of me saith :
" Sound the loud chord !
Let love be a wreath !
Death is not for ye any more, for I am the
Master of Death ! "

PARABASIS.[1]

As I sit in the sound
Of the wash of the surf,
On the long low ground,
The trees and the turf ;
In front the profound,
The warrior seas,
Upstirred of the breeze,
By the far reef bound—
I know the low music of love, I feel the
sweet murmur in me,
My soul is in tune with the sea.

The stars are above me,
The rocks are below me,
The sea is around !
Great Gods that love me
Lead me, and show me
Their powers profound.
Their lightnings move me
To stir me, to throw me
As into a swound,
The song of the infinite surf that is beaten
and bound
As a fierce wolf-hound,
The song that lures me, and lifts me, and
mingles my soul into sound !

[1] The bulk of this Book I. was written at
Waikiki, which is described in this Parabasis.

O Nature, my mother,
Heart melted on heart
At last ! Not another,
Not any shall part
Thy soul from my art.
How should it be otherwise,
Sister divine,
Lover, my mother wise,
Wiser than wine ?
Seeing I linger
Here on the beach—
Let God's own finger
Here to me reach,
Making me singer
Each unto each—
Nature and Man made one
In the light and fire of the sun,
And the sobbing tune
Of the moon,
Wedded in cyclic bonds,
Where fall the æon-fronds,
Whose large bed bears a child
(In its due period)
Not merciful and not severe,
Knowing nor love nor fear,
But majesty most mild,
Being indeed a God.

Yea, let the very ray-hand of Apollo
Lead me where none may follow
Save in blind eagle-fury and full flight
Pythian against the light,
Writing in all the sea, the trees, the flowers,
The many-fruited bowers,
The lustred lilies and arboreal scent
And fresh young element
Of blood in every osseous vein of time,
New senses more sublime !
Should it not be that the ill days are past
And my soul lost at last,
Lost in thy bosom who art mother of all
Ere the first was, to fall
After the end.   And then, O soul endued
(In this my solitude)
With all the thousand elements of life,
Shall I not call thee wife ?
O Muse long wooed !

Long called to in the forest, on the mountain,
Reached after in the fountain,
Grasped in the slumberous sea,
And yet, ever, aye, ever ! escaping me !

But here where the wise pen
And silver cadences outrunning song,
And clear sweet clean-chiselled English, sharp
    and strong,
Of the one man [1] among the latter men
Who lived with Nature, saw her face to face,
And died not : here in this consummate place,
Immortal now, though the Antarctic sent
Its mightiest coldest wave and rose and rent
The coral and annihilated land,
Or though the swarthy hand
Or foot misshapen of the Hephaestian,
(Hating the air-breathing man,
In such sweet love as dwells, above all other
    places
Here, in our hearts and faces,
Nature's and man's) if his coarse hand or
    foot,
The implacable forceful brute,
Shifted towards the bellows, and one blast
Blew through all the air aghast
And in one vast Titanic war,
Almighty avenging roar,
Oahu flung skywards blown in dust—and
    was no more—
Even then immortal stands
This loveliest of all lands,
Lovelier even than they
Know in Elysian paths, heroic bands
Treading dim gardens brighter than the day,
Even in his voice who is passed, and shall no
    pass away !
Here therefore I know Nature ; I am filled
With dew not earth-distilled
As I have prayed in vain, not vainly willed.
Now all the earth is stilled ;
But ever the monotonous sea
Keeps solemn symphony,
Tuning my lyre to her own melody,
Not understandable in colder lands
Where no man understands

[1] R. L. Stevenson.

More than the mart ; the raucous ironshod
Feet, smashing verses ; the hard heavy hands
Of time : the hateful laugh where whoredom
    trod ;
The savage snarl of man against his friend :—
How should he (such an one) perceive the end,
Or listen to the voice of Nature, know it for
    the voice of God ?

EPODE.

NATURE.

Lo ! in the interstellar space of night,
    Clothed with deep darkness, the majestic
    spaces
Abide the dawn of deity and light,
    Vibrate before the passionless pale faces
Shrined in exceeding glory, eremite.
    The tortoise skies in sombre carapaces
Await the expression and the hour of birth
In silence through the adamantine girth.

I rose in glory, gathered of the foam.
    The sea's flower folded, charioting me risen
Where dawn's rose stole from its pearl-
    glimmering home,
    And heaven laughed, and earth : and mine
    old prison,
The seas that lay beneath the mighty dome,
    Shone with my splendour.   Light did first
    bedizen
Earth with its clusters of fiery dew and spray,
When I looked forth and cried " It is the
    day ! "

The stars are dewdrops on my bosom's space ;
    The sun and moon are glances through my
    lashes,
Long, tender, rays of night ; my subtle face
    Burns through the sky-dusk, lightens, fills,
    and flashes
With solemn joy and laughter of love ; the
    grace
    Of all my body swaying stoops and dashes
Swift to the daisy's dawn of love : and
    swiftest,
O spirit of man, when unto me thou liftest !

Dawn shakes the molten fire of my delight
From the fine flower and fragrance of my
　　tresses !
Sunset bids darken all my body's light,
　　Mixing its music with the sad caresses
Of the whole world : I wheel in wingless flight
　　Through lampless space, the starless
　　wildernesses !
Beyond the universal bounds that roll,
There is the shrine and image of my soul.

Nature my name is called. O fruitless veil
　　Of the strange self of its own self begotten !
O vision laughterless ! O shadowy tale !
　　O brain that halts before its thought for-
　　gotten !
Once all ye knew me—ere the earth grew
　　pale,
　　And Time began, and all its fruit lay
　　rotten,
Once, when thou knewest me indeed, and fed
At these strong breasts—Ah ! but the days
　　are dead !

Now, in the dusty corridors of Time,
　　I am forgotten : Gaian [1] language falters
If I would teach thee half an hint sublime
　　Shed of the rayless fire upon my altars.
Vain are the light and laughter of man's
　　rime,
　　Vain the large hymns, and soaring songs
　　and psalters !
My face, my breast, no soul of man uncovers,
Nor is my bed made lovely with my lovers !

I long for purple and the holier kiss
　　Of mortal lyrist ; in these arms to gladden ;
To take him to the spring and source of bliss,
　　And in his vast embrace to rouse me,
　　madden
Once with the light of passion, not to miss
　　Uttermost rapture till the sweet loves
　　sadden
To sweeter peace thrilled with young
　　ecstasy—
Ah ! man's high spirit may not reach to Me !

[1] *I.e.*, terrestrial : from Gaia, a form of γῆ,
the earth.

I am Nature and God : I reign, I am, alone.
　　None other may abide apart : they perish,
　　Drawn into me, into my being grown.
　　None other bosom is, to bear, to nourish,
To be : the heart of all beneath my zone
　　Of blue and gold is scarlet-bright to cherish
My own's life being, that is, and is not other ;
For I am God and Nature and thy Mother.

I am the thousand-breasted milky spouse,
　　Virginal also : Tartarus and Gaia
Twinned in my womb, and Chaos from my
　　brows
　　Shrank back abashed, my sister dark and
　　dire,
Mother of Erebus and Night, that ploughs
　　With starry-sandalled feet the fields of fire ;
My sister shrank and fell, the infernal gloom
Changed to the hot sweet shadow of my
　　womb.

I am : that darkness strange and uterine
　　Is shot with dawn and scented with the
　　rose ;
The deep dim prison-house of corn and wine,
　　Flowers, children, stars, with flame far
　　subtler glows
Formless, all-piercing, death-defying, divine,
　　A sweet frail lamp whose shadow gleams
　　and shows
No darkness, is as light is where its rays
Cross, interweave, and marry with the day's !

I am : the heart that flames from central Me
　　Seeks out all life, and takes again, to
　　mingle
Its passion with my might and majesty,
　　Till the vast floods of the man's being tingle
And glow, self-lost within my soul and sea
　　Of love, and sun of utter light, and single
Keen many-veinèd heart : our lips and kisses
Marry and muse on our immortal blisses.

I am : the greatest and the least : the sole
　　And separate life of things. The mighty
　　stresses
Of worlds are my nerves twitching. Branch
　　and bole
　　Of forests waving in deep wildernesses

Are hairs upon my body. Rivers roll
To make one tear in my superb caresses,
When on myself myself begets a child,
A system of a thousand planets piled !

I am : the least, the greatest : the frail life
Of some small coral-insect still may tremble
With love for me, and call me queen and wife ;
The shy plant of the water may dissemble
Its love beneath the fronds ; reply to strife
With strife, and all its tiny being crumble
Under my rough and warrior husband-kiss,
Whose pain shall burn, and alter, and be bliss !

I am : no word beside that solemn one
Reigns in sound's kingdom to express my
station,
Who, clothed and crowned with suns beyond
the sun,
Bear on the mighty breast of foam Tha-
lassian,
Bear on my bosom, jutting plenilune,
Maiden, the fadeless Rose of the Creation !
The whole flower-life of earth and sky and sea
From me was born, and shall return to me !

I am : for men and beings passionate,
For mine own self calm as the river-cleaving
Lotus-borne lord of Silence : I create
Or discreate, both in my bosom heaving :
My lightest look is mother of a Fate :
My fingers sapphire-ringed with sky are
weaving
Ever new flowers and lawns of life, designed
Nobler and newer in mine olden mind.

I am : I am not, but all-changing move
The worlds evolving in a golden ladder
Spiral or helical, fresh gusts of love
Filling one sphere from the last sphere
grown gladder ;
All gateways leading far to the above.
Even as the bright coils of the emerald adder
Climb one by one in glory of sunlight, climb
My children to me up the steep of Time.

I am : before me all the years are dead,
And all the fiery locks of sunrise woven
Into the gold and scarlet of my head :
In me all skies and seas are shaken and
cloven :

All life and light and love about me shed
Begotten in me, in my moving moven,
Are as my tears : all worlds that ever swam
As dew of kisses on my lips : I am.

But thou, chief lover, in whose golden heart
The melody and music lifts its pæan,
Whose lyre fulfilled of me, fathered of Art
And that Sun's song beyond the Empyrèan,
Who art myself, not any more apart,
Having called my children by the call
Pandean,
Mellowed with Delphian gold, the Ephesian
quiver,
To float down Time for ever and for ever ;—

I am thy lyre and thou mine harper : thou
My music, I thy spirit : thou the lover
And I the bride : the glory of my brow
Deeper delight, new ardour, to discover
Stoops in thine heart ; my love and light endow
Thy life with fervour as I bend me over
The starry curve and surface of the sea,
And kiss thy very life out into me.

O central fountain of my yearning veins !
O mountain single-soaring, thou art blended
Into my heaven : prescient of the pains
That shall bring forth —what worlds ? my
heart is rended !
My womb reverberates the solar strains,
The lyre vibrating in me : sharp and
splendid
My face glows, gladdens ; nuptial ecstasy
Is all the guerdon and the spoil of me !

I am : the universe grown old must bear
A scion ere it sink to dædal slumber.
Thou art my strength, and I am only fair.
Our kisses are as stars ; our loves en-
cumber
With multitude the fields of space, and where
Our kisses tune the worlds, their lives out-
number
The moments of eternity : apart
I am for ever : and, in me, thou art !

EXPLICIT LIBER PRIMUS.

LIBER SECUNDUS VEL AMORIS

TO

MARY BEATON

WHOM I LAMENT

"The Kabbalists say that when a man falls in love with a female elemental—undine, sylph, gnome, or salamandrine, as the case may be—she becomes immortal with him, or otherwise he dies with her. . . . The love of the magus for such beings is insensate, and may destroy him."—*Eliphaz Levi.*

"Orpheus for the love he bare to his wife, snatcht, as it were, from him by untimely Death, resolved to go down to Hell with his harp, to try if he might obtain her of the infernal power."—*The Wisdom of the Ancients.*

ORPHEUS, FINDING EURYDICE
DEAD, STUNG BY A SERPENT,
LAMENTS OVER HER.

COME back, come back, come back, Eurydice!
    Come back to me!
Lie not so quiet, draw some faint sharp
    breath!
      It is not death:
It cannot, must not be, Eurydice.
    Come back to me!
Let me as yet lament not! Let me stoop!—
    Those eyelids droop
Not with mere death, but dreams, Eurydice!
    Come back to me!

O you that were my lover and my wife!
    Come back to life!
Come back, breathe softly from the breast of
    gold
    These arms enfold.
Give me your lips and kiss me once! O wife,
    Come back to life!
Nay, let the wind but stir the silky hair,
    (God's lesser air,
Not His full blossom of woman's breath!)
    O wife,
    Come back to life!

Stir once, move once, rise once, Eurydice!
    Be good to me!
Rise once.—O sleep not! Listen! Is not all
    Nature my thrall?
Once only: be not dead, Eurydice!
    Be good to me!
I love you—be not dead!—rise up and say
    "I feigned, I lay
Thus so you kissed me"—O Eurydice,
    Be good to me!

There is not one sweet sigh of all the old
    sighs—
    Open your eyes!
Not one warm breath of the young breast:
    no sleep
    Could be so deep.
The last pale lotus opens to the skies.
    Open your eyes!
Lift the blue eyelids under the deep lashes
    Till one light flashes!
Wake with one supreme sigh like the old
    sighs!
    Open your eyes!

I cannot leave you so, Eurydice.
    Come back to me!
Just in the triumph, in love's utmost hour,
    Life's queenliest flower—

All shattered, overblown. Eurydice,
      Come back to me !
I cannot have you dead, and live : let death
      Strangle my breath
Now as I kiss you still—Eurydice !
      Come back to me !

Fling down the foolish lyre, the witless power!
Cast the dead laurel in the dust ! The flower
   Of all the world is marred, the day's desire
Distorted in the eclipse, the sun's dead hour.

Let me fall down beside thee ! Let me take
The kisses that thou canst not give, and slake
   Despair in purposeless caresses, dire
Shames fang-wise fastened of the eternal
      snake.

Is there no warmth where beauty is so bright ?
No soul still flickering in the lambent light
   Still shed from all the body's excellence ?
No lamp unchidden of the utter night ?

Cannot my life be molten into thee,
   Or thy death fall with rosier arms on me,
      Or soul with soul commingle without sense,
As the sun's rays strike deep into the sea ?

O beauty of all beauty—central flower
Of all the blossoms in the summer's bower !
   Fades not all Nature in thy fall ? the sun
Not darken in the miserable hour ?

I hate all Nature's mockery of life.
The laugh is grown a grin ; the gentle strife
   Of birds and waves and winds at play is
      grown
A curse, a cruelty. My wife ! my wife !

I am broken, I cannot sleep, I cannot die.
Pain, pain for ever ! Nature is a lie,
   The gods a lie. Myself ? but I am found
Sole serious in the hateful comedy.

Blackness, all blackness ! How I hate the
      earth,
The curse that brought my being into birth.
   I, loving more her loveliness, am bound
And broken—thrice more bitter for my
      mirth !

Song, was it song I trusted in ? Or thou,
Apollo, was it thou didst bind my brow
   With laurel for a poison-wreath of hell
To sear my brain and blast my being now ?

A band of most corroding poison wound
Dissolving with its venom the profound
   Deep of my spirit with its terrible
Sense without speech and horror without
      sound.

A devil intertwining in my heart
Its cold and hideous lust, a twiforked dart
   Even from the fatherly and healing hand—
The double death without a counterpart

In hell's own deepest pit, far, far below
Phlegethon's flame and Styx's stifling flow,
   Far below Tartarus, below the land
Thrust lowest in the devilish vertigo.

If I could weep or slumber or forget !
If love once left me, with his eyelids wet
   With tender memory of his own despair
Or frozen to a statue of regret !

If but the chilling agony, that turns
To bitter fever-heat that stings and burns
   Would freeze me, or destroy me, or impair
My sense, that it should feel not how it
      yearns !

Or if this pain were only pain, and not
A deadness deeper than all pain, a spot
   And central core of agony in me,
One heart-worm, one plague-leprosy, one
      blot

Of death, one anguish deeper than control ?—
Then were I fit to gain the Olympian goal
   And fling forth fiery wailings to the sea,
And tune the sun's ray to my smitten soul !

How should I sing who cannot even see ?
Grope through a mist of changeless misery.
   An age-long pain—no time in wretched.
      ness !—
As of an hammer annihilating me

With swift hard rhythm, the remorseless
    clang ;
Or as a serpent loosening his fang
To bite more deeply—this inane distress
More than despair or death's detested pang.

I live—that shames me ! I am not a man.
Nothing can I to sharpen or to span
    My throat with iron fingers, or my sword
In my heart's acid where the blood began

Long since to leap, and now drops deadly slow,
Clotted with salt and sulphur and strong woe.
    I shall not die : the first sight of the sward
Stained with the spectral corpse had stung
    me so,

Not stabbed me, since I saw her and survive.
I shall not die—Ah ! shall I be alive ?
    This hath no part in either : bale and bliss
Forget me, careless if I rot or thrive.

Heaven forgot me—or she were not dead !
And Hades— or I should not raise my head
    Now, and look wildly where I used to kiss,
Gaze on the form whence all but form has fled!

I am alone in all the universe,
Changed to the shape and image of a curse,
    Muffled in self-confusion, and my brain
Wakes not nor sleeps : its destiny is worse.

It thinks not, knows not, acts not, nor
    appeals,
But hangs, remembers : it abides and feels
    As if God's vulture clung to it amain,
And furies fixed with fiery darts and wheels

Their horror, thought-exceeding, manifold,
Vertiginous within me—and the cold
    Of Styx splashed on me, making me im-
    mortal,
Invulnerable in its bitter mould ;

Leaving its own ice, penetrating streams,
Grim streaks, and dismal drops, abysmal
    beams
    Thrown from the gulph thorough the place
    and portal,
Each drop o'erladen with a curse that steams

Unnatural in the coldness : let me be
Alone, inviolate of eternity !
    Let all the winds of air leave me, nor fan :
Nor wash me all the waves of all the sea !

Let all the sun's light and the moon's be
    blind,
And all the stars be lampless to my mind,
    Until I see the destiny of man
And span the cruelty that lurks behind

Its beauty, and its glory, and its splendour !—
The girl-babe's face looks up to the mother
    tender,
    Looks for a kiss in dumb desire, and finds
Her jaws closed trap-like to expunge and
    end her !

Let all the life and dream and death be done,
And all the love and hate be woven in one,
    All things be broken of the winter winds,
No soul stand up and look upon the sun !

Save only mine !—that my voice may con-
    found
The universe, and spell the mighty sound
    To shake all heaven and earth, to mingle
    hell
In chaos, in some limitless profound ;

That it may tear Olympus from its place,
Mix it with Hades, change the Ocean space,
    Level the tides of time that sink and swell,
And curse my very father to his face !

O father, father Apollo, did I wrong
Thy chariot and thy horses in my song ?
    Why clove thine arrow the unseated air,
The heaven void of thee, why the thunder-
    thong

Slipped from the tether, and the fatal stone
Sped not to my heart, not to mine alone ?
    Ah why not ? but to hers as she lay sleep-
    ing
By hate, not fate, quelled, fallen, and over-
    thrown ?

She lies so pitiful and pure—and I,
Breast to her breast, mouth to her mouth, I
     lie,
   Hand upon hand, and foot on foot, sore
     weeping—
Can she not live again or I not die?

As the old prophet on the child I fall [1]
And breathe—but no breath answers me at
     all.
   All of my kisses stir no blush, no sigh;
She will not hear me ever if I call!

Let the far music of oblivious years
   Sound in the sea beneath!
Are not its waters one with all my tears?
Hath Atropos no comfort in her shears?
   No Muse for me one wreath?

Were I now dead and free to travel far
   Whither I will, ah me!
Not whither I must—were there no avatar
Drawn like my love from some close kindred
     star?
   No shape seen on the sea?

Were I now free of this intense desire,
   By swift magician power
I might fly westward shod with wings of fire
And find my love, and in her arms expire,
   Or wed her for an hour.

(Not for an hour as man, but even as God
   Whose day is like an aeon.
Love hath nor station, stage, nor period:
But is at once in his inane abode
   Beneath the spring Dircean.)

Alas, the will flies ere the power began.
   Lo, in the Idan grove
Invoking Zeus to swell the power of Pan,
The prayer discomfits the demented man!
   Lust lies as still as love. [2]

[1] Referring to the story of Elisha.
[2] This obscure stanza means: that the invocation of high and pure forces cannot be
diverted to low and impure ends; because the
man becomes identified with what he invokes,
of necessity.

Therefore in memory only is there life,
   And in sweet shapes of art:
The same thought for the ointment and the
     knife—
Oh lightning! blast the image of my wife
   Out of my mind and heart!

How can one hour dissolve a year's delight?
One arrow striking the full eagle-flight
   Drop him so swift, giving no time to die,
No dusk to herald and delay the night?

A serpent stung her sleeping: if the abyss
Know any cell more dolorous than this,
   Were there a sharper tooth to destiny
Than this that strikes me in the dead girl's
   kiss:—

Oh if aught bitterer could be, could know,
If ninefold Styx could gather in its flow
   Cocytus, Phlegethon, and Acheron,
All mixed to one full flood of hate and woe:

And poisoned by all venom like to his
Who kissed Eurydice the traitor-kiss:—
   Then let them sting me fourfold, nor atone
Then for the eightfold misery of this!

Is not some justice somewhere? Where is
   he
Hateful to God and man, a misery
To his own vileness by exceeding it,
Who crawls God-cursed throughout eternity

Nay! sure he lives, and licks his slavered
   lips,
Laughing to think how the sweet morsel
   slips,
   The breast-flower of my bride; the dainty
   bit
Fit for—ah God! the pearl-smooth blossom
   drips

Poisonous blood that will not poison me,
Though I drink deep its fierce intensity.
   My lips closed silent on her bosom's light,
The stung blood springs—like pearls beneath
   the sea

Whose moony glimmer hath a purple vein
Hidden—so I athirst of the sad stain
  Drink up her body's life, as if to spite
Its quiet, as if the venom were to drain

Into my life—that hurts me not at all,
Struck by a stronger buffet : let me call
  All deaths ! they come not, seeing I am broken
In this one horror where a man may fall.

I am alive, and live not : I am dead,
And die not : on my desolated head
  No dew may drop, no word of God be spoken,
None heard, if by some chance some word be said.

The wheels of Fate are over me ; quite crushed
Lies my pale body where her body blushed,
  Quite dead ! there is no single sob that stirs,
No pulse of blood of all that filled and flushed

Her cheek and mine, her breast and mine : and lo !
How sunset's bloom is faded on the snow !
  There is no laugh of all those laughs of hers,
Those tender thrills of laughter I used to know.

Nor in all nature weep the careless eyes,
Nor any soul of life may sympathise,
  All I once was in this is torn and rended—
Scorned and forsaken the lone lyre lies.

Hath that not yet some sympathy with me ?
That lyre that was myself, my heart's decree
  And ruler, subtle at the dawn, and splendid
Noonwards, and soft at day's declivity !

I flung it in my anguish to the ground.
I raise it, and its music hath not found
  One string or snapped or loosened, and the tune
Is the old triumph garlanded and crowned !

Folly and hate ! Blithe mockery of sorrow !
Shrill me no harsh lies of some sweet to-
    morrow ! [1]
  Soothe me no hateful mysteries of the moon,
How one life lends what other lives may borrow !

I hate that foolish counterfoil of grief
That one pain to its friend may give relief—
  Eurydice replace Eurydice
Long hence—no separation sharp and brief

But dwelling in the intermediate
Halls between Hades and the house of Fate :
  Atropos cut, and pass to Clotho, and she
Respin the shuttle in some other state.

What shall it boot me now to gather flowers
From this young hope to wile the angry hours ?
  That many thousand years shall pass, and show
Eurydice again amid her bowers,

Forgetting, and myself again be born,
Clasp her grave beauty in the middle corn,
  Forgetting also : Time as fallen snow
Blotting the mind and memory that adorn

At least our present littleness : nor hope
Of larger excellence, extended scope,
  Shall help me here, forgetting : nothing skills
Of this poor truth—to flatter with the trope !

Wooing in mockery !—nothing skills but this
To raise her now, and resuspire the kiss,
  United by the splendour of the will's
Success—to marry, to be made of bliss,

I care not whether here or there : to live
In memory and identity : to give
  No part of self or soul to Lethe's water :
To grapple Nature, interpose an "if"

[1] Follow references to various ancient theories of immortality, reincarnation, and so on.

In her machinery of conditioned mood ;
Suspending law, suspending amplitude
  Of all Her function ; to espouse her
    daughter
In forced embrace lasciviously rude,

Indecorous, shameful to the eternal " must " !
Law may be mercy, mercy never just !
  Thus I would alter, and divide her ways,
And let her wheels grind themselves down
    to dust.

One supernatural event—but one !—
Should scale Olympus, shattering the throne
  Of the Ægis-bearing Father : and the days
Of all the Universe be fallen and done.

Well then ? O sceptred Splendour ! dost
    Thou see
How little means Thy Universe to Me ?
  How petty looks Thy will to My desire ?
Hebe and Hera to Eurydice ?

I, knowing all the progress of the earth,
The dim procession, altering death and birth,
  The Seven Stairs, the gusts of life in fire
And Love in Life, and all the serpent girth

Of sevenfold twining worlds and sevenfold
    ways
And nights made sevenfold of the sevenfold
    days
  All the vast scheme evolving into man,
And upward, onward, through Olympian haze

Into the crowning spiritual mist,
Where spirit in the spirit may subsist,
  Evolve itself in the amazing plan
Through many planes, as shining amethyst

Melts to the sapphire's sombre indigo,
And lifts, still sapphire, to the ocean glow ;
  Thence into emerald and the golden light,
Till ruby crowns the river's living flow

And glory of colour in the sun's own flame—
Beyond, to colours without sense or name,
  Impossible to man, whose vivid sight
Would blast him with their splendour as they
    came

Flashing through spiritual space, withdrawn
Now, and now flung triumphant in the dawn
  Not of mere sun's rise, but before the birth
Of a new system on the unfolded lawn

Of space beyond the sceptre of the Gods !
I, seeing all this, would foil Time's periods
  For one small woman on this one mean
    earth,
Would spoil the plan of the inane Abodes,

Throw out of gear all Nature's enginery
For such a grain of tinsel dust as I,
  Reluctant to be mangled in the wheel—
Looks other meanness so contemptibly ?

Yet I persist. Thou knowest, O most High
    Zeus,
When Hera to thine Io did refuse
  Peace, and the gadfly bit like barbèd steel
Those limbs with dews of love once lying
    loose,

When thy vast body boarded her, wrapped
    round
Her senses with a mist of being profound,
  A flame-like penetration, serpentine,
Twining and leaping without end or bound,

Inevitable as the grasp of Fate :—
Thou, reft of her by envy of thy mate
  Didst shake the heaven with bellowings
    undivine,
And rooted stars from their primeval state.

Not without law, sayest thou ? Almighty
    Zeus,
Am I not also mothered of a Muse ?
  Let there be law ! untimely to release
This soul untinctured of the Stygian dews,

Unsprinkled of Lethean lotus-drops !
Life grows so steadily, so sudden stops—
  (Surely no part in Nature's moving peace !)
Thus, when the young, like tempest-stricken
    crops

Unripe, are blasted in the blossoming
    spring—
This is a miracle, not the other thing !
  Nature insults herself, blasphemes her God,
Thus cutting short the life's hard happening.

Nor would I suffer thus, nor she repine
Had my wife faded (as rose-tinted wine
  Bleached in the sunlight) reached her
    period
And fallen gently in the arms divine,

Caressing arms of pale Persephone,
And bathed her in death's river tenderly,
  Washing the whole bright body, the long
    limbs,
The clothing hair, the face, the witchery

Of all the smiling shape in the dark stream,
As one who gathers the first floral beam
  Of daylight by the water, dives and swims
Deep in cool alleys, softer than a dream :

So, rising to the other bank, aglow
With the bright motion and the stream's
    young flow,
  She might discover the Elysian ground,
And find me waiting, find me sad and slow

Pacing the green flower-lighted turf, and leap
Into my body's kisses, into sleep :—
  Sweeter this latter bridal than we found
The first, now lost in time's eternal deep.

It is not cruel if the ripe fruit fall—
But never an elegy funereal
  Wept for untimely burial, but cried
Aloud against the Fates, forebore to call

In pity or passion on the Gods of peace ;
But cursed, but wailed, nor bade its sharp
    tongue cease
  Until the lightning spat, sharp to divide
Bone from its marrow for their blasphemies !

So I should curse, unless indeed my grief
Be not too great to yield me such relief.
  Methinks a sob must start and mar the
    roar
Of loud harsh laughing bitter unbelief

Scarring the sky with poisonous foam of
    song.
Also, what curse might remedy the wrong?
  Are not all feuds forgotten in a war ?
All stars exhausted in Astræa's throng

When the swift sun leaps skyward ? Let
    me speak
Words rather of wisdom : hate may rage and
    wreak
  Vengeance in vain if wisdom smile beyond,
Too high to care, too ultimate to seek.

The bitterest sorrow of all sorrow is this :
I had no time to catch one last long kiss,
  Nor bid farewell, nor lay one lily-frond
Of resurrection for the sign of bliss,

Remembrance of some immortality
Affirmed if not believed : alas for me
  That might not interchange the last sad
    vows,
Nor close the blue eyes clearer than the sea

Before they darkened, and the veil of death
Shrouded their splendour: still there lingereth
  Some sad white lustre on the icy brows,
Some breast-curve surely indicating breath,

Some misty glamour of deep love within
The eye's cold gleam ! some dimple on the
    chin
  Hinting of laughter : even now she seems
A folded rosebud, where the ivory skin

Closes the ripe warm centre flower, the
    mind,
The spirit that was beautifully kind,
  The sense of beauty shadowed in deep
    dreams,
Sent through the horn gates by some sleepy
    wind.

All lingers : all is gone : a little while,
And all the live sweet rapture of the smile
  Of her whole being is discomfited,
The body broken, desolated, vile,

Till nought remains but the memorial urn
Of deep red gold, less golden than did burn
  Once the strong breast : the ash within is
    shed,
Dust given for flowers : what memory shall
    turn

Unto the flowers, think worthy to remember
How the dust scattered from their fading
    ember
Is their own sign and seal of fatherhood,
Grey seas of sorrow sun-kissed into amber.

Above me hangs the sun : horrid he hangs,
A rayless globe of hell, shooting forth fangs
    Snake-wise to parch and burn my solitude,
Nor leave me quiet lamenting, with these
    pangs

Tearing my liver, more Promethean
Than ever Titan knew—the sunbright span
    Of narrow water mocks me, brightening
Far to the indigo Ionian.

The sun hangs high, as in the Arabian tale
Enchanted palaces defy the gale,
    Perched upon airy mountains, on the wing
Of genii poised, souls suffering and pale

With their long labour : wizard spire and
    dome
That maidens grown magicians had for home,
    Where the charmed sword and graven
    talisman
Held them supremely floating on the foam

Where cloudier seas innavigably roll,
Misty with elemental shape or soul,
    Thin grey essential nebulæ of man,
Caught in the mesh of magical control !

All these are beautiful and shapen so
That every bastion flames a separate glow
    Of changing colour : all detestable,
Abhorrent, since the goodly-seeming show

Is one large lie of cruelty and lust,
Carven from spectral images of dust,
    Founded on visions of the accursed well,
And built of shame and hatred and distrust,

And all things hateful and all lying things—
O song ! where wanderest on forgetful wings?
    Shall these wild numbers help thee to thine
    own,
Or change the winter's gramarye to spring's ?

Rather beguile the tedious mourning hours
With memory of the long-forgotten bowers,
    Where loves resurged from cave and grove
    to throne,
From nuptial banquet to the bed of flowers !

Rather forget the near catastrophe,
And turn my music toward Eurydice.
    Awake in day-dream all the ancient
    days,
When love first blossomed on the springing
    tree !

Let me recall the days beyond regret,
And tune my lyre to love, sharpen and set
    The strings again to the forgotten ways,
That I may tread them over, and forget !

In child-like meditative mood
    I wandered in the dell,
Passed through the quiet glades of the
    wood,
    And sought the haunted well,
Half hopeful that its solitude
    Might work some miracle.

The oaks raised angry hands on high :
    The willows drooped for tears :
The yews held solemn ceremony,
    Magical spells of years.
I saw one cypress melancholy,
    A prince among his peers.

So, turning from the arboreal seat
    And midmost hollow of earth,
I followed Hamadryads' feet
    That made at eve their mirth
To where the streamlet wandered fleet
    To show what time was worth.

I watched the waters wake and laugh
    Running o'er pebbly beaches,
Writing amazement's epitaph
    With freshets, turns, and reaches :—
The only tale too short by half
    That nature ever teaches.

Then growing grander as it swept
Past bulrushes and ferns,
Gathering the tears that heaven had wept,
The water glows and burns
In sunlight, where no shadows crept
Around the lazy turns.

All on a sudden silence came
Athwart some avenue
Where through the trees arrowed the flame
From the exultant blue ;
And all the water-way became
One heart of glittering dew.

The waters narrowed for a space
Between twin rocks confined,
Carven like Gods for poise and grace,
Like miracles for mind :
Each fashioned like a kissing face,
The eyes for joy being blind.

The waters widened in a pool,
Broad mirror of blue light.
The surface was as still and cool
As the broad-breasted night.
Engraven of no mortal tool,
The granite glistened white.

As if to shield from mortal gaze
A nymph's immortal limbs,
The shadow of the buttress stays
And dips its head and swims,
While moss engirdles it with grays
And greens that dew bedims.

Now, at the last, the western end,
Most miracle of all !
The groves of rock dispart and rend
Their sacred cincture-wall ;
All tunes of heaven their rapture lend
To make the waterfall.

There, steaming from the haze and mist
Where dew is dashed in spray,
Rises a halo sunrise-kissed
And kissed at close of day
From ruby unto amethyst,
Within the veil of grey.

And there within the circled light
I saw a dancing thing,
Most like the tender-leavèd night
Of moonrise seen in spring,
A shadow luminous and white
Like a ghost beckoning.

And then dim visions came to me,
Faint memories of fear :
As when the Argo put on sea
Such stories we did hear,
Stories to tremble at and flee—
And others worth a tear.

I thought of how a maiden man
Might hear a deadly song
And clasp a siren in his span,
And feel her kiss grow strong
To drag him with caresses wan
Into the House of Wrong.[1]

Another :[2] how the women grew
Like vines of tender grape,
And how they laughed as lovers do,
And took a lover's shape,
And how men sought them, free to woo—
•To leave them, no escape !

Another :[3] how a golden cup
A golden girl would pour,
And whoso laughed and drank it up
Grew wise and warrior :
But whoso stayed to smile and sup
Returned—ah, never more !

And yet again[4]—a river steep,
A maiden combing light,
Her hair's enchantment—she would weep
And sing for love's delight,
Until the listener dropped to sleep
In magic of her night.

[1] See Homer's Odyssey.
[2] See Lucian.
[3] Is this a perversion of the story of Calypso ?
[4] See Goethe's " Lorelei."

And then the maiden smoothed her tresses,
  And led him to the river,
Caught him and kissed with young caresses,
  And then—her cruel smiles quiver !
Beneath the waves his life represses
  For ever and for ever !

I knew the danger of the deed
  The while enrapt I gladdened.
My eyes upon the dancer feed
As one by daylight saddened
After long night whose slumbers bleed,
  By dreams deceived and maddened !

It might be—the delusive dance,
  The shadowy form I saw,
Apollo's misty quivering lance
  Thrown to elude God's law ;
It might be—doth the maid advance,
  Evanish, or withdraw ?

So stung by certainty's mistrust,
  Or tranced in dream of sin,
Or blinded by some Panic dust,
  By Dionysian din
Deafened, arose the laughing lust
  To fling my body in !

I stood upon the rock, and cried,
  And held my body high
(Not caring if I lived or died)
  Erect against the sky :
Then plunged into the wheeling tide,
  And vanished utterly.

" O shape half seen of love, and ost
  Beneath time's sightless tide,
What obolus of the vital cost
  Remains, or may abide ?
Or what perception memory steal,
  Once passed upon the whirling wheel ?

" O hope half held of love, and fled
  Beyond the ivory gate,
A dream gone from the hapless head
  By fury of a fate !
What image of the hope returns
But stings with agony that which yearns ?

" O face half kissed in faith and fear,
  Eager and beautiful !
Drop for mortality one tear !
  For life one smile recall !
There is no passion made for me—
  Else were my water-well the sea."

Such tune my falling body snapped
  Within the sacred sides,
While the warm waves with laughter lapped,
  And changed their tunèd tides,
And all my being was enwrapped,
  A bridegroom's in a bride's.

Deep in the hollow of the place
  A starry bed I saw,
Gemmed with strange stones in many a space
  Of godlike rune and law.
Such fancies as the fiery face
  Of living Art might draw.

But rising up I lift my head
  Beyond the ripples clean :
My arms with spray dew-diamonded
  Stretched love-wise to my queen
That danced upon the light, and shed
  Her own sweet light between.

But never a mortal joy might know,
  Hold never a mortal lover !
Whose limbs like moonshine glint and glow,
  Throb, palpitate, and hover :—
Pale sunrise woven with the snow
  Athwart a larchen cover !

So danced she in the rainbow mist,
  A fairy frail and chaste,
By moon caressed, by sunlight kissed
  A guerdon vain and waste ;
And the misery of her thankless tryst
  Stole on me as she paced.

For never her lips should be caressed
  By love's exulting stings,
Whose starry shape shone in the west,
  Held of the glimmering wings.
Her shadowy soul perceived the jest
  Of man and mortal things.

And there I vowed a solemn oath
To Aphrodite fair,
Sealing that sacramental troth
With a long curl of hair,
And the strange prayer's reiterant growth
Sent shining through the air.

(*Invoking Aphrodite*)

Daughter of Glory, child
Of Earth's Dione mild
By the Father of all, the Ægis-bearing King !
Spouse, daughter, mother of God,
Queen of the blest abode
In Cyprus' splendour singly glittering.
Sweet sister unto me,
I cry aloud to thee !
I laugh upon thee laughing, O dew caught
up from sea !

Drawn by sharp sparrow and dove
And swan's wide plumes of love,
And all the swallow's swifter vehemence,
And, subtler than the Sphinx,
The ineffable iynx [1]
Heralds thy splendour swooning into sense,
When from the bluest bowers
And greenest-hearted hours
Of Heaven thou smilest toward earth, a
miracle of flowers !

Down to the loveless sea
Where lay Persephone
Violate, where the shade of earth is black,
Crystalline out of space
Flames the immortal face !
The glory of the comet-tailèd track
Blinds all black earth with tears.
Silence awakes and hears
The music of thy moving come over the
starry spheres.

Wrapped in rose, green and gold,
Blues many and manifold,
A cloud of incense hides thy splendour of
light ;

[1] An imaginary animal, sacred to Venus.

Hides from the prayer's distress
Thy loftier loveliness
Till thy veil's glory shrouds the earth from
night ;
And silence speaks indeed,
Seeing the subtler speed
Of its own thought than speech of the Pan-
dean reed !

There no voice may be heard !
No place for any word !
The heart's whole fervour silently speeds to
thee,
Immaculate ! and craves
Thy kisses or the grave's,
Till, knowing its unworthiness to woo thee,
Remembers, grows content
With the old element,
And asks the lowlier grace its earlier music
meant.

So, Lady of all power !
Kindle this firstling flower
The rainbow nymph above the waterfall
Into a mortal shade
Of thee, immortal maid,
That in her love I gather and recall
Some memory mighty and mute
In love's poor substitute
Of thee, thy Love too high, the impossible
pursuit !

Then from the cloud a golden voice
Great harmonies persuade,
That all the cosmic lawns rejoice
Like laughter of a maid ;
Till evolution had no choice,
But heard it, and obeyed.

"Show by thy magic art
The hero-story !
Awake the maiden heart
With tunes of glory !
With mortal joys and tears,
Keen woes and blisses,
Awake her faiths and fears,
Her tears and kisses !"

I caught the lavish lyre, and sate
  Hard by the waterfall,
Twisting its sweetness intimate
  Into the solemn call
Of many dead men that were great,
  The plectron's wizard thrall.

Thus as she danced, nor ceased, nor
    cared,
  I set the sacred throng
Of heroes into acts that fared
  In Argo light and long,
The foes they fought, the feats they dared,
  In shadow-show and song.

      (*The play of Argonautae is sha-
        dowed before them by Or-
        pheus' magical might.*)

So faded all the dream : so stole
Some fearful fondness in her soul ;
Even as a cloud thrilled sharply through
With lightning's temper keen and true,
Splitting the ether : so again
Grew on me the ecstatic pain,
Seeing her tremble in mid-air.
No flower so exquisitely fair
Shakes out its petals at the dawn ;
No breath so beautiful is drawn
At even by the listening vale.
For oh ! she trembled ! Frail and pale,
Her looks surpassing loveliness
Lulled its own light to fond distress,
As if the soul were hardly yet
Fit to remember or forget
New-born ! and though the goddess bade
The nymph-bud blossom to a maid,
And soulless immortality
Reach to a soul, at last to die,
For love's own sake, bliss dearly bought
For change's altering coin ill-wrought,
It seemed as though the soul were strange,
Not fledged, not capable to range
At random through the world of sense
Opened so swift and so intense
Unto the being. Thus she stood
Impatient on the patient flood
With wonder waking in her eyes.
Thus the young dove droops wing, and dies,

In wonder why the wingèd thing
Loosed from yon twanging silver string
Should strike, should hurt. But now she
    wakes,
Wreathes like a waterfall of snakes
The golden fervour of her hair
About the body brave and bare
Starred in the sunlight by the spray,
And laughed upon me as I lay
Watching the change : First dawn of fire !
First ghost of nightfall's grey desire !
First light of moonrise ! Then, as June
Leaps out of May, her lips took tune
To song most soft, a spiral spell,
A siren breathing in a shell.
The notes were clustered round the well
Like angels clustering round a god.
Let memory wake from its abode
Of dim precision lost for long
The grace and grandeur of the song !

Who art thou, love, by what sweet name I
    quicken ?
By whom, O love, my soul is subtly stricken ?
  O Love, O Love, I linger
On the dear word and know not any mean-
    ing,
Nor why I chant ; there is a whisper wean-
    ing
My soul from depths I knew to depths I
    guess,
Centred in two words only : " Love " and
    " Yes."
    What lyrist's gentle finger
Strikes out a note, a key, a chord unheard of?
What voice intones a song I know no word of?
  Who am I, Love, and where ?
What is the wonder of this troublous sing-
    ing ?
What is the meaning of my spirit's clinging
Still to the two sweet words : repeat, repeat !
" Yes, Love ! " and " Yes, Love ! " Oh the
    murmur sweet !
    The fragrance in the air !
I know not, I ; amid the choral gladness
Steals an essential tremor as of sadness,
    A grace-note to the bosom

Of music's spell that binds me, as in Panic
Dance to some grasp unthinkable, Titanic,
Unto the words fresh flowers that distil
Uttermost fragrance in the mind and will,
 The unsuspected blossom !
What is the change—new birth of spring-
 time kisses
Alone in all these water-wildernesses ?
 What change ? what loveliness !
Comes this to all ? I heard my sisters crying
No tale like this—O ! were I only lying
Asleep amid the ferns, my soul would weep
Over and over in its endless sleep ;
 "Yes, love !" and " yes !" and "yes !"

So by some spell divinely drawn
She came to me across the dawn,
With open arms to me ; and sobbed
"Yes, love !" and "Yes, love !" O how
 throbbed
The giant glory at my heart !
And I ? I drew away, apart,
Lest by mere chance to me she came.
But curling as a wind-blown flame
She turned, she found me. As the dew
Melts in the lake's dissolving blue
So to my arms she came. And now,
Now, now I hold her !
 Broke the brow
Of all wide heaven in thunder ! Hear
Tremendous vortices of fear
Swirl in the ether. What new terror
Darkens the blue pool's silver mirror ?
How bursts the mountain-chasm asunder ?
Whose voice reverberates in thunder
Muttering what curse ? The sun dissolves
In anguish ; the mad moon revolves
Like a wild thing about its cage ;
The stars are shaken in the rage
Of—who but Zeus ? Before our gaze,
(My love's in shuddering amaze,
Of birth deceived and death forlorn,
And mine in anger, ay ! and scorn !)
He stood--the mighty One ! So earth
And heaven proclaimed that fearful birth :
So they grew silent lest he curse.
Dead silence hushed the universe ;

And then in clear calm tones he spoke :
"Fools ! who have meddled, and awoke
The inmost forces of the world !
One lightning from my hand had hurled
Both to annihilation's brink.
What foolish goddess bade ye think
Ye thus could play with thunder, roll
Your wheels upon the world, control
The stately being of a soul ?
Just am I ever ! Therefore know
The unrevengeful law of woe
That ye invoke. Thou seekest life,
Child of my water ! Thou a wife,
Child of my sun ! Draw living breath,
Maiden, and gain the guerdon—death !
Thou take the wife, and risk the fate
Æons could hardly culminate
To lose thy soul ! Not two but one
Are ye. Together, as the stone,
The oak, the river, or the sea,
Mere elements of mine be ye,
Or both resolve the dreadful life,
And take death's prize ! Take thou the
 wife,
Thou, who didst know. Her ignorance
Resolve itself upon a chance !
She shall decide the double fate.
Be still, my child, and meditate !
This is an hour in heaven." He ceased
And I was silent. She released
Her soul from that tremendous birth
Of fear in gentle-minded mirth.
" Great Sir !" she cried, " the choice is made !
An hour ago I was afraid,
Knew nothing, and loved not. But I
Know now not this you say—to die.
Some doubtful change ! An hour ago
I was a nymph. I did not know
This change : but now for death or life
I care not. Am I not his wife ?
I love him. Now I would not leave
That joy once tasted ; shall not grieve
If even that should ever cease,
So great a pleasure (and a peace !)
I have therein. And by the sense
Of love's intuitive influence
I know he wills me to remain
Woman." " How frivolous and vain,

O Zeus," I cried, " art thou to rise
Out of Olympus' ecstasies !
Omnipotent ! but to control
The first breath of a human soul !—"
The thunder rolled through heaven again,
Void was the spring-delighted plain
Of that gigantic phantasy.
I turned to my Eurydice
Even as she turned. The faint breath glows,—
The lightning of a living rose.
The bright eyes gleam—night's spotless stars
Glimmering through folded nenuphars.
The red mouth moves, still to the word :
"Yes, love !" and "yes, love !"   Then I
    heard
No sound and saw no sight—the world
Folded its mighty wings, and curled
Its passion round us ; bade forget
The joy with which our eyes were wet.
All faded, folded in the bliss ;
Unfolded the first fadeless kiss.

Then my soul woke, not sundering lips,
But winged against the black eclipse
Of sense : my soul on wings did poise
Her glory in the vast turquoise
Of the whole sky : expanded far
Beyond the farthest sun or star,
Beyond all space, all time.   I saw
The very limits of the law
That hath no bounds : beheld the bliss
Of that first wonder of the kiss
In its true self : how very love
Is God, and hath its substance of
Pure light : and how love hath its cause
Beyond religions, worlds, and laws ;
Is in itself the first : and moves
All evolution, and disproves
God in affirming God : all this
In that one rapture of the kiss
I knew, and all creation's pain
Fell into nothing in my brain,
As I, remaining man, involved
All life's true purpose, and dissolved
The phantoms (of itself create)
In a mysterious sweet state,
Wherein some tune began to move
Whose likeness and whose life was love.

Roll, strong life-current of these very veins,
    Into my lover's soul, my soul that is !
Thrill, mighty life of nerves, exultant strains
Triumphant of all music in a kiss !
    Fade ! fade, oh strenuous sense
    Into the soul intense
Of life beyond your weak imagining !
    And, O thou thought, dissever
    Thy airy life for ever
While the bright sounds are lifted up to spring
    Beyond this tide of being,
    Shadows and sense far fleeing
    Into a shadow deeper than the Ocean
    When passes all the mind's commotion
To a serener sky, a mighty calm emotion !

The whole world fades, folds over its wide
    pinions
    Into a darkness deeper than its own.
Silence hath   shattered   all   the   dream-
    dominions
    Of life and light : the grey bird's soul is flown
    Into a soundless night,
    Lampless : a vivid flight
Beyond the thrones and stars of heaven down
    hurled,
    Till the great blackness heaves
    An iron breast, and cleaves
The womb of night, another mightier world.
    Lost is my soul, and faded
    The light of life that braided
    Its comet tresses into golden fire.
    Fade, fade, the phantoms of desire !
Speed, speed the song of love upon the living
    lyre !

Lo ! I abide not, and my lover's glory
    Abides not : in the swaying of those tides
Gathers beneath some mighty promontory
    One mightier wave, deep drowns it, and
        abides.
    Save that one wave alone
    Nought in the void is known,
That wave of love, that sole exultant splen-
    dour
    Throned o'er all being, supreme;
    A single-shining beam
    Burning with love, unutterably tender.

Ah! the calm wave retires.
   Down all the fearful fires
Go thundering to darkness, so dissever
Their being from pure being, that the
   river
Of love is waveless now, and is pure love for
   ever.

Then mightier than all birth of stars or suns,
   Breaks the vast flood and trembles in its
   tide.
Serene and splendid shine the mystic ones,
   Exult, appal, reiterate, abide.
   Timid and fleet the earth
   Comes rushing back to birth,
Brighter and greener, radiant with gold
   Of a diviner sun,
   An exultation
Of life to life, of light to light untold.
   I? I remain, and see
   Across eternity
My lover's face, and gaze, and know the
   worth
Of love's life to the glowing earth,
The kiss that wakes all life unto a better
   birth.

So the swoon broke. I saw the face
(Shining with Love's reverberate grace)
Of my own love across the lawn,
As warm and tender as the dawn
Tinting the snows of heaven-born hills,
Enamelling the mountain rills
With light's chameleon-coloured dyes;
So shone the love-light in grey eyes,
Changing for laughter and for tears,
Changeless for joy of myriad years.
This, this endures; there is no lover,
No loved one; all the ages cover
These things from sight: but this abides
Floating above the whelming tides
Of time and space: abides for ever
Whether the lovers join or sever.
There is no change: the love exists
Beyond the moment's suns and mists
In me, abiding: and I see
No lover in Eurydice,
Save that her kiss awoke in me

This knowledge, this supreme content,
Annihilation of the event,
The vast eternal element
Of utter being, bliss, and thought,
In dissolution direly wrought
Of sense, identity's eclipse,
The shadow of a lover's lips.
The awful steel of Death divides
The alternation of the tides
Of consciousness, and binds in bliss
The dead man to the girl's live kiss.

So sped my wooing: now I surely think
Suspended here upon the burning brink
   Of this dim agony, invading sense,
That bliss should still abide: but now I
   shrink,

Fall from the crags of memory, and abide
Now in this nature-life, basilisk-eyed,
   And serpent-stinging: yea, I perish thence.
That perishes which was: and I am tied

Unto myself: the "I" springs up again
Bound to the wheel of speedless sense and
   pain,
   None loosing me. Past is the utter bliss;
Present the strong fact of the death, the stain

Of the marred lives: I meditate awhile
Not on the mere light of the girl, the smile
   Deepening down to the extremest kiss;
Not of the long joys of the little isle

Set in Ionian waters, where the years
Passed, one long passion, too divine for tears,
   Too deep for laughter: but on that divine
Sense beyond sense, the shadow of the
   spheres

Lost in the all-pervading light of love:
That bliss all passion and all praise above;
   Impersonal, that fervour of the shrine
Changed to pure peace that had its substance
   of

Nothing but love : in vain my thoughts evoke
That light amidst the deadly night and smoke
  Of this dread hour : there's nothing serves
  nor skills
Here, since that hateful " I " of me awoke,

Making me separate from the wings of life.
Nothing avails me of the cruel strife
  With my own being : hideous sorrow fills
My heart—O misery ! my wife ! my wife !

Stay ! if I cannot be the Absolute,
Let me be man ! discard the wailing lute
  And wake the lyre : the mightier than me
Drag up the courage in me to dispute

The battle with despair : awake the strings
Stronger than earth, than the immortal kings
  Alike of death and life : invoke the sea
That I may cross her on the viewless wings

Of song, find out the desolating river
That girds the earth, unloose the silver quiver,
  Choosing an arrow of sharp song to run
Down to the waters that lament for ever :—

And cleave them ! That my song's insistent
  spell
Rive the strong gates of iron-builded hell,
  And move the heart of the ill-hearted one.
Yea ! let me break the portals terrible,

And bring her back ! come back, Eurydice !
Come back, pale wanderer to Eternity !
  Come back, my wife, my wife, again to
  love !
Come back, my wife ! come back, come back
  to me !

Enough ! my purpose holds : no feeble
  cries !
No sob shall shake these nerves : no ecstasies
  Of hope, or fear, or love avail to move
Those iron-hearted dooms and destinies.

I will be calm and firm as I were Zeus.
I will descend to Hades and unloose
  My wife : prevail on pale Persephone,
Laving her love-locks with exalted dews

Of stern grey song ; such roseate tunes
  espouse
That all the echoes of that lonely house
  Answer mé sob for sob, that she decree
With love deep-seated in her lofty brows

Forth sparkling : and with Hades inter-
  cede,
So as I stir the judgment-seat, and plead,
  The awful brows may lighten, and decree
My wife's return—a poet's lofty meed !
  •

EXPLICIT LIBER SECUNDUS.

LIBER TERTIUS VEL LABORIS

TO

THE MEMORY OF

IEHI AOUR,

WITH WHOM I WALKED THROUGH HELL, AND COMPELLED IT

" Neither were his hopes frustrated : For having appeased them with the melodious sound of his voice and touch, prevailed at length so far, as that they granted him leave to take her away with him ; but on this condition, that she should follow him, and he not to look back upon her, till he came to the light of the upper World ; which he (impatient of, out of love and care, and thinking that he was in a manner past all danger) nevertheless violated, insomuch that the Covenant is broken, and she forthwith tumbles back again headlong into Hell."—*The Wisdom of the Ancients.*

" Moody Pluto winks while Orpheus plays."—*Rape of Lucrece.*

ORPHEUS TRAVELS TO HADES.

As I pass in my flight
    On the awed storm cloud,
        Steeps steeper than sleep,
Depths deeper than night,
    I have furrowed and ploughed
        (Deep calling to deep !)
Through the spaces of light,
    The heads of them bowed
        For the fears that weep,
And the joys that smite,
    And the loves disallowed.
        They are risen ; they leap ;
They wing them in white,
    Crying aloud
        Words widowed that keep
The frost of their fires forgotten and faded
    from Memory's steep.

As I pass in my glory
    O'er sea and land,
        I smite the loud tune
From a fervid hand,
    By the promontory,
        The mountainous moon.

Vivid and hoary,
    Twin birds, as I hark,
        Take fire, understand
The ways of the dark,
    As an angel did guide me,
Waving the brand
    Of the dawn's red spark.
My measures mark
The influence fine
Of the voyage divine
Of the airy bark
Wherein I travel
O'er mountain and level,
    The land, and the sea.
And the beings of air,
    And the lives of the land,
And the daughters of fire,
    And the sons of the Ocean,
        Come unto me ;
My chariot bear,
    My tunes understand,
My love desire,
    Share my emotion.
They gather, they gather,
Apollo, O father !
    They gather around ;
    They echo the sound

Of the tune that rejoices,
　The manifold measure
Of feet tuned to voices
　Of terrible pleasure.
We pass in our courses
　Above the grey treasure
Of seas in Earth's forces,
　Her girdle, her splendour.
We bridle the horses
　Of sea as we lend her
Tunes subtle and tender
To sink in her sources.
　The air's love ?　We rend her !
We pass to the West,
We sink on the breast
Of the Ocean to rest.

As I pass, as I madden
　In fury of flight,
The sea's billows gladden
　Invoking the light.
The depths of her sadden
　Not seeing the sight
Of the glorious one,
Whose steed is the Sun,
　Whose journey is certain,
Who speeds to the gate,
　The visible curtain
Of visible fate.
My soul takes no hurt in
　Their gloom :　I await
The portals to rise
In the desolate skies.
I trust to my song
Irresistibly strong
To sunder and shatter
Those towers of matter.
They rise !　Oh !　They rise,
　The terrible towers
Of Hades : they lift
Across the white skies
　Those terrible-cliffed
Rocks, where the hours
Beat vainly : where lies
　The horrible rift
Of the earth's green bowers
Where the wan ships drift,
And the sun's rays shift,

And the river runs
　Whose banks have no flowers,
Whose waves have no suns.
　Sheer to the terror
Of heaven, the walls
　Strike ; and the mirror
Of water recalls
　No truth, but dim error.
The soul of me falls
　Down to the glamour
Of dream ; and fear
　Beats like a hammer.
Here ! it is here !
　Lost are my friends ;
The elements shrink
　Where the life-world ends
On the icy brink
　Of the sunless river ;
Ends, and for ever !

I pass to the portals
　Of death in my flight.
I sound at the gates.
I call the immortals
　Of death and of night.
I call on the Fates
By the summons of light.
　The gates are rended ;
The rocks divide ;
　My soul hath descended
Abreast of the tide.
　I, single and splendid,
Death have defied !
I pass by the terrible gates and the guardians
　dragon-eyed.

I thunder adown
　The vast abyss.
(The journey's crown
　Is a woman's kiss !),
　　What terrors to master !
　　What fear and disaster
To gain the renown
　And the fadeless bliss !
I thunder aloud
　On the rocks as I fly,
Borne on a cloud
　In the gloomy sky.

Shaped like a shroud,
Draped like a pall,
I shrink not ; I fall
To the blackness below
With my soul aglow.
No taint of a fear !
For I know, I know
Eurydice near,
Eurydice here !
The purpose divine
Thrills my soul as wine.
Now I pass to the soul of the dark, confront-
ing the innermost shrine. .

Hail to ye, warders
That guard the borders
Of Hades !   All hail to ye, dwellers
of night !
But I am the soul
In a man's control.
Ye have nought to do with the dweller
of light !

Hail to ye, hail
In the hollow vale,
Your weapons are lifted against me
in vain.
My lyre shall charm ye,
My voice disarm ye,
For I am the soul overshadowed of
pain !

Hail to ye, wardens
Of Death's grey gardens !
O flowerless and vineless your bower-
less vale !
But I must alone
To the wonderful throne.
Let fall the vain spears, shadows !
Hail to ye !   Hail !

The phantoms diminish,
The shadows fall back.
Lost in the vision
In fires that finish
Stark and black
With lust and derision ;

And all the illusion
Is fallen to the ground.
The warders are beaten
They go in confusion ;
Their place is not found.
The air hath eaten
With wide-gaping jaws
A furious folk.
Lost is the cause
In Tartarean smoke.
I, through the wall
Of impassable gloom,
Apart from the sun,
Pass as a ghost,
Bearing the lyre.
The sad notes fall
To the sorrowful womb ;
One after one
They leap as a host
With weapons of fire
On a desolate coast,
Where love is lost
And the bitterness clings of fear, and the
sadness dogs of desire !

Thrice girded with brass,
Thrice bound with iron,
The gate is in three
Pillars of gold.
But I will pass
(My heart as a lion,
My lyre as a key !)
To the gates of old,
To the place of despair
And the walls of dread,
The halls of the doomed,
The homes of the dead,
The houses where
The beautiful air
Is as air entombed.
Nothing can shake
Those terrible walls.
No man can wake
With silver calls
The home of the lost and the lone, the gate
of the Stygian thralls.

But thou, O Titan !
O splendour triform !
Gloomiest dweller
Of uttermost night !
My journey enlighten !
O soul of the storm !
Waker and queller
Of sombre delight,
Hecate ! hearken
The soul of my prayer !
Glitter and darken
Through sulphurous air !
Let the sacrifice move thee to joy, the in-
voker thy glory declare
In words that shall please
Thy terrible peace,
O speedy to save,
In flames of fine fire that bedew the deepest
Tartarean cave !

[*Invoking* HECATE]

O triple form of darkness ! Sombre splen-
dour !
Thou moon unseen of men ! Thou huntress
dread !
Thou crownèd demon of the crownless
dead !
O breasts of blood, too bitter and too tender !
Unseen of gentle spring,
Let me the offering
Bring to thy shrine's sepulchral glittering !
I slay the swart beast ! I bestow the bloom
Sown in the dusk, and gathered in the gloom
Under the waning moon,
At midnight hardly lightening the East ;
And the black lamb from the black ewe's
dead womb
I bring, and stir the slow infernal tune
Fit for thy chosen priest.

Here where the band of Ocean breaks the road
Black-trodden, deeply-stooping, to the
abyss,
I shall salute thee with the nameless kiss
Pronounced toward the uttermost abode
Of thy supreme desire.
I shall illume the fire
Whence thy wild stryges shall obey the lyre,

Whence thy Lemurs shall gather and spring
round,
Girdling me in the sad funereal ground
With faces turnèd back,
My face averted ! I shall consummate
The awful act of worship, O renowned
Fear upon earth, and fear in hell, and
black
Fear in the sky beyond Fate !

I hear the whining of thy wolves ! I hear
The howling of the hounds about thy form,
Who comest in the terror of thy storm,
And night falls faster ere thine eyes appear
Glittering through the mist.
O face of woman unkissed
Save by the dead whose love is taken ere
they wist !
Thee, thee I call ! O dire one ! O divine !
I, the sole mortal, seek thy deadly shrine,
Pour the dark stream of blood,
A sleepy and reluctant river
Even as thou drawest, with thine eyes on
mine,
To me across the sense-bewildering flood
That holds my soul for ever !

The night falls back ;
The shadows give place ;
The threefold form
Appears in the black,
As a direful face
Half seen in the storm.
I worship, I praise
The wonderful ways
Where the smitten rays
Of darkness sunder.
The hand is lifted ;
The gates are rifted ;
The sound is as thunder !
She comes to the summons,
Her face as a woman's,
Her feet as a Fear's,
Turned back on her path
For a sign of wrath :—
She appears, she appears !

I step to the river.
  The lyre-strings quiver ;
  The limbs of me shudder ;
    So cold is the mist ;
      So dark is the stream ;
        So fearful the boat ;
    So horrid the rudder ;
      So black is the tryst ;
        So frightful the beam ;
          So fearing to float ;
  The steersman so dread,
The shadowy shape of a ghost that guides
  the bark of the dead !

      Agèd and foul,
      His locks wreathe about him.
      Horrid his scowl !
        Haggard his soul !
        My songs control
  While they fear him and doubt
      him.
  I step in the boat,
      And the waters ache,
      And the old boards shake.
  I shall hardly float,
      So heavy the soul
      Of a living man
  On those waters that roll
      Nine times around
      The fatal ground ;
Yet still to my singing we move on the river
Tartarean.

    So darker and colder
      The stream as we float :
      Blacker and bleaker,
        The mist on the river !
    Stronger the shoulder
      Impels the sad boat.
        Sadder and weaker
        Shudder and quiver
    The notes of the lyre.
    Quenched is my fire
      In the fog of the air.
    Dim my desire
      Cuts through the snare.
    The cold confounds me ;

The mist surrounds me ;
  Life trembles and lowers ;
  Earth fades from my life.
The love of my wife,
  The light of the flowers,
  Earth's beautiful bowers.
Pass, and are not.
I am awed by the soul of the place, the hope-
  less, the desolate spot.

    Here is the wharf
      Wearily standing,
    Misshapen and dwarf,
      Well fit for such landing !
    Darker the bloom
      Of the night-flowers glows,
    Shadowing the tomb,
      The indicible woes.
    Dark and unlovely the cypress
      still grows
    Deformed and blistered,
      Stunted and blackened,
    Where the dead gleams glistered,
      The dusk-lights slackened.
    Such is the shore
      Who reacheth may never
      Return o'er the river !
    Here pace evermore
      The terrible ghosts
    Malignant of men,
      Whose airless hosts
        In wars unjust
    Went down to the den ;
        Whose fury and lust
    Turned poison or steel
      On their own bad lives.
    Here whirls the grim wheel
      Where the dead soul strives
    Ever to climb
      To the iron nave,
    Find Space and Time,
      Or a God to save,
      Or a way o'er the wave.
    The Fate contrives
    That he never thrives.
      Revolving anon,
      The gleam is gone,
    And the shadowy smile

Of Hecate darkens.
My sad soul hearkens ;
Moves fearfully on :-
O place of all places discrowned ! Lament-
ing, I linger awhile !

But fronting me tearful,
Me full of lament,
Shoots up the fearful
Den of the hound.
Ages they spent,
Gods, in the graving
That cavern profound,
That temple of hate,
Of horror and craving :—
O who shall abate
The moaning, the raving ?
Dark the dull flame
Of the altar, the flood
Of the black lamb's blood !
But who shall proclaim
That his soul can descry
The depth of that cavern immense where the
guardian of Orcus may lie ?

Sleepest thou, devil ?
Monster of evil !
Spawn of Typhon
By Echidna's lust !
The hateful revel
In blood and dust !
The obscene crone
And the monster's terror !
The hideous thrust
Of an unclean thirst
In the halls of error !
Expunged and accurst,
A lapping of hate,
A bride-bed rotten,
And thou, miscreate
And misbegotten !

O Hecate, hear me !
The terrors awaken,
The cavern is shaken
With horrible groanings.
Cryings and moanings
And howlings draw near me.

I tremble, I fear me !
My lyre is forsaken.
The heart of the hollow
Is helpless to bear
The notes of Apollo
Through Stygian air.

But heavier shrieking
Revolves and resounds
In the ghastly profounds ;
And the voice unspeaking
Of the hound of the damned
Runs eager, and bounds,
Malignantly crammed
In my ears, and the noise
Of infernal joys
In the houses of sin :—
Let me pass to a direr place, to the terrors
unspoken within !

Dead silence succeeds
The sound of the prayer.
Again the loud lyre
Shudders and bleeds
In the desolate air
With a sound as of fire !
The hound recedes ;
But the gates stand there,
Barring desire,
Barring the way
Of the dead unburied,
Unshrived, and unblessed ;
They stand and pray
In legions serried,
Beating the breast,
Tearing the hair,
Rending the raiment.
There is none to care.
No golden paymen
Availeth at all.
There is none to call ;
There is none to pity :
They stand in their pain
At the gate of the city.
There is none to feel
Or give relief ;
They are lost ; they are vain ;
They are eaten of grief.

They are sore afraid,
    They are weary with care.
There is none to aid.
        There is none to pity.
    They wail in despair
        At the gate of the city.

But I, shall I halt
    At the thrice-barred portal
In the lampless vault,
    I, half an immortal ?
By love of my mother,
    By might of my lyre,
        By Nature's assistance,
I, I, not another
    Demand my desire,
        Rebuke your resistance,
By mighty Apollo
    Whose power yet abides,
Though his light may not follow
Through Stygian tides !
By my power over things
    Both living and dead,
        By my influence splendid
            In heavenly court,
The song of me springs.
    My favour is dread.
        Be your portals rended !
            Your bolts be as nought !
The ethereal kings
    Encompass my head.
        My soul hath transcended
            The limits of thought !
Unbar me the gates !
    Revolve me the hinges !
Mine be the Fate !
Mine be the springes
Wherein ye have taken
The spirits forsaken !
        But I, shall I quail at a nod ?
    Shall I fail for a God ?
Is the soul of me shaken ?

Darklier winding
    And steeper the way,
Baffling and blinding
    Eyes used to the day.

Rocks cloven by thunder
    And shattered by storm
Awry or asunder
    Rise and reform
In marvellous coils
    Round the adamant road
Whose tangles and toils
    Lead on the abode,
Where dwell in the light
    Of justice infernal
The judges that smite,
    That judge men aright,
        Whose laws are eternal !
Those kings that in reigning
For bribing or feigning
    Swerved never an hair
From justice and truth ;
    Turned never a care
To wrath or to ruth ;
    Did justice, and died.

Thither I haste
    To face the austere
        Faces of peace.
        Shall the lyre cease ?
    Its music be waste ?
        Themselves not hear ?
I stride to the presence and sing : and my
    soul is not conquered of fear.

Now the road widens and grows darker still
    As if the shadow of some ancient tower
Cast its deep spell on the reluctant will.

Still tortuous winds the deep descent ; the
        hour
    Lies bitterer on my soul : I fear to fail,
To loose in vain the lyre's dissolving power

On the white souls armed in that triple mail
    Of justice, virtue, truth : percipience
Beyond the mute and melancholy veil

That covers from the drowsy eye of sense
    The subtle thought that hides behind the
        mask.
I fear indeed : but now the soul intense

Of truth precedes me and informs the task
  Of the steep ways: I gladden and go on
Ready to sing, to answer, or to ask

As all may happen : now the stern light shone
  Vivid across the blackness, and the rock
Recedes: the narrow stair is changed and
    gone

And the wide air invades : a mighty shock
  To my numbed senses void of vital air
And to my lyre reverberate to mock

With clanging echoes and discordant, where
  The dome reached up, almost to earth, so
    high
Rolled back the pillars and the walls, aglare

With iron justice' frightful symmetry
  Blazoned in blood-like flame, gushing from
    springs
Unseen, unguessed, incredible ! There fly

The dreaded banners of the demon kings
  In fearful colours, and the vast inane
Dome catches music from my mouth, and rings

Back iron curses to the blessings vain
  I pour in desperate fervour from the lyre.
So, baffled by the echoes of hell's pain,

Blinded by grisly glamour of hell's fire,
  I take my refuge in the solitude
And grandeur of that irony of ire,

That mockery of mercy : thus I brood
  Apart, alone, upon the cause of Things
And wait those fearful Three. A lifeless
    mood

Stirs my grey being : ay ! no passion springs
  In flowerless halls as these : awhile the
    mind
Wanders on void unprofitable wings

No whither : gains new strength at last to find
  Custom breed sight and hearing : in the hall
The sounds grow clear, the black fires fail to
    blind.

I see the mighty buttress of the wall
  Lost in its mighty measure : hear again
The lyre's low notes and light distinctly fall

A gentle influence in the place of pain.
  Oh now the central glory of the place
Falls splendid on the unbewildered brain,

And I am found contemplating a face
  More passionless than mortals' : central sits
Throned on pure iron, with brass for cara-
    pace,

Minos : and either side of him befits
  The mighty Rhadamanthus throned on gold
And canopied with silver : sternly knits

His brows the awful .Eacus, in cold
  Splendour of justice throned on carven
    lead ;
And o'er his head twin dragons bend and
    hold

A cobra's hood made of some metal dread
  Impossible on earth : how calm, how keen
Flash their wise eyes, those judges of the
    dead,

In silent state : how eager, how serene
  Are the broad brows : the heart shrinks up
    and sinks,
Seeing no gallery to slip between

And pass those aged ones—oft a man thinks
  He faces truth ! I know this hour, alas !
That face to face with naked truth he shrinks.

His web of woven fiction may not pass
  (Though he believes it to be truth) with
    them
Who see his mind as though it were a glass

Without a shadow. Yet the ninefold gem
  And million-facet glory of my song
Glittering, made splendid in the diadem

Of flashing music shall assoil the wrong,
  A finer truth interpret. Though the heart
And core of music hold a poisonous throng

Of lies—yet, sing it to sufficient Art,
  The lie abolishes itself—the tune
Redeems the darkness—the keen flashes start

Of truth availing though the midnight moon
  Darken, the stars be quenched in utter
    cloud,
And the high sun eclipsed at very noon.

So flash I back the glory calm and proud
  Irradiating the Three. So shall my lyre
Sweep the vast courts with acclamation loud

Of splashing music, of exulting fire
  That revels in its penetrating cover
Of azure life that smites its flickering spire

Of sworded splendour inwards, to discover
  Not justice, not discernment, not desire,
Not passion, but the sheer will of a lover !

MINOS.

Substantial, stern, and strong,
Who lifts an alien lyre ?
Confounds our echoes dire
With strange and stubborn song ?

ÆACUS.

Here in the House of Dole
Where shadows hardly dare
Stand, who doth deem to fare
Forth from the outer air
Mortal, a strenuous soul ?

RHADAMANTHUS.

The large and lordly land
Fertile of earth hath sent
With dolorous intent
Some shape or element.
What spell of might hath rent
The veil of Hell, and bent
Death's purpose to his hand ?

MINOS.

What shaft from the bow of Apollo ?

ÆACUS.

What quiver of wonder
Hath cleft the black walls of the hollow

RHADAMANTHUS.

What terror ?

MINOS.

What thunder
Hath shaken Hell's gates to the base ?

ÆACUS.

Withstanding the guards to their face ?

RHADAMANTHUS.

Hath rent him asunder
The portals of Dis in his wrath ?

MINOS.

Hath made for his will
An arrow of light for his path ?

ÆACUS.

Left stagnant and chill
The waters of Styx unappeased ?
The keys of our prison hath he seized.

RHADAMANTHUS.

A mortal !

MINOS.

An ill
Most alien to Heaven, by Zeus !

ÆACUS.

But impiety's doom,
By Poseidon, shall fill for his use
No well-omened tomb.

RHADAMANTHUS.

By Hades, our dogs let us loose !
  Let death in the gloom
Bring peace to the Hall of the Dead !

MINOS.

A passionate being !
No weal to the light of his head
In the place of the seeing !

ÆACUS.

Awake, wild justice of dread !
Lest shadows be fleeing
In fear of the portent to lurk
In a deeper-detested
Cave, ere we wake to the work.

RHADAMANTHUS.

Black snakes many-crested,
Arise ! lest the calm of the murk
From our places be wrested.

MINOS.

Who art thou ?

ÆACUS.

'What ails thee to irk
From earth tender-breasted
To the milkless dugs of the grave
And the iron breasts of the pit ?

RHADAMANTHUS.

Can a bodily presence save
Against a shadowy wit ?

MINOS.

Thy hope doth dwell, O slave,
Where thy mother fashioned it,
Oh heart of a fool, in thy breast.

ÆACUS.

Away, away to the skies !

RHADAMANTHUS.

That our dead may take their rest.

MINOS.

Arise to the air, arise !

ÆACUS.

Away to the mountain crest !

RHADAMANTHUS.

Veil, veil from the awful eyes !

MINOS.

Endure thy heart as it may,
And steel thine heart,
Thou shalt hear and know and obey
As I say "Depart";
Lest the arrow find its way
And the sternly-shapen dart.

ÆACUS.

A second our justice waits.

RHADAMANTHUS.

It falleth anon.

MINOS.

O fool of hopes and hates
Arise and begone !

ÆACUS.

O toy of the mirthless fates !
Who art thou to con
The mysteries of the dead in the black-souled
bastion ?

MINOS, ÆACUS, RHADAMANTHUS.

Away ! away ! to the light of day !
Now as it may : then as it must.
We are loath to pardon, and loath to slay,
Void of greed and anger and lust,—
But we are iron and thou art clay ;
We are marble and thou but dust.

ORPHEUS.

O iron, bow to silver's piercing note !
O marble, see the shape of ivory !
My justice fountains from a sweeter throat ;
My death is bound beyond eternity.

O wise and just, hear ye the voice of man,
Not seeking to involve in woven spells
Or trickery the decree Tartarean,
By words to blink that justice which is
Hell's !

I came indeed before this awful throne
To seek a party favour, but I wait
Shuddering and silent, steadfast and alone,
And change my music at the call of Fate.

For while ye spake in tumult, in this ear
A music rang from earth's remotest mine,
From star and comet, flaming wheel and
sphere,
From Hell's deep vault and from the
House divine.

A voice diverse, a voice identical
Called me this hour from bitterest woes
and black,
Constraining eloquence and mighty thrall
Of cosmic agony, and wrung me back

From my poor plea to challenge in my song
The whole domain of deeply-seated law,
Launch thunders not Olympic at the strong
Bars of the Order backed with strength
and awe

That men call Will of Zeus : the after scheme
And primal fate and most primordial plan
Shaped from the earth's first protoplasmic
dream
Up to the last great mischief that is man.

All this I challenge : that the suns and stars
Work in due order and procession meet
Without caprice in viewless, changeless bars,
Nor self-determinate in their wingless feet.

All nature and all consciousness and thought
He hath thrown asunder and divided them;
Fixing a gulf of agony athwart,
Where rolls a tide no soul of man may
stem.

Himself fixed high, he mocked us with his
name
Of "reconciler," and of "one beyond
all";
And cast his shadow to the deep, to shame
That oneness in its own division's thrall ;

So that Himself appears in cloud and fire
Distorted in the world's distorted mirror ;
And dark convulsion and confusion dire
Stands for his form of error and of terror.

But I perceive, I Orpheus, Lord of Song,
And every Lord of Song that me shall
follow
Down steeps of time's own agony and wrong,
Shall see the lightning bridge the dreadful
hollow

With jagged flame of master-music, hear
The blind curse thunder forth against in
vain
When the swift glory of the rolling sphere
Of song pours forth its utterance, keen
with pain,

Mad with delight, and calm beyond woe and
pleasure.
Yea, every son of this my soul shall know
In the swift concourse of his music's measure
One thing impatient of this to and fro

March of hell's dancers. I perceive a key
To lock the prison of the world on him
That built the iron walls and made decree
Long past in æons now grown gray and dim,

Like halls ancestral whence their folk have
fled,
The marbles all are broken, and the weeds
Grown o'er the bones of the unquiet dead,
And time's remorse avails not on its deeds.

I see that time is one : future and past
Are but one present ; space is one, the
North
And South and all the sixfold shame holds
fast
No more : the poet's fiat hath gone forth

And tamed the masters of division. Me
Nor sun can burn, nor moon make mad,
nor time
Alter : I drown not in the deepest sea,
Nor choke where icy mountain ridges
climb

The steeps of heaven : but these, these chil-
     dren, cry
  Their bitter cry for justice. Mighty Ones,
Lords of the Dusk, incline ye, mercifully,
  Rightly, to misery of all stars and suns

And planets and all grains of dust that
     sorrow—
  Hark ! from grim Tartarus, most doleful
     bound,
Their throats of anguish notes of triumph
     borrow
  At my loud strain's unprofitable sound.

For who are ye? Poor judges of the dead,
  In your stern eyes the sadness is mine own,
Mingled with sense that all your forces dread
  Are vain to take the spirit from one stone.

I would have called to ye in wild strong joy ;
  " Arise, O Lords of Justice, and be girt
With lightnings, and be ardent to destroy
  This Fool's creation and to heal its hurt

With swift annihilation ! " Ye are vain,
  Alas ! poor powers ! But yet the damned
     rejoice
Hearing the splendour, prophet in my strain,
  And certain comfort in my mighty voice.

For this shall be, that in the utter end
  Shall be an end, that in the vast of time
Shall come a ceasing, and the steel bar bend
  Of the God's will, himself from his sublime

Pinnacled house in heaven headlong cast
  Like his own thunder to the abyss of
     nought
When space and time and being shall be past,
  And the grim thinker perish with his
     thought.

Therefore I leave in hands unshakable
  The destinies of being, and care not
For all the miseries of the damned in hell,
  Or the vain gods' unenviable lot.

I leave the cry of chaos, and recall
  My private pang and woe particular,
One drop of water by mischance let fall
  From some white slave's divinely carven
     jar.

O Lords of Justice, universal woe
  Hath yet its shadows in a singer's soul,
He feels the arrow from a party bow
  Who yet hath strength to struggle with
     the whole.

I love my wife. The many-coloured throne
  Of Grecian meadows hath nor charm nor
     lure
Now she is gone. Lamenting and alone
  My dulled heart aches, most that it must
     endure.

Give this decree, O masters ! Few the days
  And light the hours since Heracles de-
     scended
The dusky steep, the intolerable ways,
  And one prey—Theseus—from your prisons
     rended

By might of godhead and the skill of man.
  But now with music from a Muse's breast
Sweetened with milk of tenderness, I scan
  Your eyes with hope, and with a man's
     unrest

And a man's purpose I appeal. Be just,
  O ye whom greater justice baulks and bars !
Return my lover from the unkind dust
  To the sweet light of the eternal stars !

Be kind, and from the unjust place of fear
  Return by kindness her, the innocent one,
From the grey places to the waters clear
  And meadows fair, and light of moon and
     sun !

Relent. Reverse the doom. I see your eyes
  Quiver despite ye : but your hands ye
     wring ;
Little by little bitter tears arise
  Like stubborn water from a frozen spring,

And deep unrest is seated in your limbs.
Ye pity me. Ye pity. Mute and weak
With the long trouble of persistent hymns
I bow myself and listen while ye speak.

MINOS.

Brethren, what need of wonder
That Hell is burst asunder
Shaken from base to brow, as if with Zeus'
own thunder?
What wonder if our peace
Broke, and our mysteries
Quaked at the prescience of these solemnities?

ÆACUS.

Child of the earth and heaven,
Our spirits thou hast riven
With words we must admit, with power of
song—whence given?
Neither of God nor man,
Thy song's amazing span
Hath caused strange joy among the woes
Tartarean.

RHADAMANTHUS.

Never in the centuries
Till godlike Heracles
Burst the wild bonds, hath mortal found the
fatal knees;
Nor hath the bitter cry
Of worlds in agony
Answered the groans of those who weep,
and cannot die.

MINOS.

Iron of heart and strong,
We also suffer wrong.
We know these words are just. We avail
not. Though thy song
Were the sole word of Zeus,
Should that avail to loose
The bands of Being firm, invulnerable dews
Tincturing its bitter brass,
Shielding its vital mass
From every word that cries, "Thus, and thy
day shall pass."

ÆACUS.

Typhon! Typhon! Typhon!
Heard ye that awful moan
Leap through the blackness from the miser-
able throne?
Vain as each pallid ghost,
Where is thy fatal boast,
Destroyer named of old on Khem's[1] disas-
trous coast?
Old power of evil curled
Below the phantom world,
Canst thou destroy, whose might to misery
is hurled?

RHADAMANTHUS.

What god beyond these twain
Abides or may remain
Seated, too strong to quell, exalted over
pain?
Aloof from time and chance,
Fate, will and circumstance,
Canst Thou not wither Life with one in-
dignant glance?
Thy name we know not; Thine
Is the unbuilded shrine.
We doubt us if Thou be among the powers
divine!

MINOS.

Bound by strict line and law,
Fearful with might and awe,
We hold the powerless power
For many an agèd hour.
We move not from our place.
We ask nor give not grace,
Nor change our lordly looks before a sup-
pliant's face.

ÆACUS.

Stern in all justice, we
Assent aloud to thee,
We affirm thy cause as right:
We put forth all the might
Of aid: and all is done.
Our utmost power is none
To lift one soul to live and look upon the
sun.

[1] Egypt.

RHADAMANTHUS.

For righteous thought and deed
Apportioning its meed ;
For evil act and mind
Rewarding in its kind ;
So sit we : but our power
Apportions not an hour
To light the dying lamp, revive the faded
flower.

MINOS.

But thou, be strong to sing !

ÆACUS.

Loose arrows from the string !

RHADAMANTHUS.

Bid the wild word take wing !

MINOS.

Hades hath evil fame
To suppliants—bitter shame !—
Inexorable.

ÆACUS.

                    Aim
Yet the swift prayer, abide
His word whate'er betide.
What worse ?

RHADAMANTHUS.

                    The Gods thy guide !
Go and assail him !

MINOS.

                    Stay,
The Queen of Hell !

ÆACUS.

                    That way
Leads to the light of day.

RHADAMANTHUS.

A woman's heart may yearn,
To a man's love may turn.

MINOS.

Should she, the ravished, spurn
A man whose love is reft ?

ÆACUS.

Meadows and flowers she left
To Him—O bosom cleft
With a wife's loss !—a wife.

RHADAMANTHUS.

Too doubtful is the strife.

MINOS.

Yet go ! perchance to life.

ÆACUS.

Go ! and the Gods above
Guard thee, O soul of love !

RHADAMANTHUS.

I doubt me much thereof.

ORPHEUS.

Ah me ! I find ye but ill counsellors.
For I will conquer. Have I spent these
    stores
Of will and song for nought ? Hell's heart
    may rend,
But mine endureth even to the end.

Severe and righteous Lords, O fare ye well !
Are not my feet forced forward on a road
Leading to innermost abodes of Hell

Exalted as above the green abode
Of nymphs on broad Olympus, raises high
Its head the kingly snow, gigantic load

Of sombre whiteness cleaving through the
    sky
For gods to dwell in ? So I pass the hall
And seek the gloomy thrones of majesty,

Where I may pledge my last despairing call
Unto the mightiest of the House of Dread,
And loosen Death's inexorable thrall

And bring my lover from among the dead.
Now in the blackness of the rocks that span
The dolorous way I spy a golden thread

Veined in the strength of the obsidian
Flowing and growing, joining vein to vein,
Like fresh blood in the arteries of man,

Up to the very heart.   And as I go
Loosen the knees of anguish and grow dim
The shattering flames of pain : the songs
    of woe

Flicker and alter to a solemn hymn
Chanted in slowest measure in deep awe.
Now as a yew-tree sends a mighty limb

Shooting to sunset, the black road's black
    maw
Gapes to the westward ; the great trunk
    divides
And all the armies of infernal law

Stand ranked about the venerable sides
Of the black cave : they speak not ; dumb
    they stand
And all the frost of all the air abides

Upon them, as a vampire stooped and spanned
The white throat of a maiden and held still
Her powers by virtue of its hate's command,

Somewhat like love's : so all the solemn
    chill
Invades those statued ranks of warriors,
And I pass through, the lightning of my will

A steady stream of flame : high instinct pours
Its limpid light of water on my mind,
So that I range inhospitable shores

Assured of Her I shall most surely find
Ere the end be : awake, O living lyre,
Since in the narrow way and pass confined

I see a darkness infinite as fire,
Clear as all spirit vision, lustrous yet
As ebony shows in caverns rendered dire

By dreadful magic, or as if pure jet
Had taken of itself an inner light,
And its own blackness filled night's coronet

With a new jewel : so I see aright
Where no light is like earth's.   The path
    grows broad
And lofty, till the whole hall springs to sight,

And I am standing where the dreaded Lord
And Lady of the region of the lost
Hold awful sway : yet here the flaming sword

Of sight is broken by the deadly frost
That clusters round their thrones : a mist of
    fire
Congealed to vital darkness : yet exhaust

Like a seer's magic glass of air : expire
The dumb black hours in fear : but I am
    ware,
Well ware, by instinct surer still and higher

Than the own sight of soul that they are there,
No mockery of their presence : so even
    hither
My mother's might is on me, on I flare

Into wild war of song : my keen notes wither
The flowers of frost about me and I turn
Ever the strength and mastering frenzy
    thither

With energy of madness : yea, I burn !
My soul burns up upon the lyre ! I lend
My whole life's vigour to one song, to earn

Their guerdon of the gods, a god to friend,
And seek through devious ways a single end.

[*Invoking* HADES.

Str. 1.

Now is the gold gone of the year, and gone
    The glory of the world, and gathered close
    The silver of the frost.   Far splendid snows
Shine where the bright anemone once shone.
    Ay ! for the laughter live
    Of youths and maids that strive

n amorous play, the ancient saws of eld
And wisdom mystical
From bearded lips must fall,
Old eyes behold what young eyes ne'er
beheld :
Namely, the things beyond the triple veil
Of space and time and cause, eternal woof
Of misery overproof :
And aged thoughts assail
The younger hopes, and passion stands
aloof,
And silence takes possession, and the tale
Of earth is told and done.
Then from the Sire of all the Gods, from War
And Love and Wisdom and the eternal Sun
Worship is torn afar :
While unto Thee, O Hades, turn we now,
Awful of breast and brow,
And hear thee in the sea, behold thee in the
Star.

Ant. 1 [*Echo of the Damned*].

Ay I is the earth and upper ether gone,
And all the joy of earth, and gathered close
The darkness and the death-wind and the
snows
On us on whom the sun of air once shone.
What souls are left alive
Vainly lament and strive,
For they shall join the dead of utmost eld ;
The concourse mystical
Who see the seasons fall
Shall soon behold what all we have beheld :—
The accursed stream, the intolerable veil
Of night and death and hell, disastrous
woof
Of anguish overproof
That fruitless wills assail
Ever in vain : good fortune stands aloof
And all kind gods : we, taking up the tale
Of dead men past and done,
Declare that ceaseless is the eternal war,
And victory stedfast set against the Sun.
Yet we perceive afar
Even in Hades, at the end, not now,
Some light upon his brow,
Some comfort in the sea, some refuge in the
Star.

Str. 2.

O thou I because thy chariot is golden,
And beautiful thy coursers, and their manes
Flecked with such foam as once upon
the sea
Bore Aphrodite, and thy face is olden,
Worn with dim thought and unsuspected
pains,
And all thy soul fulfilled of majesty ;
Because the silence of thy house is great,
And thy word second spoken after Fate,
And thy light stricken of thine own grim
hand ;
Because thy whisper exceedeth the command
Of Zeus ; thy dim light far outshines his
glory ;
Because, as He the first is, Thou the last :—
Therefore I take up sorrow in my hands,
And ply thine ear with my most doleful story,
Asking a future, who have lost a past :
A guerdon of my singing like the land's
When spring breaks forth from winter, and
the blood
Of the old earth laughs in every new-born
bud.

Ant. 2 [*Echo of the Damned*].

O thou I because thy lyre is keen and golden
And beautiful thy numbers through our
veins
Pouring delight, as on the starry sea
Burn gems of rapture ; though the houses
olden
Relax awhile their unredeeming pains,
And through dead slaves thrill bounteous
majesty ?
Though the strong music of thy soul be
great :—
Shall thy desire avail to alter Fate ?
Or impious hands unloose the awful hand ?
Or futile words reverse the great command ?
Or what availeth ? Though great Hades'
glory
Stoop to thy prayer, and answer thee at
last,
Should Clotho catch the thread in
weaving hands,

Respin what Atropos once cut—that story
  Were vain for thee—that which is past is
    past,
  Nor can Omnipotence avail the land's
Death—Spring's is alien though ancestral
    blood,
And a new birth is current in the bud.

Str. 3.

Think, then, the deed impossible is done
  Since Theseus fared forth to the ambient
    air !
His thread once cut—was that indeed respun
  Or patched by witchery? a deceit? a
    snare?
I tell ye ; past and future are but one,
  And present—nothing ; shall not Hades
    dare
His own omnipotence against the Sun,
  And let no tittle of his glory share
With all the earth's recuperating wheel,
And every dawn's sure falchion-flash of steel?

Ant. 3 [Echo of the Damned].

Indeed, a deed impossible was done
  Were the new Theseus heavier than the
    air.
Nay ! but a new thread phantom-frail was
    spun
  And men's blind eyes discovered not the
    snare,
Else were that elder cord and this yet one,
  Cut but in fancy. Yet, shall mortal dare
To fling a wanton word against the Sun,
  And stand forth candidate for lot and share
Where hangs Prometheus, rolls Ixion's wheel,
And the stone rolls upon the limbs of steel?

Epode.

These echoes, in my mind foul torturers,
  Present my fears, and image my distrust.
No answer comes, no voice the silence stirs
  With joyful " may " or melancholy " must."
Nor, though the gloom requicken, may I see
  Hades enthroned, my prayers who heedeth
    nought,

Nor glowing tear of bowed Persephone
  Drooped earthward for the ninefold misery
    wrought.
In utter sorrow ever bound she stays,
  Hears not my song, nor heedeth anything,
Whose mind lamenting turns to ancient days
  And Nysian meadows and the hour of
    spring.
Yea, but perchance to touch that secret chord
  Were to awake that sorrow into life ;
Sting, as a wound a deep-envenomed sword,
  The inmost soul of the Aidonean wife.
Listen ! I tune my music to that hour ;
  The careless maidens and the virgin
    laughter,
The bloom of springtide and the fatal flower,
  And all that joy the sorrow echoing after.
So that, dread Hades, thou mayst hear and
    yield,
  Thyself unmastered and inexorable,
The gentle maid as crying in that field,
  Now thy soul's keeper on the throne of
    Hell !
Hail, Hades ! Thou who hearest not my
    song,
  Repealest not the heaven's unjust decree,
Revengest not for me the woe and wrong,
  Shalt glean my sorrow from Persephone.
Hail, Hades ! In the gloom the echoing cry
  Swells, and the chorus darkens as I sing,
And all the fibres of Eternity
  Shake as I loose the loud indignant string.
Hail, Hades ! hear thy wrong proclaimed
    aloud,
  And thou the wronger safe because too
    great.
To like offence harden thy neck, and proud
  Blow thou the dismal challenge unto Fate !

In Asia, on the Nysian plains, she played,
    A slender maid,
  With the deep-bosomed Oceanides ;
    Where the tall trees
Girded the meadow with grave walls of green.
    Alone, unseen,
  The tender little lady strayed,
    Moving across the breeze.

It was a meadow of soft grass and flowers,
    Where the sweet hours
Lingered and laughed awhile ere noon re-
        poses.
    There were red roses
And crocus, and flag-flowers, and violets,
    And hyacinth, regrets
Of the ill-fortuned God, the quoit-player;
    And soft cool air
Stirred all the field—and there were jessa-
        mines
    And snaky columbines.
So all these maidens played, and gathered
        them
    From sad green stem
Rejoicing blooms with sunlight mixed therein.
    But she, for sin
And iron heart of the ill-minded Zeus,
    Caught up the dews
Deep on her ankles, and went noiselessly
    Toward the laughing sea,
And sought new blossoms—O the traitor,
        Earth,
    That brought to birth
That day, as favouring the desire that
        swelled
    Beneath her heart of eld,
Where dwelt the lonely, the detested one
    Intolerant of the sun,
Hades ! But Earth for love of him, for spite
    Of the young girl's delight,
And shame of her own age, brought forth
        that hour
    The fatal flower,
Narcissus—which what soul of man shall
        smell
    Goes down to hell,
Caught in the scent of sin—for such a doom
    Demeter's flying loom
Hath woven for revenge and punishment.
    The bright child went
Thither; an hundred heads of blossom sprang;
    The green earth sang,
And the skies laughed, and danced the sea's
        young feet
    For joy of it.
So the child went across that fairest plain
    To pluck, to strain

That blossom of all blossoms to her heart.
    Her long hands dart,
Exceeding delicate and fair, to cull
    That bloom too beautiful,
Eager to gather the fresh floral birth.
    The grim black earth
Gaped ; roared athwart the gulf the golden
        car ;
    And flaming far
The four white horses with their flashing
        manes !
    The might-resisting reins
Lay in the ghastly hands, the arms of fear
    Of that dread charioteer,
Death ; and great Hades armed stood glitter-
        ing,
    Stooped to his spring,
And whirled the child to the beneath
        abode.
    O heavy load !
O bitter harvest of rich-rolling tears !
    What cry who hears?
A shrill shrill cry to father Zeus cried she,
    Forlorn Persephone !
Heard was that agony of grief by none
    Save only by the Sun,
And Her who sat within her awful cave,
    Contemplative and grave,
Hecate, veilèd with a shining veil
    Utterly frail
As the strange web of dainty thoughts she
        wove,
    Somewhat like love.
She heard, and great Apollo : neither
        stayed
    Hades, nor stretched to aid
A pitying hand. O pitiful ! O grief
    Baffling belief !
The gentle child—the cruel god—Ah me !
    Persephone !
Thus of thy grace, thy sorrow, thy young
        way
    Torn from the day
Of all thy memory of soft shining flowers
    And happy-hearted hours,
Mayst thou be very pitiful to me
    Who aye have pitied thee,
        Persephone !

PERSEPHONE.

Ah me ! I feei a stirring in my blood.
Pours through my veins a delicate pale flood
Of memory.   Not the pale and terrible
Goddess whose throne is manifest in Hell
—I am again a child, a playful child.

ORPHEUS.

And therefore, O most beautiful and mild
Sweet mother ! art the girl beloved again
Of Hades mighty on the Nysian plain.
And therefore are thine eyes with sorrow dim
For me, and thy word powerful with Him.

PERSEPHONE.

Ah me ! no fruit for guerdon,
Who bore the blossom's burden ;
There shines no sunlight toward Persephone.
Ravished, O iron-eyed !
From my young sisters' side,
Torn and dragged down below the sundered
sea,
No joy is mine in all thy bed,
And all thy sorrow shaken on my head.

Cursed above gods be thou
Whose blind unruffled brow
Rules the grim place of unsubstantial things !
Hated, to me thy face
Turns not the glance of grace.
I rule unloved above the infernal kings,
And only thee in all deep Hell
I charm in vain, despair my royal spell.

By might of famine long
And supplication strong
Demeter won the swift Hermetic word :
In bitter days of eld
Thus by great force compelled
The glad earth saw me, careless of my lord,
Rise to her crystal streams and sapphire
seas,
And Theseus thus owed life to Heracles.

Thou mockest me with power ;
Thy sceptre's awful dower
Avails me nothing.   Shall a mortal bring
Such pity wrapped in song
And Echo's choral throng
Of all things live and dead to hear me sing ;—
And I by pity moved and love
Have not thy voice to grant him grace
thereof ?

Inexorable Lord !
Accursèd and abhorred
Of men, begin in Hell to show thy grace !
Not to a man's weak life,
Not to thy shuddering wife,
But to the queen's unfathomable face
Dread beyond sorcery and prayer,
And fearful even because it is so fair !

Yea, from the ghastly throne
Unchallenged and unknown
Let the fierce accents roll athwart the skies !
My voice is given, my power
Fares forth to save the flower
Broken but plucked not by these fingers wise.
I love the song—be thou not mute,
But turn a lucky lot towards the suit !

ORPHEUS.

In vain, O thou veiled
Immutable queen !
Thy strong voice bewailed,
Thy fair face was seen !
It flushed up and paled ;
The song echoed clean—
But alas ! for the veil of the night and the
fear that is ever between !

Of pity unfilled
And void of remorse,
He moves unappealed
In the terrible course.
But the lyre is unchilled :—
By force unto force
He shall answer me power unto power at the
source of its source !

Dost thou hear how the weight
Of the earth and the moon
Shudder, as if fate
Were involved in the tune?
The portals of hate
Shake at the rune
Of the magical nature-cry, the song from the
mountains hewn!

Alecto! I call thee,
My words ring thee round.
My spells enwall thee.
My lyre is crowned
With might to appal thee
With terror profound.
Arise! O Alecto, arise! for my song hath
compelled thee and bound.

To the horrible hollow
In Tartarus steep,
O song of me, follow!
I flee to the deep.
That word of Apollo
Shall shudder and leap;
That word in the uttermost night shall awake
them who know not of sleep.

Ye furies of Hell!
Ye terrors in Heaven!
The strength of the spell
Is as thunder at even
The rocks of the fell
That hath blasted and riven.
Come forth! I invoke ye, Erinyes, the
charm of the One that is seven.

Hear, O ye Three,
In the innermost pit
Dwellers that be!
Tartarus, split!
Arise unto me
For I call ye with wit
Of the words that constrain and compel, of
the summons ordered and fit!

By the Five that are One,
And the One that is Ten;
By the snake in the sun
And her mirror in men;
By the Four that run
And return them again;
By the fire that is lit in the Lion, the wave
in the Scorpion den!

O daughter of Earth,
Tisiphone dread,
The ophidian girth,
And the blood-dripping head,
In hideous mirth
Bring living and dead
To torture! Arise! I conjure by the might
of the words I have said.

By the One that is Seven,
The whirling eyes;
The Two made Eleven,
The dragon's devise;
The Eight against Heaven,
All crowns of lies;
Come forth! I invoke ye, Erinyes, move,
answer, take shape and arise!

Megæra, thou terror,
O daughter of Night
Whose sight in a mirror
Is death of affright,
Wingèd with error,
I chain thee, and cite
The words that thy soul must obey if a
mortal but say them aright!

By the cross and the wheel
I call ye to hear;
By the dagger of steel
I command ye, give ear!
By the word that ye feel,
The summons of Fear;
Come forth! I invoke ye, Erinyes, move,
answer, arise and appear!

N

For my purpose is swift,
And my vengeance strong ;
I shall not shift ;
I shall cry the wrong.
My voice I uplift
In terrible song
As your forms take shape before me in the
likeness for which ye long.

The shape of my passion
And bitter distress
Shall clothe ye, and fashion
An equal dress.
Ye shall force compassion
With awful stress
From the soul that hath mocked me, and
turned his heart from my song's excess.

The ruler of Hell,
The invisible Lord,
Hath laughed at my spell,
Hath slept at my word.
He hath heard me well—
Awake, O Sword !
Shall he flout a suppliant thus and no answer
of favour accord ?

If mercy be sundered
From splendour and power ;
If he answer with thunder
The plaint of a flower ;
Shall justice wonder
If Furies devour
So bitter a heart, set a term to his date that
was aye but an hour ?

Avenge me, ye forces
Of horror and wrath !
Clear the dread courses !
Split open the path !
With cruel remorse is
His heart brought to scath.
And a terror is on him at last, the seed of his
hate's aftermath.

MEGÆRA.

Ha ! who invokes ? What horror rages
Here, to compel our murderous hands to
smite ?

ALECTO.

What mortal summons ?   Who his battle
wages
So strongly as to call the seed of Night ?

TISIPHONE.

Ha !   The grim tyrant of despair engages
Our deadly anguish with his useless might.

HADES.

Detested fiends ! avaunt !

MEGÆRA.

He speaks !

ALECTO.

He thunders !

TISIPHONE.

His lightnings split the living rock.

MEGÆRA.

Hell sunders
The livid walls and iron-bound prisons of
death.

HADES.

Thus ! to your towers and wail !

ALECTO.

He speaks !

TISIPHONE.

His breath
Is cold as ours.

HADES.

Depart !   Due silence keep,
Lest I enchain ye in a fouler deep
Than aught your horror pictures !

MEGÆRA.

Dost thou hear,
Sister ?

ALECTO.

Sweet sister !

TISIPHONE.
Dost thou think we fear
Who are all fear? or feel, who are but pain?

MEGÆRA.
Creep round his heart, and cluster in his
brain,
Ye serpents of my hair!

ALECTO.
His blood shall drip
For sweet warm juice on my decaying lip.

TISIPHONE.
My fearful wings enfold him!

ALECTO.
My foul eyes
Hold his in terror!

MEGÆRA.
All my agonies
Crawl in his vitals!

TISIPHONE.
He is mine, mine, mine!
Pour forth of Thebes' abominable wine!
Mine, O thou god, detested and adored!

MEGÆRA.
Mine! he is mine! my lover and my lord!

ALECTO.
Mine! I am in his shape!

MEGÆRA.
Despair! Dispute
Never my passion!

TISIPHONE.
Sisters! Be ye mute!
I am the livid agony that starts
Damp on his brow; the horror in his heart's
Envenomed arteries! and I the fear,
The torment, and the hate!

MEGÆRA.
Be of good cheer!
Rend him apart! Hunger and lust we sate,
Equal in terror on that heart of hate.

ALECTO.
Hell's throne be kingless!

TISIPHONE.
Mortal! is it well,
Our vengeance on the impious lord of Hell!

ORPHEUS.
Well! it is well! And yet my eyes are wet
To see such anguish.

MEGÆRA.
Tear the fatal net!

ALECTO.
Bite with strong acid his congealing blood!

TISIPHONE.
Rend out the bowels!

MEGÆRA.
Pour the monstrous flood
Of unclean wisdom in his soul!

PERSEPHONE.
Desist!

ALECTO.
O face of woman wretched and unkissed,
What hast thou here to do with us?

TISIPHONE.
Be quiet!

MEGÆRA.
Quench not the fire of murder!

ALECTO.
Loose the riot
Of worms beneath the skull!

TISIPHONE.

Tear wide apart

The jaws !

MEGÆRA.

Force fear against the inmost heart !

PERSEPHONE.

Mercy ! I plead, sweet sisters !

ORPHEUS.

And I plead
Vengeance, and help in my extremest need.
Pile up the torture ! Had he not the power,
And silence mocked me ?

MEGÆRA.

Urge us hour by hour,
Thou couldst not add one particle of pain.

ALECTO.

He speaks not ! Bid his torture speak again !

TISIPHONE.

Speak, murderer !

MEGÆRA.

Hades ! answer us !

ALECTO.

Expel
These torments from thy being, us from Hell,
Or Zeus from Heaven !

TISIPHONE.

Or else obey !

MEGÆRA.

Obey !

ALECTO.

Obey !

HADES.

O throne of Hell ! O night ! O day
Of anguish exquisite beyond control,
Fibre and substance of my inmost soul !
There is a power not mine, and yet in me
Burning its cold and cruel agony

With icy flames, its cutting poison fangs
Striking my being with detested pangs.
Alas ! of me and not to be expelled,
Conjured, assuaged, averted. Grey as eld
The juice of blood that stagnates in my veins
Appals their current with avenging pains :—
O pain ! O pitiful and hateful sense
Of agony and grief and impotence !
O misery of the day when Orpheus bore
First his loud lyre across the Stygian shore !
Hath Hell no warders ? Is the threefold gate
Brazen in vain against the foot of Fate ?
Now is but little choice—abase my pride,
Or sink for ever to the gloomy tide
Of fire beneath the utmost reach and span
Of Stygian deeps and walls Tartarean.
Yet I abide.

MEGÆRA.

Fall ! Fall !

ALECTO.

Descend the abyss !

TISIPHONE.

Link the lewd fiend with your incestuous
kiss !

MEGÆRA.

Hither !

ALECTO.

O hither !

HADES.

Steams a newer shape
Of threefold terror.

TISIPHONE.

Shall the god escape
The monstrous wedlock ?

ALECTO

Let him turn again
His horrid passion to the Nysian plain !

MEGÆRA.

Echidna !

ALECTO.

Mother of the Sphinx and snake
Of Colchus, and the marsh-beast of the lake
Lernean, of Chimaera and Hell's hound—

TISIPHONE.

Answer!

ALECTO.

Arise!

MEGÆRA.

Awake from the profound!

TISIPHONE.

Here is a worthy partner unto thee
To wake thy womb with monstrous progeny,
Yet more detested and detestable
Than all the shapeless brood of hate and Hell.

ECHIDNA.

Ha! rose-lipped lover! Welcome to this
bed!

MEGÆRA.

She plays with words of love!

ALECTO.

Her black eyes shed
Disease for tears.

TISIPHONE.

Her fangs and lips are red
With gouts of putrid blood.

MEGÆRA.

Her guile employs
The sweet soft shape of words of upper joys
More bitterly to rack his soul.

ALECTO.

Ha, sister,
The embrace!

TISIPHONE.

She conquers.

MEGÆRA.

He hath moved.

ALECTO.

He hath kissed her!

TISIPHONE.

Ha! the worse hate of hate in love's white
dress.

MEGÆRA.

And lewdness tricked to look like loveliness.

ALECTO.

Uttermost pain in pleasure's hour supreme.

MEGÆRA.

Hate's nightmare waking love's unreal dream.

ALECTO.

Claws, teeth, and poison!

TISIPHONE.

How she plies her pest!

MEGÆRA.

Strangling she holds him.

ALECTO.

In the inmost breast
Her hands defile him.

TISIPHONE.

In his rotting brain
He teeth, her breath, pass all imagined pain.

MEGÆRA.

Sisters!

ALECTO.

We conquer!

TISIPHONE.

Have we power?

MEGÆRA.

The king
Endures, and is not moved at anything.

ALECTO.

He will not now relent.

TISIPHONE.

He's ours for ever !

HADES.

Ai ! Ai !

MEGÆRA.

Hark !

ALECTO.

Listen !

TISIPHONE.

Now he yields—or never !

HADES.

Release ! Relent !

ECHIDNA.

Fair lover, let my embrace
Still gladden thee to rapture ! let my face
Be like a garden of fresh flowers to cull,
And all thy being and thy body full
As mine of gentle love—then sink to sleep !

MEGÆRA.

Ha ! Ha ! She mocks him ! In the utter
deep,
Her house of evil, sleep is stranger there.

ALECTO.

She sings !

TISIPHONE.

The final misery ! Beware !

ECHIDNA.

O tender lover !
My wings still cover
Thy face, and my lips

Are on thine, and my tresses
Like Zephyr's caresses
When the twilight dips.

HADES.

This passes all. Relent. Release ! Depart !
I yield : my power is broken, and my heart
Riven, and all my pride ruined, and me
Compelled to earth to loose Eurydice.

ORPHEUS.

Depart !

ERINYES.

Baffled ! O misery ! Bethink,
Proud Hades, ere thy torture gar thee drink
Humiliation's utmost dregs !

HADES.

I spake.
Depart ye ! lest my power regained awake,
And smite ye with a terror more than ye.

MEGÆRA.

We are borne on bitter winds.

ALECTO.

We sink.

TISIPHONE.

We flee !

MEGÆRA.

To the abyss !

ALECTO.

Descend !

TISIPHONE.

Nor hope in vain
The ill-hearted one shall feel our fangs again.

MEGÆRA.

Murder and violation, deafened ear
To suppliants, these our friends are.

ALECTO.

Hate and fear
Leave not for long that bosom.

TISIPHONE.

Now away !
Back from this night more splendid than our
day !

MEGÆRA.

We may not drag him down this chance.

ALECTO.

Despair
Not, O my sisters !

TISIPHONE.

The next suppliant's prayer
Rejected—

MEGÆRA.

Come, my sisters, we'll be there.

HADES.

Well, be it so.   O wizard, by this strength
Thou hast availed in deepest Hell at length.
I grant thy prayer.   Eurydice be given
To the sweet light and pleasant air of heaven !
Even on this wise.   With Hermes for a
guide
Up the dread steeps there followeth thee thy
bride,
And thou before them singing.   If thou yearn
Towards her, if thy purpose change or turn
While in these realms ; if thou thy face
revert ;
That shall be hostage unto me for hurt
Of further magic : she shall fade and flee
A phantom frail throughout Eternity,
Driven on my winds, adrift upon my seas !
These are thy favours, and thy duties these.
Invoke thou Hermes, and thy lyre restring !

ORPHEUS.

This I accept and this shall be, O king !

[Invoking HERMES.]

O Light in Light ! O flashing wings of fire !
The swiftest of the moments of the sea
Is unto thee
Even as some slow-foot Eternity
With limbs that drag and wheels that tire.
O subtle-minded flame of amber gyre,
It seems a spark of gold
Grown purple, and behold !
A flame of gray !
Then the dark night-wings glow
With iridescent indigo,
Shot with some violet ray ;
And all the vision flames across the horizon
The millionth of no time—and when we
say :
Hail !—Thou art gone !

The moon is dark beside thy crown ; the Sun
Seems a pale image of thy body bare ;
And for thine hair
Flash comets lustrous with the dewfall
rare
Of tears of that most memorable One,
The radiant Queen, the veilèd Paphian.
The wings of light divine
Beneath thy body shine ;
The invisible
Rayed with some tangible flame,
Seeking to formulate a name,
A citadel ;
And the winged heels are fiery with enormous
speed,
One spurning heaven ; the other tramp-
ling hell ;
And thou—recede !

O Hermes ! Messenger of inmost thought !
Descend ! Abide ! Swift coursing in my
veins
Shoot dazzling pains,
The Word of Selfhood integrate of Nought,
The Ineffable Amen ! the Wonder wrought.
Bring death if life exceed !
Bid thy pale Hermit bleed,
Yet Life exude ;
And Wisdom and the Word of Him

Drench the mute mind grown dim
  With quietude !
Fix thy sharp lightnings in my night !   My
    spirit free !
  Mix with my breath and life and name thy
    mood
    And self of Thee.

[HERMES *appears:* ORPHEUS *departs.*

The magical task and the labour is ended ;
  The toils are unwoven, the battle is done ;
My lover comes back to my arms, to the
    splendid
  Abyss of the air and abode of the sun.
The sword be assuaged, and the bow be un-
    bended !
  The labour is past, and the victory won.

The arrows of song through Hell cease to
    hurtle.
  Away to the passionate gardens of Greece,
Where the thrush is awake, and the voice of
    the turtle
  Is soft in the amorous places of peace,
And the tamarisk groves and the olive and
    myrtle
  Stir ever with love and content and release.

O bountiful bowers and O beautiful gardens !
  O isles in the azure Ionian deep !
Ere ripens the sun, ere the spring-wind
    hardens
  Your fruits once again ye shall have me to
    keep.
The sleep-god laments, and the love goddess
    pardons,
  When love at the last sinks unweary to sleep.

The green-hearted hours shall burst into
    flowers.
  The winds shall waft roses from uttermost
    Ind.
Our nuptial dowers shall be birds in our
    bowers,
  Our couches the delicate heaps of the wind,
Where the lily-bloom showers all its light,
    and the powers
  Of earth in our twinning are wedded and
    twinned.

So singing I make reverence and retire ;
Not with high words of worship fairly flung
To that sad monarch from the magic lyre,

And half the triumphs in my heart unsung,
Surpassing, as such triumphs must, all praise
Of golden strings and human - fashioned
    tongue.

But now I follow the uprising ways
By secret paths indubitably drawn
Straight from the centre of the trackless maze

To light of earth and beauty of the dawn,
A sure swift passage taught of wit divine
To the wide ocean, the Achæan lawn.

For, wit ye well, not easy is that shrine
Of access to the mortal, as some tell,
Not knowing : easy and exact the line

Of light to upper air : but awful spell
And dire demand the inward journey needs :
That is the labour, that the work : for Hell

Is not designed for men's aspiring deeds.
The air is fatal, and the fear unspanned,
Even ere the traveller fronts the Stygian
    meads

And utmost edge of the detested land.
Wherefore already doth the light appear
Shaped in the image of a little hand

Far up the rocky cavern : warm and clear
The good air sends its fragrance : glory then
To the great work accomplished even here,

Promise and purpose unto little men
Bound in life's limits : death indeed I sever
By will's efficiency and speechless ken

Of power not God's but man's.   Forget this
    never,
O mortals chained in·life's detested den !
I leave this heritage to you for ever.

        O light of Apollo !
        O joy of the sky !
      We see thee, we follow,
        We draw to thee nigh.

We see thee unclouded,
Whose hearts have been thinned,
Whose souls have been shrouded,
Whose ears are bedinned
By hell's clamour. How did
The strength that has sinned
Avail in the crowded
Abodes of the wind?

By lightning of rapture
The soul of my song
My love doth recapture ;
Lead up to the long
Years in blithe measure
Of summer and ease ;
Linger at leisure
For passion and peace.
Sadness and pleasure
Relent and release :—
A torrent, a treasure,
A garden of Greece !

Selene, our sister,
• Our lover and friend,
Thy light hath long missed her :
That hour hath an end.
All æons to squander
We chance at our will :
We may woo, work or wander
Through time to our fill,
Hither or yonder
By fountain or hill,
Each day growing fonder,
Each night growing still !

Bright Hermes behind me
Caduceus-armed
Guides : shall he blind me ?
My spirit be charmed ?
The song shall not swerve her,
Its glory shall shed
Respite, deserve her
From gulfs of the dead.
Ah me ! let it nerve her
These conduits to tread
That lead to the fervour
Of earth overhead !

Fire, thou dear splendour
Of uppermost space,
Turn to me tender
Thine emerald face !
Thy rubies be blended
With diamond light !
Thy sapphires be splendid,
Extended to sight !
The portals be rended
That govern the night,
And the guardians bended
To magical might !

O air of the glorious
Garb of the globe,
Don thy victorious
Glittering robe !
The sun is before us ;
The moon is above.
Rise and adore us
Ye dwellers thereof !
The Muses restore us
To Greece : as we move
Swell the wild chorus
Of welcome and love !

Alas ! that ever the dark place
Should from its rocky base
Give up no echo of the god's strong stride,
And no one whisper steal and thrill
My heart, dissolve the ill
That gathers close and fears me for my bride.

I were no worse if I were blind.
I may not look behind
To catch one glimpse of the dear face that
    follows,
Lest I should gain forbidden lore
And wisdom's dangerous store
Of the black secrets of those heights and
    hollows.

Alas ! the way is over long,
And weary of my song
I sing who yearn to catch my love, and hold
In such ten-thousandfold caress
As shall annul distress,
And from the iron hours bring the years of
    gold.

Alas ! my soul is filled with fear,
Is the hard conquest here?
Where is Eurydice ?   The god hath faded
Back to invisible abodes
And on these rocky roads
Comes no deep perfume of her hair light-
braided.

Alas ! I listen ! and no breath
Assures the walls of death
That life remembers, that their hate is quelled.
My ears, my scent avail me nought ;
My slavish eyes are bought
By the command wherewith I am compelled.

Alas ! my heart sinks momently.
Fear steals and misery.
From faith in faith of Hell my thoughts dis-
sever.
Yet, O my heart ! abide, endure !
Seek not by sight to assure,
Or she is lost to thee and lost for ever !

Now breathes the night-air o'er the deep,
And limb-dissolving sleep
Laps my own country, and the maiden moon
Gleams silver barley from the sea,
And binds it royally
Into a sheaf that waves to the wind's tune.

The rocky portals rise above.
Here I may clasp my love,
Here Hermes shall deliver.   Ah ! how shook
Yon cliff at the wind's ardent kiss !
This is the hour of bliss—
The sea ! The sea ! Eurydice ! Look, Look !

Ai ! but like wind-whirled flowers of frost
The flying form is lost !
Cancelled and empty of Eurydice
The black paths where she trod !
Ai ! Ai ! My God ! My God !
Apollo, why hast thou forsaken me ?

EXPLICIT LIBER TERTIUS

LIBER QUARTUS VEL MORTIS

TO

MY WIFE

LYSANDER (*reads*).

" The riot of the tipsy Bacchanals
Tearing the Thracian singer in their rage."

THESEUS.

That is an old device.
Midsummer Night's Dream.

What could the Muse herself that Orpheus bore
The Muse herself, for her enchanting son
Whom universal Nature did lament
When by the rout that made the hideous roar
His gory body down the stream was sent
Down the swift Hebrus to the Lesbian shore?
Lycidas.

A brighter Hellas rears its mountains
From waves serener far ;
A new Peneus rolls his fountains
Against the morning star.
Where fairer Tempes bloom, there sleep
Young Cyclads on a sunnier deep.

.   .   .   .   .   .

Another Orpheus sings again
And loves, and weeps, and dies.
Hellas.

MOUNT IDA.

THE COMPANY OF THE MÆNADS.

MÆNADS.

Evoe ! Evoe Ho ! Iacche ! Iacche !

Hail, O Dionysus ! Hail !
Wingèd Son of Semelé !
Hail, O Hail ! The stars are pale.
Hidden the moonlight in the vale ;
Hidden the sunlight in the sea.

Blessed is her happy lot
Who beholdeth God ; who moves
Mighty-souled without a spot,
Mingling in the godly rout
Of the many mystic loves.

Holy maidens, duly weave
Dances for the mighty mother !
Bacchanal to Bacchus cleave !
Wave his narthex wand, and leave
Earthy joys to earth to smother !

Io ! Evoe ! Sisters, mingle
In the choir, the dance, the revel !
He divine, the Spirit single,
He in every vein shall tingle.
Sense and sorrow to the devil !

Mingle in the laughing measure,
Hand and lip to breast and thigh !
In enthusiastic pleasure
Grasp the solitary treasure !
Laughs the untiring ecstasy !

Sisters ! Sisters ! Raise your voices
In the inspired divine delight !
Now the sun sets ; now the choice is
Who rebels or who rejoices,
Murmuring to the mystic night.

Io ! Evoe ! Circle splendid !
Dance, ye maids serene and subtle !
Clotho's task is fairly ended.
Atropos, thy power is rended !
Ho, Lachesis ! ply thy shuttle !

Weave the human dance together
With the life of rocks and trees !
Let the blue delirious weather
Bind all spirits in one tether,
Overwhelming ecstasies !

Io Evoe! I faint, I fall,
Swoon in purple light ; the grape
Drowns my spirit in its thrall.
Love me, love me over all,
Spirit in the spirit shape !

All is one ! I murmur. Distant
Sounds the shout, Evoe, Evoe !
Evoe, Iacche ! Soft, insistent
Like to echo's voice persistent :—
Hail ! Agave ! Autonoe !

AGAVE.
Evoe Ho ! Iacche ! Hail, O Hail !
Praise him ! What dreams are these ?

AUTONOE.
Sisters, O sisters !

AGAVE.
Say, are our brethren of the rocks awake ?

AUTONOE.
The lion roars.

MÆNADS.
O listen to the snake !

AUTONOE.
Evoe Ho ! Give me to drink !

AGAVE.
Run wild !
Mountain and mountain let us leap upon
Like tigers on their prey !

MÆNADS.
Crush, crush the world !

AGAVE.
Tread earth as 'twere a winepress !

AUTONOE.
Drink its blood,
The sweet red wine !

MÆNADS.
Ay, drink the old earth dry !

AGAVE.
Squeeze the last drops out till the frame
collapse
Like an old wineskin !

AUTONOE.
So the sooner sup
Among the stars !

AGAVE.
The swift, swift stars !

MÆNADS.
O night !
Night, night, fall deep and sure !

AUTONOE.

Fall soft and sweet !

AGAVE.

Moaning for love the woods lie.

AUTONOE.

Sad the land
Lies thirsty for our kisses.

MÆNADS.

All wild things
Yearn towards the kiss that ends in blood.

AGAVE.

Blood !   Blood !
Bring wine !   Ha !   Bromius, Bromius !

MÆNADS.

Come, sweet God,
Come forth and lie with us !

AUTONOE.

Us, maidens now
And then and ever afterwards !

AGAVE.

Chaste, chaste !
Our madness hath no touch of bitterness,
No taste of foulness in the morning mouth.

AUTONOE.

O mouth of ripe red sunny grapes !   God !
    God !
Evoe !   Dwell !   Abide !

AGAVE.

I feel the wings
Of love, of mystery ; they waft soft streams
Of night air to my heated breast and brow.

MÆNADS.

He comes !   He comes !

AGAVE.

Silence, O girls, and peace !
The God's most holy presence asks the hymn
The solemn hymn, the hymn of agony,
Lest in the air of glory that surrounds
The child of Semelé we lose the earth
And corporal presence of the Zeus-begot.

AUTONOE.

Yea, sisters, raise the chant of riot !   Lift
Your wine-sweet voices, move your wine-
    stained limbs
In joyful invocation !

MÆNADS.

Ay, we sing.

Hail, child of Semelé !
To her as unto thee
Be reverence, be deity, be immortality !

Shame !   treachery of the spouse
Of the Olympian house,
Hera !   thy grim device against the sweet
    carouse !

Lo !   in red roar and flame
Did Zeus descend !   What claim
To feel the immortal fire had then the
    Theban dame !

Caught in that fiery wave
Her love and life she gave
With one last kissing cry the unborn child
    to save.

And thou, O Zeus, the sire
Of Bromius—hunter dire !—
Didst snatch the unborn babe from that
    Olympian fire :

In thine own thigh most holy
That offspring melancholy
Didst hide, didst feed, on light, ambrosia,
    and moly.

Ay ! and with serpent hair
And limbs divinely fair
Didst thou, Dionysus, leap forth to the
　　nectar air !

Ay ! thus the dreams of fate
We dare commemorate,
Twining in lovesome curls the spoil of mate
　　and mate.

O Dionysus, hear !
Be close, be quick, be near,
Whispering enchanted words in every curving
　　ear !

O Dionysus, start
As the Apollonian dart !
Bury thy hornèd head in every bleeding heart !

AGAVE.
He is here ! He is here !

AUTONOE.
Tigers, appear !

AGAVE.
To the clap of my hand
And the whish of my wand,
Obey !

AUTONOE.
　　I have found
A chariot crowned
With ivy and vine,
And the laurel divine,
And the clustering smell
Of the sage asphodel,
And the Dædal flower
Of the Cretan bower ;
Dittany's force,
And larkspur's love,
And blossoms of gorse
Around and above.

AGAVE.
The tiger and panther
Are here at my cry.
Ho, girls ! Span there
Their sides !

MÆNADS.
　　　　Here am I !
And I ! We are ready.

AGAVE.
Strong now and steady !

FIRST MÆNAD.
The tiger is harnessed.

SECOND MÆNAD.
The nightingale urges
Our toil from her far nest.

THIRD MÆNAD.
Ionian surges
Roar back to our chant.

FOURTH MÆNAD.
Aha ! for the taunt
Of Theban sages
Is lost, lost, lost !
The wine that enrages
Our life is enforced.
We dare them and daunt.

AGAVE.
The spirits that haunt
The rocks and the river,
The moors and the woods,
The fields and the floods,
Are with us for ever !

MÆNADS.
Are of us for ever.
Evoe ! Evoe !

AUTONOE.
Agave ! He cometh !

AGAVE.
Cry ho ! Autonoe !

ALL.
Ho ! Ho ! Evoe Ho ! Iacche ! Evoe ! Evoe !

The white air hummeth
With force of the spirit.
We are heirs : we inherit.
Our joys are as theirs ;
Weave with your prayers
The joys of a kiss !
Ho ! for the bliss
Of the cup and the rod.
   He cometh ! O lover !
O friend and O God,
Cover us, cover
Our faces, and hover
Above us, within us !
   Daintily shod,
   Daintily robed,
His witcheries spin us
A web of desire.
Subtle as fire
He cometh among us.
   The whole sky globed
      Is on fire with delight,
Delight that hath stung us,
   The passion of night.
Night be our mistress !
That tress and this tress
Weave with thy wind
Into curls deep-vined !
Passionate bliss !
Rapture on rapture !
Our hymns recapture
The Bromian kiss.
Blessèd our souls !
Blessèd this even !
We reach to the goals
Of the starriest heaven.
Daphnis, and Atthis, and Chrysis, and Chloe,
Mingle, O maidens ! Evoe ! Evoe !

DIONYSUS.

I bring ye wine from above,
   From the vats of the storied sun ;
For every one of ye love,
   And life for every one.
Ye shall dance on hill and level ;
   Ye shall sing in hollow and height
In the festal mystical revel,
   The rapturous Bacchanal rite !

The rocks and trees are yours,
   And the waters under the hill,
By the might of that which endures,
   The holy heaven of will !
I kindle a flame like a torrent
   To rush from star to star ;
Your hair as a comet's horrent,
   Ye shall see things as they are !
I lift the mask of matter ;
   I open the heart of man ;
For I am of force to shatter
   The cast that hideth—Pan !
Your loves shall lap up slaughter,
   And dabbled with roses of blood
Each desperate darling daughter
   Shall swim in the fervid flood.
I bring ye laughter and tears,
   The kisses that foam and bleed,
The joys of a million years,
   The flowers that bear no seed.
My life is bitter and sterile,
   Its flame is a wandering star.
Ye shall pass in pleasure and peril
   Across the mystical bar
That is set for wrath and weeping
   Against the children of earth ;
But ye in singing and sleeping
   Shall pass in measure and mirth !
I lift my wand and wave you
   Through hill to hill of delight :
My rosy rivers lave you
   In innermost lustral light.
I lead you, lord of the maze,
   In the darkness free of the sun ;
In spite of the spite that is day's
   We are wed, we are wild, we are one !

FIRST MÆNAD.

O sweet soul of the waters ! Chase me not !
What would'st thou ?

A VOICE AS OF RUNNING BROOKS.

Love !

FIRST MÆNAD.

               Love, love, I give, I give.
I yield, I pant, I fall upon thy breast,

O sacred soul of water.   Kiss, ah kiss,
With gentle waves like lips my breast, my
      two small breasts,
Rose flames on ivory seas !

SECOND MÆNAD.

                  Nay !   Nay !   O soul
Of ivy, clingst thou so for love ?

A VOICE AS OF THE RUSTLING OF IVY.

                              For love.

SECOND MÆNAD.

Cling not so close !   O no !   cling closer then !
Let thy green coolness twine about my limbs
And still the raving blood : or closer yet,
And link about my neck, and kill me so !

THIRD MÆNAD.

Soul of the rock !   Dost love me ?

A VOICE AS OF FALLING ROCK.

                     I love thee.

THIRD MÆNAD.

                        Woo me then !
Let all the sharp hard spikes of crystal dart,
Press hard upon my body !   O, I fall,
Fall from thy crags, still clinging, clinging so,
Into the dark.   Oblivion !

A DISTANT VOICE.

                  Io Evoe !
                          [ORPHEUS enters.

CROWD OF MÆNADS.

Evoe !   Evoe !   It is a lion !

FOURTH MÆNAD.

                        Lion,
O lion, dost thou love me ?

FIFTH MÆNAD.

                  Thee I love,
O tawny king of these deep glades !

SIXTH MÆNAD.

                        What wood
Were worthy for thy dwelling ?

CHORUS.

                  Come, come, come,
O lion, and revel in our band !

ORPHEUS.

                              Alas !
I sorrow, seeing ye rejoice.

FIRST MÆNAD.

                  O lion !
That is not kind.

ORPHEUS.

                  Too kind.   Since all is sorrow,
Sorrow implicit in the purest joy,
Sorrow the cause of sorrow ; evil still
Fertile, and sterile love and righteousness.
Eurydice, Eurydice !

SECOND MÆNAD.

                  Drink wine !

ORPHEUS.

Ay, mask the grisly head of things that are
By drowning sense.   Such horror as is hid
In life no man dare look upon.   Woe !   Woe !

AGAVE.

Call then reproach upon these maiden rites !

ORPHEUS.

Nay !   virtue is the devil's name for vice,
And all your righteousness is filthy rags
Wherein ye strut, and hide the one base
      thought.
To mask the truth, to worship, to forget ;
These three are one.

AGAVE.

What art thou then ? a man ?

ORPHEUS.

No more.

AGAVE.

No longer?

ORPHEUS.

Nothing.

AGAVE.

What then here
Dost thou amid these sacred woods?

ORPHEUS.

I weep.

AGAVE.

Weep then red wine!

AUTONOE.

Or we will draw thy tears,
Red tears of blood.

AGAVE.

On, girls! this bitter fool
Would stop our revel!

ORPHEUS.

Nay! ye bid me cease
Weeping.

AGAVE.

Then listen! drink this deep full cup,
Or here we tear thee limb from limb!

ORPHEUS.

Do so!
Ay, me! I am Orpheus, poor lost fool of
    Fate!
Orpheus, can charm the wildest to my lyre.
Beasts, rocks, obey—ah, Hades, didst thou
    mock,
Alone of all, my songs? Thee I praise not.
                [AUTONOE *embraces him.*
Audacious woman!

AGAVE.

Tear the fool in shreds!
Then to the dance!
VOL. III.

ORPHEUS. [1]

The old Egyptian spell!
Stir, then, poor children, if ye can! Ah me!
                [*Sings.*
Unity uttermost showea,
    I adore the might of thy breath,
Supreme and terrible God
    Who makest the Gods and death
        To tremble before thee:—
        I, I adore thee!

O Hawk of gold with power enwalled,
Whose face is like an emerald;
Whose crown is indigo as night;
    Smaragdine snakes about thy brow
Twine, and the disc of flaming light
Is on thee, seated in the prow
Of the Sun's bark, enthroned above
With lapis-lazuli for love
    And ruby for enormous force
Chosen to seat thee, thee girt round
With leopard's pell, and golden sound
    Of planets choral in their course!
O thou self-formulated sire!
Self-master of thy dam's desire!
Thine eyes blaze forth with fiery light;
    Thine heart a secret sun of flame!
I adore the insuperable might:
    I bow before the unspoken Name.

For I am Yesterday, and I
    To-day, and I to-morrow, born
Now and again, on high, on high
    Travelling on Dian's naked horn!
I am the Soul that doth create
    The Gods, and all the Kin of Breath.
I come from the sequestered state;
    My birth is from the House of Death.

Hail! ye twin hawks high pinnacled
    That watch upon the universe!
Ye that the bier of God beheld!
    That bore it onwards, ministers
Of peace within the House of Wrath.

[1] Much of the following invocation is a free
rendering of several fine passages in the
Egyptian Book of the Dead.

O

Servants of him that cometh forth
At dawn with many-coloured lights
Mounting from underneath the North,
The shrine of the celestial Heights!

He is in me, and I in Him!
Mine is the crystal radiance
That filleth æther to the brim
Wherein all stars and suns may dance.
I am the beautiful and glad,
Rejoicing in the golden day.
I am the spirit silken-clad
That fareth on the fiery way.
I have escaped from Him, whose eyes
Are closed at eventide, and wise
To drag thee to the House of Wrong :—
I am armed! I am armed! I am strong!
I am strong!
I make my way : opposing horns
Of secret foemen push their lust
In vain : my song their fury scorns ;
They sink, they grovel in the dust.

Hail, self-created Lord of Night!
Inscrutable and infinite!
Let Orpheus journey forth to see
The Disk in peace and victory!
Let him adore the splendid sight,
The radiance of the Heaven of Nu ;
Soar like a bird, laved by the light,
To pierce the far eternal blue!

Hail! Hermes! thou the wands of ill
Hast touched with strength, and they are
shivered!
The way is open unto will!
The pregnant Goddess is delivered!

Happy, yea, happy! happy is he
That hath looked forth upon the Bier
That goeth to the House of Rest!
His heart is lit with melody ;
Peace in his house is master of fear ;
His holy Name is in the West
·When the sun sinks, and royal rays
Of moonrise flash across the day's!

I have risen! I have risen! as a mighty
hawk of gold!
From the golden egg I gather, and my wings
the world enfold.
I alight in mighty splendour from the thronéd
boats of light ;
Companies of Spirits follow me ; adore the
Lords of Night.
Yea, with gladness did they pæan, bowing
low before my car,
In my ears their homage echoed from the
sunrise to the star.
I have risen! I am gathered as a lovely
hawk of gold,
I the first-born of the Mother in her ecstasy
of old.
Lo! I come to face the dweller in the sacred
snake of Khem ;
Come to face the Babe and Lion, come to
measure force with them!
Ah! these locks flow down, a river, as the
earth's before the Sun,
As the earth's before the sunset, and the God
and I are One.
I who entered in a Fool, gain the God by
clean endeavour ;
I am shaped as men and women, fair for
ever and for ever.

(*The* MÆNADS *stand silent and quiet.*)

ORPHEUS.[1]

Worship with due rite, orderly attire,
The makers of the world, the floating souls
Whence fell these crystals we call earth.
    Praise Might
The Limitless; praise Pallas, by whose
    Wisdom
The One became divided. Praise ye Him,
Chronos, from whom, the third, is form per-
ceived.
Praise ye Poseidon, his productive power,
And Juno, secret nature of all things,
On which all things are builded : praise ye
Love,

[1] The following is paraphrased from one of
the writings (falsely) attributed to Orpheus.

Idalian Aphrodite, strong as fair,
Strong not to loosen Godhead's crown by
    deed
To blind eyes not a God's : and praise pure
    Life,
Apollo in his splendour, whom I praise
Most, being his, and this song his, and his
All my desire and all my life, and all
My love, albeit he hath forsaken me.
These are One God in many : praise ye Him !

AGAVE.

We praise indeed who made the choral world
And stars the greatest, and all these the least
Flowers at our feet : but also we may praise
This Dionysus, lord of life and joy,
In whom we may perceive a subtle world
Hidden behind this masquerade of things.
O sisters, thither, thither !

ORPHEUS.

          All deceit.
Delusive as this world of shadows is,
That subtler world is more delusive yet,
Involving deeper and still deeper : thought,
Desire of life, in that warm atmosphere
Spring up and blossom new, rank poisonous
    flowers,
The enemies of peace. Nay ! matter's all,
And all is sorrow. Therefore not to be,
Not to think, love, know, contemplate, exist ;
This Not is the one hope.

AGAVE.

          Believe it not !
Here is true joy—the woodland revellings,
The smile, the kiss, the laughter leaping up,
And music inward, musings multiform,
Manifold, multitudinous, involved
Each in the deep bliss of the other's love ;—
Ay me ! my sisters. Thither !

AUTONOE.

          Wake the dance !

MÆNADS.

Pour luscious wine, cool, sweet, strong wine !
    Bring life,
Life overflowing from the cup !

ORPHEUS.

          Hush ! Hush !
I hymn the eternal matter, absolute,
Divided, chaos, formless frame of force,
Wheels of the luminous reach of space that
    men
Know by the name of Pan.

MÆNADS.

          Hail ! Hail !
Pan ! Son of Hermes ! God of Arcady
And all wild woodlands !

ORPHEUS.

          Neither Son, nor Sire,
Nor God : but he is all : all else in him
Is hidden : he the secret and the self
Shrined central in this orb of eyeless Fate,
Phantom, elusive, permanent. In all,
In spirit and in matter immanent,
He also is the all, and all is ill.
Three forms and functions hath the soul ;
    the sea
Murmurs their names repeating : *Maris* call
The soul as it engendereth things below ;
Neptune the soul that contemplateth things
Above ; and *Ocean* as itself retracts
Itself into itself : choose ye of these ! [1]
But I hymn Pan. Awake, O lyre, awake !
As if it were for the last time, awake !
                [*He sings.*

In the spring, in the loud lost places,
    In the groves of Arcadian green,
There are sounds and shadowy faces
    And strange things dimly seen.
Though the face of the springtide as grace is,
    The sown and the woodland demesne
Have a soul caught up in their spaces,
    Unkenned, and unclean !

[1] Again from pseudo-Orpheus.

It takes up the cry of the wind.
Its eyes with weeping are blind.
A strong hate whirls it behind
    As it flees for ever.
Mad, with the tokens of Fear ;
Branded, and sad, without cheer;
Year after ghastly year,
    And it endeth never.

And this is the mystical stranger,
    The subtle Arcadian God
That lurks as for sorrow and danger,
    Yet rules all the earth with his rod.
Abiding in spirit and sense
    Through the manifold changes of man,
This soul is alone and intense
    And one—He is Pan.

More subtle than mass as ye deem it
    He abides in the strife that is dust.
Than spirit more keen as ye dream it,
    He is laughter and loathing and lust.
He is all.   Nature's agonies scream it ;
    Her joys quire it clear ; in the must
Of the vat is His shape in the steam.   It
    Is Fear, and Disgust.

For the spirit of all that is,
The light in the lover's kiss,
The shame and sorrow and bliss ;
    They are all in Pan ;
The inmost wheel of the wheels,
The feeling of all that feels,
The God and the knee that kneels,
    And the foolish man.

For Pan is the world above
And the world that is hidden beneath ;
He grins from the mask of love ;
    His sword has a jewelled sheath.
What boots it a maiden to gird her?
    Her rape ere the æons began
Was sure ; in one roar of red murder
    She breaks: He is Pan.

He is strong to achieve, to forsake her ;
He is death as it clings to desire,
Ah, woe to the Earth!   If he wake her,
    Air, water and spirit and fire

Rush in to uproot her and break her :—
    Yet he is the broken ; the pyre,
And the flame and the victim ; the maker,
    And master and sire !

And all that is, is force.
A fatal and witless course
It follows without remorse
    With never an aim.
Caught in the net we strive ;
We ruin, and think we thrive ;
And we die—and remain alive :—
    And Pan is our name !

For the misery catches and winds us
    Deep, deep in the endless coil ;
Ourself is the cord that binds us,
    And ours is the selfsame toil.
We are ; we are not ; yet our date is
    An age, though each life be a span ;
And ourself and our state and our fate is
    The Spirit of Pan.

O wild is the maiden that dances
    In the dim waned light of the moon !
Black stars are her myriad glances:
    Blue night is the infinite swoon !
But in other array advances
    The car of the holier tune ;
And our one one chance is in mystical
    trances ;—
Thessalian boon !

For swift as the wheels may turn,
And fierce as the flames may burn,
The spirit of man may discern
    In the wheel of Will
A drag on the wheels of Fate,
A water the fires to abate,
A soul the soul to make straight.
    And bid " be still ! "

But ye, ye invoke in your city
    And call on his name on the hill
The God who is born without pity,
    The horrible heart that is chill ;

The secret corruption of ages
Ye cling to, and hold as ye can,
And abandon the songs of the sages
For Passion—and Pan !

O thou heart of hate and inmost terror !
O thou soul of subtle fear and lust !
Loathsome shape of infamy, thy mirror
Shown as spirit or displayed as dust !
O thou worm in every soul of matter
Crawling, feasting, rotting; slime of hell !
Beat and batter ! shear and shatter !
Break the egg that hides thee well !
Pan ! I call thee ! Pan ! I see thee in thy
whirling citadel.

I alone of all men may unveil thee,
Show the ghastly soul of all that is
Unto them, that they themselves may hail
thee,
Festering corruption of thy kiss !
Thou the soul of God ! the soul of demon !
Soul of matter, soul of man !
Show the gross fools, thine, that think them
freemen,
What thou art, and what thy heart,
And what they are, that they are thee,
All creation, whole and part,—
Thine and thee, near and far :—
Come ! I call thee, I who can.
Pan ! I know thee ! Pan ! I show thee !
Burst thy coffin open, Pan !

What have I said ? What have I done ?

MÆNADS.

Pan ! Pan !
Evoe, Iacche ! Pan !

AGAVE.
The victim !

AUTONOE.

Rend
The sole pure thing in this impure gross
lump,
The shapeless, formless horror that is us
And God—Ah ! rend him limb from limb !

ORPHEUS.

Apollo !
This is the night. This is the end of all.
No force detains. No power urges on.
I am free ! Alas ! alas !—Eurydice !
*(He is torn to pieces. A faint
voice—like his—is still heard,
ever receding and failing.)*
O night !
Fade, love ! Fade, light !
I pass beyond Life's law.
I melt as snow ; as ice I thaw ;
As mist I dissipate : I am borne, I draw
Through chasms in the mountains : stormy
gusts
Of ancient sorrows and forgotten lusts
Bear me along : they touch me not : I waste
The memory of long lives interlaced
Fades in my fading. I disintegrate,
Fall into black oblivion of Fate.
My being divides : I have forgot my name.
I am blown out as a thin subtle flame.
I am no more.

A SPIRIT.

What is ? what chorus swells
Through these dark gorges and untrodden
dells !
What whisper through the forest ? Far
entwines
The low song with the roses and the vines,
The high song with the mountains and the
pines,
The inmost song with secret fibre of light,
And in the boiling pools and quorns and
chasms
Chases the stryges, Death's devote phantasms,
Into a brilliant air wherein they are lost.
Deep in the river moans the choral roar,
Till the deep murmur of the Lesbian shore
Washed of the luminous sea gives answer,
while
The angry wail of Nature doth beguile
The hours, the wrath of Nature reft of one,
The sole strong spirit that was Nature's sun,
The orb she circled round, the one thing
clean
From all her gross machinery, obscene

And helpless:—and the lonely mother-cry,
The Muse, her hope down-stricken. Magi-
cally
The full deep chorus stirs the sky ;
Hark ! one voice beyond all
Gives love's own call,
Not hers, Eurydice's,
But thine, thou sweet blood-breasted nightin-
gale
Waking thy choral wail
From Mitylene to remotest seas !

THE RIVER HEBRUS.

Was e'er a stream before
So sad a burden bore
Rolling a melancholy sorrow down from
shore to shore ?

CALLIOPE.

O this is bitterness beyond belief,
Grief beyond grief.
Boots it to weep? I holp him not
with force :
What should avail—remorse?

RIVER HEBRUS.

Hear upon high the melancholy
Antistrophe
Matching the strophe's agony !
Tides on a terrible sea !

CALLIOPE.

Bear, bear the laurelled head
Of him I loved, him dead,
O Hebrus, ever downward on thy bosom
iron-red !

RIVER HEBRUS.

All Nature's tunes are dull.
The beautiful,
The harmony of life is null.

CALLIOPE.

What unto us remains
But in these broken strains
To hymn with voices jarred the jarred world's
shriek of woe?

O ! O !

RIVER HEBRUS.

This discord is an agony
Shuddering harsh in me ;
My waters will empoison the fair fresh-water
sea !

CALLIOPE.

Nay ! all is ended now.
Cover the beaten brow !
Carry the brain of music into the wide
Ægean !
No priest pronounce thy pæan
Ever again, Apollo,
Thou false, thou fair, thou hollow !
Die to a groan within a shrine !
Despair thy force divine !
Thou didst achieve this ruin ; let the
seas
Roar o'er thy lost name of Musagetes !

THE LESBIAN SHORE.

Welcome, O holy head !
Welcome, O force not dead !
Reverberating joy of music subtly
shed !
Welcome, O glorious, O laurelled one !
Own offspring of the Sun,
The ancient harmony was hardly yet
begun.
By thee and by thy life
Arose the Lesbian maiden.
Thou art perished as thy wife ;
My shores with magic loves and songs of life
are laden.

CALLIOPE.

Weep, weep no more !
O loyal Lesbian shore,
I hear a murmur sound more sweet than
murmur ever bore.
Not ocean's siren spell
Soft-sounded in a spiral shell
Were quite so exquisite, were all so admir-
able !

LESBIAN SHORE.

Nay ! but the agony of the time
Rings in the royal rime !
She hath touched the intimate, and chanced
on the sublime.

CALLIOPE.

Ay ! Ay ! a woman's silky tone
Makes music for eternity her own,
Till all men's victories in song seem a dis-
cordant groan.

LESBIAN SHORE.

Upon my cliffs of green,
Beneath the azure skies,
She stands with looks of fire,
Sappho. Her hands between
Lies the wild world ; she flies
From agony to agony of desire.

CALLIOPE.

Him, Orpheus, him she sings ;
Loosing the living strings,·
Till music fledged fares forth sunward on
moon-wrought wings.

LESBIAN SHORE.

Yea, by the solar name,
Orpheus her lips acclaim,
The centre and the silence ! O ! the torrent
of fine flame
Like hair that shooteth forth
To the ensanguine North
Whence ran the drunken crew, Bassarids in
their wrath.

SAPPHO.

Woe is me ! the brow of a brazen morning
Breaks in blood on water athirst of Hebrus.
Sanguine horror starts on her hills tenebrous :
Hell hath not heard her !

Dumb and still thy birds, O Apollo, scorning
Song ; yells drown them, lecherous anthems
gabbled,
Laughter splashed of Bassarids, blood-be-
dabbled,
Mad with their murder !

O thou many-coloured immortal maiden,
Dawn ! O dew, delight of a world ! A
sorrow
Hides your holy faces awhile. To-morrow
Comes for your calling ?

Still the notes of musical Orpheus, laden
Never now of pain or of failing, follow ;
Follow up the height, or adown the hollow
Fairy are falli

O my hopeless misery mind of longing !
O the anguish born in a breast unlovered !
Women, wail the face of a God uncovered,
Brain dead and breath dumb !

Wail the sense of infinite ardours thronging
Fast and fast and faster athwart the heaven,
Keen as light and cruel as fire, as levin
Swift and as death dumb !

Freedom, rapture, victory, fill the chorus,
Dying, ever dying, among the billows ;
Whispered, ever whispered among the
willows :—
Pour the libation !

Now springs up a notable age. Adore us
Masters now of music above his magic,
Lords of change, leaps pastoral up to tragic,
Thanks to the Thracian !

Ah, my pain ! what desolate female bosoms,
Smitten hearts of delicate males, uncover ;
Grip not life for poet or sage or lover,
Feed on derision.

Yea, in these mature me avenger blossoms
Swift as swords to sever the subtle ether,
Lift the earth, see infinite space beneath her,
Swoon at the vision.

This, O Orpheus, this be a golden guerdon
Unto thee for gift of amaze and wonder !
This thy sorrow, sword of a heart asunder,
Beareth a flower.

This the heart of woman—a bitter burden !—
Thou hast filled with seed—O a seed of
madness !
Seed of music ! seed of a royal sadness !—
This be our dower !

Ah ! the bitter legacy left of lyre-light !
Thou wast Nature's prophet, a wise magician;
Magic fails, and love is a false physician :—
　　Deep our disease is !

Now to us the crouching over the firelight,
Eating out for hunger of love our vitals !
(Eaten out the hollower for respitals
　　Swift as the breeze is.)

Ay ! the golden age is a broken vessel.
All the golden waters exhale, evanish.
Joy of life and laughter of love we banish :
　　Damned is the will dead.

Now with brass and iron we writhe and
　　wrestle.
Now with clay the torrent of fire is tainted.
Life apes death : the lily is curled and
　　painted ;
　　Gold is regilded.

Master, we lament thee, as awful anguish
Seizes on the infinite maze of mortals.
See we love that yearns to the golden portals
　　Bound of the grey god.

Love, thy children, laughter and sunlight,
　　languish.
Aphrodite, miracle of the flashed foam,
Burns with beaten agony in the lashed foam ;
　　Down is the day-god.

Ay ! this first of Lesbian lamentations
Still shall burn from æon to idle æon !
(Chorus, epithalmy, ode, and pæan
　　Dumb or dishevelled !)

Still my songs shall murmur across the
　　nations,
Gain their meed of misery, praise, and
　　yearning,
Smite their stroke on centuries foully burning,
　　Drunk or bedevilled.

Song ? No beauty shine in a sphere of music !
Me ? my voice be dull, be a void, be toneless !
Match me, sea ! than me thou hast many a
　　moan less,
　　Many a million !

Sun, be broken ! Moon, be eclipsed ; be
　　dew sick !
Ocean flat and poisonous, earth demented !
Living souls go shuddering through the tented
　　Air, his pavilion !

Ay ; the pectis clangs me a soulless discord :—
Let me break my visible heart a-weeping !
Loving ?　Drinking ?　Misery.　Singing,
　　sleeping
　　Touch not my sorrow.

Orpheus, turn the sorrow-chord to the bliss-
　　chord !
All may rise the easier that the one set.
So our eyes from saddening at the sunset
　　Turn to to-morrow.

CALLIOPE.

　　Silence.　I hear a voice
　　That biddeth me rejoice.
　　I know the whole wise plan
　　Of Fate regarding Man.

THE LESBIAN SHORE.

It is the sun's dark bride
Nuith, the azure-eyed.
No longer Sappho sings her spell ;
His heart divorced, her heart insatiable.
There is deep silence.　Earth hath passed
To a new kingdom.　In a purpose vast
Her horoscope is cast.

NUITH.

Enough.　It is ended, the story
　　Of magical æons of song ;
The sun is gone down in his glory
　　To the Houses of Hate and of Wrong.
　　Would ye see if he rise ?
　　In Hesperian skies
Ye may look for his rising for long.

The magical æon beginneth
　　Of song in the heart of desire,
That smiteth and striveth and sinneth,
　　But burns up the soul of the lyre :—
　　There is pain in the note :—
　　In the sorcerer's throat
Is a sword, and his brain is afire !

Long after (to men : but a moment
 To me in my mansion of rest)
Is a sundawn to blaze what the glow meant
Seen long after death in the west ;
 A magical æon !
 Nor love-song nor pæan,
But a flame with a silvery crest.

There shall rise a sweet song of the soul
Far deeper than love or distress ;
Beyond mortals and gods shall it roll ;
It shall find me, and crave, and caress.
 Ah ! me it shall capture
 In torrents of rapture ;
It shall flood me, and fill, and possess.

For brighter from age unto age
The weary old world shall renew
Its life at the lips of the sage,
 Its love at the lips of the dew.
 With kisses and tears
 The return of the years
Is sure as the starlight is true.

Yet the drift of the stars is to beauty,
 To strength, and to infinite pleasure.
The toil and the worship and duty
 Shall turn them to laughter and leisure.
 Were the world understood
 Ye would see it was good,
A dance to a delicate measure.

Ye fools, interweaving in passion
 The lyrical light of the mind !
Go on, in your drivelling fashion !
 Ye shall surely seek long and not find.
 From without ye may see
 All the beauty of me,
And my lips, that their kisses are kind.

For Eurydice once I lamented ;
For Orpheus I do not lament :
Her days were a span, and demented ;
 His days are for aye, and content.
 Mere love is as nought
 To the love that is Thought,
And idea is more than event.

O lovers ! O poets ! O masters
 Of me, ye may ravish my frown !
Aloof from my shocks and disasters !
 Impatient to kiss me, and crown !
 I am eager to yield.
 In the warrior field
Ye shall fight me, and fasten me down.

O poets ! O masters ! O lovers !
 Sweet souls of the strength of the sun !
The couch of eternity covers
 Our loves, and our dreams are as done.
 Reality closes
 Our life into roses ;
We are infinite space : we are one.

There is one[1] that hath sought me and
 found me
 In the heart of the sand and the snow :
He hath caught me, and held me, and
 bound me,
 In the lands where no flower may grow.
 His voice is a spell,
 Hath enchanted me well !
I am his, did I will it or no.

But I will it, I will it, I will it !
 His speck of a soul in its cars
Shall lift up immensity ! fill it
 With light of his lyrical bars.
 His soul shall concentre
 All space ; he shall enter
The beautiful land of the stars.

He shall know me eternally wedded
 To the splendid and subtle of mind ;
For the pious, the arrogant-headed,
 He shall know they nor seek me nor find.
 O afloat in me curled !
 Cry aloud to the world
That I and my kisses are kind !

O lover ! O poet ! O maiden
 To me in my magical way !
Be thy songs with the wilderness laden !
 Thy lyre be adrift and astray :—
 So to me thou shalt cling !
 So to me thou shalt sing
Of the beautiful law of the day !

[1] Possibly intended as a reference to the
poet himself.

I forbid thee to weep or to worship ;
　I forbid thee to sing or to write !
The Star-Goddess guideth us her ship ;
　The sails belly out with the light.
　　Beautiful head !
　　We will sing on our bed
Of the beautiful law of the Night !

We are lulled by the whirr of the stars ;
　We are fanned by the whisper, the wind ;
We are locked in unbreakable bars,
　The love of the spirit and mind.
　　The infinite powers
　　Of rapture are ours ;
We are one, and our kisses are kind.

EXPLICIT LIBER QUARTUS

EPILOGUE AND DEDICATION

November 18, 1906.

MY DEAR ION,—I address you by the unfamiliar title in giving you, a man self-damned, God knows how unjustly, as the author of the phrase, "I am not an appreciator of poetry, and I have no Keats," these volumes. For the matter thereof is already in great part yours and as such cannot be given. The rest I offer because it is hardly possible to close definitely, as I do now, a period of many years' work, without reflecting upon that period as a whole. And, when I do so, I find you at the beginning like Ladas or Pheidippides of old, running —ready to run until you achieve the goal or your heart burst; but you are among a crowd. I join you. Eight years ago this day you, Hermes, led me blindfold to awake a chosen runner of the course. "In all my wanderings in darkness your light shone before me though I knew it not." To-day (one may almost hope, turning into the straight) you and I are alone. Terrible and joyous! We shall find companions at the End, at the banquet, lissome and cool and garlanded; companions with a Silver Star or maybe a Jewelled Eye mobile and uncertain—as if alive—on their foreheads. We shall be bidden to sit, and they will wreathe us with immortal flowers, and give us to drink of the seemly wine of Iacchus—well! but until then, unless my heart deceives me, no third shall appear to join us. Indeed, may two attain? It seems a thing impossible in nature. May it not be that—near as the resounding roar of the viewless spectators sounds to our dust-dimmed ears—there stands some awful opposer in the way, some fear or some seduction? Why do you grip that bar in your left hand? Does not this loin-cloth irk my limbs? We should have shaved our heads before the race—the curls are moist and heavy! Why did we cumber ourselves with sandals? Long ere now our feet would have grown hard. Well, if my heart bursts, it bursts; you must give these volumes to the young athletes, that they may learn wherefore I failed—wherefore it was given unto me to run thus far. For, if I have put nothing else therein, most surely that is there.

ALEISTER CROWLEY.

EPILOGUE AND DEDICATION OF

VOLUMES I., II., III.

ELEUSIS.

THOSE who are most familiar with the spirit of fair play which pervades our great public schools will have no difficulty, should they observe, in an obscure corner, the savage attack of Jones minor upon Robinson minimus, in deducing that the former has only just got over the "jolly good hiding" that Smith major had so long promised him, the determining factor of the same being Smith's defeat by Brown maximus behind the chapel, after Brown's interview with the Head-Master.

We are most of us aware that cabinet ministers, bishops, and dons resemble each other in the important particular that all are still schoolboys, and their differences but the superficial one produced by greasing, soaping, and withering them respectively; so that it will meet with instant general approval if I open this paper by the remark that Christianity, as long as it flourished, was content to assimilate Paganism, never attacking it until its own life had been sapped by the insidious heresies of Paul.

Time passed by, and they bullied Manes and Cerinthus; history repeated itself until it almost knew itself by heart; finally, at the present day, some hireling parasites of the decaying faith—at once the origin and the product of that decay—endeavour to take advantage of the "Greek movement" or the "Neo-pagan revival" in the vain hope of diverting the public attention from the phalanx of Rationalism—traitorously admitted by Luther, and now sitting crowned and inexpugnable in the very citadel of the faith —to their own dishonest lie that Paganism was a faith whose motto was "Carpe diem,"[1] and whose methods were drink, dance, and Studio Murder.[2] Why is Procopius cleaner than Petronius? Even a Julian could confute this sort of thing; but are we to rest for ever in negation? No: a Robinson minimus ipse will turn, and it is quite time that science was given a chance to measure itself against bulk. I shall not be content with giving Christian apologists the lie direct, but proceed to convict them of the very materialism against which they froth. In a word,

to-day Christianity is the irreligion of the materialist, or if you like, the sensualist; while in Paganism, we may find the expression of that ever-haunting love— nay, necessity!—of the Beyond which tortures and beautifies those of us who are poets.

πάντα καθαρὰ τοῖς καθαροῖς—and, while there is no logical break between the apparently chaste dogma of the Virgin Birth and the horrible grossness of R. P. Sanchez in his De Matrimonio, Lib. ii. Cap. xxi., "Utium Virgo Maria semen emiserit in copulatione cum Spiritu Sancto," so long as we understand an historical Incarnation : the accomplishment of that half of the Magnum Opus which is glyphed in the mystic aphorism "Solve!" enables an Adept of that standing to see nothing but pure symbol and holy counsel in the no grosser legends of the Greeks. This is not a matter of choice : reason forbids us to take the Swan-lover in its literal silliness and obscenity; but, on the other hand, the Bishops will not allow us to attach a pure interpretation to the precisely similar story of the Dove.[1]

So far am I, indeed, from attacking Christian symbolism as such, that I am quite prepared to admit that it is, although or rather because it is the lowest, the best. Most others, especially Hinduism and Buddhism, lose themselves in metaphysical speculations only proper to those who are already Adepts.

The Rosicrucian busies himself with the Next Step, for himself and his pupils; he is no more concerned to discuss Nibbana than a schoolmaster to "settle the doctrine of the enclitic Δή" in the mind of a child who is painfully grappling with the declension of Νεανίας. We can read even orthodox

---

[1] "Gather ye roses!" is the masterpiece of a Christian clergyman.—A. C.

[2] A peculiarly gross case of psychopathic crime which occurred in 1906.

[1] Recently, a certain rash doctor publicly expressed his doubts whether any Bishop of the twentieth century was so filthy-minded a fool. They were, however, soon dispelled by telegrams from a considerable section of the entire Bench, couched in emphatic language.

Christian writers with benefit (such is the revivifying force of our Elixir) by seeking the essence in the First Matter of the Work; and we could commend many of them, notably St. Ignatius and even the rationalising Mansel and Newman, if they would only concentrate upon spiritual truth, instead of insisting on the truth of things, material and therefore immaterial, which only need the touch of a scholar's wand to crumble into the base dust from which their bloodstained towers arose.

Whoso has been crucified with Christ can but laugh when it is proved that Christ was never crucified. The historian understands nothing of what we mean, either by Christ or by crucifixion, and is thus totally incompetent to criticise our position. On the other hand, we are of course equally ill-placed to convert him; but then we do not wish to do so; certainly not *quâ* historian. We leave him alone. Whoso hath ears to hear, let him hear! and the first and last ordeals and rewards of the Adept are comprised in the maxim "Keep silence!"

There should be no possible point of contact between the Church and the world: Paul began the ruin of Christianity, but Constantine completed it. The Church which begins to exteriorise is already lost. To control the ethics of the state is to adopt the ethics of the state: and the first duty of the state will be to expel the rival god Religion. In such a cycle we in England seem to be now revolving, and the new forced freedom of the Church is upon us.

If only the destruction is sufficiently complete, if only all England will turn Atheist, we may perhaps be able to find some Christians here and there. As long as "church" means either a building, an assembly, or even has any meaning at all of a kind to be intelligible to the ordinary man, so long is Christ rejected, and the Pharisee supreme.

Now the materialism which has always been the curse of Christianity was no doubt partly due to the fact that the early disciples were poor men. You cannot bribe a rich man with loaves and fishes: only the overfed long for the Simple Life. True, Christ bought the world by the promise of Fasts and Martyrdoms, glutted as it was by its surfeit of Augustan glories; but the poor were in a vast majority, and snatched greedily at all the gross pleasures and profits of which the educated and wealthy were sick even unto death. Further, the asceticism of surfeit is a false passion, and only lasts until a healthy hunger is attained; so that the change was an entire corruption, without redeeming aspect. Had there been five righteous men in Rome, a Cato, a Brutus, a Curtius, a Scipio, and a Julian, nothing would have occurred; but there was only the last, and he too late. No doubt Maximus, his teacher, was too holy an Adept to mingle in the affairs of the world; one indeed, perhaps, about to pass over to a higher sphere of action: such speculation is idle and impertinent; but the world was ruined, as never before since the fabled destruction of Atlantis, and I trust that I shall take my readers with me when I affirm so proud a belief in the might of the heart whose integrity is unassailable, clean of all crime, that I lay it down as a positive dictum that only by the decay in the mental and moral virility of Rome and not otherwise, was it possible for the slavish greed and anarchy of the Faith of Paul to gain a foothold. This faith was no new current of youth, sweeping away decadence: it was a force of the slime: a force with no single salutary germ of progress inherent therein. Even Mohammedanism, so often accused of materialism, did produce, at once, and in consequence, a revival of learning, a crowd of algebraists, astronomers, philosophers, whose names are still to be revered: but within the fold, from the death of Christ to the Renaissance — a purely pagan movement—we hear no more of art, literature, or philosophy.[1]   But we do hear—well, what Gibbon has to say.

There is surely a positive side to all this; we agree that Pagans must have been more spiritual than their successors, if only because themselves openly scoffed at their mythology without in the least abandoning the devout performance of its rites, while the Christian clung to irrelevant historical falsehood as if it were true and important.   But it is justifiable —nay, urgent—to inquire how and why? Which having discovered, we are bound to proceed with the problem : " Wherewithal shall a young man cleanse his way?" receive the answer : " By taking heed thereto accord-

[1] Such philosophy as does exist is entirely vicious, taking its axioms no more from observed fact, but from "Scripture" or from Aristotle.   Barring such isolated pagans as M. Aurelius Antoninus, and the neo-Platonists, those glorious decadents * of paganism.

ing to thy word," and interpret "thy word " as " The Works of Aleister Crowley."

But this is to anticipate ; let us answer the first question by returning to our phrase " The Church that exteriorises is already lost." On that hypothesis, the decay of Paganism was accomplished by the very outward and visible sign of its inward and spiritual grace, the raising of massive temples to the Gods in a style and manner to which history seeks in vain a parallel.   Security is mortals' chiefest enemy ; so also the perfection of balanced strength which enabled Hwang-sze to force his enemies to build the Great Wall was the mark of the imminent decay of his dynasty and race— truly a terrible " Writing on the Wall." An end to the days of the Nine Sages ; an end to the wisdoms of Lao Tan on his dun cow ; an end to the making of classics of history and of odes and of ethics, to the Shu King and the Shih King, and the Li-Ki,

* Decadence marks the period when the adepts, nearing their earthly perfection, become true adepts, not mere men of genius.   They disappear, harvested by heaven : and perfect darkness (apparent death) ensues until the youthful forerunners of the next crop begin to shoot in the form of artists.   Diagrammatically :

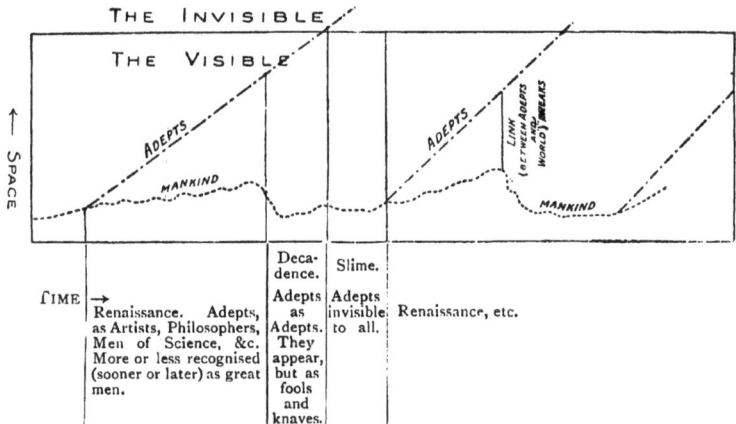

	Deca-dence.	Slime.	
TIME →	Adepts as Adepts. They appear, but as fools and knaves.	Adepts invisible to all.	Renaissance, etc.
Renaissance. Adepts, as Artists, Philosophers, Men of Science, &c. More or less recognised (sooner or later) as great men.			

By the Progress of the World we mean that she is always giving adepts to God, and thus losing them ; yet,. through their aid, while they are still near enough to humanity to attract it, she reaches each time a higher point.   Yet this point is never very high ; so that Aeschylus, though in fact more ignorant than our schoolboys, holds his seat besides Ibsen and Newton in the Republic of the Adepti—a good horse, but not to be run too hard.—A. C.

and the mysterious glories of the holy Yi King itself! Civilisation, decadence, and the slime. Still the Great Wall keeps the Barbarians from China : it is the wall that the Church of Christ set up against science and philosophy, and even to-day its ruins stand, albeit wrapped in the lurid flames of Hell. It is the law of life, this cycle ; decadence is perfection, and the perfect soul is assumed into the bosom of Nephthys, so that for a while the world lies fallow. It is in failing to see this constant fume of incense rising from the earth that pessimistic philosophies make their grand fundamental error : in that, and in assuming the very point in dispute, the nature of the laws of other worlds and the prospects of the individual soul. Confess, O subtle author, that thou thyself art even now in the same trap ! Willingly, reader ; these slips happen when, although one cannot prove to others, one knows.[1] Thou too shalt know, an thou wilt :—ask how, and we come suddenly back to our subject, just as a dreamer may wander through countless nightmares, to find himself in the end on the top of a precipice, whence falling, he shall find himself in bed.

Hear wisdom ! the Lord answered Job out of the whirlwind.

A man is almost obliged to be in communion with God when God is blowing his hat off, drenching him to the skin, whistling through his very bones, scaring him almost to death with a flash of lightning, and so on. When he gets time to think, he thinks just that. In a church all is too clearly the work of man : in the matter of man's comfort man's devices are so obviously superior to God's : so that we compare hats and languidly discuss the preacher.

Religion is alive in Wales, because people have to walk miles to chapel.

[1] Let me run wild for once, I beg ; I am tired of emulating Mr. Storer Clouston's Sir Julian Wallingford, " whose reasoning powers were so remarkable that he never committed the slightest action without furnishing a full and adequate explanation of his conduct."—A. C.

Religion is alive among Mohammedans, who pray (as they live) out of doors, and who will fight and die for their ideas ; and among Hindus, whose bloody sacrifices bring them daily face to face with death.

Pan-Islam is possible ; pan-Germany is possible ; but pan-Christendom would be absurd. There were saints in the times of the Crusades, and Crusaders in the times of the Saints : for though the foe was more artificial than real, and the object chimerical, a foe and an aim of whatever sort assist the concentration which alone is life.

So that we need not be surprised to see as we do that religion is dead in London, where it demands no greater sacrifice than that of an hour's leisure in the week, and even offers to repay that with social consideration for the old, and opportunities of flirtation for the young.

The word " dear " has two senses, and these two are one.

Pressing the " out-of-doors " argument, as we may call it, I will challenge each of my readers to a simple experiment.

Go out one night to a distant and lonely heath, if no mountain summit is available : then at midnight repeat the Lord's Prayer, or any invocation with which you happen to be familiar, or one made up by yourself, or one consisting wholly of senseless and barbarous words.[1] Repeat it solemnly and

[1] I am ashamed to say that I have devoted considerable time to the absurd task of finding meanings for, and tracing the corruptions of, the " barbarous names of evocation " which occur in nearly all conjurations, and which Zoroaster warns his pupils not to change, because " they are names divine, having in the sacred rites a power ineffable."

The fact is that many such names are indeed corruptions of divine names. We may trace Eheieh in Eie, Abraxas in Abrae, Tetragrammaton in Jehovah.

But this, an initiate knows, is quite contrary to the true theory.

It is *because* the names are senseless that they are effective. If a man is really praying he cannot bring himself to utter ridiculous things to his God, just as Mark Twain observes that one " cannot pray a lie." So that it is a sublime

aloud, expectant of some great and mysterious result.

I pledge myself, if you have a spark of religion in you, that is, if you are properly a human being, that you will (at the very least) experience a deeper sense of spiritual communion than you have ever obtained by any course of church-going.

After which you will, if you are worth your salt, devote your life to the development of this communion, and to the search for an instructed master who can tell you more than I can.

Now the earlier paganism is simply over-flowing with this spirit of communion. The boy goes down to the pool, musing, as boys will; is it strange that a nymph should reward him, sometimes even with wine from the purple vats of death?

Poor dullards! in your zeal to extinguish the light upon our altars you have had to drench your own with the bitter waters of

test of faith to utter either a lie or a jest, this with reverence, and that with conviction. Achieve it; the one becomes the truth, the other a formula of power. Hence the real value of the Egyptian ritual by which the theurgist identified himself with the power he invoked. Modern neophytes should not (we think) use the old conjurations with their barbarous names, because, imperfectly un-derstanding the same, they may supersti-tiously attribute some real power to them; we shall rather advise "Jack and Jill went up the hill," "From Greenland's icy moun-tains," and such, with which it is impossible for the normal mind to associate a feeling of reverence.

What may be the mode of operation of this formula concerns us little; enough if it succeeds. But one may suggest that it is a case of the will running free, i.e. un-checked, as it normally is, by the hosts of critical larvæ we call reason, habit, sensation, and the like.

But the will freed from these may run straight and swift; if its habitual goal has been the attainment of Samadhi, it may under such circumstances reach it. It will require a very advanced student to use this type of faith. The Lord's Prayer and the minor exaltation are the certainties for this event.—A. C.

most general unbelief. Where are the witches and the fairies and the angels, and the visions of divine St. John? You are annoyed at my mention of angels and witches; because you know yourselves to be sceptics, and that I have any amount of "scriptural warrant" to throw at your heads, if I deigned; you are all embar-rassed when Maude Adams leans over the footlights with a goo-goo accent so ex-cessive that you die of diabetes in a week, and asks you point-blank: "Do you believe in fairies?" while, for your visions, you do not go to St. John's Island, and share his exile; but to his Wood, and waste your money.

The early pagan worships Demeter in dim groves: there is silence; there is no organisation of ritual; there the worship is spontaneous and individual. In short, the work of religion is thrown upon the religious faculty, instead of being dele-gated to the quite inferior and irrelevant faculties of mere decorum or even stage-craft. A Christian of the type of Brown-ing understands this perfectly. True, he approves the sincerity which he finds to pervade the otherwise disgusting chapel; but he cares nothing whatever for the "raree-show of Peter's successor," and though I daresay his ghost will be shocked and annoyed by my mention of the fact, Browning himself does not get his illumi-nation in any human temple, but only when he is out with the universe alone in the storm.

Nor does Browning anywhere draw so perfect and so credible a picture of the inter-course between man and God as the exquisite vision of Pan in "Pheidippides." It is all perfectly natural and therefore miraculous; there is no straining at the gnats of vestment in the hope of swallowing the camel of Illumination.

In the matter of Pentecost, we hear only, in the way of the "conditions of the experiment," that "they were all with one accord in one place." Now, this being the only instance in the world's history of more than two people in one place being of one accord, it is naturally also the only instance of a miracle which happened in church.

The Quakers, arguing soundly enough that women were such a cause of contention chiefly on account of their tongues, and getting a glimpse of these truths which I have so laboriously been endeavouring to expound, hoped for inspiration from the effects of silence alone, and strove (even by a symbolic silence in costume) to repeat the experiment of Pentecost.

But they lacked the stimulus of Syrian air, and that of the stirring times of the already visible sparks of national revolt: they should have sought to replace these by passing the bottle round in their assemblies, and something would probably have happened, an 'twere only a raid of the police.

Better get forty shillings or a month than live and die as lived and died John Bright !

Better be a Shaker, or a camp-meeting homunculus, or a Chatauqua gurl, or a Keswick week lunatic, or an Evan Roberts revivalist, or even a common maniac, than a smug Evangelical banker's clerk with a greasy wife and three gifted children—to be bank clerks after him !

Better be a flagellant, or one who dances as David danced before the Lord, than a bishop who is universally respected, even by the boys he used to baste when he was headmaster of a great English public school !

That is, if religion is your aim : if you are spiritually minded : if you interpret every phenomenon that is presented to your sensorium as a particular dealing of God with your soul.

But if you come back from the celebration of the Eucharist and say, " Mr. Hogwash was very dull to-day," you will never get to heaven, where the good poets live, and nobody else ; nor to hell, whose inhabitants are exclusively bad poets.

There is more hope for a man who should go to Lord's and say he saw the angels of God ascending and descending upon C. B. Fry.

It is God who sees the possibility of Light in Chaos ; it is the Churches who blaspheme the superb body of Truth which Adepts of old enshrined in the Cross, by degrading the Story of the Crucifixion to a mere paragraph in the *Daily Mail* of the time of Pontius Pilate.

Bill Blake took tea with Ezekiel : Tennyson saw no more in the Arthurian legends than a prophecy of the Prince Consort (though Lancelot has little in common with John Brown), and the result of all is that Tennyson is dead and buried—as shown by the fact that he is still popular —and Blake lives, for poets read and love him.

Now when Paganism became popular, organised, state-regulated, it ceased to be individual : that is to say, it ceased to exist as a religion, and became a social institution little better than the Church which has replaced it. But initiates—men who had themselves seen God face to face, and lived --preserved the vital essence. They chose men ; they tested them ; they instructed them in methods of invoking the Visible Image of the Invisible. Thus by a living chain religion lived—in the Mysteries of Eleusis.

Further, recognising that the Great Work was henceforth to be secret, a worship of caverns and midnight groves and catacombs, no more of open fields and smiling bowers, they caused to be written in symbols by one of the lesser initiates the whole Mystery of Godliness, so that after the renaissance those who were fitted to the Work might infallibly discover the first matter of the Work and even many of the processes thereof.

Such writings are those of the neo-Platonists, and in modern times the God-illumined Adept Berkeley, Christian though he called himself, is perhaps the most distinguished of those who have understood this truth.[1]

But the orthodox Christian, confronted with this fact, is annoyed; just as the American, knowing himself to be of the filthiest dregs of mankind, pretends that there is no such thing as natural aristocracy, though to be sure he gives himself away badly enough when confronted with either a nigger or a gentleman, since to ape

---

[1] EXTRACTS FROM BERKELEY'S LIFE

[1] " There is a mystery about this visit to Dublin. ' I propose to set out for Dublin about a month hence,' he writes to ' dear Tom,' ' but of this you must not give the least intimation to any one. It is of all things my earnest desire (and for very good reasons) not to have it known I am in Dublin. Speak not, therefore, one syllable of it to any mortal whatsoever. When I formerly desired you to take a place for me near the town, you gave out that you were looking for a retired lodging for a friend of yours ; upon which everybody surmised me to be the person. I must beg you not to act in the like manner now—but to take for me an entire house in your own name, and as for yourself; for, all things considered, I am determined upon a whole house, with no mortal in it but a maid of your own getting, who is to look on herself as your servant. Let there be two bedrooms ; one for you, another for me, and as you like you may ever and anon lie there.
" ' I would have the house with necessary furniture taken by the month (or otherwise as you can), for I propose staying not beyond that time, and yet perhaps I may.
" ' Take it as soon as possible. . . . Let me entreat you to say nothing of this to anybody, but to do the thing directly. . . . I would of all things have a proper place in a retired situation, where I may have access to fields, and sweet air, provided against the moment I arrive. I am inclined to think one may be better concealed in the outermost skirt of the suburbs, than in the country or within the town. A house quite detached in the country I should have no objections to, provided you judge I shall not be liable to discovery in it. The place called Bermuda I am utterly against. Dear Tom, do this matter cleanly and cleverly, without waiting for further advice. . . . To the person from whom you hire it (whom alone I would have you speak to of it) it will not be strange at this time of the year to be desirous for your own convenience, or health, to have a place in a free and open air ! '
" This mysterious letter was written in April. From April till September Berkeley

EXTRACTS FROM THE BOOK OF THE SACRED MAGIC OF ABRAMELIN THE MAGE

I resolved to absent myself suddenly and go away . . . and lead a solitary life.

I am about here to set down in writing the difficulties, temptations, and hindrances which will be caused him by his own relations . . . beforehand thou shouldest arrange thine affairs in such wise that they can in no way hinder thee, nor bring thee any disquietude.

I took another house at rent . . . and I gave over unto one of my uncles the care of providing the necessaries of life.

" Should you perform this Operation in a town, you should take a house which is not at all overlooked by any one, seeing that in this present day curiosity is so strong that you ought to be upon your guard ; and there ought to be a garden (adjoining the house) wherein you can take exercise."

" Consider then the safety of your person, commencing this operation in a place of safety, whence neither enemies nor any disgrace can drive you out before the end."

" the season of Easter. . . . Then first on the following day . . . I commenced this Holy

dominance is the complement of his natural slavishness. So the blind groveller, Mr. Conformity, and his twin, Mr. Nonconformity, agree to pretend that initiates are always either dupes or impostors; they deny that man can see God and live. Look! There goes John Compromise to church, speculating, like Lot's wife, on the probable slump in sulphur and the gloomy outlook for the Insurance Companies. It will never do for his Christ to be a man of like passions with himself, else people might expect him to aim at a life like Christ's. He wants to wallow and swill, and hope for an impossible heaven.

So that it will be imprudent of you (if you want to be asked out to dinner) to poin out that if you tell the story of the life of Christ, without mentioning names, to a Musulman, he will ask, "What was the name of that great sheikh?" to a Hindu, "Who was this venerable Yogi?" to a Buddhist, "Haven't you made a mistake or two? It wasn't a dove, but an elephant with six tusks: and He died of dysentery."

The fact being that it is within the personal experience of all these persons that men yet live and walk this earth who live in all essentials the life that Christ lived, to whom all His miracles are commonplace, who die His death daily, and partake daily in the Mysteries of His resurrection and ascension.

Whether this is scientifically so or not is of no importance to the argument. I am not addressing the man of science, but the man of intelligence: and the scientist himself will back me when I say that the evidence for the one is just as strong and as weak as

again disappears. There is in all this a curious secretiveness of which one has *repeated examples in his life*.[1] Whether he went to Dublin on that occasion, or why he wanted to go, does not appear."

[2] "I abhor business, and especially to have to do with great persons and great affairs."

[3] "Suddenly, and without the least previous notice of pain, he was removed to the enjoyment of eternal rewards, and although all possible means were instantly used, no symptom of life ever appeared after; nor could the physicians assign any cause for his death."

Operation . . . the period of the Six Moons being expired, the Lord granted unto me His grace . . ."

"a solitary life, which is the source of all good . . . once thou shalt have obtained the sacred science and magic the love for retirement will come to thee of its own accord, and thou wilt voluntarily shun the commerce and conversation of men, &c."

"a good death in His holy Kingdom."

It is surely beyond doubt that Berkeley contemplated some operation of a similar character to that of Abramelin. Note the extreme anxiety which he displays. What lesser matter could so have stirred the placid and angelic soul of Berkeley? On what less urgent grounds would he have agreed to the deceptions (harmless enough though they are) that he urges upon his brother?

That he at one time or another achieved success is certain from the universal report of his holiness and from the nature of his writings. The repeated phrase in the Optics, "God is the Father of Lights,"[2] suggests an actual phrase perhaps used as an exclamation at the moment of a Vision to express, however feebly, its nature, rather than the phrase of a reasoner exercising his reason.

This mysterious letter which so puzzles his biographer is in fact the key to his whole character, life, and opinions.

This is no place to labour the point; I have at hand none of the necessary documents; but it might be worth the research of a scholar to trace Berkeley's progress through the grades of the Great Order.—A. C.

[1] The italics are ours.—ED.

[2] It occurs in James i. 17.

for the others. God forbid that I should rest this paper on a historical basis ! I am talking about the certain results of human psychology : and science can neither help nor hinder me.

True, when Huxley and Tyndall were alive, their miserable intelligences were always feeding us up with the idea that science might one day be able to answer some of the simpler questions which one can put : but that was because of their mystical leanings ; they are dead, and have left no successors. To-day we have the certitude, " Science never can tell," of the laborious Ray Lankester

" Whose zeal for knowledge mocks the curfew's call,
And after midnight, to make Lodge look silly,
Studies anatomy—in Piccadilly."

Really, we almost echo his despair. When, only too many years ago, I was learning chemistry, the text-books were content with some three pages on Camphor : to-day, a mere abstract of what is known occupies 400 closely printed pages : but Knowledge is in no wise advanced. It is no doubt more difficult to learn " Paradise Lost " by heart than " We are Seven " ; but when you have done it, you are no better at figure-skating.

I am not denying that the vast storehouses of fact do help us to a certain distillation (as it were) of their grain : but I may be allowed to complain with Maudsley that there is nobody competent to do it. Even when a genius does come along, his results will likely be as empirical as the facts they cover. Evolution is no better than creation to explain things, as Spencer showed.

The truth of the matter appears to be that as reason is incompetent to solve the problems of philosophy and religion, *à fortiori* science is incompetent. All that science can do is to present reason with new facts. To such good purpose has it done this, that no modern scientist can hope to do more than know a little about one bud on his pet twig of the particular branch he has

chosen to study, as it hangs temptingly from one bough of the Tree of Knowledge.

One of the most brilliant of the younger school of chemists remarks in the course of a stirring discourse upon malt analysis : " Of extremely complex organic bodies the constitution of some 250,000 is known with certainty, and the number grows daily. No one chemist pretends to an intimate acquaintance with more than a few of these . . ." Why not leave it alone, and try to be God ?

But even had we Maudsley's committee of geniuses, should we be in any real sense the better ? Not while the reason is, as at present, the best guide known to men, not until humanity has developed a mental power of an entirely different kind. For to the philosopher it soon becomes apparent that reason is a weapon inadequate to the task. Hume saw it, and became a sceptic in the widest sense of the term. Mansel saw it, and counsels us to try Faith, as if it was not the very fact that Faith was futile that bade us appeal to reason. Huxley saw it, and, no remedy presenting itself but a vague faith in the possibilities of human evolution, called himself an agnostic : Kant saw it for a moment, but it soon hid itself behind his terminology ; Spencer saw it, and tried to gloss it over by smooth talk, and to bury it beneath the ponderous tomes of his unwieldy erudition.

I see it, too, and the way out to Life.

But the labyrinth, if you please, before the clue : the Minotaur before the maiden !

Thank you, madam ; would you care to look at our new line in Minotaurs at 2s. 3d. ? This way, please.

I have taken a good deal of trouble lately to prove the proposition "All arguments are arguments in a circle." Without wearying my readers with the formal proof, which I hope to advance one day in an essay on the syllogism, I will take (as sketchily as you please !) the obvious and important case of the consciousness.

A. The consciousness is made up exclusively of impressions (The tendency to certain impressions is itself a result of impressions on the ancestors of the conscious being). Locke, Hume, &c.

B. Without a consciousness no impression can exist. Berkeley, Fichte, &c.

Both A. and B. have been proved times without number, and quite irrefutably. Yet they are mutually exclusive. The "progress" of philosophy has consisted almost entirely of advances in accuracy of language by rival schools who emphasised A. and B. alternately.

It is easy to see that all propositions can, with a little ingenuity, be reduced to one form or the other.[1]

Thus, if I say that grass is green, I mean that an external thing is an internal thing: for the grass is certainly not in my eye, and the green certainly *is* in it. As all will admit.

So, if you throw a material brick at your wife, and hit her (as may happen to all of us), there is a most serious difficulty in the question, "At what point did your (spiritual) affection for her transform into the (material) brick, and that again into her (spiritual) reformation?"

Similarly, we have Kant's clear proof that in studying the laws of nature we only study the laws of our own minds: since, for one thing, the language in which we announce a law is entirely the product of our mental conceptions.

While, on the other hand, it is clear enough that our minds depend upon the laws of nature, since, for one thing, the apprehension that six savages will rob and murder you is immediately allayed by the passage of a leaden bullet weighing 230 grains, and moving at the rate of 1200 feet per second, through the bodies of two of the ringleaders.

[1] Compare the problems suggested to the logician by the various readings of propositions in connotation, denotation, and comprehension respectively; and the whole question of existential import.—A. C.

It would of course be simple to go on and show that after all we attach no meaning to weight and motion, lead and bullet, but a purely spiritual one : that they are mere phases of our thought, as interpreted by our senses : and on the other that apprehension is only a name for a certain group of chemical changes in certain of the contents of our very material skulls : but enough ! the whole controversy is verbal, and no more.

Since therefore philosophy and *à fortiori* science are bankrupt, and the official receiver is highly unlikely to grant either a discharge; since the only aid we get from the Bishops is a friendly counsel to drink Beer —in place of the spiritual wine of Omar Khayyam and Abdullah el Haji (on whom be peace !)—we are compelled to fend for ourselves.

We have heard a good deal of late years about Oriental religions. I am myself the chief of sinners. Still, we may all freely confess that they are in many ways picturesque : and they do lead one to the Vision of God face to face, as one who hath so been led doth here solemnly lift up his voice and testify ; but their method is incredibly tedious, and unsuited to most, if not all, Europeans. Let us never forget that no poetry of the higher sort, no art of the higher sort, has ever been produced by any Asiatic race. We are the poets ! we are the children of wood and stream, of mist and mountain, of sun and wind ! We adore the moon and the stars, and go into the London streets at midnight seeking Their kisses as our birthright. We are the Greeks —and God grant ye all, my brothers, to be as happy in your loves !—and to us the rites of Eleusis should open the doors of Heaven, and we shall enter in and see God face to face ! Alas !

"None can read the text, not even I ;
And none can read the comment but myself."[1]

[1] Tennyson must have stolen these lines ; they are simple and expressive.

The comment is the Qabalah, and that I have indeed read as deeply as my poor powers allow : but the text is decipherable only under the stars by one who hath drunken of the dew of the moon.

Under the stars will I go forth, my brothers, and drink of that lustral dew : I will return, my brothers, when I have seen God face to face, and read within those eternal eyes the secret that shall make you free.

Then will I choose you and test you and instruct you in the Mysteries of Eleusis, oh ye brave hearts, and cool eyes, and trembling lips ! I will put a live coal upon your lips, and flowers upon your eyes, and a sword in your hearts, and ye also shall see God face to face.

Thus shall we give back its youth to the world, for like tongues of triple flame we shall brood upon the Great Deep—Hail unto the Lords of the Groves of Eleusis !

END OF VOL. III

APPENDICES

APPENDIX A

NOTES

TOWARDS AN OUTLINE OF A BIBLIOGRAPHY OF THE WRITINGS IN PROSE AND VERSE OF ALEISTER CROWLEY *

EDITIONES PRINCIPES

(I)

[ACELDAMA: 1898]

Aceldama, | a Place to Bury Strangers in. | a philosophical poem | by | a gentleman of the University of Cambridge. | privately printed. | London : | 1898.

Collation:—Crown 8vo, pp. 29, consisting of Half-title, quotation on reverse from "Songs of the Spirit," p. 13, ll. 1-4; Title-page as above, quotation on reverse St. John xii. 24, 25; prose Prologue, quotation on reverse Acts i. 18, 19; Dedication dated "Midnight, 1897-1898," on reverse "*à toi* "; second half-title, quotation on reverse from Swinburne's "The Leper"; "Poems and Ballads," 1866, pp. 1-10; Text, pp. 11-27; no headline; Epilogue p. 28; no imprint, but printed by an obscure printer in the Brompton-road, London.

Edition: 2 copies on vellum, numbered 1, 2 ; [1] 10 copies on Japanese vellum, numbered 3-12; [2] 88 copies on hand-made paper, numbered 13-100.

Issued in Japanese vellum turned-in wrapper repeating title-page.

[THE TALE OF ARCHAIS: 1898]

The | Tale of Archais | a Romance in Verse | by a Gentleman of the University | of Cam-

bridge | London | Kegan Paul, Trench, Trübner & Co. | MDCCCXCVIII.

Collation : —Pott 4to, pp. viii + 89, consisting of Half-title, Title-page in red and black as above (with imprint : "Chiswick Press : —Charles Whittingham & Co. | Tooks Court, Chancery Lane, London." on reverse), pp. iii–iv. ; Dedication "To | The White Maidens of England | this Tale of Greece | is | dedicated " (with blank reverse), pp. v–vi; continued in verse, pp. vii–viii. ; Prologue in verse, pp. 1-5 ; second Half-title, p. 7; Text, pp. 8-84 ; Epilogue, pp. 85-89. There are headlines throughout. The imprint — " Chiswick Press :—Charles Whittingham and Co. | Tooks Court, Chancery Lane, London."— is repeated at the foot of the last page.

Edition : 2 copies on Roman vellum, 250 on hand-made paper.

Issued in slate-blue, dull-green, and brick-red boards with white holland backs, and white paper back label. The published price was five shillings.

[THE HONOURABLE ADUL-TERERS: 1899]

The | Honourable Adulterers | a tragedy | by | A. E. C. | 1899.

Collation :—Demy 8vo, cut edges, pp. 8, pagination from 119-126,[1] consisting of Title

---

[1] These large-paper copies measure 7½ × 10, printed on thick vellum, wrapper of Japanese vellum.
[2] These large-paper copies measure 7½ × 10, on thick Japanese vellum, wrapper of thin Japanese vellum.

[1] The pagination is accounted for by the fact that these three pamphlets were printed off from the paged type of *Jephthah and Other Mysteries*, then in the press, and issued separately.

* For the bulk of these notes we are indebted to the late Mr. L. C. R. Duncombe-Jewell.

as above; Text, pp. 119-126. Headlines throughout. No imprint.

Edition: 5 copies, on smooth purplish paper.

Issued in blue paper wrapper, repeating title-page.

[JEPHTHAH AND OTHER MYSTERIES : 1899]

Jephthah | and other mysteries | lyrical and dramatic | by Aleister Crowley | London : Kegan Paul, Trench, | Trübner and Company, Ltd. | 1899 | *all rights reserved.*

Collation:—Demy 8vo, pp. xxii + 223, consisting of Half-title, quotation on reverse from *Il Penseroso*; Title-page as above, quotation on reverse from SAPPHO; Quotation from *The Book of the Sacred Magic of Abra-Melin the Mage;* on reverse "The dedication | is to | Algernon Charles Swinburne"; Dedication in verse, pp. vii-xii; Contents, pp. xiii-xiv; Prelude, xv-xxi; second Half-title, "Jephthah, | a tragedy," on reverse quotation from *Hamlet;* second Dedication, "To | Gerald ·Kelly, | poet and painter, | I dedicate | this tragedy"; dated "Cambridge, November, 1898." Text, pp. 5-221; Epilogue, pp. 222-223. On reverse, imprint "Chiswick Press :—Charles Whittingham and Co. | Tooks Court, Chancery Lane, London," surmounted by colophon, upon a mound, *a lion rampant, grasping an anchor entwined with a dolphin, the flukes and head in base.* Advertisements at end of book, pp. 8. Headlines throughout.

Editions : 1000 copies on machine-made paper, 6 copies on India paper.

Issued in brick-red boards, linen backs, white paper label, "Crowley | Jephthah | & other | mysteries | lyrical & | dramatic | Kegan Paul, | Trench | Trübner & | Co. Ltd. | 1899 | Price 7s. 6d." The six India-paper copies issued in old gold coloured buckram, lettered on cover "Jephthah" in red.

[SONGS OF THE SPIRIT : 1898]

Songs of the Spirit | by | Aleister Crowley | "Sublimi feriam sidera vertice" HOR. | London | Kegan Paul, Trench, Trübner & Co. | MDCCCXCVIII.

Collation:—Pott 8vo, pp. x + 109. Half-title ; on reverse, quotation from *The Tale of*

Archais ; Title in red and black as above ; reverse, quotation from *Ecclesiastes,*" a fool also is full of words," p. iv. Dedication in verse to J. L. B.,[1] pp. v-vii. Contents, pp. ix-x ; Second Half-title ; Text, pp. 3-104 ; Epilogue, pp. 105-109. Imprint on last page,"Chiswick Press:—Charles Whittingham and Co. | Tooks Court, Chancery Lane,London " ; surmounted by colophon. No headlines.

Edition : 1 copy on vellum, 50 copies on hand-made paper numbered and signed,[2] 300 copies on machine-made paper.

Issued in Japanese vellum with gold lettering on front of cover " Songs of the Spirit " for copies printed on hand-made paper ; and in grey cloth boards, lettered on back " Songs | of the | Spirit | Aleister Crowley | 1898 " in crimson for those printed on machine-made paper. Priced 3s. 6d.

[THE POEM : 1898]

The Poem | a little drama in four scenes | by | Aleister Crowley | printed privately | London | 1898.

Collation:—Demy 8vo, cut edges, pp. 20, pagination 99-118 * ; consisting of Half-title, "The Poem. | a little drama in four scenes"; Dedication, p. 101 ; Text, pp. 103-117. Headlines throughout. No imprint.

Edition : 10 copies on smooth paper.

Issued in Japanese vellum wrapper repeating title-page.

[JEZEBEL : 1898]

Jezebel | and other | Tragic Poems | By Count Vladimir Svareff | Edited, with an Introduction and Epilogue, by | Aleister Crowley | Vignette of Armorial Design of Chiswick Press | London | Privately printed at the Chiswick Press | 1898.

Collation:—Demy 4to, pp. 23, with 8 unnumbered preliminary pages printed from the Caxton fount of antique type ; Half-title ; Title as above, " Jezebel " and " London " in red ; Dedication in verse dated, " Londres, Juin 1898," in French,

---

[1] J. L. Baker, the alchymist.
[2] Carelessly done or not done at all.

"à Gerald"; Contents; Introduction in verse signed "A. C." p. i.; Text, pp. 3–22; Epilogue signed "A. C." p. 23; colophon, printer's mark, *argent, a printer's maul in pale*, the shield surrounded by a scroll; below the imprint, "Chiswick Press: Tooks Court, Chancery Lane, London." No headlines.

Edition : 2 copies on vellum, 10 copies on Japanese vellum, 40 copies on hand-made paper.

Issued in Japanese vellum turned-in wrapper, with legend "Jezebel | and other Tragic Poems" enclosed in ornamental border on front of cover in gold. Unpriced : copies were sold at half-a-guinea.

[AN APPEAL TO THE AMERICAN REPUBLIC : 1899]

Price Sixpence | An Appeal | to the | American Republic | design of Union Flag and United States Ensign crossed | by | Aleister Crowley | London | Kegan Paul, Trench, Trübner & Co. Ltd. | 1899.

Collation : — Demy 4to, pp. 12. Crimson wrapper and Title-page in one. Text, pp. 1–12. Imprint at foot of last page, "Chiswick Press: Charles Whittingham and Co., Tooks Court, Chancery Lane, London."

Edition : 500 copies on machine-made paper.

[JEPHTHAH : 1898]

Jephthah | a Tragedy | by | a gentleman of the University of | Cambridge | (Aleister Crowley) | London | 1898 | [not for sale].

Collation :—Demy 8vo, cut edges, pp. 71; consisting of Half-title, "Jephthah | a tragedy," on reverse quotation from *Hamlet ;* Dedication " To | Gerald Kelly, | Poet Painter, | I dedicate | this tragedy; because his friendship was the turquoise, which I had of him before I was a bachelor; and which I would not have given for a wilderness of monkeys."[1] Dated "Cambridge, November 1898";

[1] The reference is to *The Merchant of Venice*, Act III. Scene 1. "Bachelor" refers to the degree of " B.A.," which the Author was expecting to take at the time of writing the Dedication ; but which in fact he did not take.

Text, pp. 5–69; "A Note on Jephthah," pp. 70–71. Headlines throughout. No imprint.

Edition : 25 copies on machine-made paper.

Issued in grey paper with an auto-lithograph in black ink, "Aleister Crowley | Jephthah," on cover.

[THE MOTHER'S TRAGEDY : 1901]

The Mother's | Tragedy | and | Other Poems | by | Aleister Crowley | Privately printed | 1901.

Collation :—Medium 8vo, pp. xii+111 ; consisting of Half-title ; Title as above ; Contents, pp. v–vi ; Prologue, pp. vii–xii ; Text, pp. 1–106; Epilogue, pp. 107–111. No imprint. Headlines throughout.

Edition : 500 copies on machine-made paper.

Issued in blue boards, linen backs, white paper back-label, "Crowley | The | Mother's | Tragedy | and other | Poems." Priced at 5s. od.

[THE SOUL OF OSIRIS : 1901]

The Soul of Osiris | a history | by | Aleister Crowley | London : Kegan Paul, Trench | Trübner and Company, Ltd. | 1901 | *All rights reserved.*

Collation :—Medium 8vo, pp. ix+129 ; consisting of Half-title ; Title as above, on reverse imprint "Chiswick Press: Charles Whittingham and Co. | Tooks Court, Chancery Lane, London " ; Contents, pp. v–vi ; Prologue, pp. vii–ix ; Text, pp. 3–129 ; Epilogue, " The Epilogue is silence," on reverse imprint of Chiswick Press as before.

Edition : 500 copies on machine-made paper, 6 copies on India paper.

Issued in brick-red boards, linen backs, white paper back-label, "Crowley | The | Soul | of | Osiris | Kegan Paul, Trench | Trübner & | Co. Ltd. Price 5s. od.

[CARMEN SAECULARE : 1901]

Carmen Saeculare | by | St. E. A. of M. and S. | London | Kegan Paul, Trench, Trübner

& Co. Ltd. | Paternoster House, Charing Cross Road | 1901.

Collation:—Demy 4to, pp. 30; consisting of Half-title; Dedication to "'The Countess of Glenstrae" ; Title as above ; Prologue, pp. 5-7 ; Text pp. 9-25 ; Epilogue, pp. 27-30, dated "s.s. Pennsylvania, July 4, 1900." No headlines.

Edition : 450 copies on machine-made paper, 6 copies on Roman vellum and 50 copies (?) on hand-made paper with title-page, "Carmen Saeculare | by | St. E. A. of M. and S. | Privately issued | London, 1901."

Issued in green paper wrapper repeating title-page with design of shamrock in centre. Price 1s. od.

[TANNHAUSER : 1902]

Tannhäuser | A story of all time | by | Aleister Crowley | London | Kegan Paul, Trench, Trüber & Co. Ltd. | Paternoster House, Charing Cross Road | 1902.

Collation : — Demy 4to, 142 pp., consisting of Half-title, quotation on reverse from Browning's *Master Hughes of Saxe-Gotha ;* Title-page as above, on reverse " all rights reserved " ; Dedication in verse, pp. 5-7 ; Prose preface, pp. 9-16, dated " Kandy, Ceylon, Sept. 1901." Second Half-title ; Text, pp. 18-142. Imprint at foot, " Turnbull and Spears, Printers, Edinburgh." Two pages of advertisements at end. No headlines.

Edition: 6 copies on Japanese vellum, 500 copies on machine-made paper.

Issued in royal-blue boards, linen backs, white paper back-label, "Crowley | Tannhäuser [1] | a story of | all time | Kegan Paul, | Trench, | Trübner & | Co. Ltd. | 1902. Price 5s. od.

[NEW YEAR'S CARD, 1903]

New Year, 190

A sonnet printed in gold on fly-sheets of Roman vellum (12) and hand-made paper (50) within a broad scarlet border, size 5⅞ × 6⅞, "from Aleister Crowley, | wishing you a speedy termination of existence." Printed throughout in capital letters.

1 Note the misprint "aü " for " äu."

[BERASHITH : 1903]

A.B. 2447, | Paris | בראשׁת | an Essay | in | ontology | with some remarks on ceremonial magic | by | Abhavananda | (Aleister Crowley) | Privately printed for the Sangha of | the West.

Collation :—Size 9 × 7⅞, pp. 24, consisting of Title-page and wrapper in one as above, on reverse, Number of Copy and Errata ; Text, pp. 1-24 ; Imprint at foot of last page, " Clarke & Bishop, Printers, Etc., 338, Rue St. Honoré, Paris." No headlines.

Edition : 200 copies on China paper numbered.

Issued in wrapper and title in one on machine-made paper 10⅝ × 8¹⁄₁₆. Price 5 francs.

[SUMMA SPES : undated]

Summa | Spes | Aleister | Crowley.

Collation :—Single poem on Japanese vellum 9 × 7¼, printed in red with a green ornamental border. Photograph by Haweis and Coles in front, and colophon by T. Spicer Simpson on back.

[BALZAC : 1903]

Balzac | *Hommage à Auguste Rodin.*

A sonnet which occurs in *Ahab* in a slightly altered form. Was issued in Paris by request, on a single unfolded sheet of Japanese vellum 14⅝ × 9¼ inches : 3 copies printed vertically, and 15 horizontally on the right half of the paper ; also 6 copies on China paper 12⅝ × 9½ inches printed vertically in the upper moiety of the sheet. No imprint.

[AHAB : 1903]

Ahab | and other Poems | By Aleister Crowley | with an introduction and Epilogue by | Count Vladimir Svareff | Design of the Chiswick Press, vignette | London. Privately printed at the Chiswick Press | 1903.

Collation :—Demy 4to, pp. 35, and 6 unnumbered preliminary pages, consisting of Half-title ; Title in red and black as above ; Dedication in verse to G. C. J., [1] dated Paris, December 9, 1902 ; Contents ;

1 George Cecil Jones, the Theurgist.

Rondel, p. 1; Text, pp. 3-33; Epilogue, signed "V.S.," p. 35. Printed from the Caxton fount of antique type : no headlines : no imprint.

Edition : 2 copies on vellum, 10 copies on Japanese vellum, 150 copies on handmade paper.

Issued in Japanese vellum turned-in wrapper with legend "Ahab | and other poems" enclosed in ornamental border on front of cover in gold. Price 5s. od.

[ALICE : 1903]

Alice : an | Adultery | privately printed | 1903.

Collation :—Fcp. 8vo, pp. xx+95, consisting of Half-title ; Title as above ; Introduction by the Editor dated "Yokohama, April, 1901," pp. i-xii ; Critical Essay on *Alice* signed "G. K.,"[1] pp. xiii-xx. Prefatory poems, pp. 1-17. Second Half-title ; Text, pp. 21-95. No headlines. No imprint.

Edition : 100 copies on China paper. Price to subscribers, 10s. 6d. ; published price, 21s. od.

Issued in green camel-hair, turned-in wrapper lettered on front cover, " Alice," in white.

[THE GOD-EATER : 1903]

The God-Eater | A Tragedy of Satire | by | Aleister Crowley | Watts & Co. | 17 Johnson's Court, Fleet Street, London, E.C. | 1903.

Collation :—Cr. 4to, pp. 32, consisting of Half-Title, on reverse announcement of works " by the same author "; Title-page as above ; Dedication ; Text, pp. 7-32. Imprint " R. Clay and Sons, Ltd., Bread St. Hill, E.C., and Bungay, Suffolk," at foot of last page.

Edition : 2 copies on Roman vellum, 300 on machine-made paper.

Issued in green camel-hair wrapper lettered in red, "The | God-eater | A Tragedy | of Satire | By | Aleister Crowley | Watts & Co. | 17 Johnson's Court, Fleet Street, London, E.C. | 1903." Price 2s. 6d.

[1] Gerald Kelly. Both the Introduction and Critical Essay are the result of the collaboration of four men—A. C., G. K., D. J.-F., and I. B.

[THE STAR AND THE GARTER : 1903]

The Star & | The Garter | By Aleister | Crowley | Watts & Co. | 17 Johnson's Court | London | 1903.

Collation :—Demy 4to, pp. 89, consisting of Half-title ; Title-page as above ; Invocation in Greek ; Text, pp. 7-77 ; Appendix, prose and verse, pp. 79-86 ; Press Notices, pp. 87-89 ; reply to Invocation in Greek, p. 78 ; advertisement one page. Imprint in centre of last page, "printed, by Turnbull and Spears, Edinburgh."

Edition : 2 copies on Roman vellum, fifty copies on hand-made paper.

Issued in green camel's-hair wrapper, lettered in white on front of cover, "The | Star & | The Garter | by Aleister | Crowley."

[THE ARGONAUTS : 1904]

The Argonauts | by | Aleister Crowley | Society for the Propagation of Religious Truth | Boleskine, Foyers, Inverness | 1904.

Collation :—Crown 8vo, pp. 102, consisting of Half-title ; Title-page as above ; sub-title, "Jason,"[1] dedication on reverse ; Text of "Jason," pp. 3-17 ; sub-title of "Argo," dedication on reverse ; Text of "Argo," pp. 3-19 ; sub-title " Medea," dedication on reverse ; Text of " Medea," pp. 3-19 ; sub-title " Sirenæ," dedication on reverse ; Text of " Sirenæ," pp. 3-24 ; sub - title " Ares," dedication on reverse ; Text of " Ares," pp. 3-23. Imprint at foot of last page, " Chiswick Press : printed by Charles Whittingham and Co | Tooks Court, Chancery Lane, London." Announcement of works by the same author on reverse. No headlines.

Edition : 2 copies on Roman vellum, 200 copies on machine-made paper.

Issued in green camel's-hair wrapper, lettered in red on front of cover, "The Argonauts | by | Aleister Crowley." Price 5s. od.

[1] Each Act is a separate play on the Greek model separately paginated.

[THE SWORD OF SONG : 1904]

The Sword of Song | called by Christians | The Book of the Beast | Aleister Crowley | Society for the Propagation of Religious Truth | Benares | 1904.

Collation :—Post 4to, pp. ix + 194, printed in red and black, consisting of Half-title, parody of passage from *Through the Looking Glass* on reverse ; Title-page as above, Dedication on reverse ; Introductory poem *Nothung ;* Half-title ; Prose Introduction to "Ascension Day and Pentecost," pp. iii–ix ; Text, pp. 1–62 ; Notes, pp, 63–91 ; Appendices, pp. 93-121 ; "בראשית | an essay | in | ontology | with some remarks on | ceremonial magic," pp. 123–148 ; "Science and Buddhism," pp. 149–192 ; Epilogue in verse, pp. 193–194 ; Index on last page, imprint on reverse, "printed | by | Philippe Renouard | 19, rue des Saints-Pères, 19 | Paris." Headlines throughout.

Editions : 100 copies on a glazed foreign paper.[1]

Issued in navy blue wrapper front page lettered in gold "Ye Sword | of Song," with design in centre "666" thrice repeated on a golden square (*vide* pp. 4–5 of book), on reverse publishers' advertisement ; back of cover author's name in Hebrew characters adding up to "666," in gold ; inside of back page of cover list of author's works in gold ; back of cover "The | Sword | of | Song." Price 10s. od.

[GOETIA : 1904]

The Book of the | Goetia | of | Solomon the King | translated into the English Tongue by a | Dead Hand | and | adorned with divers other matters germane | delightful to the wise | the whole | edited, verified, introduced and commented | by | Aleister Crowley | Society for the Propagation of Religious Truth | Boleskine, Foyers, Inverness | 1904.

Collation :—Demy 4to, pp. ix + 65, consisting of Half-title, Invocation in Greek on reverse ; Frontispiece ; Title-page as above, talisman on reverse ; Prefatory Note, pp. v–vi ;_ Preliminary Invocation, pp. vii–ix ; Text, pp. 1–65 ; colophon of Chiswick

[1] There were 10 advance copies issued in a crimson wrapper repeating title-page, on back "The Sword of Song" lengthwise, on back outside of cover colophon Louis Seize design, initials of designer "L. M."

Press Mark on reverse of last page. No headlines. Two illustrations besides Frontispiece.

Edition : 200 copies on machine-made paper, 1 copy on vellum, 10 copies on Japanese vellum.

Issued in green camel's-hair wrapper, lettered in red "Goetia" in centre, surrounded by the legend "Goetia vel clavicula Salomonis Regis" frequently repeated. Price 21s. od., raised from subscription price of 10s. od.

Japanese vellum copies in white and gold. Japanese vellum turned-in wrapper, same lettering.

[WHY JESUS WEPT : 1904]

Why | Jesus Wept | a Study of Society | and of | The Grace of God | by | Aleister Crowley | Privately Printed | 1904.

Collation :—Post 4to, pp. 16 + 80. Half-title; advertisement (of the 21s. edition) ; Title as above ; letter from author's mother, 2 pp. ; Persons studied ; Quotation from *Times* newspaper and John xi. 35. Dedications 6 pp. to various persons (all these pages unnumbered) ; Text, pp. 1-80; inset, a slip "Note to pp. 75-76" ; also, loose inset, a pamphlet "Mr. Crowley and the Creeds" and "The Creed of Mr. Chesterton, &c. &c." No imprint, but printed by Philippe Rénouard.

Edition : 100 copies on hand-made paper, 20 in Japanese vellum ; 1 on Roman vellum.

Issued in turned-in Japanese wrapper ; front, "Why | Jesus | Wept | Aleister | Crowley | " ; reverse, colophon of Press ; back, "Why Jesus Wept."

[ORACLES : THE BIOGRAPHY OF AN ART : 1905]

Oracles | the biography of an art | unpublished fragments of the work of Aleister Crowley with | explanatory notes by R. P. Lester and the Author | 1905 | Society for the Propagation of Religious Truth | Boleskine, Foyers, Inverness.

Collation :—Demy 8vo, pp. viii + 175 + 16 advertisements, consisting of Half-title ; Title as above ; prefatory note "To Explain" ; Contents, pp. vii, viii ; Text, pp. 1–175 ;

Advertisement, pp. 1 - 16. Headlines throughout.

Edition : 500 copies on machine-made paper.

Issued in green camel-hair paper, on back in large white letters, ORACLES ALEISTER CROWLEY The price was 5s.

[ORPHEUS : 1905]

Orpheus | a lyrical legend by | Aleister Crowley in two volumes of which | this is volume { one / two } each one crown | *Left*. Society | for the | Propagation of | Religious | Truth | *Right*. Boleskine | Foyers | Inverness | 1905.

Printed in Red and Black.

Collation :—Demy 8vo, pp. 156, consisting of Half-title ; Title as above ; Contents, pp. 7-9 ; Warning, pp. 11-14 ; Exordium, pp. 15-19 ; Half-title, Liber Primus vel Carminum, p. 21 ; Dedication " To Oscar Echenstein," &c., p. 23 ; Quotations, p. 24 ; Text, pp. 25-106 ; Half-title, Liber Secundus vel Amoris, p. 107 ; Dedication " To Mary Beaton," &c., 109 ; Quotations, p. 110 ; Text, pp. 111-155 ; Printer's name, p. 156. Headlines throughout.

Volume ii. similarly arranged. Dedications to " The Memory of Jehi Aour," &c., and " To my Wife," p. 148.

Edition : 1 copy on Roman vellum, 500 copies on hand-made paper.

Issued in white boards, linen backs, white label " ORPHEUS | I. (or II.") | Two volumes | Ten Shillings | Boards | CROWLEY.

[COLLECTED WORKS]

The Works | of | Aleister Crowley | Volume I. | Foyers | Society for the Propagation of | Religious Truth | 1905 | [*All rights reserved*].

Collation :—Extra crown. In Three Volumes. Vol. I., pp. x+269, consisting of Half-title ; Title as above ; Preface ; Contents, pp. vii-ix ; Text, pp. 1-269 ; Vol. II., pp. viii+283, consisting of Half-title ; Title as above ; Contents, v-vii ; Text, pp. 1-283. Vol. III., pp. vii+230, consisting of Half-title ; Title as above ; Contents, pp. v-vii ; Text, pp. 1+230. Appendices, half-title, and pp. 233-248.

Edition : 1 copy on vellum, 1000 copies on India paper.

Issued in camel-hair paper cover ; on front cover, in large white letters, " The Collected Works of Aleister Crowley."

[GARGOYLES : 1906]

Gargoyles | being | Strangely Wrought Images | of Life and Death | by | Aleister Crowley | Foyers | Society for the Propagation of Religious Truth | 1906.

Collation :—Pott 8vo, pp. vi+113. Half-title [reverse ∵ Fifty copies only, &c., on the hand-made paper]; Title as above in red and black ; Contents, pp. v, vi.

Prose Dedication (" To Lola Bentrovata ") in red and black, pp. 1, 2, and Text, pp. 3-112 ; (presumably) Dedicatory Epilogue, p. 113, printed in red. Chiswick Press imprint, p. 114.

Edition : 2 copies on Roman vellum, 50 on hand-made paper numbered and signed, 300 copies on machine-made paper.

Issued in facsimile to " Songs of the Spirit." No price, but sold at 3s. 6d. net cash to the trade.

[ROSA MUNDI : 1905]

Rosa Mundi | a poem | by | H. D. Carr | with an original composition by | Auguste Rodin | prix : vingt francs | price : sixteen shillings net | Paris : Ph-Renouard, rue des Saints Pères | London—of H. D. Carr, care of E. Dennes, 22 Chancery Lane | and through all booksellers | 1905.

Collation :—Foreign glazed paper, measuring 13″ × 10″ approximately. Half-title, reverse *tirage ;* 2 copies on vellum, 10 copies on China paper, 488 copies on hand-made paper ; Lithograph by Clot from A. Rodin, woman seated, her arms clasping her knees. Title as above ; Text, pp. 1-15 ; p. 17, printer's imprint ; Edition as above.

Issued in rose wrappers ; front, Auguste Rodin | Rosa Mundi | H. D. Carr ; reverse, design of curves.

APPENDIX B

INDEX OF FIRST LINES TO

VOLUMES I., II., III.

Q

Milton Keynes UK
Ingram Content Group UK Ltd.
UKHW021621030823
426219UK00001B/7